THE

TRANSFORMATION

OF

THE SCHOOL

THE

TRANSFORMATION

OF

THE SCHOOL

PROGRESSIVISM

IN AMERICAN EDUCATION,

1876–1957

LAWRENCE A. CREMIN

VINTAGE BOOKS

A DIVISION OF RANDOM HOUSE
New York

V519

9B

FOR

Charlotte

Preface

THE DEATH of the Progressive Education Association in 1955 and the passing of its journal, *Progressive Education*, two years later marked the end of an era in American pedagogy. Yet one would hardly have known it from the pitifully small group of mourners at both funerals. Somehow a movement that had for half a century enlisted the enthusiasm, the loyalty, the imagination, and the energy of large segments of the American public and the teaching profession became, in the decade following World War II, anathema, immortalized only in jokes that began, "There was this mixed-up youngster who went to an ultra-progressive school"; in cartoons like H. T. Webster's classic drawing in the "Life's Darkest Moment" series picturing the day little Mary got a D in blocks and sand piles; in comedies like *Auntie Mame* with its delightful caricature of a Freud-oriented Greenwich Village private school of the 1920's; in vitriolic attacks on John Dewey, mostly by people who had never read him (he was too often defended by people who had not read him either); and in the rhetoric and jargon of professional educators.

What was this progressive education movement that in two generations worked a transforming influence on American education? When did it begin? Who sponsored it? What were its contributions? What happened to it? And what, if anything, remains of it? Is it quite as dead as its critics believe, or are the reports of its demise, in Mark Twain's words, very much exaggerated?

There is currently afoot a simple story of the rise of progressive education, one that has fed mercilessly on the fears of anxious parents and the hostilities of suspicious conservatives. In it John Dewey, somewhat in the fashion of Abou Ben Adhem, awakes one night with a new vision of the American school: the vision is progressive education. Over the years, with the help of a dedicated group of crafty professional lieutenants at Teachers College, Columbia University, he is able to foist the vision on an unsuspecting American people. The story usually ends with a plea for the exorcising of this devil from our midst and a return to the ways of the fathers. This kind of morality play has always been an influential brand of American political rhetoric, used by reformers and conservatives alike. But it should never be confused with history!

Actually, progressive education began as part of a vast humanitarian effort to apply the promise of American life— the ideal of government by, of, and for the people—to the puzzling new urban-industrial civilization that came into being during the latter half of the nineteenth century. The word *progressive* provides the clue to what it really was: the educational phase of American Progressivism writ large. In effect, progressive education began as Progressivism in education: a many-sided effort to use the schools to improve the lives of individuals. In the minds of Progressives this meant several things.

First, it meant broadening the program and function of the school to include direct concern for health, vocation, and the quality of family and community life.

Second, it meant applying in the classroom the pedagogical principles derived from new scientific research in psychology and the social sciences.

Third, it meant tailoring instruction more and more to the different kinds and classes of children who were being brought within the purview of the school. In a sense, the revolution Horace Mann had sparked a generation before—the revolution inherent in the idea that everyone ought to be educated —had created both the problem and the opportunity of the Progressives. For if everyone was to attend school, the Progressives contended, not only the methods but the very meaning of education would have to change. It was all very well for some educators to say, in effect: "We know what good education is; take it or leave it"—in much the same fashion that Henry Ford told customers they could have their cars in any color they wished so long as it was black. What happened was that youngsters in droves deserted the schools as irrelevant to the world of here and now.

Finally, Progressivism implied the radical faith that culture could be democratized without being vulgarized, the faith that everyone could share not only in the benefits of the new sciences but in the pursuit of the arts as well. Jane Addams, that noble lady who founded Hull House and led its efforts for fully forty years, once remarked: "We have learned to say that the good must be extended to all of society before it can be held secure by any one person or any one class; but we have not yet learned to add to that statement, that unless all men and all classes contribute to a good, we cannot even be sure that it is worth having." Here was the spiritual nub of progressive education, and it simply negates contemporary nonsense about the movement being narrowly practical and nothing else.

The story of the progressive education movement· of its genesis in the decades immediately following the Civil War; of its widespread appeal among the intellectuals at the turn of the century; of its gathering political momentum during the decade before World War I; of its conquest of the organized teaching profession; of its pervasive impact on American schools and colleges, public and private; of its fragmentation during the 1920's and 1930's; and of its ultimate collapse after World War II; is the substance of this volume. Seen in the large, the movement constitutes a crucial chapter in the recent history of American civilization; to ignore it is to miss one whole facet of America's response to industrialism.

Two caveats might well be entered at the start. First, the movement was marked from the very beginning by a pluralistic, frequently contradictory, character. The reader will search these pages in vain for any capsule definition of progressive education. None exists, and none ever will; for throughout its history progressive education meant different things to different people, and these differences were only compounded by the remarkable diversity of American education. And second, while the effort here is to write a chapter in American social and intellectual history, the reader will quickly recognize that what happened was clearly part of a much larger worldwide response to industrialism, and that while the American movement proceeded in terms of the American experience, many of its elements were similar to, and indeed influenced by, contemporary developments in other industrial nations.

During the course of this study some heavy scholarly debts have been incurred which it is a pleasure here to acknowledge. Ann M. Keppel, Judy F. Suratt, Patricia A. Graham, Sheila L. Tuchman, and Nancy S. Shulman provided expert research assistance. Merle L. Borrowman, Merle E. Curti, and the late Howard K. Beale of the University of Wisconsin, and John F. C. Harrison of the University of Leeds contributed invaluably by listening and criticizing during the early period of conceptualization. My colleagues in the Department of Social and Philosophical Foundations at Teachers College asked their usual searching questions from the beginning, as did my long-time friend and associate, Martin S. Dworkin. R. Freeman Butts was also kind enough to read and criticize the penultimate draft. Many of the persons discussed in the study readily granted interviews and access to unpublished papers, notably William H. Kilpatrick, George S. Counts, Frederick L. Redefer, Archibald W. Anderson, H. Gordon Hullfish, Stanwood Cobb, Eugene Randolph Smith, Margaret Naumburg, and the late Harold Rugg. What strength this study may possess can be traced in large measure to these generous contributions; responsibility for its shortcomings is most assuredly mine.

The staff of the Wisconsin Historical Society, especially John Colson, was most helpful during a year of residence in Madison, as were the librarians at Teachers College throughout the course of the research. My secretary, Helen D. Zolot, typed the manuscript with intelligence and devotion. Finally, grants from the Columbia University Council for Research in the Social Sciences and the Teachers College Dean's Research Fund aided the initial investigations; while a Fellowship from the John Simon Guggenheim Memorial Foundation enabled me to spend a full year of research and writing in a carrel blessedly devoid of a telephone. My debt to my beloved wife is reflected in the dedication.

Parts of this volume appeared initially in the *Harvard Educational Review* (1957), *The School Review* (1959), the *Teachers College Record* (1959) and *The Educational Forum* (1960).

L. A. C.

Contents

PART I : *The Progressive Impulse in Education,*
1876–1917

1 Traditions of Popular Education   3
2 Education and Industry   23
3 Culture and Community   58
4 Science, Darwinism, and Education   90
5 Pedagogical Pioneers   127

PART II : *The Progressive Era in Education,*
1917–1957

6 Scientists, Sentimentalists, and Radicals   179
7 The Organization of Dissent   240
8 The Changing Pedagogical Mainstream   274
9 The Crisis in Popular Education   328

Bibliographical Note   355
Index   *follows page* 387

PART · I

The Progressive Impulse

in Education

1876–1917

1

Traditions of
Popular Education

THE circulation of *The Forum* was climbing in 1892—and no wonder. The stuffy, moribund New York monthly had suddenly sprung to life under the imaginative editorship of Walter Hines Page. Energetic, knowledgeable, uncompromising in his journalistic standards, the progressive young southerner was running article after article that the would-be conversationalist simply could not afford to miss: Henry Cabot Lodge and Jacob Schiff on politics, Jane Addams and Jacob Riis on social reform, and William James on psychical research. Well-nigh anything *The Forum* printed was likely to be discussed, but Page himself never anticipated the controversy destined to arise over Joseph Mayer Rice's series on the schools.

The year 1892 was much like any other, and Dr. Johnson's injunction about the fatal dullness of education was as pertinent as ever. Yet Page had been intrigued by Rice's pedagogical criticism. Apparently all was not right with the nation's much vaunted schools, and Page, ever the journalist, sensed news. Moreover, if anyone could come up with some first-rate articles, it was Rice. Astute, opinionated, and sharp in his judgments, Rice was a young New York pediatrician whose interest in prophylaxis had led him to some searching questions about the city's schools—questions so pressing that he spent the period between 1888 and 1890 studying pedagogy at Jena and Leipzig.[1] He returned bearing some fairly definite ideas about a "science of education"—dangerous luggage for a young man of thirty-three—and spent 1891 looking for a means of publicizing them. A series of columns in *Epoch*, a small New York weekly, and a piece in the December *Forum* provided his first opportunities. His pungent writing inevitably attracted comment, and near the end of 1891 Page offered him a novel proposal.

On behalf of *The Forum* Rice was to prepare a firsthand appraisal of American public education. From Boston to Washington, from New York to St. Louis, he was to visit classrooms, talk with teachers, attend school board meetings, and interview parents. He was to place "no reliance whatever" on reports by school officials; his goal was to render an objective assessment for the public. The proposal could not have been more welcome. Rice left on January 7, 1892. His tour took him to thirty-six cities; he talked with some 1200 teachers; he returned late in June, his notes crammed with statistics, illustrations, and judgments. The summer was given to writing, and the first article appeared in October. Within a month he and Page both knew they had taken an angry bull by the horns. By the time the final essay had been published the following June, Rice's name had become a byword—frequently an epithet—to schoolmen across the nation.[2]

Rice's story bore all the earmarks of the journalism destined to make "muckraking" a household word in America. In city after city public apathy, political interference, corruption, and incompetence were conspiring to ruin the schools. A teacher in

[1] A short biography of Rice appears in *The National Cyclopædia of American Biography*, XII, 203–4.

[2] The articles ran in nine consecutive issues from October, 1892, through June, 1893. They were subsequently republished as *The Public-School System of the United States* (New York, 1893).

Baltimore told him: "I formerly taught in the higher grades, but I had an attack of nervous prostration some time ago, and the doctor recommended rest. So I now teach in the primary, because teaching primary children does not tax the mind." A principal in New York, asked whether students were allowed to move their heads, answered: "Why should they look behind when the teacher is in front of them?" A Chicago teacher, rehearsing her pupils in a "concert drill," harangued them with the command: "Don't stop to think, tell me what you know!" In Philadelphia the "ward bosses" controlled the appointment of teachers and principals; in Buffalo the city superintendent was the single supervising officer for 700 teachers. With alarming frequency the story was the same: political hacks hiring untrained teachers who blindly led their innocent charges in singsong drill, rote repetition, and meaningless verbiage.

But the picture was not uniformly black; here and there Rice found encouraging departures from the depressing rule. In Minneapolis "a very earnest and progressive corps of teachers" was broadening the school program around the three R's and dealing sympathetically with children from "even the poorest immigrant homes." In Indianapolis, where politics had been firmly excluded from the management of schools, competent "progressive" teachers were attempting to introduce "the idea of unification" into the curriculum, combining the several subjects "so they may acquire more meaning by being seen in their relations to one another." At LaPorte, Indiana, Rice saw exciting progress in drawing, painting, and clay modeling, as well as encouraging efforts to teach pupils "to be helpful to each other." And finally, at Francis Parker's world-famous Cook County Normal School, "one of the most progressive as well as one of the most suggestive schools" he had seen, Rice found examples par excellence of the "all-side" education of children: nature study, art, social activities, and the three R's all taught by an inspired, enthusiastic staff.

The final article in the June *Forum* was a call to action. All citizens could have the life and warmth of the "progressive school" for their children. The way was simple and clear: led by an aroused public, the school system would have to be "absolutely divorced from politics in every sense of the word"; direct, thorough, and scientific supervision would have to be introduced; and teachers would have to endeavor constantly to improve their professional and intellectual competence. "The general educational spirit of the country is progressive," Rice concluded; it remained only for the public in local communities throughout the nation to do the job.

The response to Rice's series was electric. Newspaper reaction was about what one would expect—a rather general sympathy typified, perhaps, by a January editorial in the *Boston Daily Advertiser:* ". . . it must be admitted that the examples which he has cited do show a regrettable condition of affairs, and one that decidedly demands improvement. There is far too much of the mechanical in the existing system, especially in the 'busy work,' which here, as almost everywhere else, means a hindrance rather than a help to child education." [3] The Chicago *Dispatch* thought it "a shame and a disgrace that Chicago's public schools cannot be kept above the level of ward politics"; while the Detroit *Free Press* believed Rice's criticisms "so full of sound sense and of suggestion for improvement that they must commend themselves even to those who have been hit the hardest, and result sooner or later in correction of the defects and abuses pointed out." [4]

Much more intriguing, however, was the reaction of the professional press—a reaction that ranged from chilling disdain to near-hysteria. Boston's *Journal of Education* characterized Rice as a young man who had "demonstrated beyond cavil that he is merely a sensational critic. . . ." [5] *Education*, widely read by classroom teachers in New England, ran a searing editorial in December, picturing Rice as a carping journalist who had "recently abandoned the work of physicking his patients for a course in pedagogy in Germany." [6] Comments in succeeding months only elaborated this theme, pil-

[3] *Boston Daily Advertiser*, January 27, 1893, p. 4.
[4] Both quotations are taken from a series of extracts on "Dr. Rice's Visits" quoted in *The School Journal*, XLVI (1893), 450.
[5] *Journal of Education*, XXXVII (1893), 72.
[6] *Education*, XIII (1892–93), 245.

lorying the *Forum* series as radical, high-university, expert-type criticism by an intellectual snob who had completely missed the point of American public education.[7]

In New York the editor of *The School Journal* early adopted a wait-and-see attitude, writing in a November issue: "Dr. Rice has entered a new field. We have said repeatedly that at some time the schools would have the electric light turned on them, and have asked if they were ready. We ask it again." [8] Two months later, after Rice's article on New York had appeared, *The School Journal* was less concerned with illumination. Rice's criticisms were "weak and inconsequential"; if the schools produced results, that was all that could be asked of them.[9] Not to be outdone by its older and more respected competitor, the magazine *School* excoriated the series from the beginning. It interspersed barbed editorials with letters from self-appointed defenders of the schools who contended that Rice's foreign training, lack of classroom experience, inadequate evidence, and anti-public-school bias had rendered him unfit to judge American education.[1] By March the editor of *School* had vowed he would provide the self-styled "expert" no more free advertising by commenting on his errors—a pledge he broke only once (in April) to castigate *The School Journal* for giving "timid, half-hearted support to the cheap criticisms and the charlatanism of an alleged expert in *The Forum.* . . ." [2]

And so the criticism mounted—along with the circulation of *The Forum*. The appearance of the essays in book form in October only fanned the fires, which burned brightly into the summer of 1894 and then died down. Rice himself remained undaunted. He continued to write for *The Forum*, and some of his later articles such as "The Futility of the Spelling Grind" (providing evidence from tests on 33,000 schoolchildren that there is no significant correlation between amount of time de-

---

[7] Ibid., 306–7, 354–7, 377–8, 501–3, 567.
[8] *The School Journal*, XLV (1892), 444.
[9] Ibid., XLVI (1893), 153.
[1] *School*, IV (1893), 180, 193, 199, 210, 211, 250, 260.
[2] Ibid., 322.

voted to spelling homework and competence in the high art itself) were widely read and quoted.[3] In 1897 he became editor of the magazine—with disheartening results in the business office. Two more books flowed from his pen: one on *Scientific Management in Education* (1913), the other on municipal government.[4] He even founded a society for educational research. But when he died, in 1934, he was virtually unknown, remembered only—when at all—as one of the founders of the American testing movement. An unfortunate fate for this erstwhile progressive, but an occupational hazard of those who would father reform. For reform movements are notoriously ahistorical in outlook. They look forward rather than back; and when they do need a history, they frequently prefer the fashioning of ideal ancestors to the acknowledgment of mortals.

I I

Rice's disclosures must have come as a bitter pill to Americans of the nineties; for if anything had been established in the public mind by a half-century of public-school propaganda, it was the sense of an inextricable relationship between education and national progress. The great pre-Civil War architects of universal schooling—Horace Mann in Massachusetts, Henry Barnard in Connecticut, John Pierce in Michigan, and Samuel Lewis in Ohio—had hammered relentlessly at this theme in their quest for political support, picturing each local district school as a bulwark of the Republic and a repository of popular hopes and aspirations.[5]

Consider Mann, as the leading example. The commanding figure of the early public-school movement, he had poured into his vision of universal education a boundless faith in the perfectibility of human life and institutions. Once public

[3] *The Forum*, XXIII (1897), 163–72.

[4] The one on municipal government was a plea for scientific public administration called *The People's Government* (Philadelphia, 1915). Rice also published a *Rational Spelling Book* for the schools in 1898.

[5] See Lawrence A. Cremin: *The American Common School* (New York, 1951); and E. I. F. Williams: *Horace Mann* (New York, 1937).

schools were established, no evil could resist their salutary influence. Universal education could be the "great equalizer" of human conditions, the "balance wheel of the social machinery," and the "creator of wealth undreamed of." Poverty would most assuredly disappear, and with it the rancorous discord between the "haves" and the "have-nots" that had marked all of human history. Crime would diminish; sickness would abate; and life for the common man would be longer, better, and happier. Here was a total faith in the power of education to shape the destiny of the young Republic—a kind of nineteenth-century vision of ancient Athenian *paideia*. Little wonder that it fired the optimism of the American public.

The theory supporting Mann's faith represented a fascinating potpourri of early American progressivism, combining elements of Jeffersonian republicanism, Christian moralism, and Emersonian idealism. Mann understood well the relationship between freedom, self-government, and universal education. Like Jefferson, he believed that freedom could rest secure only as free men had the knowledge to make intelligent decisions. But for Mann the problem went deeper; it was fundamentally one of moral elevation. "Never will wisdom preside in the halls of legislation," he once wrote, "and its profound utterances be recorded on the pages of the statute book, until Common Schools . . . create a more far-seeing intelligence and a purer morality than has ever existed among communities of men." [6] Mann recognized that knowledge was power, but the power to do evil as well as good. Hence, the education of free men could never be merely intellectual; values inevitably intruded.

To raise the question of values, though, was to raise other problems. Mann was tremendously impressed with the diversity of the American people. Yet he feared that conflicts of value might rip them apart and render them powerless. Dreading the destructive possibilities of religious, political, and class difference, he sought a common value system within which

[6] *Twelfth Annual Report of the Board of Education, Together with the Twelfth Annual Report of the Secretary of the Board* (Boston, 1849), p. 84.

diversity might flourish. His quest was for a new public philosophy, a sense of community to be shared by Americans of every
background and persuasion. And his instrument in this effort
would be the common school.

Mann's school would be common, not as a school for the
common people—for example, the nineteenth-century Prus-
sian *Volksschule*—but rather as a school common to all people.
It would be open to all, provided by the state and the local
community as part of the birthright of every child. It would be
for rich and poor alike, not only free but as good as any private
institution. It would be nonsectarian, receiving children of all
creeds, classes, and backgrounds. In the warm associations of
childhood Mann saw the opportunity to kindle a spirit of
amity and respect which the conflicts of adult life could never
destroy. In social harmony he located the primary goal of
popular education.

The genius of Mann's design, and the hub of a built-in
dynamism that has characterized American public education
ever since, was the vesting of political control in the people.
Through state legislatures and local boards of education, popu-
larly elected representatives rather than professional schoolmen would exercise ultimate oversight. The manifest reason
was that public supervision must follow public support, and
this, of course, was reason enough. Yet the relationship went
far deeper. For by the artful device of lay control the public
was entrusted with the continuing definition of the public
philosophy taught its children. When Mann himself set out to
define this philosophy, what emerged was a not uncommon
nineteenth-century blend of natural law, faith in progress,
capitalistic morality, and liberal Protestantism. But Mann's
own definition is less important than the enterprise he set in
motion, for it is in this political process by which the public
defines the commitments of the schools that one finds the decisive forces in American educational history.

In the realm of curriculum Mann's thinking was ordinary
enough. He was inclined to accept the usual list of reading,
writing, spelling, arithmetic, English grammar, and geography,
with the addition of health education, vocal music (singing

would strengthen the lungs and thereby prevent consumption)
and some Bible reading. In the realm of pedagogy, however,
his ideas were of a different order, reaching again and again for
fresh solutions to the age-old problem of how to educate free
men. To begin, Mann was one of the first after Rousseau to
argue that education in groups is not merely a practical necessity, but a social desideratum. Rousseau had contended in
Émile that the ideal pedagogical situation is one teacher, one
child; yet even he had counseled his readers to turn to Plato's
Republic for guidance on mass education. Now Mann was
arguing that the tutorial relationship could never serve the social ends of education, that only with a hetcrogeneous group
of students could the unifying goals of the common school be
achieved.

Once this is granted, however, other problems arise. A free
society concerns itself with individuals, not masses. How, then,
can the values of individuality be reconciled with the teaching
of children in groups? Mann by no means solved the problem,
but—to his great credit—he did recognize it. He counseled,
for example, that children differ in temperament, ability, and
interest, and that lessons should be adapted to these differences. He insisted that the discipline of a free school must be
the self-discipline of the individual. "Self-government," "self-
control," "a voluntary compliance with the laws of reason and
duty," are the phrases he used to describe the ends of republican education. He rejected blind obedience on the one hand
and anarchic willfulness on the other. For Mann the essence
of the moral act was free self-choice; and insofar as his ultimate
purposes were moral, only in the arduous process of training
children to self-discipline did he see the common school fulfilling its commitment to freedom.

Granted these insights, Mann's resolution is still not without
its theoretical difficulties. He was attracted to the naturalistic
pedagogy of the Swiss reformer Pestalozzi, but like Pestalozzi
himself, was deeply committed to moral instruction. How does
one free a child and shape him at the same time? The problem
goes back to Rousseau, and ultimately to Plato. Rousseau, of
course, never solved it. Mann sought his answers in the

"science" of phrenology, as popular an intellectual fad as any that swept nineteenth-century America.[7] Phrenologists assumed that the mind is composed of thirty-seven faculties—for example, aggressiveness, benevolence, and veneration—that govern the attitudes and actions of the individual. Behavioristic in outlook, the theory maintained that human character can be modified, that desirable faculties can be cultivated through exercise and undesirable faculties inhibited through disuse. Remembered too much today as merely an entertaining method of reading character from the contours of the skull, the theory provides important insights into the pedagogical reformism of the 1840's. It reached for a naturalistic explanation of human behavior; it stimulated much-needed interest in the problem of child health; and it promised that education could build the good society by improving the character of individual children. What a wonderful psychology for an educational reformer! Emerson himself called a foremost treatise on the subject "the best Sermon I have read for some time."[8]

The struggle to achieve popular schooling is one of the fascinating chapters in American history. Under Mann's aggressive leadership Massachusetts in many ways taught the nation the ideals of universal education. In almost every state citizens organized to do battle in the cause of public schools. The political coalitions they formed frequently drew together the oddest collections of otherwise disparate interests. As Howard Mumford Jones has pointed out, the successful school leader was one who could with consummate skill simultaneously touch the hurt pride of the workingman, the pocketbook nerve of the wealthy, the status aspirations of the poor, and the timid defensiveness of the cultured before the onslaught of the unlettered masses.[9] Yet the very strangeness of these coalitions holds

[7] One of the first books Mann read after accepting the post as Secretary of the Massachusetts Board of Education was James Simpson's *Necessity of Popular Education* (Edinburgh, 1834). The volume leaned heavily on the writings of Pestalozzi and the English phrenologists.

[8] Ralph L. Rusk, ed.: *The Letters of Ralph Waldo Emerson* (6 vols., New York, 1939), I, 291. See also John D. Davies: *Phrenology: Fad and Science* (New Haven, 1955).

[9] Howard Mumford Jones: "Horace Mann's Crusade," in Daniel Aaron, ed.: *America in Crisis* (New York, 1952), pp. 91–107.

the key to understanding them; for the politics of education, while related to larger political crosscurrents, has exhibited unique tendencies over the past century, tendencies too often blurred by the commonly held fiction that education is non-political.

The fight for free schools was a bitter one, and for twenty-five years the outcome was uncertain. Local elections were fought, won, and lost on the school issue. The tide of educational reform flowed in one state, only to ebb in another. Legislation passed one year was sometimes repealed the next. State laws requiring public schools were ignored by the local communities that were supposed to build them. Time and again the partisans of popular education encountered the bitter disappointments that accompany any effort at fundamental social reform.

Yet by 1860 a design had begun to appear, and it bore upon it the marks of Mann's ideal. A majority of the states had established public school systems, and a good half of the nation's children were already getting some formal education. Elementary schools were becoming widely available; in some states, like Massachusetts, New York, and Pennsylvania, the notion of free public education was slowly expanding to include secondary schools; and in a few, like Michigan and Wisconsin, the public school system was already capped by a state university. There were, of course, significant variations from state to state and from region to region. New England, long a pioneer in public education, also had an established tradition of private education, and private schools continued to flourish there. The Midwest, on the other hand, sent a far greater proportion of its school children to public institutions. The southern states, with the exception of North Carolina, tended to lag behind, and did not generally establish popular schooling until after the Civil War.

On the whole, universal education had won clear—if sometimes grudging—acceptance from the society at large; and visitors from abroad were already accepting it as a characteristic American innovation. Thus, the Polish revolutionary Count De Gurowski could observe enthusiastically in 1857: "On the common schools, more than any other basis, depends and is fixed the future, the weal and the woe of American society, and they are the noblest and most luminous manifestations of the spirit, the will, and the temper of the genuine American communities and people. . . . Europe has polished classes; learned societies; but with less preponderating individual training, America, the Free States—stimulated, led on by New England, by Massachusetts—they alone possess intelligent, educated masses." [1]

I I I

Victories must be consolidated, and it fell to the teachers of a succeeding generation to confirm the pioneering work of Mann and his contemporaries. In the red brick buildings of the cities, in the white frame schoolhouses of the countryside, and in the roughhewn cabins of the newly settled frontier, the teachers of the seventies and eighties sought to translate the mandate of universal education into real schooling for real children. Their work has not been well remembered, for historians in their zeal for crusading pioneers sometimes ignore the equally important, if less colorful, figures who succeed them. The decade following the Civil War brought new schoolmen to the fore: Barnas Sears of Massachusetts, J. L. M. Curry of the Peabody Education Fund, Edward Sheldon of the Oswego (N. Y.) Normal School, John Eaton of the Federal Bureau of Education. Towering above them all, however, and undoubtedly the commanding figure of his pedagogical era, was William Torrey Harris.

Harris, a New Englander who had gone West as a young man of twenty-two, distinguished himself first as superintendent of the St. Louis public schools (1868–80) and subsequently as United States Commissioner of Education (1889–1906). From 1859 until his death in 1909, his career represents a rather remarkable marriage of the intensely idealistic philosopher and the eminently practical schoolman. The same Harris who worked for years to master Hegel's *Logic* and who founded

[1] Adam G. De Gurowski: *America and Europe* (New York, 1857), pp. 292, 308.

the *Journal of Speculative Philosophy,* the first periodical of its kind in the United States, was also the man who more than any other professionalized the art of school administration. He is quickly identified by American philosophers as the spiritual heir to Emerson's idealism, as the foremost Hegelian of his time, and as a leading spirit of the intellectual revival called the St. Louis movement in philosophy. To American educators he remains the great consolidator of pre-Civil War victories, the man who ultimately rationalized the institution of the public school. When he began his work—almost the very year of Mann's death—universal education was a radical notion shared by a shaky alliance of farmers, workers, and businessmen; when he concluded it, universal education had been made the nub of an essentially conservative ideology.[2]

Fully to understand Harris's work, one must view him primarily as a transitional figure in the history of educational thought. The nation that heard his powerful addresses and read his intricate theoretical analyses had entered into a stormy period of early industrial growth. Spurred on by protective tariffs, cheap labor, abundant raw materials, and a spreading network of railroad communication, American manufacturing was expanding at an unprecedented rate. People were on the move. A steady stream of immigrants poured through the gates of eastern seaports, and Americans themselves shifted westward and to the cities. It is not insignificant that Harris's platform during the first years of his pedagogical eminence was the thriving midwestern city of St. Louis. For it was ultimately in the city that teeming numbers, ethnic and religious diversity, and the insistent demands of commerce and industry were destined to test the claims of the common school.

To view Harris as a figure between two eras is to begin to comprehend his terrific fascination with the abstruse writings of Hegel. Harris, along with many of his mid-nineteenth-century countrymen, was suffering through a profound religious

[2] See Merle Curti: *The Social Ideas of American Educators* (New York, 1935) ch. ix; Brian Holmes: "Some Writings of William Torrey Harris," *British Journal of Educational Studies,* V (1956–7), 47–66; and Kurt F. Leidecker, *Yankee Teacher* (New York, 1946).

crisis. Clues appear in the very first issue of the *Journal of Speculative Philosophy*, in which Harris observed that the "tendency to break with the traditional, and to accept only what bears for the soul its own justification, is widely active, and can end only in the demand that Reason shall find and establish a philosophical basis for all those great ideas which are taught as religious dogmas." [3] For Harris neither naturalism nor mysticism would suffice; but in Hegel's rationalistic doctrines of the dialectic, of absolute truth, and of self-activity, he found a way—however tortuous—of reconciling his boyhood Christian beliefs with the methods and findings of science. More generally, Harris used Hegel to confirm what was worth conserving in a society pervaded by change; Hegel enabled him to accept a new America without repudiating the old. In Hegel's rationalism Harris found religion.

Much that Harris believed and did in education can be understood in simple pragmatic terms. He had the sensitivities and abilities of a natural-born administrator. But his most fundamental contributions can only be grasped in light of his Hegelian commitments. Consider, for example, his confirmation of the public-school ideal. That he should echo the faiths of Mann and Barnard is only natural for a man born and reared in ante-bellum Connecticut. "The spirit of American institutions is to be looked for in the public schools to a greater degree than anywhere else," he wrote in 1871. "If the rising generation does not grow up with democratic principles, the fault will lie in the system of popular education." [4] A year later he cautioned: "An ignorant people can *be* governed, but only a wise people can *govern itself*." [5] Common schools increased opportunity; they taught morality and citizenship; they encouraged a talented leadership; they maintained social mobility; they promoted popular responsiveness to social evolution. Mann and his contemporaries would have nodded in hearty approval.

[3] *Journal of Speculative Philosophy*, I (1867), 1.
[4] *Sixteenth Annual Report of the Board of Directors of the St. Louis Public Schools* (St. Louis, 1871), p. 28.
[5] *Seventeenth Annual Report of the Board of Directors of the St. Louis Public Schools* (St. Louis, 1872), p. 58.

But as one reads on, subtle differences appear. While the reformism of the 1840's is preserved, it takes on a new tone. The school is the "great instrumentality to lift all classes of people into a participation in civilized life." [6] But what is civilized life? For Harris it is a life of order, self-discipline, civic loyalty, and respect for private property. The civilized man possesses the view of the world entertained by the society of which he is part. "Education is the process of adoption of this social order in place of one's mere animal caprice"; it is "a renunciation of the freedom of the moment for the freedom that has the form of eternity." [7] Hence, the purposes of education must be tied to time-honored principles deeply imbedded in the wisdom of the race. While the free individual contributes his share to social evolution, what he proffers can be but an infinitesimal addition to a vast social whole.

Yet had not Mann also assured the businessman that public schools would preserve order, extend wealth, and secure property? Of course, he had; his Fifth Report to the Massachusetts Board of Education is a classic example of such reasoning. And Mann, too, had ventured his definition of the civilized life. But the difference between Mann and Harris is a crucial difference of emphasis. Mann's common school was to contribute substantially to fashioning an emerging social order governed by a new public philosophy; Harris's was merely to play a part in confirming an order that had already come into existence.

The difference becomes clearer on analyzing Harris's recommendations regarding the school program. To begin, much more than Mann he recognized that the school is but one of several educative institutions, and thus sharply limited in power. The child is molded by family, church, civil community, and state before he ever comes to school, and their influence continues unabated during his years as a student. What then

[6] William T. Harris: "The Pedagogical Creed of William T. Harris," in Ossian H. Lang, ed.: *Educational Creeds of the Nineteenth Century* (New York, 1898), p. 43.

[7] William T. Harris: *Psychologic Foundations of Education* (New York, 1898), p. 282.

becomes the distinctive task of formal education? Harris replied with four principles: schooling must always be deemed
preliminary to the larger education of life—an education continuing through adulthood; the school should teach only what
the pupil is not likely to pick up from intercourse with the
family circle, with his playmates, or with his fellow workmen;
the school program should embrace only such matters as have
a general theoretical bearing on the world in which the pupil
lives; and lastly, the school must not trespass on the just do-
main of the Church—moral education, yes, religious education, categorically no.[8]

Harris never forgot these principles in dealing with the content of education. "The question of the course of study. . . ,"
he once wrote, "is the most important question which the educator has before him"; [9] the curriculum was to be the means by
which the child would be brought into orderly relationship
with his civilization. Harris agreed with Rousseau that the
child is born weak, but from that point forward their thought
diverged. Rousseau's naturalism was to Harris "the greatest
heresy in educational doctrine." [1] Institutions, Hegel taught,
are not opposed to man; they enable man to achieve his truest
expression. Hence in Harris's view the school must lead the
child to freedom by leading him away from his primitive self.
The goals of the process could only be determined by orderly
study of adult life and institutions; education would have to
be social science par excellence. The key to the process is
the Hegelian doctrine of self-estrangement. The natural self,
the self of instinct and impulse, must be connected with the
larger society; its transient likes and dislikes must be subordinated to civilized wants—"rational objects." In the process new
versions of the self emerge and are joined to the primitive
self in a continuing dialectic of alienation and return. The essence of the enterprise is discipline, a discipline stressing or-

[8] See Neil G. McCluskey: *Public Schools and Moral Education* (New
York, 1958), Part III; and Carl Lester Byerly: *Contributions of William
Torrey Harris to Public School Administration* (Chicago, 1946).
[9] National Education Association: *Addresses and Proceedings, 1880,*
p. 174.
[1] "The Pedagogical Creed of William T. Harris," op. cit., p. 37.

derly behavior in the kindergarten; mastery of the fundamentals in the elementary school (Harris called them the "five windows of the soul"—mathematics, geography, literature and art, grammar, and history); and concentration on the classics, languages, and mathematics in the high schools and colleges. The end product is the self-active individual, the reasoning person who can exercise true freedom in the terms of his own civilization.

Harris the administrator, however much the practical man, was ultimately guided by Harris the theorist. Like his counterparts in New York, Boston, Philadelphia, and Chicago, his concerns began and ended with the ever-pressing problem of numbers. It is one thing to sing the praises of universal education; it is quite another to provide it. The city superintendent of the seventies was faced with thousands of children eager for education and too few teachers and classrooms to serve them. Moreover, he had at his command few precedents for classifying and grouping his flood of charges. Harris's answer was the graded school, organized by years and quarter-years of work, with pupils moving through on the basis of regular and frequent examinations. For the system to function at all, planning and order were needed; and Harris's superb sense of detail never rested as he sought constantly to improve economy and efficiency. He devoted himself to attendance reports, to textbooks, to the collection of school statistics, to the standardization of pedagogical terminology, to the lighting, heating, and ventilation of school buildings, to teacher salary schedules, and to the continuing supervision of instruction. And his Hegelian love of institutions sustained him through every step of the way, for in the completely evolved system would lie the finest educational expression of the new urban civilization.

Ultimately, Harris's social philosophy became an apology for the new urban industrial order, while his pedagogy rendered service to its educational needs. But it is futile to contend that his pedagogy is wholly static. The doctrine of self-activity cannot but leave the way open to change, while the social analysis he deemed central to the determination of educational policy allows for reform as well as reaction. Moreover, the continuing tension between social adjustment on the one hand and individuality on the other—a tension so dear to Harris—lends an unmistakable dynamism to his system. Yet granted this, the temper of Harris's pedagogy is patently conservative. His emphasis is on order rather than freedom, on work rather than play, on effort rather than interest, on prescription rather than election, on the regularity, silence, and industry that "preserve and save our civil order." His attempt to define the precise functions of the school tended inevitably toward formalism, while his steadfast resistance to demands for trade and vocational education made him the *bête noire* of those pressing for change. In the end, Harris consolidated the revolution Mann had wrought; but as if in the terms of his own Hegelianism, his pedagogy itself became the target of a succeeding generation of protest.

I V

Whatever the high-minded philosophies that justified them, the schools of the 1890's were a depressing study in contrast. Everywhere, mundane problems of students, teachers, classrooms, and dollars had become overwhelming. Rural schools, built during the educational renaissance of the forties and fifties, had been allowed to fall into disrepair and disrepute. Cut off from the pedagogical mainstream and frequently beset by problems of rural decline, they remained ungraded and poorly taught. Recitations averaged ten minutes per subject per class, and untrained teachers continued to concentrate on "the same old drill in the same old readers." McGuffey had been good enough for mother and dad; he would certainly do for the youngsters.[2]

In the cities problems of skyrocketing enrollments were compounded by a host of other issues. In school buildings badly lighted, poorly heated, frequently unsanitary, and bursting at

[2] For the sorry picture of the rural schools, see the "Report of the Committee on Rural Schools," National Educational Association: *Addresses and Proceedings*, 1897, pp. 385–583; Hervey White: "Our Rural Slums," *Independent*, LXV (1908), 819–21; and Martha van Rensselaer: "A Rural School," *The Chautauquan*, XXXIV (1901–2), 428–32.

the seams, young immigrants from a dozen different countries swelled the tide of newly arriving farm children. Superintendents spoke hopefully of reducing class size to sixty per teacher, but the hope was most often a pious one. Little wonder that rote efficiency reigned supreme. It needed none of Harris's elaborate Hegelian justifications; it was simply the basis of survival.

As school budgets mounted, politicians were quick to recognize one more lucrative source of extra income. In the continuing consolidation of hamlets into villages, villages into towns, and towns into cities, school boards grew to fifty, seventy, or indeed, more than a hundred members. Responsibility being difficult to define, corruption reared its ugly—if familiar—head. Teaching and administrative posts were bought and sold; school buildings—like city halls and public bathhouses—suddenly became incredibly expensive to build; and politics pervaded everything from the assignment of textbook contracts to the appointment of school superintendents. In short, the school system, like every other organ of the urban body politic, was having its growing pains.[3]

Joseph Mayer Rice was not the first to protest against these unspeakable conditions. Francis W. Parker, called by Dewey the father of progressive education, had undertaken the reform of the Quincy, Massachusetts, schools as early as 1875; and while he himself had made little effort to publicize the work, the "Quincy System" had attracted national—indeed worldwide—interest. Following upon the revelations of the Russian system of technical instruction at the Philadelphia Centennial Exposition of 1876, businessmen in New York, St. Louis, and Chicago had sharply criticized the narrow intellectual emphases in the secondary school program, demanding a central place for manual training and vocational education. And no early Grange convention was complete without its resolutions

[3] Rice gives the best journalistic picture of the urban schools. In 1903 Walter Hines Page, then editor of *The World's Work*, sent Adele Marie Shaw on a school-appraisal expedition similar to Rice's. Her series was much like the earlier one in *The Forum*, and testified eloquently to the persistence of the conditions Rice had exposed a decade earlier. See *The World's Work*, VII (1903–4), 4204–21, 4460–6, 4540–53; VIII (1904), 4795–8, 4883–94, 4996–5004, 5244–54, 5405–14; IX (1904–5), 5480–5.

deploring the lack of practical agricultural training in the rural schools and colleges.

Yet pedagogical protest during the seventies and eighties was local, intermittent, and frequently innocuous. By contrast the nineties brought a nationwide torrent of criticism, innovation, and reform that soon took on all the earmarks of a social movement. And it is at this point that Rice's articles appear to mark a beginning. His *Forum* series was the first to weave the many strands of contemporary protest into a single reform program; it was the first to perceive the educational problem as truly national in scope; and it was the first to apply the technique of muckraking in attacking the political corruption and professional intransigence infecting the schools. The progressive movement in education begins with Rice precisely because he saw it as a movement. It is this growing self-consciousness more than anything else that sets the progressivism of the nineties apart from its sources in previous decades.

Once under way, the movement manifested itself in a remarkable diversity of pedagogical protest and innovation; from its very beginning it was pluralistic, often self-contradictory, and always closely related to broader currents of social and political progressivism. In the universities it emerged as part of a spirited revolt against formalism in philosophy, psychology, and the social sciences. In the cities it was but one facet of a wider program of municipal clean-up and reform. Among farmers it became the crux of a moderate, liberal alternative to radical agrarianism. It was at the same time the "social education" demanded by urban settlement workers, the "schooling for country life" demanded by rural publicists, the vocational training demanded by businessmen's associations and labor unions alike, and the new techniques of instruction demanded by avant-garde pedagogues. It embraced the kindergartens of St. Louis and the State University of Wisconsin, venerable Harvard, and an *arriviste* New York professional school named Teachers College, Columbia University. It enlisted parents and teachers, starry-eyed crusaders and hardheaded politicians. And in less than two generations it transformed the character of the American school.

2

Education
and Industry

AMERICANS have always loved a fair, and the great Philadelphia Centennial Exposition of 1876 was one of the best of them. Five years in the making, it had cost over $11 million; fifty-eight governments had been represented; and almost ten million persons had been in attendance. Besides providing the sort of once-in-a-lifetime extravaganza so dear to the popular heart, the Exposition had testified eloquently to worldwide progress under the benevolent influence of science and technology. It had served its hosts as "a school of incomparable excellence" in manufactures, in agriculture, and especially in the arts; and there was no denying that American industry itself had scored an impressive triumph. Whatever else the Centennial contributed to a not reticent national pride, it had demonstrated conclusively that in the worldwide competition for industrial supremacy the United States was a power to be reckoned with.[1]

[1] United States Centennial Commission: *Report of the Director-General* (Washington, 1880), I, 13, 438.

From the beginning, the relation of education to national progress had been a key theme of the Centennial. The Exposition had boasted literally hundreds of displays, varying all the way from a case of botanical specimens contributed by the schoolchildren of Indiana to a full-scale model of a Swedish country schoolhouse. It is not surprising, though, that pedagogical innovations associated rather directly with industrial prosperity had come under the closest scrutiny. In the end, a few displays of tools from Moscow and St. Petersburg literally stole the show; for these objects showed the West for the first time that Russian educators had finally scored a breakthrough on the thorny problem of how to organize meaningful, instructive shop training as an essential adjunct of technical education.

The key to their solution lay in the work of Victor Della Vos, director of the Moscow Imperial Technical School. When the School had been created by royal decree in the spring of 1868, the effort had been to complement the work in mathematics, physics, and engineering with on-the-job training in *construction* shops built expressly for teaching purposes. These workshops were actually designed to produce saleable goods, but their primary task was to provide apprenticeships by which students at the Technical School might master the practical phases of their work. Della Vos from the beginning had regarded the workshop method as inefficient and overly expensive, and in order to ready the boys for their apprenticeships, he had organized *instruction* shops separate from and preliminary to the *construction* shops. It was in working out a program for these *instruction* shops that Della Vos had happened upon his radical pedagogical innovation.[2]

"Everybody is well aware," he reasoned, "that the mastery of any art—drawing, music, painting—is readily attained only when the first attempts are subject to a law of gradation, the pupil following a definite method or school, and surmounting, little by little and by certain degrees, the difficulties encoun-

[2] Charles Alpheus Bennett: *History of Manual and Industrial Education, 1870–1917* (Peoria, 1937), ch. i.

tered." [3] Why not work out similar methods for teaching the mechanic arts? Della Vos and his assistants set out to do just this. They organized an instruction shop for each distinctive art or trade—one for joinery, one for blacksmithing, one for carpentry, and so on; they analyzed each trade into its component skills and arranged these in pedagogical order; and they combined drawings, models, and tools into a series of graded exercises by which a student could, under supervision, progress toward a requisite standard of skill. That the new system quickly proved itself was compellingly demonstrated by the swift disappearance of the *construction* shops from the Moscow Imperial Technical School.

It was the drawings, the models, and the tools illustrating the Della Vos methods that the Russians exhibited at Philadelphia. It is said that President John D. Runkle of the Massachusetts Institute of Technology was strolling through Machinery Hall one day when he happened upon the Russian display cases.[4] American education was never the same thereafter. Runkle had been wrestling with the shop problem at M.I.T., and for him the Russian solution held "the philosophical key to all industrial education." [5] As soon as he returned from Philadelphia, he recommended the organization of instruction shops at the Institute, and on August 17, 1876, the trustees established not only shops for the engineering students, but a new School of Mechanic Arts to provide manual education "for those who wish to enter upon industrial pursuits, rather than to become scientific engineers." [6]

Runkle himself became an enthusiastic promoter of manual training, and in reports to the Massachusetts Board of Educa-

[3] Victor Della Vos: *Description of the Collections of Scientific Appliances Instituted for the Study of Mechanical Art in the Workshops of the Imperial Technical School of Moscow* (Moscow, 1876).

[4] Runkle to Charles H. Ham, May 22, 1884, quoted in Ham: *Manual Training* (New York, 1886), pp. 331–2.

[5] John D. Runkle: "The Manual Element in Education," in Massachusetts Board of Education: *Forty-First Annual Report, 1876–77* (Boston, 1878) p. 188.

[6] Ibid., p. 192.

tion as well as to his own trustees, he soon elaborated a more general theory of education based on the manual training idea. In the early days of the Republic, he reasoned, apprenticeship had properly joined mental and manual education; this ideal education, however, had been torn asunder by the rise of an industrial system overcommitted to specialization and a public school system overconcerned with mental training. In manual instruction lay the key to a new balanced schooling that would again marry the mental and the manual, thereby preparing people realistically for life in an industrial society.

Runkle may have begun to generalize Della Vos's discovery into a new vision of the school; but it was Calvin M. Woodward of Washington University (St. Louis) who made a new philosophy of it. A Harvard-educated New Englander, Woodward had joined the faculty of Washington University in 1865 as vice-principal of the academic department and instructor in mathematics. The next year he associated himself also with the O'Fallon Polytechnic Institute, a local school dedicated to evening instruction for the city's apprentices and journeymen, and in 1868 he was authorized to establish an engineering department in the University. According to Woodward, it was in the course of teaching certain difficult problems in applied mechanics that he decided to have his students prepare a number of illustrative wooden models. Upon bringing in the college carpenter to supervise the boys in their work, he quickly realized their appalling ignorance in the simplest use of tools. Deciding to put first things first, he laid aside thoughts of mathematical models and set to teaching tool work, thus embarking on his first venture in shop teaching *with no immediate vocational goal.*

During the 1870's Woodward became an outspoken critic of the public schools, charging them with adherence to outmoded ideals of gentlemanliness and culture. "There has been a growing demand," he wrote in 1873, "not only for men of knowledge, but for men of skill, in every department of human activity. Have our schools and colleges and universities been equal to the demand? Are we satisfied with what they have produced? Or are we compelled reluctantly to admit, that, after filling to overflowing the three traditionally learned professions, they yield little else but candidates for Milton's class of 'gentlemen,' inasmuch as they are fitted for no kind of work, and consequently must spend their lives in ease and enjoyment if it be possible?" The old style of education is useless, he concluded; it "oftener *unfits* than *fits* a man for earning his living." [7]

Obviously Woodward was ready for Della Vos's revelations at Philadelphia. Within a year he was enthusiastically commending the Russian methods to university officials, warning that the desire to eliminate all narrow utilitarian motives had "sometimes run to the other extreme and excluded from our schools important and essential branches of study because they were suspected of being useful." [8] The subtle distinction here between the "narrowly utilitarian" and the "essential and useful" held the key to Woodward's emerging educational ideal. Sincerely committed to a broad and liberal curriculum, he was unwilling to make preparation for a specific trade the goal of general schooling. The trades are many but the arts are few, he contended. The genius of Della Vos had been to provide a method whereby mechanical processes might be abstracted, systematized, and efficiently taught; the genius of Runkle had been to see meaning in Della Vos's discovery for the liberal education of *all* students. Woodward set out to build an institution that would embody both principles. The Manual Training School of Washington University, established on June 6, 1879 as the first of its kind in the United States, represented the fruit of his efforts.

The object of the new school was to provide a three-year secondary program divided equally between mental and manual labor. Mathematics, drawing, science, languages, history, and literature were to be combined with instruction in car-

[7] Calvin M. Woodward: *The Manual Training School* (Boston, 1887), pp. 243–5. See also Charles Penney Coates: *History of the Manual Training School of Washington University* (United States Bureau of Education, Bulletin, 1923, No. 3), pp. 8–11; and Bennett: op. cit., p. 318.

[8] *Manual Education in the Polytechnic School of Washington University* (1877).

pentry, wood turning, patternmaking, iron chipping and filing, forge work, brazing and soldering, and bench and machine work in metals. The goal of the course was liberal rather than vocational; the emphasis throughout was to be on education rather than production for sale, on principle rather than narrow skill, on art rather than the tradesman's competence. The school opened in September 1880 with fifty pupils; by June of 1883, when the first class was graduated, the enrollment had climbed to 176.[9]

With the Manual Training School successfully launched, Woodward was quickly projected before the public as the protagonist of a new movement, and the 1880's saw both the extension and elaboration of his philosophy. Espousing change, he was inevitably pushed to sharper criticism of the existing system. To Woodward it was lopsided and impractical. It trained a handful of youngsters for the "so-called learned professions" but cared little for the "productive, toiling classes." It taught young people to think without teaching them to work; indeed, it actually taught them to abhor work. Ignoring the hard realities of life, it concentrated on aimless, grinding booklearning to the detriment of true education. The most eloquent testimony to its inadequacy was its failure to hold more than an infinitesimal percentage of the population beyond the eighth grade.

What was the remedy? Manual training. "Put the whole boy in school," Woodward urged, and educate him equally "for all spheres of usefulness." There would be no end to the ensuing benefits. Young people would remain in school longer. Dull intellectual subjects would be invested with new vigor and meaning. Young people, unprejudiced by false notions of gentility, would make more sensible occupational choices. And labor problems—inevitably associated with uneducated, unintelligent workmen—would rapidly disappear. "The system I advocate sets up no false standards," Woodward assured; ". . . it aims to elevate, to dignify, to liberalize, all the essential elements of society; and it renders it possible for every honorable

[9] Coates: op. cit., p. 39.

calling to be the happy home of cultivation and refinement." [1]

Woodward's contentions could hardly go unchallenged, and during the late seventies the National Educational Association became an arena in which the manual-training issue was hotly debated. From the beginning, there was spirited interest. When President Runkle explained the Russian system of tool instruction at the NEA meetings of 1877, an Ohio schoolman called it the most important thing he had heard at an NEA gathering since the Association had been organized. Yet most of the new enthusiasts agreed that the new methods belonged in higher technical institutions like M.I.T., but certainly not in the public schools. "I have little expectation that the workshop will ever have an important place in the public school," advised President Emerson White of Purdue. Public schools, being common to all, needed to teach a cultural education useful to all. White had no objection to including certain "general forms of technical knowledge," but to teach trades or trade processes was to subvert the proper and primary work of public education.[2]

The issue thus drawn became the crux of the most vigorous pedagogical battle of the eighties. When Woodward put forward his notion of manual training as part of a balanced general education for all, many joined White in his cry of subversion. Superintendent Albert P. Marble of the Worcester, Massachusetts, school system, for example, was unceasing in

[1] Woodward: *The Manual Training School*, p. 239. The notion of "dignifying" manual labor, so much an aspect of the "self-help" theme sounded by Americans like Horace Mann and their Victorian counterparts like Samuel Smiles, was for many the core of the manual-training idea. The notion is nowhere better expressed than in the work of Charles H. Ham, journalist, author, appraiser of customs for the Port of Chicago, and one of the moving spirits in the founding of Chicago's Manual Training School in 1884. See Ham's book: *Manual Training*.

[2] White had become a well-known figure in the councils of American education by the late 1870's. He assumed the presidency of Purdue in 1876, after serving as state superintendent of common schools in Ohio, and as president of the NEA in 1872. He thought it ridiculous for public schools to devote their energies to handicraft training at a time when the machine was assuming an ever-greater burden of production, a penetrating criticism of Woodward's position. See National Educational Association: *Addresses and Proceedings*, 1880, p. 225.

his public criticism of what he deemed the exaggerated claims and misguided sentimentalism of the manual-training enthusiasts. In an 1882 debate before the NEA, he made short shrift of the new idea, claiming that "the schools we have to conduct are to train boys and girls in those directions that are common to everybody, and one of the things that the boys and girls ought to learn in those schools is how to get information from books. There is no information stored up in the plow, hoe handle, [or] steam engine; but there *is* information stored up in books. . . . The saw is brought into the recitation room, and the teacher says, 'now, saw.' It is a thing that does not belong to the school at all. It belongs outside, and ought to be attended to outside." [3]

As might be expected, the heaviest blast at the manual-training idea came from William T. Harris himself. Harris had left the St. Louis superintendency for the Concord School of Philosophy just as Woodward's school was getting under way; hence there is little in the record of his reaction to the Washington University experiment. As early as 1884, in a brief remark to the NEA, Harris rejoiced that preparation for work was becoming a matter of schooling rather than apprenticeship, but denied any need to introduce manual training into the general common-school program. [4]

As Woodward further elaborated his own position, it was almost inevitable that Harris would cross swords with him. The occasion finally came at the full-dress debate planned for the 1889 gathering of the NEA's Department of Superintendence. Harris's paper, "The Psychology of Manual Training," cut deeply into the philosophical issues at stake. Schoolmen, Harris began, tend to divide themselves into conservatives and progressives, the former holding by the heritage of the past, the latter constantly critical and casting about for remedies and radical changes. Both, of course, were necessary to the dialectical process inherent in educational progress. Without experi-

[3] United States Bureau of Education: *Report of the Commissioner of Education for the Year 1893–94*, I, 887.
[4] National Educational Association: *Addresses and Proceedings*, 1884, p. 85.

ment there could be no advance; yet even progressives would admit that only one in a hundred experiments gains real results. Hence, the need for searching debate on all proposals for change.

What, then, of manual training? Harris viewed Woodward's notion of putting the "whole boy" in school as a dangerous "survival of Rousseauism," one that failed to distinguish between higher and lower faculties in the individual. And as for tool work being educative, Harris noted that so were marbles, quoits, baseball, and jackstraws, but this did not command for them a place in the school. The difference between man and animal, Harris insisted, lay in man's ability to generalize, comprehend, relate, and idealize; and it was the business of the school to cultivate these abilities, to begin a lifelong process of education through self-activity. To teach a child carpentry, Harris warned, is to give him a limited knowledge of self and nature; to teach him to read is to offer him the key to all human wisdom. "It is the difference between a piece of baked bread, which nourishes for the day, and the seed-corn, which is the possibility of countless harvests. Education that educates the child in the art of self-education is that which the aggregate experience of mankind has chosen for the school." [5]

Four months after Harris delivered his rather caustic analysis to the Department of Superintendence, he took occasion to reiterate his views at the July convention of the NEA.[6] That same gathering also heard a similar report from the Committee on Pedagogics of the National Council of Education, a kind of laureate group within the NEA organized in 1880 to debate high policy.[7] Woodward prepared a detailed rejoinder to the Committee's assertions and published it in 1890 as part of his

[5] *Proceedings of the Department of Superintendence of the National Educational Association*, 1889 (United States Bureau of Education, Circular of Information No. 2, Washington, 1889), pp. 126–7.

[6] "The Intellectual Value of Tool-Work," in National Educational Association: *Addresses and Proceedings*, 1889, pp. 92–8.

[7] The similarity of the two reports was hardly surprising, Harris being one of the four-man Committee. See Isaac Edwards Clarke, ed.: *Education in the Industrial and Fine Arts in the United States* (Washington, 1892), Part II, pp. 931–36.

Manual Training in Education. He need not have gone to the trouble, for he had clearly won the debate by 1889, and little in the way of articulate opposition appeared thereafter.[8]

Moreover, if results were to be judged, Woodward had won more than the debate. The year 1884 had seen the establishment of manual training in three cities in ways destined to set the pattern of subsequent development. Under the prodding of Charles Ham and Colonel Augustus Jacobson, the Chicago Commercial Club had organized a private manual-training school modeled closely along the lines of Woodward's institution, though without university affiliation.[9] A month later the Baltimore School Board had responded to demands from businessmen and labor unions by opening the first public manual-training school in the United States.[1] Meanwhile, Peru, Illinois, an industrial city of 6,500, had decided to introduce manual-training courses into its general high school, the pattern destined to become most common in American education.[2]

All three lines of work quickly expanded. Private manual-training schools, most often sponsored by businessmen, were established in Toledo (1885), Cleveland (1886), Cincinnati (1886), New Orleans (1886), New York (1887), and Cambridge, Massachusetts (1888). Philadelphia founded a public manual-training school in 1885; St. Paul opened one in 1888. And city after city established manual classes as adjuncts to the general school program. An 1890 survey by the United States Bureau of Education found thousands of boys and girls studying carpentry, metal and machine work, sewing, cook-

[8] Calvin M. Woodward: "The Rise and Progress of Manual Training," in United States Bureau of Education: *Report of the Commissioner of Education for the Year 1893–94,* I, 903–4.

[9] Jacobson, a Cook County judge, had written as early as 1874: "I should build schoolhouses, fill them with steam engines and machinery, and in them I would train young America, male and female, fully up to the present state of knowledge in everything there is to be known." Ibid., 889.

[1] Charles Hirschfeld: *Baltimore, 1870–1890: Studies in Social History* (Baltimore, 1941), ch. iii.

[2] Clarke: op. cit., Part II, pp. 191–4.

ing, and drawing in thirty-six cities representing fifteen states and the District of Columbia.

Moreover, the survey, in classifying this broad range of studies as "manual training," revealed the rather striking extension that had occurred in the common definition of manual education.[3] In addition to the tool work espoused by Runkle and Woodward, correlative studies in homemaking had entered the high school. And largely influenced by Swedish instruction in *slöjd* (handwork, usually in wood), manual training had moved downward into the grades, appearing as a variety of arts and crafts in the elementary school. By 1890 some educators were contending that if the ordinary activities of the kindergarten could be joined to *slöjd* at the elementary level and tool exercises or homemaking in the secondary school, the result would be an orderly progression of manual work to parallel intellectual activities throughout the twelve-year period of general education. In a proper balance of the two they saw a new vision of popular schooling suitable to the demands of an industrial age.[4]

The fabulous advance of manual training during the nineties only further corroborated Woodward's position. Yet his victory was in many ways a Pyrrhic one. The businessmen who advocated and supported manual education may have spoken in Woodward's rhetoric, but what they wanted was practical trade training to free them from growing union regulation of apprenticeships. And the students themselves seemed to care less about dignifying manual labor than they did about using the manual-training school to escape to some higher technical occupation.[5] As tool work moved from wood to metals, par-

[3] United States Bureau of Education: *Report of the Commissioner of Education for the Year 1889–90*, II, 1351–6. Undoubtedly the range of studies also revealed a simple confusion as to the meaning of manual education.

[4] An early example is Felix Adler, founder of the New York Society for Ethical Culture. See Robert H. Beck: "Progressive Education and American Progressivism: Felix Adler," *Teachers College Record*, LX (1958–59), 77–89.

[5] When Woodward listed the occupations of graduates of the St. Louis Manual Training School as of October, 1894, few were engaged

ticularly steel, the machine gradually replaced the hand tool, and productive skill rather than artistic handcraft became the guiding ideal. And as the schools themselves fell into the hands of a new class of administrators imbued with reformist enthusiasm for manual training, talk about a liberalizing balance between manual and intellectual activities became increasingly academic.

Ultimately, Woodward's own formulation embodied a dilemma that cast it at best in the role of transition philosophy. On the one hand, he had been forced to deny vocational aspirations to make his viewpoint acceptable to the educational fraternity at large; on the other, the very tool work he was espousing—tied as it was to a sentimental handicraft ideal— led the school to the brink of vocational training. Students and sponsors, less troubled with an historic commitment to culture than the educators, hardly saw reason not to take the plunge. In the end, the voracious manpower demands of an expanding industrial economy resolved the dilemma. The same Woodward who in 1890 denied that manual-training schools had any concern with vocation boasted thirteen years later that "by multiplying manual-training schools we solve the problem of training all the mechanics our country needs." [6]

I I

Throughout the eighties there had been schools frankly vocational in character and purpose. In 1881, for example, just a year after the St. Louis Manual Training School had opened its doors, Colonel Richard T. Auchmuty, a well-to-do architect and scion of an old New York family, had organized the New York Trades Schools for the express purpose of providing trade instruction in bricklaying, plastering, plumbing, carpentry, stonecutting, blacksmithing, tailoring, and printing. Based on

---

in manual labor; most had gone into clerical and technical occupations, the professions, or supervisory work.

[6] Calvin M. Woodward: "Manual, Industrial, and Technical Education in the United States," in United States Bureau of Education: *Report of the Commissioner of Education for the Year 1903*, I, 1039.

a theory closely paralleling the discoveries of Della Vos, the schools made no pretense at providing education with a larger cultural value. The courses were short and intensely practical, each one culminating in a rigorous certifying examination. The effort was avowedly to replace a deteriorating, overly specialized, and stringently limited apprenticeship training with a combination of technical and trade instruction specifically designed to produce qualified journeymen.[7]

Auchmuty minced no words about the forces that had called his schools into being. Under the modern factory system, apprenticeship had deteriorated into a haphazard arrangement in which masters no longer cared to teach, in which boys were unready to accept prolonged periods of indenture, and in which child labor had therefore become exploitive rather than educative. To compound the difficulty, labor unions, controlled overwhelmingly by "foreigners," were conspiring drastically to limit the number of apprenticeships, thereby restricting the flow of American boys into the trades. For Auchmuty the solution was clear: owing to the modern subdivision of labor, the workshop was no longer the best place to learn a trade. Schools would have to assume the classical functions of apprenticeship.[8] As one might expect, Auchmuty

[7] *The Century*, New Series, I (1881–82), 286; and *Fourth Annual Report of the Bureau of Statistics of Labor of the State of New York, 1886*, pp. 392–7. Vocational education, of course, was not new in the eighties; it had been central to schools like Rensselaer Polytechnic Institute and Michigan Agricultural College, both founded before the Civil War, and central to the purposes of the agricultural and mechanic arts colleges founded under the Morrill Act of 1862. All of these institutions featured manual work in a shop or on an institutional farm. But insofar as Auchmuty's schools offered trade rather than technical training, and disavowed any pretense at collegiate status, they were new.

[8] Richard T. Auchmuty: "An American Apprentice System," *The Century*, New Series, XV (1888–9), 401–5. *The Century* was quite taken with Auchmuty's arguments and gave continuing attention to the problem of trade education and apprenticeship. A series of editorials in 1893 was largely inspired by Auchmuty, and proof sheets of the articles were read and revised by him. For a rejoinder to Auchmuty's arguments as they pertained to labor unions, see Edward W. Bemis: "Relation of Labor Organizations to the American Boy and to Trade Instruction," *Annals of the American Academy of Political and Social Science*, V (1894–5), 209–41.

turned initially to employers for support for his ideas, holding out the promise that his graduates would work at lower wage scales and remain relatively free of union control. A $500,000 grant by J. P. Morgan to the New York Trades Schools in 1892 symbolized a rather general concurrence on the part of the business community.

The unions, on the other hand, were ambivalent from the beginning. A New York survey in 1886 revealed that the state's labor organizations favored both manual training and trade schools by a plurality of about two to one. The majority saw in industrial education a needed practicalizing of the schools, and many—especially those representing skilled tradesmen—commented that there need be no incompatibility between what they thought of as *preparatory* industrial education and a "healthy, practicable apprenticeship system." A highly vocal minority, though, was both acrimonious and adamant in its opposition. The secretary of Cigarmakers' Union No. 144 wrote: "The trade schools thus far in existence have been nothing more nor less than the breeding schools for scabs or rats. . . ." A carpenters local warned that school training made "half-fledged" mechanics; while a carpet worker feared that trade instruction would deprive children of general education, already too brief to begin with. The Secretary of the Twist and Warp Lace Makers' Association predicted that trade education "would be rather a curse than a blessing by placing at the disposal of every capitalist bent on grinding down wages to the lowest point, an unlimited number of skilled operatives out of work, to supersede those who might resist his tyranny." The arguments were many, but the point was clear: to relinquish control over apprenticeship was to relinquish a hard-won right crucial in the struggle for higher wages and improved working conditions.[9]

The 1890's witnessed not only an extension of the trade-school idea but a number of efforts to come to terms with

[9] *Fourth Annual Report of the Bureau of Statistics of Labor of the State of New York*, 1886, pp. 398–405. Labor Commissioner Peck's reports were among the earliest to refer to industrial education as progressive education.

labor opposition. The early history of Pratt Institute in Brooklyn, New York, provides an excellent case in point. From its
first years, Pratt provided full-fledged training in bricklaying,
stonecarving, and plumbing, modeled along the lines of Auchmuty's program. The Institute soon encountered hostility from
local unions in connection with its trade courses, but in the
absence of Auchmuty's vigorous antilabor bias, the result was
more armed neutrality than continuing warfare. In at least
one field, plumbing, the trustees entered into an arrangement
with the Brooklyn Journeymen Plumbers' Association whereby
a committee of the Association formally examined candidates
for graduation in the arts of plumbing and a knowledge of
trade union methods. Relations with the bricklayers' and
plasterers' unions were less friendly, though, and during the
early 1890's there were intermittent threats to withdraw journeymen who were serving as instructors. Eventually, however,
the situation was adjusted.[1]

In the case of New York's Baron de Hirsch School, founded
in 1891 to fit boys in as brief a time as possible to be helpers
in the mechanical and building trades, the authorities actually
leaned over backward in friendliness toward labor, urging
each graduate to join the union in his trade. Even so, Samuel
Gompers opposed it along with all trade schools as naturally
hostile to the interests of the labor movement. "It is not only
ridiculous but positively wrong for trade schools to continue
their turning out 'botch' workmen who are ready and willing,
at the end of their so-called 'graduation,' to take the places of
American workmen far below the wages prevailing in the
trade," Gompers wrote in the early nineties. "With practically
half of the toiling masses of our country unemployed, the con-
tinuance of the practice is tantamount to a crime." [2]

With the organization of the National Association of Manufacturers in 1896 and its early espousal of trade education as
an economic weapon, labor hostility sharpened considerably.
At their very first convention (1897), NAM members visited
the Pennsylvania Museum's School of Industrial Art at the

[1] Clarke: op. cit., Part III, pp. 449–59; and Bemis: op. cit., p. 227.
[2] Bemis: op. cit., pp. 233–6.

invitation of their President, Theodore C. Search, and impressed with what they saw, subsequently approved a resolution supporting "practical arts, industrial, manual training or other technical schools." [3] The following year Search devoted a substantial portion of his presidential address to the larger question of industrial education, warning that Germany's rising industrial power was founded squarely on a system of excellent technical schools, that England was rapidly learning the lesson from Germany, and that the United States had better do likewise. It was all good and well to hold fast to classical and literary studies, Search granted, but it was "unfair and unjust to the great material interests of the land to leave out of account the obvious demands of industry and commerce." Wherever possible, he advised, "considerable sums should be diverted from the main educational channels to be put into commercial and technical schools." His sentiments were adopted as the views of the convention. [4]

Search's advice set the pattern of NAM demands for at least a decade, and during the 1900's the Association was the nation's most outspoken exponent of trade education. Resolutions favoring commercial and technical training were passed virtually every year. A Committee on Industrial Education was appointed in 1905, and its reports, following in the intellectual footsteps of Auchmuty, pictured an industrial America locked in mortal commercial combat with Germany and England yet hamstrung by hidebound high schools, monopolistic union regulation of apprenticeship, and "the outrageous opposition of organized labor" to trade education. "It is plain to see," the Committee concluded, "that trade schools properly protected from the domination and withering blight of organized labor are the one and only remedy for the present intolerable conditions." [5]

NAM–AF of L antagonism on this issue might well have become irreconcilable during the next few years had it not

[3] National Association of Manufacturers: *Proceedings*, 1897, pp. 81, 92.
[4] Ibid., 1898, pp. 20–2, 62–3.   [5] Ibid., 1906, pp. 57–83.

been for the establishment in 1906 of the National Society
for the Promotion of Industrial Education. Organized largely
through the efforts of Charles R. Richards of Teachers College, Columbia University, and James P. Haney, Director of
Manual Training for the New York City public schools, the
National Society was frankly conceived as a political effort
"to unite the many forces making toward industrial education
the country over." [6] Like many a similar effort, it served during
its early years largely as a clearinghouse for information and
propaganda from the many agencies concerned with vocational education. But as is often the case, its enthusiasm
spilled over and made many a convert to the movement.

In 1907 Richards himself went to the AF of L convention
in Norfolk, Virginia, to explain the Society's aims and to enlist
support for the cause. The Federation was less than enthusiastic, responding with a resolution condemning the use of trade
schools as a weapon against the trade-union movement but
endorsing "any policy, or any society or association having
for its object the raising of the standard of industrial education and the teaching of the higher technique of our various
industries." More important, perhaps, the Committee on Education recommended that the Executive Council further consider the matter to determine the wisest policy for the Federation.[7]

The Council came into the 1908 Convention with a recommendation that the problem be given still further study by
the Federation's Committee on Education. The education
committee in turn produced a strongly worded resolution
warning that two groups with opposing methods and antago-
nistic ends were advocating industrial education for the nation: one, composed largely of nonunion employers, was
seeking such training as a special privilege to produce half-
educated scab laborers and strikebreakers; the other, embrac-

[6] National Society for the Promotion of Industrial Education: *Pro-*
ceedings of the Organization Meetings (Bulletin No. 1, New York,
1907).
[7] American Federation of Labor: *Proceedings, 1907,* pp. 318–9.

ing "great educators, enlightened representatives of organized labor and persons engaged in genuine industrial service," was urging industrial education as a common right of all children under public auspices. The resolution went on to state that industrial education was "necessary and inevitable" and that the Federation should throw its political weight on the side of the angels. It concluded with a call for a special AF of L Committee to investigate the whole matter. The Convention went along, leaving the selection of the committee to President Gompers.[8]

Gompers, collaborating with the Executive Council, appointed a strong group with John Mitchell, former President of the United Mine Workers, as chairman and himself as a member. In the course of its deliberations, the Committee scrutinized the public state technical schools of New Jersey; the Massachusetts program of independent, four-year public vocational schools; New York's plan of public industrial schools for pupils between fourteen and sixteen, and public trade schools for pupils between sixteen and eighteen; the Milwaukee School of Trades, the first to be supported by a special tax; the cooperative arrangement in Cincinnati whereby two groups of pupils alternated between shop and school; the Inland Printer Technical School run by the International Typographical Union; several endowed trade schools; the apprenticeship schools of the New York Central Railroad and the General Electric Company; and a number of federally sponsored industrial training programs.

The Committee's recommendations paralleled those of organized business to a point. Old-time apprenticeship, they granted, had become wasteful, inefficient, and exploitive; some other educational arrangement would have to replace it. But at this juncture agreement ended. The Committee was scathing in its attack on cooperative arrangements between manufacturers and school authorities, contending "that there is justification in condemning any system of public instruction privately controlled, or any scheme of private selection of pu-

[8] Ibid., 1908, p. 234.

pils. . . ." It then went on to recommend three kinds of
schools: first, public continuation schools for those who had
already entered the trades; second, union-sponsored supple-
mental trade schools patterned after the work of the ITU;
and third, public trade schools—not necessarily in separate
school buildings—in which a balanced combination of general education and shop instruction would be provided. To
keep such schools in close touch with the trades themselves,
the Committee further recommended the creation of local
advisory boards representing industry and organized labor.
Finally, the Committee appended a proposed bill providing
for an annual federal appropriation of $11,000,000 to the
states, territories, and the District of Columbia for secondary-
school instruction in agriculture, home economics, and the
trades, and for teacher-training courses in each of these subjects.[9]

The Committee's report marked a new era in labor's attitude toward vocational education. Before 1910 many individual unions and unionists had favored it, but the most articulate
of the national spokesmen, Gompers among them, had been
hostile. From 1910 on, the Federation supported vocational
education, assuming that the question was no longer *whether*
the school would offer vocational training, but *how*. It remained only for labor to assure itself a role in determining
answers to the latter question.

III

Historians of education have long tended to portray the vocational education movement as essentially urban in character,
and to assume that once labor had been converted to the cause,
the battle was all but won.[1] The difficulty with this view is

[9] American Federation of Labor: *Industrial Education* (Washington,
1910).

[1] The view is advanced by Charles Alpheus Bennett in his *History of
Manual and Industrial Education, 1870–1917*, ch. xiii; and by Ellwood P.
Cubberley in *Public Education in the United States*, rev. ed. (Boston,
1934), ch. xix.

that it virtually ignores the telling support that derived from a half-century of agrarian protest and innovation. Vocational-ism, after all, had been at the heart of the farmers' institute idea, begun formally with the work of the Massachusetts State Agricultural Board in 1852 and taken up by at least thirteen states during the 1860's and 1870's.[2] It had been central to the agricultural colleges founded under the Morrill Act of 1862. And it had been implicit in Oliver H. Kelley's initial concep-tion of the National Grange, founded in 1867 as a social and educational fraternity for "the resuscitation of the country and the recuperation of its farmers." As early as 1874 the Grange had proclaimed its interest in the teaching of "prac-tical agriculture, domestic science, and all the arts which adorn the home";[3] and two years later a standing committee on education had been created to pronounce from year to year on matters pedagogical and to direct the attention of state Granges to similar concerns.

During the eighties, despite farmer preoccupation with poli-tics, the vigor of educational reform never flagged. More than a score of states organized farmers' institutes on a more or less permanent basis, most of them aided by some sort of public appropriation. A powerful lobby, begun in 1882, secured pas-sage five years later of the so-called Hatch Act, providing for federally assisted agricultural experiment stations "to aid in ac-quiring and diffusing among the people of the United States useful and practical information on subjects connected with agriculture." The year 1887 also witnessed a coalescing of the groups that had obtained this legislative victory into the Asso-ciation of American Agricultural Colleges and Experiment Stations, an organization destined to lend powerful support to the drive for agricultural education in the years ahead.

[2] Alfred Charles True: A *History of Agricultural Extension Work in the United States*, 1785–1923 (Washington, 1928). True traces the roots of the farmers' institutes back to the early nineteenth-century agri-cultural societies and farmers' clubs.

[3] National Grange of the Patrons of Husbandry: *Proceedings, 1874*, p. 58. For a general treatment of education in the early program of the Grange, see Solon Justus Buck: *The Granger Movement: 1870–1880* (Cambridge, 1913), ch. viii.

In 1890, the very year People's Parties were beginning to appear in the Midwest, Congress passed the "Second Morrill Act," bestowing further federal largesse upon the A. & M. Colleges for "instruction in agriculture, the mechanic arts, the English language and the various branches of mathematical, physical, natural and economic science, with special reference to their application in the industries of life. . . ." By 1896, the year of Bryan's ill-fated campaign, there were over 25,000 students in the land-grant institutions, studying everything from metallurgy to dairy husbandry to domestic science, eloquent testimony to the vigor of the enterprise Senator Morrill had sponsored three decades before.[4]

With the collapse of political populism, educational reform seemed to gain new vigor, and pleas for the reconstitution of the school could suddenly be heard on every side.[5] Most of them sounded the common theme that rural education was unimaginative and irrelevant, that it dealt too much with books and too little with life, that it educated away from the country and toward the city, and that only a massive infusion of agricultural studies could save it from complete decay.

Consider, for example, the efforts of some of the more popular farm journalists; "Uncle Henry" Wallace, editor of the influential *Wallace's Farmer*, provides an excellent case in point. A farm boy originally trained for the ministry, Wallace waged an unceasing campaign to enlighten his readers on school affairs. Until his death in 1916 his journal editorialized on education, printed letters from interested subscribers, quoted significant speeches, and reported new developments in pedagogy. He extolled the virtues of country living and expounded on the necessity of fusing the interests of teachers

[4] United States Bureau of Education: *Report of the Commissioner of Education for the Year 1895–96*, II, 1272.

[5] The shift of agrarian reform from the polls to the schools after 1896 has not been generally noted. See Theodore Salutos and John D. Hicks: *Agricultural Discontent in the Middle West, 1900–1939* (Madison, 1951); Grant McConnell: *The Decline of Agrarian Democracy* (Berkeley, 1953); and Ann M. Keppel: "Country Schools for Country Children: Backgrounds of the Reform Movement in Rural Elementary Education, 1890–1914" (Unpublished Doctoral Thesis, University of Wisconsin, 1960).

and farmers. Above all, he sought to overcome time-honored suspicions about education and to prod farmers into active concern for the schooling of their children. Regeneration would only occur when teachers had been imbued with the "spirit of agriculture," and such a spirit could only emanate from the farmers themselves.[6]

Wallace agreed with the contributor who insisted on abandoning "the cut-and-dried formula of a period when a man was 'educated' only when he knew Greek and Latin," and suggested that there be less adherence to textbooks, more concern with the all-around development of children, and unceasing attention to the rudiments of agriculture.[7] "It is hard," he wrote, "for many a middle-aged farmer to get a clear idea of what is meant by protein, carbohydrates, nitrogen-free extract, etc. Now, these terms are no harder than many which the pupils learn and which are of no earthly use to them in their everyday lives."[8] The teachers' guides should come not from high schools, normal schools, or colleges, but from farmers themselves, who know best what their children need. Instead of depending on textbooks, teachers should experiment in the classroom with seeds, with the Babcock milk tester, with honeycombs, or with any other practical material, being careful to "get the fodder down low enough for the lambs."[9] Once begun, such practices would not only capture the attention of youngsters; they would undoubtedly interest adults in better education. Parents might even be prompted to visit their schools—if only to object!

Wisconsin's counterpart of Wallace was William Dempster Hoard. Editor of a local newspaper and of *Hoard's Dairyman*, one-term governor of the state, and a member of the University's Board of Regents, Hoard rested his hopes for a genuinely scientific agriculture squarely with the younger generation. "Us old fellows—our eyes are 'sot,' and it ain't much

[6] *Wallace's Farmer*, December 18, 1908, p. 1564.
[7] Ibid., January 19, 1913, p. 68.
[8] Ibid., March 6, 1908, p. 338.
[9] Ibid., February 18, 1910, p. 322, and August 28, 1914, p. 1165.

use to bother with us," he announced to the dairy farmers
of the state. "The country has got no hope through the old
farmers." [1] With dismay he reported instances of boys seeking
his aid when their fathers refused to employ new agricultural
techniques, or even to hear of them. Eventually he came to
despair of adult intransigence; the future lay with the youngsters in the schools.

Granted this, the schools would have to change. Hoard cast
a jaundiced eye at the "cheap miserable character" of existing
education: ". . . as it was 60 years ago in our boyhood, so it
is today in 99 out of every 100 schools. Not a grain of progress
that will help the country boy to a better understanding of
the problems of agriculture." [2] A whole new outlook was
needed. Teachers would have to master elementary botany,
sanitation, and agricultural chemistry; textbooks would have
to make sense to rural readers. Only then would farmers realize the value of schooling and abandon their traditional
apathy.

Hoard worked tirelessly for county normal schools that
would train farm-oriented rural teachers. Unlike Wallace, who
tried to influence farmers themselves, Hoard saw conservative
educators as the primary obstacles to change. "The old idea of
culture," he wrote, "was to have something the great mass of
humanity did not have. Men possessing an understanding
of Greek and Latin used to constitute the cultured people.
How narrow and selfish was this conception." Hoard would
have extended it to embrace the girl who had learned to care
for the sick and beautify her home and the boy who had mastered soil chemistry and the "habits of dumb animals." [3] In his
mind, a democracy of culture meant more than mere access
to education; it transformed the very meaning of education,
making it nothing less than the intelligent pursuit of happiness.

These urgings in the agricultural press—*Wallace's Farmer*

---

[1] *32nd Annual Report of the Wisconsin Dairyman's Association, 1904.*
p. 25; and *33rd Annual Report . . . , 1905,* p. 19.

[2] *Hoard's Dairyman,* July 19, 1895, p. 419.

[3] Ibid., April 10, 1914, p. 416.

and *Hoard's Dairyman* were certainly representative, if superior, examples—echoed widely through organizations purporting to speak for the farmer. The National Grange intensified its pressure for "practical knowledge" in the common schools and for agricultural education at all levels, contending that the land-grant colleges in particular had been too dominated by conservative pedagogical interests in the state universities to serve their true vocational purposes. The Farmers' Union and the American Society of Equity, both organized in 1902, gave continuing attention to educational questions during their early years. The first constitution of the Union explicitly committed it "to educate the agricultural classes in scientific farming"; [4] and rural schoolteachers were made eligible for membership so long as they were not engaged in banking, merchandising, law, or speculation—no doubt a stringent screen for the pedagogues. The Union's national convention of 1906 recommended an increase in agricultural and industrial education in the public schools as well as a course of reading on economic and governmental affairs, [5] while delegates to the Georgia State Conventions of 1907 and 1908 proclaimed their vigorous support of agricultural high schools. [6] Equity, organized initially as a giant farmer monopoly, early declared in favor of "institutions for educating farmers, their sons and daughters, and the general advancement of agriculture." [7] The Wisconsin branch of the society, probably the most active of all after 1907, waged a running guerrilla warfare with the state's education system, calling the university "a cold-storage institution of dead languages and useless learning which costs several millions of bushels of wheat each year"; [8] and there is no doubt that continued criticism from the *Wisconsin Equity News* was a potent force in

[4] Charles Simon Barrett: *The Mission, History and Times of the Farmers' Union* (Nashville, 1909), pp. 107–8.
[5] Ibid., p. 257.
[6] Ibid., pp. 215–21.
[7] Carl C. Taylor: *The Farmers' Movement, 1620–1920* (New York, 1953), p. 369.
[8] Salutos and Hicks: op. cit., p. 128.

triggering the 1914 legislative investigation into university affairs.[9]

As might be expected, farmers' institutes also performed yeoman's service in the cause of educational reform. Institute workers organized a national association in 1896, and from the beginning their annual conventions pondered the problems of the rural school.[1] At the Buffalo meeting of 1901, William Dempster Hoard urged institute people to impress farmers with the need for agricultural instruction at the elementary level, insisting that it was the only way to keep boys on the farm.[2] At the 1902 gathering, delegates were assured that once they succeeded in getting agriculture and domestic science into the schools, the farm kitchen would become a "vestibule of Paradise" and the garden "a second edition of that garden which the Lord planted eastward of Eden." [3]

Whatever the importance of these national meetings, it was at the state level that the institutes really made a difference. If the Wisconsin Institute may be taken as a case in point— and it is a good one, since it worked with legislative funds but was actually managed by farmers—local institutes were sounding boards par excellence for the educational reform movement. Farmers and their wives were lectured unceasingly on the need for a reoriented rural school. School gardens, field trips, and practical courses in the work of farm and kitchen

[9] Ibid., pp. 129–30; and Merle Curti and Vernon Carstensen: *The University of Wisconsin. A History 1848–1925* (2 vols., Madison, 1949), II, 267–94.

[1] The organization was founded in Watertown, Wisconsin and was first known as the International Association of Farmers' Institute Workers. It later became the American Association of Farmers' Institute Workers. A brief history is given in its *Proceedings*, 1901 (United States Department of Agriculture, Office of Experiment Stations, Bulletin No. 110). See also John Hamilton: *A History of Farmers' Institutes in the United States* (United States Department of Agriculture, Office of Experiment Stations, Bulletin No. 174).

[2] American Association of Farmers' Institute Workers: *Proceedings*, 1901, pp. 20 ff.

[3] American Association of Farmers' Institute Workers: *Proceedings*, 1902 (United States Department of Agriculture, Office of Experiment Stations, Bulletin No. 120), pp. 109 ff.

were the answers to an overly bookish program which overemphasized the accumulation of useless knowledge. "Grammar, history, geography are bundles of abstractions, while the child is interested in the world of realities," one speaker inveighed. "Rotation of crops is as inspiring as the position of the preposition; the fertilization of apples and corn as interesting as the location of cities and the course of rivers; the economy of the horse and cow and sheep as close to life as the duties of the President and the causes of the Revolutionary War." [4] In agriculture alone lay the salvation of rural education.[5]

Granted this many-sided demand for the reform of rural schools and colleges, those entrusted with the teaching of agriculture soon found themselves facing many of the same problems as Runkle and Woodward. What is the distinctive content of agriculture courses, and what are appropriate methods for teaching them? The Association of American Agricultural Colleges and Experiment Stations could hardly avoid such questions, and the early proceedings of the organization are replete with addresses on "Whither Agricultural Education?" Between 1897 and 1901 the Association's Committee on Methods of Instruction actually hammered out a uniform agriculture curriculum to replace the widely divergent improvisations of the land-grant colleges.[6] It divided the field into

[4] Wisconsin Farmers' Institute: *Bulletin No. 15, 1901*, p. 65.

[5] The importance of the Grange and the Institutes in promoting educational reform is discussed in Kenyon L. Butterfield: "A Significant Factor in Agricultural Education," *Educational Review*, XX (1901), 301–6.

[6] The seventies and eighties were decades of trial and error for the newly established A. & M. colleges. Almost all of them had established demonstration farms and attempted to relate their efforts to classroom work in agriculture, horticulture, and animal husbandry. Much of this work was little more than apprenticeship under a superintendent farmer-professor; some of it, on the other hand, became a highly abstruse business of classifying the memorizing that had little to do with the practicalities of agriculture. These early gropings are described in Edward Danforth Eddy, Jr.: *Colleges for Our Land and Time* (New York, 1957), chs. ii, iv; Alfred Charles True: *A History of Agricultural Education in the United States, 1785–1929* (Washington, 1929), Parts III, IV; and Earle D. Ross: *Democracy's College* (Ames, 1942), chs. v–vi.

appropriate topics; it offered recommendations as to time allot-
ments for each in the four-year college program; and it suggested appropriate correlative work on demonstration farms
and gardens.[7] While the Committee advanced its formulations
as tentative at best, they were rapidly taken up by agriculture
professors eagerly seeking the comfort of a well-defined body
of subject matter.

Having completed its endeavors at the college level, the
Committee turned to secondary and elementary education. A
1902 report discussed secondary agriculture courses in colleges
(on-campus preparatory courses were quite common at the
turn of the century), in special agricultural high schools, and
in ordinary township high schools, contending that such
courses would enable graduates to profit from the work of
farmers' institutes and experiment stations, thereby rendering
them "more intelligent and progressive farmers." [8] Two years
later, the Committee produced a widely circulated plea for
the teaching of agriculture in rural common schools. Its effort was to locate agricultural instruction within William T.
Harris's broadly cultural conception of the elementary program. Agriculture, in the Committee's view, was simply a
phase of the larger study of geography, one of Harris's "five
windows on the soul." At best, it would "awaken interest in
the work and life of the farm, show the progress being made
in the improvement of farming, indicate the rational and scientific basis of agriculture, and give the pupil an outlook toward the work of the experiment stations, agricultural schools
and colleges, and other agencies for his future education or
assistance in his life work." [9]

The 1900's, then, brought not only a powerful rural demand
for vocationalism as the key to educational reform, but a

[7] The reports of the Committee are carried in United States Department of Agriculture, Office of Experiment Stations: *Bulletins* No. 41
(1897), No. 49 (1898), No. 65 (1899), No. 76 (1900), No. 99
(1901), and No. 115 (1902).

[8] The report is carried in United States Department of Agriculture,
Office of Experiment Stations: *Bulletin* No. 123 (1903).

[9] United States Department of Agriculture, Office of Experiment Stations: *Circular* No. 60 (1904).

sharpening definition of the content of agricultural studies and their place in a reconstituted school curriculum. Notwithstanding traditional rural-urban antipathy, it was inevitable that this rural phase of the larger industrial education movement would eventually join forces with its urban counterpart. The two streams tended to run parallel during the first years of the twentieth century; but the National Society for the Promotion of Industrial Education did its work well, and after 1906 they began to converge. Groups that were at best strange political bedfellows found themselves lobbying together in Congress toward the common goal of a federal vocational education bill.

I V

For a number of reasons, 1910 marks a turning point in the vocational education movement. With the acceptance of the Mitchell Committee's report, the American Federation of Labor joined the National Association of Manufacturers in lobbying for outright trade instruction in the schools. The Grange and the Association of American Agricultural Colleges and Experiment Stations intensified their pressure for expanded agricultural studies at all levels. And the National Education Association came forward that year with a vigorous statement referring to vocational training as "the central and dominant factor" in the education of pupils headed for industry.[1] Sparked by the National Society for the Promotion of Industrial Education, a progressive coalition as polyglot as any during the Progressive era, the movement was beginning to roll up an enviable legislative record in state capitols across the country.

A 1910 survey, undertaken by the Society in collaboration with the American Association for Labor Legislation, revealed that twenty-nine states had provided for some form of industrial education; of these, ten had provided for technical high schools, eighteen for manual training, eleven for domestic sci-

[1] National Education Association: *Addresses and Proceedings, 1910,* p. 657.

ence, nineteen for agricultural training, and eleven for industrial and trade courses. Some, like Illinois, had simply authorized localities to establish manual-training departments in
township high schools. Others, like Wisconsin, had made elaborate provision for many kinds of industrial education, including county schools of agriculture and domestic science, manual-training departments in public high schools and in the
upper grades of common schools, and trade schools in the
cities. The Society found the movement to be largely of recent
origin, twenty-five of the states having enacted their laws since
1900. "No other educational movement calling for large expenditures and involving sweeping changes in curriculum and
method has received such prompt legislative recognition," the
Society concluded.[2]

Yet granted these successes, the Society's leaders were already beginning to suffer the impatience characteristic of reformers. Convinced that vocational education held the key
to industrial progress, they began to dream of by-passing an
arduous state-by-state campaign with a massive bid for federal
assistance. Their notion was not a new one; bills with this purpose in mind had been in the hoppers of Congress since 1906
at least. Generally, they had followed two lines. Those like
the Davis Bill of 1907 had sought federal support for secondary-
school instruction in agriculture, home economics, and the
mechanic arts; while those like the McLaughlin Bill of 1909
had sought federal support for extension work under the auspices of the agricultural colleges. In 1910, just as the AF of L
was committing itself to vocational education, Senator Jonathan P. Dolliver of Iowa introduced a new measure seeking
to combine both programs into a single piece of legislation.
The bill had strong backing from the NEA, the Grange, and
the AF of L but was vigorously opposed by elements in the
Association of American Agricultural Colleges and Experiment Stations on the grounds that federal aid to secondary
schools would ultimately weaken the work of the land-grant

[2] National Society for the Promotion of Industrial Education: *Legislation upon Industrial Education in the United States* (Bulletin No. 12,
New York, 1910), p. 25.

colleges. A bid was made to obtain National Society support just as the Society itself was deciding to undertake an intensive lobbying effort. Inevitably, the drama moved onto the stage of federal politics.[3]

The story of the campaign that began in earnest with the Dolliver Bill and culminated in 1917 with the passage of the Smith-Hughes Act, providing federal aid for vocational secondary education, is an exciting chapter in the politics of American education. The details have been told elsewhere at length[4] and will not be repeated here. Suffice it to say that the campaign was the work of many hands, with the National Society providing the principal leadership. Coordinating a lobby that included the AF of L and the NAM proved no easy matter, as the Society early discovered. NAM President John Kirby railed in 1911 that the Federation had about as much business in the industrial education movement as "a tarantula a rightful place on the bosom of an angel"; [5] and as if in rejoinder to the Mitchell Committee's report, the Association reversed its decade-old position on trade schools. Probably influenced by the well-publicized lecture tour of Dr. Georg Kerschensteiner, Germany's foremost exponent of continuation education,[6] the NAM abandoned advocacy of trade schools for vigor-

[3] Lloyd E. Blauch: *Federal Cooperation in Agricultural Extension Work, Vocational Education, and Vocational Rehabilitation* (United States Office of Education, Bulletin, 1933, No. 15, Washington, 1935), pp. 52–71.

[4] Ibid.

[5] National Association of Manufacturers: *Proceedings, 1911*, pp. 73–4. The antipathy was not new. When Charles Richards of the NSPIE wrote the NAM in 1906 about plans for the Society, Chairman Anthony Ittner of the NAM's Committee on Industrial Education replied: "To invite labor leaders affiliated with the American Federation of Labor to become members of the Society would be tantamount to inviting the devil and his imps to participate in a movement for the promotion of the Christian religion as taught by the lowly Nazarene while on earth." Richards prevailed, though, and Ittner joined the Society. See National Association of Manufacturers: *Proceedings, 1909*, p. 19.

[6] See National Society for the Promotion of Industrial Education: *The Continuation Trade Schools of Munich* (Bulletin No. 14, New York, 1911); and Georg Kerschensteiner: *Three Lectures on Vocational Training* (Chicago, 1911). Kerschensteiner, Director of Education in Munich, came to the United States in 1910 under the auspices of the National

ous espousal of continuation education. The "old-time" trade school was pronounced impractical, overly expensive, and unsuited to the needs of the people. The real answer to America's need for vocational training was a practical part-time continuation school managed by "men of affairs." Let the educators care for word-minded children, the NAM's Education Committee maintained in 1913, but let independent boards of vocational education, composed mainly of employers and employees, manage the training of the hand-minded half of the population. Wisconsin's independent vocational-school system, controlled by a separate board of industrial education, was the model to follow.[7]

In the face of this revised NAM position the AF of L hewed even closer to the recommendations of its special committee. The nation needed some combination of regular trade instruction and continuation schooling, and both should be supported with public funds. While the Federation agreed that committees representing employers and organized labor might well serve in an advisory capacity, it was adamant in its insistence that vocational education for the great body of the people remain under public control, that it not be separated from the public school system. For the Federation, apparently, the ineptness of the educators was less to be feared than the self-seeking of the businessmen.[8]

Society. His visit exemplifies the continuing interrelationship between the European and American phases of the industrial education movement. Moreover, insofar as his lectures were interpreted by some as "proving that the Germans were ahead of us," they served as propaganda for the proponents of vocational training. The misuse of comparative data for political ends is common in the history of American education.

[7] To comprehend the magnitude of the shift, compare the report of the Committee on Industrial Education for 1910 (National Association of Manufacturers: *Proceedings,* 1910, pp. 258–68) with its report for 1911 (National Association of Manufacturers: *Proceedings,* 1911, pp. 185–94).

[8] American Federation of Labor: *Proceedings,* 1912, pp. 269–76. The possibility of splitting the public school system along class lines occasioned a vigorous debate in the professional and the public press. See, for example, Dewey's exchange with Edwin G. Cooley, a spokesman of the Chicago Commercial Club—John Dewey: "An Undemocratic Proposal,' *Vocational Education,* II (1913), 374–7; and Edwin G. Cooley: "Pro,

The National Society, increasingly a lobbying organization, in 1912 employed Charles A. Prosser as its full-time secretary. Following upon the work of the pioneering Douglas Commission, which had alerted Massachusetts to the urgent need for public industrial training,[9] Prosser had been called to organize a new division of vocational education for the Commonwealth. As secretary of the National Society from 1912 to 1915, he was literally indefatigable in its cause, traveling from city to city and from state to state, formulating programs, exciting individuals, and corralling legislators. No one worked as efficiently in marshaling the congressional support that eventually pushed through the Smith-Hughes Bill.[1]

The appointment of a Commission on National Aid to Vocational Education in 1914 marked the beginning of the final phase of the campaign.[2] The Commission was authorized by congressional resolution on January 20, 1914, and asked to report by June 1. The AF of L and the National Society voiced concern lest "poor appointments" jeopardize the whole effort; but once President Wilson announced the membership, there was little doubt as to the outcome. The four congressional members, Senators Hoke Smith and Carroll S. Page and Representatives Dudley M. Hughes and S. D. Fess, had all declared previously in favor of federal aid to vocational education; the five noncongressional members—Prosser was

fessor Dewey's Criticism of the Chicago Commercial Club and Its Vocational Education Bill," ibid., III (1914), 24–9. See also Dewey: "Splitting up the School System," *New Republic*, II (1915), 283–4.

[9] The Massachusetts Legislature in 1905 authorized Governor William L. Douglas to appoint a commission to "investigate the needs for education in the different grades of skill and responsibility in the various industries of the Commonwealth." The Commission reported in 1906, a date which for many marks the beginning of the vocational education movement in the United States. See *Report of the Commission on Industrial and Technical Education* (Boston, 1906); and Bennett: op. cit., p. 507.

[1] William T. Bawden: "Leaders in Industrial Education," *Industrial Arts and Vocational Education*, XLI (1952), 219–20.

[2] "Report of the Commission on National Aid to Vocational Education," 63rd Congress, 2nd Session, House of Representatives Document No. 1004.

one of them—were all members of the National Society, two having served on the Board of Managers.

The Commission, as Prosser once pointed out at a business meeting of the National Society, was unique in congressional history. It submitted its report on time and it spent only two-thirds of its appropriation. It submitted questionnaires to hundreds of schoolmen, to 104 national labor unions, and to seventy representative employers; and it held round-the-clock hearings during the week of April 20, taking testimony from officers of federal departments, representatives of interested national organizations, and well-known individuals. The report it submitted on June 1 noted a "great and crying need" for vocational education, insisted that federal funds were necessary to meet this need, and recommended that the national government aid in a continuing study of the problem.

Specifically, the Commission recommended that federal money support part of the salaries of teachers and supervisors of trade, industrial, and agricultural subjects and assist in the training of teachers in agricultural, trade, industrial, and home economics subjects. The Commission further recommended that aid be confined to public institutions of less-than-college grade and suggested that three types of school might properly be included: all-day secondary schools in which about half the time would be devoted to actual training for a vocation; part-time schools for young workers over fourteen years of age designed to extend either their vocational skill or their general "civic or vocational intelligence"; and evening schools to extend the vocational knowledge of mature workers over sixteen years of age.

To administer the grants, the Commission recommended that the states designate or create public boards that would act as their agents to deal with the federal government. More important, perhaps, the Commission suggested that a federal board, consisting of the Postmaster-General and the Secretaries of the Interior, Agriculture, Commerce, and Labor, with the Commissioner of Education as executive officer, be appointed to administer the funds and to cooperate with the states in promoting vocational education. Finally, the Commission recommended that states and local communities be required to match any federal grants dollar for dollar, and also to pay all costs of plant, equipment, and maintenance.

The Commission's report signaled the final phase of the drive for legislative action. Businessmen, trade unionists, and educators were now squarely behind the principle of federal aid for vocational education; and the signing of the Smith-Lever Act, providing for a federally assisted agricultural extension program, had removed the opposition of the Association of American Agricultural Colleges and Experiment Stations. As the war in Europe progressed, vocational education was increasingly viewed as an aspect of the nation's preparedness program; President Wilson portrayed it as such in his 1916 message to Congress. In June, 1916, the Chamber of Commerce added its voice to the supporting chorus by publishing the results of an April survey of local chambers overwhelmingly in favor of the legislation. Finally, in February, 1917, just two months before the United States entered the war, a bill proposed by Senator Smith and Representative Hughes became law. The final version bore a striking resemblance to the proposals of the 1914 Commission, differing at only two principal points: home economics was included with agricultural, trade, and industrial subjects as a vocational study to be supported; and the composition of the Federal Board of Vocational Education was altered to include the Secretaries of Agriculture, Labor, and Commerce, the United States Commissioner of Education, and three citizens—representing respectively manufacturing and commerce, agriculture, and labor—to be appointed by the President with the advice and consent of the Senate.

Like many a federal law, the Smith-Hughes Act confirmed more than it innovated. Had the Act never been passed, the unmistakable trend in state legislation that the National Society found in 1910 would undoubtedly have continued until it affected most of the nation's schools. What the Act did, of course, was to accelerate the process and standardize it along certain lines. It was not too long before the insights of

Victor Della Vos had become an ingrained aspect of the American school, while the objections of William T. Harris had all but disappeared.

As is so often the case, however, Harris's protestations would not down for good. As Paul Douglas pointed out in a perceptive criticism written shortly after World War I, the very sort of craft-oriented instruction to which the Smith-Hughes Act had committed the nation had already been left behind by the onrush of technological advance.[3] The craftsmen who left industry to become the teachers of vocational subjects too easily isolated themselves from the mainstream of industrial innovation; while the machinery purchased for school use was itself soon outmoded by technological improvement. It took less than forty years for American industry, facing a new apprenticeship crisis after World War II, to reclaim for itself educational responsibilities it had so easily abandoned in the early decades of the century.[4]

[3] Paul H. Douglas: *American Apprenticeship and Industrial Education* (New York, 1921), ch. v.

[4] See Harold F. Clark and Harold S. Sloan: *Classrooms in the Factories* (Rutherford, New Jersey, 1958).

3

Culture
and Community

WHEN Theodore Roosevelt first read Jacob Riis's *How the Other Half Lives*, he found it "an enlightenment and an inspiration" for which he would remain forever grateful.[1] As for the untold millions Riis described, the poverty, the squalor, the disease, and the desperation of the urban slum were simply the drab facts of everyday existence. In the cities of the 1890's a new generation of Americans was coming into abrasive contact with the ills of industrial civilization. They swarmed in droves into New York, Chicago, Philadelphia, and Detroit, seeking jobs, wealth, excitement, a better life. What they found too often was the hard grinding misery of the tenement, in which hopes corroded and dreams turned rapidly to nightmares.

Poverty, squalor, and disease were hardly new in the nineties. They date, after all, from the beginning of history. What was new was the growing number of Riises and Roosevelts who

[1] *Theodore Roosevelt: An Autobiography* (New York, 1926), p. 169.

suddenly seemed to care.[2] To look back on the nineties is to
sense an awakening of social conscience, a growing belief that
this incredible suffering was neither the fault nor the inevitable
lot of the sufferers, that it could certainly be alleviated, and
that the road to alleviation was neither charity nor revolution,
but in the last analysis, education.

The awakening assumed a vast variety of institutional forms.
There were civic commissions, charity associations, church
leagues, and reform societies galore, but none symbolized the
new spirit of conscience more dramatically than the social settlement. Settlements originated in England during the 1880's
as a response to the appalling conditions of industrialism. Inspired by the social philosophies of Charles Kingsley, Frederick
Denison Maurice, and John Ruskin, a number of University
men under the leadership of the Reverend Samuel A. Barnett
resolved to live as "neighbours of the working poor, sharing
their life, thinking out their problems, learning from them the
lessons of patience, fellowship, self-sacrifice, and offering in response the help of their own education and friendship."[3] In
1884 they obtained a building in Whitechapel, a London
slum, and named it Toynbee Hall after a recently deceased
friend of Barnett who had done much to inspire the movement.[4]

The idea spread rapidly, not only through England but to
the United States as well. In 1886 a young Amherst graduate
named Stanton Coit, who had actually lived for two months
in Toynbee Hall, established the first American settlement at
146 Forsyth Street on New York's lower East Side. Others
followed in swift succession. The plans of four Smith College
alumnae under the leadership of Jane Robbins and Jean Fine
blossomed into New York's College Settlement in the fall of
1889. And almost simultaneously—again influenced by Canon

[2] Robert H. Bremner: From the Depths: The Discovery of Poverty
in the United States (New York, 1956).

[3] Canon Barnett: His Life, Work, and Friends, by His Wife (2 vols.,
London, 1919), I, 310.

[4] Canon and Mrs. S. A. Barnett: Towards Social Reform (London,
1909), Part III; and Werner Picht: Toynbee Hall and the English
Settlement Movement (London, 1914), Parts I–II.

Barnett's work in London—Jane Addams and Ellen Gates Starr opened what was destined to become the most famous of the American settlements, Hull House of Chicago. In 1891 Everett Wheeler's East Side House (New York City) and Charles Zueblin's Northwestern University Settlement were established, while in 1892 William J. Tucker opened Andover House in Boston with Robert Woods as headworker. Thus were founded within five years the half-dozen seminal institutions of the American settlement movement.[5]

These young reformers came to their work convinced that the real curse of industrialism lay not so much in its physical blight as in its shattering of historic human associations. True, they were sharp and uncompromising in their attack on "the malefactors of great wealth"; but their deeper plaint was what Morton Grodzins has aptly called "the gemeinschaft grouse" —the cry that industrialism had dissolved the fabric of community leaving alienation in its wake, and that this ultimately had caused the deterioration of life in the slum.[6] Such reasoning led them inevitably to seek solutions through education as well as politics; hence their assumption that by sharing their knowledge and ideals with the underprivileged they could lead in the rebuilding of community and thereby release the forces of social alleviation. Settlement workers talked in terms of neighborhood regeneration, but their ultimate goal was the humanizing of industrial civilization. In this, education would always be a primary instrument.

In divising their initial programs, the residents took their cues directly from neighborhood needs. Were the streets dirty and the tenements infested with vermin? Settlements founded antifilth societies to induce people to rid their rooms of bedbugs, lice, cockroaches, and rats. Were gangs of street urchins a menace to life and property? Settlements established boys' and girls' clubs to channel the ebullient energy of adolescence into athletics, arts and crafts, and constructive recreation.

[5] Robert A. Woods and Albert J. Kennedy. *The Settlement Horizon* (New York, 1922), ch. iv.

[6] Morton Grodzins: *The Loyal and the Disloyal* (Chicago, 1956), pp. 238–42.

Were death and disease rates in the slum pitifully high? Settlements became first-aid centers, clinics, headquarters for visiting nurses, and schools of preventive medicine. Were young men unable to obtain jobs? Settlements experimented not only with trade education but with devices for fitting individuals to the trades for which they were best suited. Were mothers required to work? Settlements introduced kindergartens and day nurseries. Were workingmen illiterate? Settlements taught them to read. Was summer oppressive in the city? Settlements established playgrounds and vacation centers. No effort that might contribute to human betterment went untried; their cause was nothing less than the total regeneration of society.[7]

As the work progressed, the residents found themselves more and more in the business of education. Consider Hull House as the leading example. Almost from the beginning there were kindergartens for toddlers and clubs for boys and girls, men and women. There was a venture in dietetics closely connected with the effort to encourage women to purchase cheap but nutritious cuts of meat. A Working People's Social Club was founded, as was a Hull House Labor Museum. There were drama and choral groups, and a Hull House Music School. There were adult activities of every sort and variety: English classes for immigrants, a Shakespeare Club, a Plato Club, and various courses in cooking, dressmaking, millinery work, child care, and the trades.[8]

Jane Addams liked to think of this program of "socialized education" as ultimately a protest against a restricted view of the school.[9] She lashed out bitterly against the elitism of the wealthy, who believed the underprivileged had little to contribute to the spiritual life of the community, and the provincialism of the educators, whose own narrow view of culture

[7] See, for example, Jane Addams: *Twenty Years at Hull-House* (New York, 1910); Stanton Coit: *Neighbourhood Guilds* (London, 1891); Mary Kingsbury Simkhovitch: *Neighborhood* (New York, 1938); Lillian Wald: *The House on Henry Street* (New York, 1915); and Robert A. Woods: *The Neighborhood in Nation-Building* (Boston, 1923).

[8] Jane Addams: op. cit.

[9] "The Subjective Necessity for Social Settlements," in Jane Addams *et al.: Philanthropy and Social Progress* (New York, 1893), p. 10.

kept them from grasping the rich pedagogical possibilities in the productive life of the city. "We are impatient with the schools which lay all stress on reading and writing," she wrote in *Democracy and Social Ethics*, "suspecting them to rest upon the assumption that all knowledge and interest must be brought to the children through the medium of books. Such an assumption fails to give the child any clew to the life about him, or any power to usefully or intelligently connect himself with it."[1] To become a force for social good, the school would have to cast itself into the world of affairs, much as the settlement had done, and exert its influence toward the eventual humanizing of the productive system. Industry, she concluded, would have to be seized upon and conquered by the educators.

How might this be done? Her answer lay in imparting to young people a deeper, more humane understanding of the industrial world of which they were part. In addition to manual training and domestic science, she wanted the factory-bound child to study the history of industry and the relation of each facet of labor to all others, so that sensing "the historic significance of the part he is taking in the life of the community,"[2] he might be spared the dehumanizing meaninglessness of industrial labor. A spirit of art, nurtured by the school, could ultimately infuse the whole productive process, raising it from the narrowest domination of men by machines to a genuinely human enterprise. Educated workmen, given the free exercise of cultivated imagination, would demand more artful products, which in turn could only be produced by educated workmen. In the end, artist-laborers, trained by a socially conscious school, would subordinate the machine to ever nobler purposes.

Miss Addams deeply believed that her formulations went beyond the sentimental impracticalism of a Woodward on the one hand and the selfish practicalism of an Auchmuty on the

[1] Jane Addams: *Democracy and Social Ethics* (New York, 1902), pp. 180–1.
[2] Ibid., p. 192.

other. Assuming that factories were here to stay, she pondered the human problems associated with them. "It takes thirty-nine people to make a coat in a modern tailoring establishment," she argued, "yet those same thirty-nine people might produce a coat in a spirit of 'team work' which would make the entire process as much more exhilarating than the work of the old solitary tailor, as playing in a baseball nine gives more pleasure to a boy than afforded by a solitary game of hand ball on the side of the barn." [3] In effect, she sought to socialize Ruskin's dictum that labor without art brutalizes; industrial civilization, she maintained, "needs the solace of collective art inherent in collective labor." [4]

Whether or not her outlook suffered from the same romanticism as Ruskin's is, of course, a moot point.[5] She claimed that associated in labor unions, workers could eventually realize any ends they legitimately set for themselves. Whatever the difficulties, however, her view was essentially liberating and always equalitarian. She wanted the school to bathe the surroundings of the ordinary individual with a truly human significance, assuming "that unless all men and all classes contribute to a good, we cannot even be sure that it is worth having." [6] There may have been more coldly realistic notions of education in her time, but certainly none more humane.[7]

As protestors against a restricted view of the school, it was inevitable that settlement workers would end up lobbying for

[3] Jane Addams: The Spirit of Youth and the City Streets (New York, 1909), p. 127.

[4] Addams: Democracy and Social Ethics, p. 219.

[5] For a relevant commentary on Ruskin, see Raymond Williams: Culture and Society (London, 1958), ch. vii.

[6] Addams: Democracy and Social Ethics, pp. 219–20.

[7] There is a patent similarity between Jane Addams's educational outlook and John Dewey's, a similarity that undoubtedly derives from their close association at Hull House during Dewey's tenure at the University of Chicago. Jane Dewey—Jane Addams's namesake—wrote of her father in 1939: "Dewey's faith in democracy as a guiding force in education took on both a sharper and a deeper meaning because of Hull House and Jane Addams." See her "Biography of John Dewey," in Paul Arthur Schilpp, ed.: The Philosophy of John Dewey (New York, 1939), pp. 29–30.

pedagogical innovation, and it is no surprise that during and after the nineties, they played a central role in the educational reform movement. It was Lillian Wald of New York's Henry Street Settlement, for example, who persuaded the City Health Department to appoint the first school physicians in 1897, while her colleague Elizabeth Farrell inaugurated the first classes for handicapped children under Board of Education auspices. Henry Street was also instrumental in promoting the first "practical housekeeping centers" in New York, an experiment that led eventually to a city-wide school-lunch program. In Chicago the Commons aided in the establishment of school libraries, while the City's first experiments with school nurses were undertaken in cooperation with the University Settlement. The Roadside Settlement in Des Moines and the Locust Point Settlement in Baltimore convinced their school boards to introduce evening classes for adults, while Whittier House in Jersey City and Neighborhood House in Fort Worth took the lead in sponsoring public-school kindergartens.

Jane Robbins and Elisabeth Irwin of New York's College Settlement assumed important duties with the Public Education Association, while Charles B. Stover, James K. Paulding, and James B. Reynolds served as school trustees during their residence at the University Settlement. Julia Richman, an officer of the Educational Alliance as well as a district superintendent of schools, established a Teachers House, whose residents pressed for school lunch programs, special classes for mental and physical defectives, and curriculum revisions "to make the course of study fit the child." And Jane Addams served four years as a member of the Chicago Board of Education, laboring unremittingly for smaller classes, improved facilities, and better trained teachers.[8]

[8] These data, along with a wealth of detail about the settlements, are given in Robert A. Woods and Albert J. Kennedy, eds.: *Handbook of Settlements* (New York, 1911). See also Mary Simkhovitch: "The Enlarged Function of the Public School," in National Conference of Charities and Correction: *Proceedings, 1904,* pp. 471–86; and Morris Isaiah Berger: "The Settlement, the Immigrant and the Public School" (Unpublished Doctoral Thesis, Columbia University, 1956), ch. iv.

Settlement workers were also influential in the establishment and early direction of the United States Children's Bureau. The idea originated with Lillian Wald and Florence Kelley, an early associate of Jane Addams; and it was the National Child Labor Committee, of which Miss Wald, Miss Addams, and Mrs. Kelley were trustees, that eventually pushed it through the Congress.[9] In 1912 President Taft appointed Julia Lathrop, another long-time Hull House resident, as first Chief of the Bureau; and armed with broad statutory authority to investigate and report "upon all matters pertaining to the welfare of children and child life among all classes of our people," she played a decisive part in shaping its early program.[1]

The very establishment of the Bureau, of course, represented a victory for the profession of social work; and as such, it could not help but mark a substantial advance for the concept of "socialized education."[2] As the Bureau proceeded with its investigations into child welfare, it leaned heavily on the ideas and assumptions of the settlement workers, among them the notion of an educational program designed to serve any and all needs of children. Inevitably, its reports and pamphlets, which circulated in the hundreds of thousands, embodied the settlement view of the school; and into homes and agencies across the country there flowed a steady stream of potent propaganda for the expanded view of education that Jane Addams and her confreres had long seen as the ultimate meaning of the social settlement movement.

[9] See Bremner: op. cit., pp. 218–22; Josephine Goldmark: *Impatient Crusader: Florence Kelley's Life Story* (Urbana, 1953), chs. vii–viii; Alice Elizabeth Padgett: "The History of the Establishment of the United States Children's Bureau" (Unpublished Master's Thesis, University of Chicago, 1936); and Jane Addams: *My Friend, Julia Lathrop* (New York, 1935). The tie between child-labor legislation and educational reform was an early and continuing theme of the settlement workers, especially the group at Hull House.

[1] Dorothy E. Bradbury: *Four Decades of Action for Children: A Short History of the Children's Bureau* (United States Children's Bureau Publication No. 358, Washington, 1956), pp. 5–17, 87.

[2] The tie has been reflected in the continued commitment of professional social workers to educational reform in the period since World War I.

I I

To work with the underprivileged was to work with the immigrant, and to work with the immigrant was to be immediately conscious of the historic problem of Americanization. Well before the Civil War nationalist-minded educators had called upon the school to train newcomers to American ways of life and thought. As early as 1849, the President of Middlebury College had queried whether the flood of immigrants would become part of the body politic or indeed prove to the Republic what the Goths and Huns had been to the Roman Empire. The answer, he thought, would depend in large measure "upon the wisdom and fidelity of our teachers." [3] Many, in the fashion of those whose own loyalty is so new and untested as to need reaffirmation, loudly seconded his sentiments, and from its earliest years the public school was viewed as an instrument par excellence for inducting newcomers into the "responsibilities of citizenship."

With the profound shift in the character of American immigration during the latter years of the nineteenth century, this Americanizing function was again called to the fore. Before 1880 most immigrants had come from northwestern Europe, particularly England, Ireland, Germany, and Scandinavia. Except for the Irish, they had tended to push inland, settling the rich, fertile territories of the middle-Atlantic, midwestern, and northwestern states. During the 1880's, however, the percentage of immigrants from southern and eastern Europe began to rise perceptibly, presaging the vast number from these areas destined to come between 1890 and 1920. [4] These "new immigrants" settled in ways different from their predecessors. They tended to remain in the cities, congregating in self-contained slum neighborhoods that perpetuated the life and customs of the old world. As one immigrant reminisced

[3] Benjamin Labaree: "The Education Demanded by the Peculiar Character of Our Civil Institutions," in American Institute of Instruction: *Lectures and Proceedings*, 1849, p. 34. See also my book: *The American Common School* (New York, 1951), pp. 44–7; and Merle Curti: *The Roots of American Loyalty* (New York, 1946).
[4] Bureau of the Census: *Historical Statistics of the United States, 1789–1945* (Washington, 1949), pp. 33–6.

about his arrival in New York: ". . . my problem was to fit myself in with the people of Vaslui and Roumania, my erstwhile fellow-townsmen and my fellow-countrymen. It was not America in the larger sense, but the East Side Ghetto that upset all my calculations, reversed all my values, and set my head swimming." [5]

For settlement workers laboring in the ghetto-slums of the cities, the fundamental problems remained wealth, corruption, and the unwillingness of the privileged to share their knowledge and ideals with the poor. For others equally dedicated to reform, however, the problems lay more directly with the unfortunates themselves. Social Gospel ministers denounced the high rates of crime and immorality among the immigrants, speaking vaguely in the language of racial origins; unionists blamed the newcomers for unemployment and declining wage rates; while municipal leaders voiced alarm over the boss-ridden immigrant vote. A growing chorus of voices began to demand restrictionist laws as the most rapid and painless way of combating the corruption, the squalor, and the injustice of urban industrialism.[6]

Education was immediately involved, for whatever the fate of restrictionism, there was the ever-present need to Americanize those who had already come. Yet the very statement of the need raised many more problems than it solved, since there was little agreement as to what Americanization was and what it meant. Professor Ellwood P. Cubberley of Stanford, for example, was an eloquent spokesman for the view that to Americanize was to Anglicize. The southern and eastern Europeans, Cubberley declared, were essentially different from the immigrants who had preceded them. "Illiterate, docile, lacking in self-reliance and initiative, and not possessing the Anglo-Teutonic conceptions of law, order, and government,

[5] Marcus Ravage: *An American in the Making* (New York, 1917), p. 61. The differences between the "old" and "new" immigrants are significant, but they have too often been exaggerated. See Oscar Handlin: *Race and Nationality in American Life* (Boston, 1957), ch. v; and Maldwyn Allen Jones: *American Immigration* (Chicago, 1960), ch. vii.

[6] John Higham: "Origins of Immigration Restriction, 1882–1897: A Social Analysis," *Mississippi Valley Historical Review*, XXXIX (1952–3), 77–88, and *Strangers in the Land* (New Brunswick, 1955), chs. iii–vii.

their coming has served to dilute tremendously our national stock, and to corrupt our civic life." The first task of education, he concluded, was break up their ghettos, "to assimilate and amalgamate these people as a part of our American race, and to implant in their children, so far as can be done, the Anglo-Saxon conception of righteousness, law and order, and popular government, and to awaken in them a reverence for our democratic institutions and for those things in our national life which we as a people hold to be of abiding worth." [7] To Americanize, in this view, was to divest the immigrant of hi ' ethnic character and to inculcate the dominant Anglo-Saxon morality. Americanization meant taking on the ways and beliefs of those who embodied the true, historic America, the America worth preserving. "What kind of American consciousness can grow in the atmosphere of sauerkraut and Limburger cheese," asked a representative of the Daughters of the American Revolution. "Or, what can you expect of the Americanism of the man whose breath always reeks of garlic?" [8] There was no room in the United States for "hyphenated Americans."

Others, primarily the foreign-born themselves, argued that the promise of unity lay less in any purely Anglo-Saxon tradition than in a new nationality that was slowly emerging from the drama of American life. "America is God's Crucible," proclaimed the protagonist in Zangwill's play *The Melting-Pot*: "Here you stand, good folk, think I, when I see them at Ellis Island, here you stand in your fifty groups, with your fifty languages and histories, and your fifty blood hatreds and rivalries. But you won't be long like that, brothers, for these are the fires of God you've come to—these are the fires of God. A fig for your feuds and your vendettas! Germans and Frenchmen, Irishmen and Englishmen, Jews and Russians—into the Cruci-

[7] Ellwood P. Cubberley: *Changing Conceptions of Education* (Boston, 1909), pp. 15–16. Cubberley's is a typical progressive tract of the era, sketching in lyrical terms an educational awakening commensurate with the great crusade of the 1840's.

[8] Edward Hale Bierstadt: *Aspects of Americanization* (Cincinnati, 1922), pp. 114–5.

ble with you all! God is making the American." [9] And in 1912 Mary Antin in her autobiography wrote in rhapsodic terms of being "made over" by the cosmopolitan conditions of "the promised land." [1]

Finally, a small group of intellectuals advanced a notion of cultural pluralism that would preserve the best of the old world while introducing the immigrant into the new. In this view, ethnic minorities would be encouraged to cultivate and extend their own unique traditions at the same time as they contributed to the broader mainstream of American life. "The general culture of the land stands before us like an iron wall," wrote Israel Friedlaender of New York's Jewish Theological Seminary, "and we shall be cracked like a nutshell if we attempt to run our heads against it. The only solution left to us is that of adaptation, but an adaptation which shall sacrifice nothing that is essential to Judaism, which shall not impoverish Judaism but enrich it, which . . . shall take fully into account what the environment demands of us, and shall yet preserve and foster our Jewish distinctiveness and originality." [2] The position was a noble and courageous one in the face of mounting pressure for undivided loyalty during the war years, but it was neither widely heard nor widely heeded by the nation at large.

Given this heady flow of rhetoric, how did the actual work of Americanization go forward? We know far less about the process than we should like, though there is ample evidence that educators were in the business of Americanizing long before Americanization became a national issue. Settlement workers, for example, early discovered that to attempt to help the underprivileged was to contend with all of the problems

[9] Israel Zangwill: *The Melting-Pot* (New York, 1909), p. 37.

[1] Mary Antin: *The Promised Land* (Boston, 1912), p. 12.

[2] Israel Friedlaender: *Past and Present* (Cincinnati, 1919), p. 317. Friedlaender had formulated his position as early as 1907 in an address entitled "The Problem of Judaism in America," ibid., pp. 253–78. The viewpoint was also eloquently stated by Horace Kallen in *The Nation* (February 18 and 25, 1915) and by Isaac B. Berkson in *Theories of Americanization* (New York, 1920).

later debated under the "Americanization question." Yet the residents attacked these problems with their usual zeal, less concerned with formal definitions than with doing the work of social improvement. Throughout the nation, wherever there were large immigrant communities, neighborhood houses could be found seeking to assist the inhabitants. Hull House early established a Labor Museum, designed as an "educational enterprise, which should build a bridge between European and American experiences in such wise as to give them both more meaning and a sense of relation."[3] New York's Greenwich House staged French, Italian, and Irish musicals to dramatize the immigrants' gifts to American life, and the Bethlehem Institute in Los Angeles maintained El Club Belen, featuring a school of citizenship for Spanish, Italian, Syrian, and Slavonic pupils.[4] By 1910 virtually all of the houses were committed in one way or another to interpreting America for new arrivals.

Benefit and cultural societies, like the German *turn verein*, the Scandinavian *turners*, the Bohemian *sokol*, and the Polish *falcons*, were also involved in Americanization, sponsoring libraries, clubs, and classes to ease the acculturation of their countrymen.[5] New York's Educational Alliance, founded by well-established German-born Jews to assist in the adjustment of east-European coreligionists, developed an amazingly diverse educational program: by 1894 it could boast a kindergarten with an average attendance of 100, Hebrew classes, an industrial school, a free circulating library with some 15,000 volumes, a lecture program, and classes in English, civics, sewing, cooking, and dressmaking. In 1898, under the sponsorship of the Alliance, Thomas Davidson founded his Breadwinners' College to bring the benefits of culture to the workingman, a pedagogical experiment much in the tradition of Ruskin and the other spiritual fathers of the English settlement.

Older and more established institutions were also drawn

[3] Addams: *Twenty Years at Hull-House*, pp. 235–6.
[4] Woods and Kennedy: *Handbook of Settlements*, pp. 10, 200.
[5] John Daniels: *America via the Neighborhood* (New York, 1920), chs. ii, iv, v. See also Berger: op. cit., chs. ii–iii.

into the work. Churches became the headquarters for literacy training, citizenship classes, and a broader effort at "socialized education"; political clubs, newspapers, and public libraries found themselves similarly compelled to adapt to immigrant needs. Each in its own way took part in the business of Americanization—the short stories in the foreign-language press, the YWCA sewing circle, and the local precinct glee club, all Americanized, willy-nilly.[6]

And what of the schools? The picture was again one of historic institutions seeking to transform the immigrant and being inexorably modified in the process. The teachers of New York, for example, found themselves giving hundreds of baths each week.[7] The syllabi said nothing about baths, and teachers themselves wondered whether bathing was their charge. But there were the children and there were the lice! In Massachusetts twenty-six cities and towns organized "steamer classes" as school reception centers, designed to provide immigrant youngsters with enough English to get on at least haltingly in regular classrooms.[8] Roman Catholic, Lutheran, and Greek Orthodox Churches in a number of cities set up bilingual schools, staffed by teachers who were themselves foreign-born.[9] Several states required localities to provide voluntary evening classes.[1] And in Chicago the Immigrants' Protective League, founded at Hull House, obtained the names, addresses, and nationalities of all children between six and sixteen who came to Illinois by way of Ellis Island and referred them to the appropriate school authorities.[2]

[6] Daniels: op. cit.; Robert E. Park: *The Immigrant Press and Its Control* (New York, 1922); and Mordecai Soltes: *The Yiddish Press: An Americanizing Agency* (New York, 1924).

[7] Adele Marie Shaw: "The True Character of New York Public Schools," *The World's Work*, VII (1903–4), 4204–21.

[8] *Report of the Commission on Immigration on the Problem of Immigration in Massachusetts* (Boston, 1914), pp. 115–17.

[9] Grace Abbott: *The Immigrant and the Community* (New York, 1917), pp. 231–2.

[1] H. H. Wheaton: "Survey of Adult Immigrant Education," *The Immigrants in America Review*, June, 1915, pp. 42–65.

[2] Ibid., p. 228; and United States Bureau of Education: *Report of the Commissioner of Education*, 1916, p. 350.

These were the "visible" changes. But the transformation went far beyond. By 1909, when the United States Immigration Commission made its massive study, 57.8 per cent of the children in the schools of thirty-seven of the nation's largest cities were of foreign-born parentage. In Chelsea, Massachusetts, and Duluth, Minnesota, the percentage ran as high as 74.1; in New York it was 71.5, in Chicago 67.3, and in Boston 63.5. Moreover, the foreign-born group itself embraced some sixty distinct ethnic (the Commission used the term "racial") varieties.[3] Schools that really wanted to educate these youngsters could not get by with surface changes. The mere fact that children in a single schoolroom spoke a half-dozen different languages, none of them English, inevitably altered the life of that schoolroom. And the problem went far beyond language, for each language implied a unique heritage and unique attitudes toward teacher, parents, schoolmates—indeed, toward the school itself. Not only baths, but a vast variety of other activities that could not be found in any syllabus began to appear. Manners, cleanliness, dress, the simple business of getting along together in the schoolroom—these things had to be taught more insistently and self-consciously than ever. And long before Spencerian talk about "health," "citizenship," and "ethical character" began to replace "mental discipline" in the ponderous reports of NEA committees, teachers found themselves pursuing these ends in the day-to-day business of teaching.[4]

[3] United States Immigration Commission: *Abstract of the Report on the Children of Immigrants in Schools* (Washington, 1911), pp. 18–19.

[4] Mary Antin: op. cit., ch. x; Edward Bok: *The Americanization of Edward Bok* (New York, 1922), pp. 2–4; Leonard Covello: *The Heart Is the Teacher* (New York, 1958), pp. 24–5; A. R. Dugmore: "New Citizens for the Republic," *The World's Work*, V (1903), 3323–6; Marion Hill: "The Star Spangled Banner," *McClure's Magazine*, XV (1900), 262–7; W. H. Maxwell: "Stories from the Lives of Real Teachers," *The World's Work*, XVIII (1909), 11877–80; Angelo Patri: *A Schoolmaster of the Great City* (New York, 1917); Jacob A. Riis: *The Children of the Poor* (New York, 1892), chs. xi–xii; Mark Sullivan: *The Education of an American* (New York, 1938), p. 30; Winthrop Talbot: "A Public School in the Slums That Does Its Job," *The World's Work*, XVIII (1909), 11567–72; and Frank V. Thompson: *Schooling the Immigrant* (New York, 1920). The immigrant character of American society may

As the first specific pressures for Americanization began to appear, many schoolmen thought the problem could be solved with a few courses in English. John Daniels relates the story of a man who told him: "We used to have an Americanization problem, but we haven't got one any longer. Several years ago we got all the foreigners in our town in some English and civics classes and in two or three months we Americanized 'em all." [5] Others, with all the good will in the world, set up evening work totally inappropriate to immigrant needs. A survey of the Cleveland school system in 1916 pictured the activities in the classrooms of a single school. In the first husky laboring men were copying: "I am a yellow bird. I can sing. I can fly. I can sing to you." In a second the teacher ended a lesson by having his adult male pupils read a selection about making pickles from cucumbers. In a third the instructor spent most of an hour trying to teach inflections, voices, moods, tenses, numbers, and persons, and ended his lesson with a story about a robin that said: "God loves the flowers and birds too much to send the cold to freeze them." In a fourth the lesson concerned "Little drops of water, Little grains of sand." And in a fifth fourteen men were reading a selection beginning: "Oh baby, dear baby, Whatever you do, You are the king of the home, And we all bend to you." [6] With this kind of pedagogical abomination repeated in city after city —and recall that Cleveland was one of the few cities with any program at all—there is no wonder at the widespread complaint that immigrants avoided the night schools in droves,

---

explain in part why American schools seemed more receptive to educational reform than their European counterparts. But this is not to argue that either the extent or the particular directions of educational reform were foreordained, a common assumption among progressive educators who came to believe their own propaganda. See my essay: "The Revolution in American Secondary Education, 1893–1918," *Teachers College Record*, LVI (1954–5), 295–308; and Alan M. Thomas, Jr.: "American Education and the Immigrant," ibid., LV (1953–4), 253–67.

[5] Daniels: op. cit., p. 5.

[6] Herbert A. Miller: *The School and the Immigrant* (Cleveland, 1916), pp. 91–4. For a classic good-humored account, see also [Leo Rosten]: *The Education of H*y*m*a*n K*a*p*l*a*n* (New York, 1937).

Much of this would undoubtedly have continued had not "Americanization" become a burning national issue. With the publication of the United States Immigration Commission's multivolume study in 1911, schoolmen, social workers, and government officials intensified their search for fresh solutions to the problem. A 1913 conference sponsored by the North American Civic League for Immigrants heard a variety of speakers urge special approaches to English, civics, hygiene, home economics, and recreation for the immigrant child. Schools were encouraged to transcend their traditional limitations and become all-day neighborhood centers coordinating the larger work of Americanizing.[7] A National Conference on Immigration and Americanization held three years later heard many of these same themes, as well as a proposal by the United States Commissioner of Education that the federal government recognize Americanization as a national problem and contribute "funds and directions" to its solution.[8]

Commissioner Claxton's suggestion reflected the growing influence of his Bureau in the Americanization movement. Sparked by a new Division of Immigrant Education, the Bureau redoubled its efforts, gathering up-to-date statistics, sponsoring conferences of schoolmen and civic workers, organizing poster campaigns for night schools, and disseminating a constant stream of information about promising innovations. Gradually, as Americanization became first a preparedness and then a war measure, a point of view crystallized that bore striking resemblance to the settlement notion of "socialized education." [9] "The schools," argued one widely distributed pamphlet, "should be the wheel upon which all other activities

[7] *Education of the Immigrant* (United States Bureau of Education, Bulletin, 1913, No. 51).

[8] *The Immigrants in America Review*, April, 1916, pp. 38–45.

[9] Winthrop Talbot: *Teaching English to Aliens* (United States Bureau of Education, Bulletin, 1917, No. 39); *Americanization as a War Measure* (United States Bureau of Education, Bulletin, 1918, No. 18); *Proceedings Americanization Conference* (Washington, 1919); Fred Clayton Butler: *Community Americanization* (United States Bureau of Education, Bulletin, 1919, No. 76); and John J. Mahoney: *Training Teachers for Americanization* (United States Bureau of Education, Bulletin, 1920, No. 12).

may turn. This means that they will have to realize that education does not consist merely of 'book learning.' " [1] Local boards were to turn schoolhouses into neighborhood centers for every sort and variety of community activity; the school would be meeting place, public forum, recreation house, civic center, home of all formal and informal education. Ultimately, Americanization came to be viewed as a venture in social education, immigrant education, a cooperative effort to improve the quality of neighborhood life. The settlement theme of regeneration was patent; Jane Addams must have nodded in hearty approval.

I I I

However brutal their slums, their ugliness, and their corruption, the cities of the nineties continued to beckon; and young people in droves fled the hardship, the loneliness, and the deepening poverty of the farm. Their departure symbolized the sickness of rural America. For three generations the farmer had been fed a steady diet of sweet Arcadian fare, about the primacy of agriculture, the superiority of the yeoman, and the inextricable connection between farming and democracy. Those who labored in the soil had been "God's chosen people." Now, somehow, the old slogans rang a bit hollow as farm prices hovered at pitiful lows and the number of abandoned homesteads multiplied. Despite all the talk about the nobility of agriculture, there was no ignoring the hard facts of life: the cheap land was gone; the jobs, the money, and the opportunity had moved to the city. "The farmer's burden is heavy, painful, and without reward," a student wrote Dean Liberty Hyde Bailey of Cornell's Agriculture School, "with no prospect of change in condition. Life is short and uncertain. Why spend it performing a painful task, which is at the same time a thankless one?" [2]

In a sense, Bailey spent a lifetime answering that student's query. An early graduate of Michigan's State Agricultural Col-

[1] Fred Clayton Butler: op. cit., p. 66.
[2] L. H. Bailey: *The Training of Farmers* (New York, 1909), p. 98.

lege, Bailey had come to Cornell in 1888 as the institution's first professor of horticulture.[3] There, for over a quarter-century, his prolific pen poured forth a flood of books, tracts, articles, and pamphlets which, taken together, constituted the most elaborate justification of agriculture attempted in his time. The earth is holy, Bailey proclaimed; it is good, kindly, unselfish. To be close to the earth is to set one's life in order, to return to the simplicities that are the moral bulwarks of civilization. Agriculture is not only the rock foundation of democracy; it is the very basis of humanity, morality, and justice. Mysticism, romanticism, nostalgia, religiosity, even a measure of fanaticism—Bailey used them all in the service of his cause. And in an age when Americans were coming to know the seamy side of city life, his efforts could not but leave their mark.

As a champion of country life, Bailey had no peer. It was the farm that had given America its greatness, and it was the farmer who would continue to be the "moral mainstay" of the nation. That cities must grow he readily acknowledged; they were the nerve centers of the new industrial order. But cities alone could never build a lasting civilization, for they depended on a strong, healthy country for men, materials, and spiritual sustenance. In the past the cities had sat like parasites, running their roots into the open country and draining it of its strength. The result was only too apparent in the tragic deterioration of rural America. For Bailey the moral was clear. City and country could no longer afford the luxury of historic antagonism; both would have to strive for that vast regeneration of country life and institutions which alone could guarantee the continued progress of civilization.

Regeneration—the eternal theme of the nineties! How would it be achieved? For Bailey, as for Jane Addams, the answer from beginning to end lay in education. In 1893, the very year Rice's exposés were appearing in *The Forum*, Bailey elaborated his vision before a crowded meeting of Cornell's

[3] The standard biographies are Andrew Denny Rodgers III: *Liberty Hyde Bailey* (Princeton, 1949); and Philip Dorf: *Liberty Hyde Bailey* (Ithaca, 1956).

Agricultural Association. Tracing the pedagogical revolution which had begun when Harvard had established a chemistry professorship a hundred years before, he sketched the pressing need for a "new species of curriculum" that would exploit every known scientific tool—experiments, laboratory work, and farm demonstrations—in the search for a truly reliable body of agricultural principles. Once discovered, these principles would be diffused as widely as possible among practicing farmers. "All the late developments of educational methods," he indicated, "have tended uniformly in one direction—towards popularizing academic work, towards bringing it before the people that its influence may be felt by all men." [4] Properly seized with a missionary spirit, education could be the great lever in the struggle for rural uplift; all other reforms would follow in its beneficent wake.

Over the next twenty years Bailey worked ceaselessly to extend and refine his vision. During the nineties he became a foremost exponent of nature study, first in New York and then in the nation at large. By 1900 Cornell was the bustling headquarters of hundreds of nature-study clubs, issuing a steady stream of pamphlets, leaflets, and periodicals carrying the message of the new movement. For Bailey himself nature study quickly became the jumping-off point for a pedagogy extending far beyond the birds, the bees, and the flowers. Properly taught, nature study was the great remedy for the alienation of man from the land and from his neighbor. It educated "country-ward," toward "naturalness," "simplicity of living," and "sympathy with common things." Children who studied the Creator's work first-hand would hardly join the flight to the artificialities of the city. [5]

With the appearance of *The Nature-Study Idea* in 1903, Bailey embarked on an ambitious effort to unify his outlook on education and tie it more closely to the larger regeneration

[4] L. H. Bailey: *Agricultural Education and Its Place in the University Curriculum* (Ithaca, 1893), pp. 10–11.

[5] L. H. Bailey: *The Nature-Study Idea, Being an Interpretation of the New School-Movement to Put the Child in Sympathy with Nature* (New York, 1903). For the Cornell work, see Ruby Green Smith: *The People's Colleges* (Ithaca, 1949), chs. v–vi.

of country life. Within eight years he had produced four widely read volumes [6] and a host of shorter essays calling for nothing less than the total redirection of rural education. Traditional schools had failed to teach information and attitudes that would keep graduates on the farm. They had isolated themselves from the community, dealing with time-honored irrelevancies bearing little relation to agriculture. No wonder youth fled the country! The school of the future, Bailey insisted, must take its cues from life; it must abandon "sit-still methods" and "screwed-down seats" for active learning in shops, fields, and gardens. It must be broad rather than narrow, spontaneous rather than formal. Most important, it must be of, by, and for the country, oriented to rural needs, concerned with rural problems, seeking at every juncture to cultivate a love of agriculture and the land. Working closely with church, library, fair, and farmers' institute, it must tie the community together and make it a better place to live in. Ultimately, Bailey's "school of the future" would be the hub of a massive effort to coordinate agricultural colleges, experiment stations, federal and state agencies, and local organizations of every sort and variety in the uplift and regeneration of rural community life.

Visionary that he was, Bailey was not unaware of the Herculean problems posed by his ideal. Yet he could look about him in the 1900's and take a good deal of satisfaction from the progress he saw. His Cornell experiments were widely applauded, and nature-study clubs made rapid headway in all parts of the country. City school systems also caught the new enthusiasm, and supported by the American Civic Association, school gardens became a fairly common phenomenon in slum neighborhoods. Meanwhile, agriculture slowly found its way into primary-school curricula, and laws encouraging or requiring it began to appear on state statute books.

At the secondary level most of the states established preparatory courses in connection with their agricultural colleges,

---

[6] *The Outlook to Nature* (New York, 1905), *The State and the Farmer* (New York, 1908), *The Training of Farmers* (New York, 1909), and *The Country-Life Movement in the United States* (New York, 1911).

while Alabama, Georgia, Wisconsin, and California pioneered
in state-aided agricultural high schools. In addition, a number
of private schools also introduced country-life subjects. A Roman Catholic school at Rutherford, California, used the vine-
yards, orchards, and stock pens of a thousand-acre ranch to
train students from the San Francisco area. A school of horticulture just outside Hartford, Connecticut, offered work in
gardens and greenhouses to the children of that city; and the
National Farm School at Doylestown, Pennsylvania, prepared
boys for farm careers in an impressive array of greenhouses,
barns, dairies, and chemistry laboratories.[7]

As might be expected, some of the most promising innovations appeared quite apart from the formal confines of the
school. The development of boys' and girls' agricultural clubs
is an excellent case in point. The clubs seem to have sprung
up independently in a variety of places. Superintendents Albert B. Graham of Clark County, Ohio, and O. J. Kern of
Winnebago County, Illinois, probably share the honors for
making the first extensive use of them. Once begun, they were
quickly taken up as a ready-made device for breathing life into
moribund rural schools. A Farm Boys' and Girls' Progressive
League was organized in Texas by the *Farm and Ranch* magazine "to relieve the narrowness of farm life of our young people
and to dignify and ennoble the agriculture of the future."
Wallace's Farmer began to distribute superior seed corn to
boys in 1904, offering prizes for the best yields at the State
Farm Institute in Des Moines. And farming, sowing, and baking projects introduced by Superintendent E. C. Bishop in
the York County, Nebraska, schools proved so successful that
he was called to Lincoln in 1905 to organize these activities
on a statewide basis. By 1906 literally thousands of boys and
girls the country over were tending gardens, raising chickens,
collecting insects and wild flowers, and cooking, canning,

---

[7] James Ralph Jewell: *Agricultural Education, Including Nature Study
and School Gardens* (United States Bureau of Education, Bulletin, 1907,
No. 2); and A. C. True and Dick J. Crosby: *The American System of
Agricultural Education* (United States Department of Agriculture, Office
of Experiment Stations, Circular No. 83, Washington, 1909).

and baking, all under the sponsorship of local school authorities.[8]

Closely paralleling the efforts of these informal clubs was
the pioneering demonstration work of Seaman A. Knapp,
justly remembered as "the schoolmaster of American agriculture." [9] Long an ardent proponent of scientific farming as the
answer to rural economic distress, Knapp discovered early in
1903 that the one sure way to get local farmers to adopt scientific methods was to have one of their neighbors actually
demonstrate the superiority of these methods on his own farm
under Department of Agriculture tutelage. The idea would
undoubtedly have spread on its own merit, but when the
Mexican cotton boll weevil created a statewide panic in Texas
during the summer of 1903, Knapp's technique was seized
upon as an emergency measure. Congress voted financial assistance, and Knapp was asked to organize what became the Farmers' Cooperative Demonstration Work.[1]

His program proceeded at a phenomenal pace. In 1904, as-

[8] Dick Crosby: "Boys Agricultural Clubs," *Department of Agriculture
Yearbook*, 1904, pp. 488–96; Alfred Charles True: *A History of Agricultural Education in the United States, 1785–1925*, pp. 393–4; and Franklin M. Reck: *The 4-H Story* (Ames, Iowa, 1951), pp. 11–16. The clubs
were actually a schoolchild's potpourri of the best in the Grange, the
farmers' institute, and university extension, and were at one point or
another closely tied to all three. The idea of a Juvenile Grange antedates
the school clubs by more than a decade, the first one having been
organized in Texas in 1888. See C. M. Freeman: *Juvenile Grange Information* (Tippecanoe City, Ohio, 1914), p. 3.

[9] Joseph Cannon Bailey: *Seaman A. Knapp: Schoolmaster of American
Agriculture* (New York, 1945).

[1] Seaman A. Knapp: *The Work of the Community Demonstration
Farm at Terrell, Texas* (United States Department of Agriculture,
Bureau of Plant Industry, Bulletin No. 51, Part II, Washington, 1905);
and O. B. Martin: *The Demonstration Work: Dr. Seaman A. Knapp's
Contribution to Civilization* (Boston, 1921). Knapp made his discovery
almost by accident on the farm of one Walter Porter in Terrell, Texas.
The arrangement was that Porter would continue to own and operate his
farm, using Department of Agriculture seeds and techniques, that Porter
would keep any profit he made, and that a committee of local merchants
would raise a special fund to cover Porter in case of any loss. By minimiz-
ing the government's share in the enterprise, by enhancing the role of the
individual farmer, and by enlisting local support and interest, Knapp converted the demonstration farm from an agency of Washington into a local
community activity.

sisted by two dozen special agents of the Department of Agriculture, he was able to organize some 7,000 demonstrations and to sponsor over 1,000 meetings. As the work spread beyond Texas, it soon allied itself with the club idea. In 1907 W. H. Smith, a teacher who had successfully launched corn-growing clubs in Holmes County, Mississippi, was charged by the Department of Agriculture with extending the demonstration idea to work with schoolboys; while in 1909 Marie S. Cromer, who had organized canning clubs in a South Carolina country school, was asked to undertake parallel activities for girls. The latter activity quickly enlarged into the Department's Home Demonstration Work, a program that employed enterprising women agents to do for the farm home what the cooperative demonstrations were doing for the farm itself.

The success of the demonstration work quickly made Knapp an almost legendary figure. In 1905 President David F. Houston of Texas A. & M. College chanced the remark in a conversation with Wallace Buttrick: "There are two universities here in Texas, one is at Austin; the other is Dr. Knapp." [2] The remark made history. Buttrick was then Secretary of the General Education Board, created by John D. Rockefeller in 1902 as the vehicle for educational philanthropy on a hitherto undreamed of scale. The Board was deeply involved in the progressive effort to reconstruct the South through education,[3] and at the time of President Houston's remark Buttrick was actually in search of promising ways for using the Board's resources in the cause of southern regeneration. Once he had met Knapp, he was convinced he had found his answer; and after the usual series of conferences, an agreement was reached by which the General Education Board became "a silent partner" with the Department of Agriculture in sponsoring Knapp's work. Beginning with a grant of $7,000 for 1906, the Board raised its contribution year by year until 1914, when

[2] Bailey: *Seaman A. Knapp: Schoolmaster of American Agriculture,* p. 214.
[3] The story is told in Charles William Dabney: *Universal Education in the South* (2 vols., Chapel Hill, 1936), II; and Louis R. Harlan: *Separate and Unequal* (Chapel Hill, 1958), ch. iii.

passage of the Smith-Lever Act rendered private assistance no longer necessary.[4]

By 1908 both the rising pressure for rural-school reform and the heightening tempo of rural educational innovation had created an interested public extending far beyond the farmers and teachers directly involved. Spurred on by magazines like *The World's Work*, which ran article after article graphically portraying the plight of the rural community, concern for the renewal of country life had gained considerable support among socially conscious businessmen and professionals in the eastern cities, thereby taking on the character of a national movement. Sensitive to a fertile field in which Progressivism might work its uplifting influence, Theodore Roosevelt appointed a Commission on Country Life and charged it with gathering information and formulating recommendations for alleviating rural distress. Broadly representative of farmers, educators, conservationists, and urban progressives—witness the presence of Liberty Hyde Bailey, chairman; Henry Wallace; Walter Hines Page; President Kenyon Butterfield of Massachusetts Agricultural College, a powerful figure in the Association of American Agriculural Colleges and Experiment Stations; Gifford Pinchot of the United States Forest Service; Charles S. Barrett of the Farmers' Union; and William A. Beard of California's *Great West Magazine*—the Commission quickly crystallized national sentiment on the rural-life problem.[5] And given its

[4] *The General Education Board: An Account of Its Activities, 1902–1914* (New York, 1915), ch. iii. For the extent to which the GEB borrowed Bailey's pedagogical agrarianism, see Frederick T. Gates: *The Country School of To-Morrow* (New York, 1913), published by the GEB.

[5] In his letter of appointment to the several members of the Commission, Roosevelt mentioned favorably the demonstration work of Seaman Knapp and also quoted at some length from his own address, "The Man Who Works With His Hands," delivered at the semicentennial of Michigan Agricultural College in 1907. Bailey's biographers report that his initial response to Roosevelt's invitation was negative, but that he subsequently changed his mind in an interview with the President after making the appointment of Butterfield a condition of his acceptance. Butterfield was later a key figure in convincing the Association of American Agricultural Colleges and Experiment Stations to support the Smith-Lever Act of 1914. Barrett and Beard were appointed after the others, apparently to lend further geographical scope to the Commission.

membership, its recommendations for sweeping educational
changes were only to be expected.

Much of the Commission's effort centered in a rather
lengthy questionnaire sent to over half a million farmers and
rural spokesmen throughout the nation. The one question on
education—"Are the schools in your neighborhood training
boys and girls satisfactorily for farm life?"—elicited a loud and
nearly unanimous, "No." "Everywhere," the Commission
noted, "there is a demand that education have relation to living, that the schools should express the daily life, and that in
rural districts they should educate by means of agriculture and
country life subjects." Only a drastic overhaul of rural education would suffice. Teaching would have to be "visual, direct,
and applicable," related always to the immediate needs of
farm, home, and community; and schooling would need to be
supplemented by a vast national extension program embracing farm demonstrations, boys' and girls' clubs, reading circles,
traveling teachers, farmers' institutes, and publications of every
sort and variety. Only such a program could generate the personal ideals and local leadership that the Commission saw
crucial to any genuine, long-term revival of country life.[6]

Despite the enthusiasm and publicity that surrounded it,
the work of the Country Life Commission "died aborning."
The Commission's findings were ultimately condensed into
one brief report to Congress which never really achieved wide
circulation. Congress, true to what had become form by the
end of Roosevelt's administration, not only refused the $25,-
000 requested for printing and distributing the report, but expressly prohibited the Commission from publishing its investigations. State commissions patterned after the national model
did continue the work, recruiting farmers in many communities for round-table discussions on rural life; and the educational ideas of the national report did remain alive. But no
legislation was immediately forthcoming.

Yet the direct outcome of the report was prodigious. To begin, there followed in its wake a flood of literature on the

[6] *Report of the Country Life Commission* (Senate Document No. 705,
6oth Congress, 2nd Session, Washington, 1909).

country school, the country church, the social aspects of agriculture, and the uplift of the farm home. A superb example of
what came the teacher's way is Mabel Carney's book, *Country
Life and the Country School*, first published in 1912.[7] After
introducing her reader to the "farm problem" in general, Professor Carney quickly got down to business. The rural teacher
would have to assume leadership in the revival of country life.
She could do this only by (1) improving the physical environment of her school; (2) making it a community center; (3) "vitalizing and enriching the course of study" with agriculture,
domestic science, and elementary rural sociology; and (4) wag-
ing outspoken campaigns for the consolidation of overly small
school districts. For the teacher ready to roll up her sleeves
and go to work, Professor Carney provided everything: a plan
for a modern schoolhouse ("Among the furnishings suggested
for this building are Napier matting rugs. They save nerve-
wear in the schoolroom and are easily cleaned."); a plan for
daily school work; a suggested library of rural literature, art,
and music; and a minimum list of manual training tools with
prices. The book undoubtedly trained a new breed of country-
school teacher.

More importantly, perhaps, although legislation did not
come immediately, it did come eventually. After much hag-
gling over who would administer the program, Congress in
1914 finally passed the Smith-Lever Act establishing a national
system of extension work in agriculture and home economics.
The provisions of the law differed in a number of ways from
the proposals of the Commission, but the Commission's influence was manifest. Bailey had been consulted in the formulation of the bill, and though it fell far short of what he
thought needed to be done, he approved it as a useful step in
the right direction. The Act itself received widespread com-
mendation, proving an extraordinarily imaginative device for
coordinating federal, state, and local effort in the cause of
education. And the demonstration program spread rapidly,

---

[7] The book was widely used as a text for rural teachers. Professor
Carney subsequently joined the faculty of Teachers College, Columbia
University.

with vast implications for country life in general, and the country schools in particular.[8] For the rest of his life Senator Smith considered the extension bill the most important single piece of federal legislation he had ever sponsored.[9]

I V

The theme of these discussions—namely, the inextricable relationships between social reform, reform *through* education, and the reform *of* education—may now be generalized. Proponents of virtually every progressive cause from the 1890's through World War I had their program for the school. Humanitarians of every stripe saw education at the heart of their effort toward social alleviation. "Do you see how the whole battle with the slum is fought out in and around the public school?" cried Jacob Riis. "The kindergarten, manual training, the cooking school, all experiments in their day, cried out as fads by some, have brought common sense in their train. When it rules the public schools in our cities . . . we can put off our armor; the battle with the slum will be over."[1] His friend, the Reverend William S. Rainsford, New York's chief spokesman for reform Protestantism, seconded him, contending that "the one way to bring better times, better civilization, better men, better women is education."[2]

In the universities there was growing agreement among liberal social scientists that popular schooling held the key to rational social progress. But it could never be routinized mass

[8] Grant McConnell in *The Decline of Agrarian Democracy* (Berkeley, 1953) argues that the national extension system created by the Smith-Lever Act provided a new basis of political power for the farmer symbolized by the American Farm Bureau Federation, thereby accomplishing through education what the populists had failed to gain in their head-on political assault.

[9] Dewey W. Grantham, Jr.: *Hoke Smith and the Politics of the New South* (Baton Rouge, 1958), p. 263.

[1] Jacob A. Riis: *The Battle with the Slum* (New York, 1902), pp. 404, 410. See also Robert Hunter: *Poverty* (New York, 1905), ch. v; John Spargo: *The Bitter Cry of the Children* (New York, 1906); and Joseph Lee, *Constructive and Preventive Philanthropy* (New York, 1902).

[2] *The New York Times*, March 15, 1895, p. 16.

education; it would have to be schooling "in contact with reality"—critical, scientific, and charged with social meaning. "The problem of the twentieth century" wrote sociologist Frank Tracy Carlton of Albion College, "is to make education an engine for social betterment. Hitherto, educational progress has been conditioned by economic and social changes. Have we advanced far enough on the path of civilization to make it, in a measure, a directive agent?"[3] In the South Walter Hines Page lectured up and down the countryside, calling for educational reconstruction as the prime remedy for the region's social and economic distress, and in widely quoted addresses like "The Forgotten Man" (1897) and "The School That Built a Town" (1901) paved the way for the dramatic work of the great philanthropic foundations in succeeding years.[4]

In the case of municipal reform movements, there were frequently educational adjuncts. Thus, in New York the women's auxiliary of Club E of the Federation of Good Government Clubs in 1895 actually organized itself into the Public Education Association and plunged into the fight for evening schools, playgrounds, vocational studies, free lunches, visiting teachers, and special classes for mentally and physically defective children.[5] In 1898 eleven such organizations from as many cities organized a regional conference in New York, devoting

[3] Frank Tracy Carlton: *Education and Industrial Evolution* (New York, 1908), p. 17.

[4] Walter Hines Page: *The Rebuilding of Old Commonwealths* (New York, 1902); and Burton J. Hendrick: *The Life and Letters of Walter H. Page* (Garden City, 1925), ch. iii.

[5] *First Annual Report of the Public Education Association* (New York, 1895). The Association enlisted the efforts of some of the City's leading reformers, among them Jacob Riis, Felix Adler, Nicholas Murray Butler, the Reverend W. S. Rainsford, and Mrs. Schuyler van Rensselaer, and worked closely with the League for Political Education, the Child Labor Committee, the Ethical Culture Society, the National Municipal League, the Women's Municipal League, and the Association for the Improvement of the Condition of the Poor. The fact that it started as a women's group is not surprising; at the Louisville conference of the General Federation of Women's Clubs in 1896 a motion was adopted urging member clubs to turn their primary effort to the betterment of public education. See Jennie Cunningham Croly: *The History of the Women's Club Movement in America* (New York, 1898), pp. 154, 181–3.

several days of discussion to the improvement of school buildings, the education of juvenile offenders, the reform of school
board politics, and the publicizing of educational needs. The
meetings were filled with familiar figures in the municipal-
reform organizations of the era.[6]

At the state level, Wisconsin during the La Follette era provides a classic example of the marriage between political and
educational reform. There were notable advances in elementary and secondary education beginning in the nineties, and by
1910 the schools of Menomonie and Milwaukee had become
pedagogical showplaces of the nation. Yet it was the interplay
between university and capitol that really captured the popular
imagination as the heart of the Wisconsin idea. "The State wel-
comes the ever increasing tendency to make the university
minister in a direct and practical way to the material interests
of the state," La Follette declared in 1904.[7] The work of Professors Ely, Commons, Gilmore, Reinsch, and others—not
only their contribution to the actual business of government
but the larger influence of their teaching—was the University's
response.[8]

At the national level, the Country Life Commission serves
as an excellent case in point. So, too, does the National Society
for the Promotion of Industrial Education. Embracing among
its diverse leadership businessmen like James Phinney Monroe,
labor leaders like John Golden of the United Textile Workers,

    [6] *Fourth Annual Report of the Public Education Association* (New
York, 1898); Mrs. William E. D. Scott: "The Aims and Work of the
Conference of Public Education Associations," *The Annals*, XXV
(1905), 371–4; and "Public Education Societies," *The School Journal*,
LXXIV (1907), 395–404. The confederation called itself the Conference of Eastern Public Education Associations. Borrowing the general
assumptions of the municipal reform movement, it argued that the
primary problem of good school management is to divorce the schools
from "politics," and that this is best accomplished by centralizing
educational authority in an expert superintendent of schools, reserving
business matters to a small, public-spirited lay board of education. Recall
that these had also been Rice's assumptions in 1892.

    [7] Merle Curti and Vernon Carstensen: *The University of Wisconsin:
A History 1848–1925*, II, 90.

    [8] For the more general movement in the Midwest, see Russel B. Nye's
chapter on "The Capture of the Ivory Tower" in *Midwestern Progressive
Politics* (East Lansing, 1951).

municipal reformers like Henry Bruere of the New York Citizens' Union, settlement workers like Jane Addams and Robert Woods, and reformist educators like Charles R. Richards, the Society came as close as any in the years before 1917 to being an association for the advancement of progressive education. No wonder it took the group only eleven years to push a national vocational education bill through the Congress!

Other examples are legion, but perhaps the point has been made. Progressive education [9] began as part and parcel of that broader program of social and political reform called the Progressive Movement. Contrary to the widespread misconception that it dates from the advent of the Progressive Education Association in 1919, the idea had its origin during the quarter-century before World War I in an effort to cast the school as a fundamental lever of social and political regeneration.[1] It began as a many-sided protest against a restricted view of the school, but it was always more than this; for essentially it viewed education as an adjunct to politics in realizing the promise of American life.

To grasp this relationship between progressive education and progressivism is to sharpen significantly our understanding of both. On the one hand, it extends the purview of the progressive movement in education far beyond the common caricature of the Bohemian school where children run wild in orgies of naturalistic freedom. While the seeds of such romanticism undoubtedly go back to the nineties and earlier, it is patently unjust to a great deal of tough-minded pedagogical thinking to contend that the caricature sums up the movement.

[9] The phrase *progressive education* was in fairly common use during the decade before World War I, most frequently referring to industrial education of one sort or another and to the movement to transform the school into a social center.

[1] In their conceptions of regeneration, progressive educators reflected many of the same contradictions as progressivism writ large, looking wistfully back to a golden age of *Gemeinschaft* at the same time as they militated for realistic social legislation. The contradictions are a persistent theme of the recent literature on the progressive movement. See, for example, Richard Hofstadter: *The Age of Reform* (New York, 1955); and David W. Noble: *The Paradox of Progressive Thought* (Minneapolis, 1958).

On the other hand, to sense the relationship between progressivism and progressive education is to gain new insight into the meaning of Progressivism itself. Richard Hofstadter has observed that the Progressive mind was characteristically a journalistic mind, and that its characteristic contribution was that of a socially responsible reporter-reformer. One might well paraphrase his statement to contend that the Progressive mind was ultimately an educator's mind, and that its characteristic contribution was that of a socially responsible reformist pedagogue. As moralists, the Progressives might be expected to turn to education; and as journalists concerned with purveying information, they would certainly view the mass school as an adjunct to the mass press. When Governor La Follette sermonized, "Ye shall know the truth and the truth shall make you free," he meant the schools as well as *La Follette's Magazine*. For only an educated public would move from the revelations of the exposé to the informed political action in which the Progressives so deeply believed.

Finally, and perhaps most important, the Progressives were fundamentally moderates, and for all their sense of outrage, moderates take time. It is this as much as anything that usually separates them from their more radical contemporaries. The real radicals of the nineties—men like Eugene Victor Debs and Daniel De Leon—had little patience for reform through education: they directed their energy to the drive for political power which they saw as the only real source of genuine social alleviation.[2] But for the much larger group impelled by conscience yet restrained by conservatism, education provided a field par excellence for reform activities untainted by radicalism. Their predicament was not a new one. A half-century earlier Horace Mann, certainly no radical, had refashioned the school as an engine to create a new republican America. It should hardly be surprising that a generation which followed him would again view education as an instrument to realize America's promise.

[2] The impatience persists in more recent Socialist assessments of progressive education, as, for example, William F. Warde: "John Dewey's Theories of Education," *International Socialist Review*, XXI (1960), 5–8, and "The Fate of Dewey's Theories," Ibid., 54–7, 61.

❧ *4* ❧

Science, Darwinism,
and Education

HENRY STEELE COMMAGER has likened the nineties to a great watershed in American history, a decade in which "the new America came in as on flood tide." [1] His metaphor is as apt for pedagogy as for any other realm. The era was truly a brilliant one, vastly fruitful for the development of American scholarship. Virtually every field of knowledge quickened under the influence of science in general and Darwinism in particular. Psychology, social theory, and philosophy were as deeply affected as physics, chemistry, and biology.[2] And as new notions of man and society came to the fore, pedagogy too was

[1] Henry Steele Commager: *The American Mind* (New Haven, 1950), ch. ii.

[2] Stow Persons, ed.: *Evolutionary Thought in America* (New Haven, 1950); Richard Hofstadter: *Social Darwinism in American Thought* (Philadelphia, 1945); and Bert J. Loewenberg: "The Reaction of American Scientists to Darwinism," *American Historical Review*, XXXVIII (1933), 687–701, and "Darwinism Comes to America," *Mississippi Valley Historical Review*, XXVIII (1941), 339–69.

inevitably caught up in the ferment. The year 1890 saw the appearance of William James's *Principles of Psychology*, an epochal work that had been twelve years in the making. There followed an extraordinary succession of seminal publications: Francis W. Parker's *Talks on Pedagogics* (1894), Edward L. Thorndike's *Animal Intelligence* (1898), James's *Talks to Teachers on Psychology* (1899), and John Dewey's *The School and Society* (1899). By the turn of the century a revolution was clearly at hand, and progressives found themselves with a growing body of theory to support the pedagogical reformism they so dearly espoused.

If the revolution had a beginning, it was surely with the work of Herbert Spencer. No philosopher seemed to promise greater hope or deeper insight into the mysteries of the universe for post-Civil War Americans. His first book, *Social Statics* (1850), was known and discussed in the United States almost as soon as it was published; and with the appearance of the early volumes of the *Synthetic Philosophy* after 1862, his influence grew steadily, reaching a peak in 1882 when he came to America for a series of lectures and celebrations in his honor. Broadly comprehensive and reassuringly based on the new theory of evolution, his theories seemed admirably suited to a generation uncertain of its religious convictions and desperately seeking solace in the revelations of science. "I believe there is great work to be done here for civilization," Edward L. Youmans wrote Spencer in 1863. "What we want are ideas—large, organizing ideas—and I believe there is no other man whose thoughts are so valuable for our needs as yours are." [3]

Of Spencer's many books—and they were legion—the one on education was probably the most widely read in America. A collection of four essays originally published in English periodicals between 1854 and 1859, the treatise propounded notions that must have sounded supremely sensible to a people nurtured on the aphorisms of Poor Richard. "To prepare us for complete living," Spencer declared, "is the function which education has to discharge; and the only rational mode of judging

[3] Youmans to Spencer, December 14, 1863, in John Fiske: *Edward Livingston Youmans* (New York, 1894), 169–70.

of any educational course is, to judge in what degree it discharges such function." [4] And what was complete living? Spencer classified it into five categories: (1) those activities ministering directly to self-preservation, (2) those that secure the necessaries of life, (3) those concerned with the rearing and disciplining of offspring, (4) those that maintain proper social and political relations, and (5) those devoted to the gratification of tastes and feelings. The ideal education, he concluded, is simply "complete preparation in all these divisions."

Measured against this yardstick, Spencer found conventional schooling sadly deficient. Time and again he saw first principles sacrificed to inferior ends; elegance had become the goal, to the exclusion of the most important learning a man could pursue. What knowledge was of most worth? Spencer's unqualified answer was science. For the maintenance of health, for earning a living, for parenthood, for civic duty, for the perfect production and highest enjoyment of the arts, and for discipline in all its forms—intellectual, moral, and religious—science was the most efficient and economical study of all.

The immediate effect of Spencer's work was to accelerate tendencies that had long been in evidence on the American scene. It lent potent support to Charles W. Eliot's indefatigable campaign for a "new education" based on the pure and applied sciences, the modern European languages, and mathematics.[5] It was obviously influential in the formulations of the NEA's Committee of Ten (1893), which gave parity to the

---

[4] Herbert Spencer: *Education: Intellectual, Moral, and Physical* (New York, 1860), p. 31. The reception among educators was not unqualified. Thus, while reviews in *The New York Teacher*, X (1860), 141–2, and *The Ohio Educational Monthly*, X (1861), 30, were generally favorable, a commentator in *The Pennsylvania School Journal* disposed of the treatise as "the materialistic speculations of a metaphysical transcendentalist." IX (1861), 197–9.

[5] Charles W. Eliot: "The New Education," *The Atlantic Monthly*, XXIII (1869), 203–20, 358–67, and *Educational Reform* (New York, 1898). For the influence of Spencer on Eliot, see Henry James: *Charles W. Eliot* (2 vols., Boston, 1930), I, 349–51. Eliot himself wrote the introduction for the Everyman's edition of Spencer's *Education* in 1910, observing there that Spencer's ideas "have been floated on a prodigious tide of industrial and social change, which necessarily involved wide-spread and profound educational reform."

natural sciences in the secondary school program.[6] And it was crucial in the report of the NEA's Commission on the Reorganization of Secondary Education (1918), a document that pronounced health, command of fundamental processes, worthy home-membership, vocation, citizenship, worthy use of leisure, and ethical character as the seven "main objectives" of American secondary education.[7]

The larger effect of Spencer's work was more elusive, but perhaps more important.[8] Spencer, after all, was the great proponent of evolution to the American people, the teacher of what later came to be called social Darwinism. In the *Social Statics*, published fully nine years before Darwin's *Origin of Species*, he had stated an evolutionary thesis that was to remain fairly constant in the many works that followed—namely, that history is the progressive adaptation of constitution to conditions, or, put another way, the adjustment of human character to the circumstances of living. In the course of history human perfection is ultimately attainable, but men are infinitely more the creatures of history than its creators.

Applying this general thesis to the realm of education, Spencer drew a number of conclusions. Some were pedagogical maxims very much in the modernist stream of Bacon, Locke, Rousseau, and Pestalozzi. Thus the aim of education is preparation for life. Instruction ought to begin with objects rather than abstractions. Morals are best taught by connecting acts with consequences. The health of the body is essential to the health

[6] *Report of the Committee on Secondary School Studies Appointed at the Meeting of the National Educational Association, July 9, 1892* (Washington, 1893). Eliot, as chairman of the committee, had much to do with its pronouncements. The influence of Spencer is patent, though Edward Krug has pointed out to me that while Spencer viewed the sciences as directly functional, Eliot saw them much more as "disciplinary" subjects which, by training the mind, would contribute indirectly to intelligent action. The difference was already evident in Eliot's 1869 pronouncements in *The Atlantic Monthly*.

[7] *Cardinal Principles of Secondary Education* (United States Bureau of Education, Bulletin, 1918, No. 35, Washington, 1918). See my essay: "The Revolution in American Secondary Education, 1893–1918," *Teachers College Record*, LVI (1954–5), 295–308.

[8] See Elsa Peverly Kimball: *Sociology and Education* (New York, 1932), chs. i–iii.

of the mind. Play is a central activity of childhood and should be encouraged. These and similar pronouncements appear throughout his work, supported always by general observations on the "laws of nature."

But there were deeper social teachings that merit close examination. The development of mind, Spencer insisted, follows evolutionary processes. And because evolutionary processes work themselves out over long periods of time, according to laws independent of immediate human acts, education can never be an important factor in social progress. The best the teacher can do is provide the knowledge that will enable people to adapt more readily to the circumstances that surround them. Any changes in these circumstances must await the inexorable operations of evolutionary progress, and men had best not meddle.

Closely allied to this belief in the futility of reform was Spencer's unalterable opposition to public—or national—education. From *Social Statics* until his death in 1903, he was an adamant proponent of private schooling, contending that state education could only undermine parental freedom and corrupt the body politic with the poison of public welfare. Social improvement was exasperatingly slow, he granted, but no measure of human tampering could hasten it. Indeed, the very impatience of reformers, in supposing there were artificial roads to progress, could only invite disaster.

Spencer's works were widely pondered by educated Americans of his generation, and his influence unassisted would certainly have been profound. But it was rendered even more powerful by the energetic discipleship of William Graham Sumner. Sumner, who held a professorship of political and social science at Yale from 1872 until his death in 1910, was for most of that time the commanding figure of the new field of sociology. And his wholehearted espousal of social Darwinism undoubtedly did much to enhance the stature of that creed both within and without the community of scholars.

Like Spencer, Sumner combined a vigorous laissez-faire individualism with an unshakable belief that true scientific progress could only come through the inexorable natural workings of the evolutionary process. Like Spencer, too, he assumed that those who held power had gained it by being "fittest," that their survival in the competition of society was the most eloquent testimony to their suitability for leadership. And like his mentor, he was on the side of curricular reform in the schools, but ended up essentially pessimistic about any melioristic powers of education.[9]

In essays like "The Absurd Attempt to Make the World Over" and "What Social Classes Owe to Each Other," Sumner placed himself squarely in the ranks of those who resisted most reform. Richard Hofstadter notes that he opposed almost every reform movement of his day, save in education, where he was a progressive influence. Yet except for his advocacy of the sciences and the elective system, he seems as antiprogressive there as elsewhere. He maintained a healthy bias against public education in general, and state universities in particular, contending that the right to vote did not imply any right to free schooling.[1] And while he supported limited compulsory education, he believed in it more as a guarantee of public order than a lever of social uplift.[2] He inveighed unceasingly against pedagogical faddists of every sort and variety, assuming that most proposals for reform were nostrums designed to avoid the irksome labor essential to true mental discipline. And he was equally caustic in his criticism of all public plans for popularizing knowledge among the masses.[3] Ultimately, he placed his faith in the processes of nature. The principal contribution of sociology, he concluded, would be to awaken men to the enormous complex-

[9] Sumner's pessimism was not unqualified. In *Folkways*, his magnum opus, he conceived of the school as society's prime agency for transmitting the heritage of the race. "The transmission ought to be faithful," he went on to say, "but not without criticism. The reaction of free judgment and taste will keep the mores fresh and active, and the schools are undoubtedly the place where they should be renewed through an intelligent study of their operation in the past." (Boston, 1906), p. 635.

[1] William Graham Sumner: *What Social Classes Owe to Each Other* (New York, 1883), pp. 40–2.

[2] William Graham Sumner: *Earth-Hunger and Other Essays*, Albert Galloway Keller, ed. (New Haven, 1913), pp. 100–3.

[3] William Graham Sumner: *The Forgotten Man and Other Essays*, Albert Galloway Keller, ed. (New Haven, 1918), pp. 409–19.

ity of the social organism, and hence to the slim prospects of any scheme for the rapid alleviation of social problems.

I I

Eleven years after Sumner assumed his professorship at Yale, a new book appeared from the pen of an obscure government paleontologist named Lester Frank Ward. Entitled *Dynamic Sociology*, it undertook to deal with evolution in a way diametrically opposed to the approach of the stern Yale scholar. Like two litigants who enter a courtroom armed with conflicting views of the same facts, Ward and Sumner began alike with Spencer and proceeded to vastly differing conclusions. Out of their differences grew controversies about the nature of education and social reform that have continued to plague theorists and men of affairs right down to the present day.

Ward was for all intents and purposes self-educated.[4] Although he earned three degrees at George Washington University, then known as Columbian College, his real learning came from voracious reading and from the tireless observation of natural phenomena. He was abreast of nearly all of the great scientific treatises of his day, and he made himself thoroughly familiar with Spencer's works as they appeared. Yet as Ward observed the phenomenon of evolution, he soon concluded that there was more to it than the inexorable operation of natural selection throughout the universe. Spencer, he argued, had described merely physical, or animal, or *genetic* evolution, a process essentially planless in character. But Spencer had ignored the crucial fact that with the emergence of mind the very character of evolution changes. For mind is "telic." It has purposes; it can plan. And in so doing, it supplants the relatively static phase of genetic evolution with a new dynamic phase. "The office of mind," Ward counseled, "is to direct society into unobstructed channels, to enable these forces to continue in free play, to prevent them from being neutralized by collision with obstacles in their path. In a word, mind has for

[4] Samuel Chugerman: *Lester F. Ward: The American Aristotle* (Durham, 1939), ch. i.

its function in civilization to preserve the dynamic and prevent the statical condition of the social forces, to prevent the restoration of equilibrium between the social forces and the natural forces operating outside of them." [5] With mind at work, evolution is no longer blind, but instead telic, purposeful, and consciously directed toward worthy social ends.

Given this formulation, Ward, unlike Spencer and Sumner, conceived of education as the foremost activity of mankind, the "great panacea" for all social ills.[6] Following Auguste Comte, he argued that social salvation lay in a vast diffusion of information, especially scientific information, among the citizenry at large. The popularization of knowledge would inevitably create widespread understanding of man's relations with nature; this, in turn, would enable men in their daily lives to harmonize natural phenomena with human advantage; and this, ultimately, would lead to the greatest happiness for the greatest number. Education that was scientific, popular, and universal could be the "mainspring of progress," the "piston of civilization," the "embodiment of all that is progressive."

In the matter of opportunity Ward was overwhelmingly equalitarian. Borrowing heavily from Claude-Adrien Helvetius, he tended to dispose of the classical problem of the differences among men by arguing first, that there were no class variations in intellect, and second, that given individual variations, the ordinary capacity for knowledge was far in excess of the knowledge possessed. Fundamentally an environmentalist, he preferred to emphasize general potentialities rather than comparative limitations, thereby shifting the burden of proof to the elitist in the controversy over popular education.[7]

In the matter of control Ward again followed Enlightenment lore, contending that the state alone had sufficiently

[5] Lester F. Ward: *Dynamic Sociology* (2 vols., New York, 1883), I, 698.

[6] Ward left a long unpublished manuscript on education, written between 1871 and 1873 and now in the Brown University library, which, *inter alia*, disposes of Spencer's pedagogical essays as essentially treatises on home training.

[7] Lester F. Ward: *Pure Sociology* (New York, 1903), pp. 447–8, and *Dynamic Sociology*, I, 405–8.

broad means and motives to sponsor universal schooling. Whereas Spencer and Sumner saw public education as a corrosion of parental responsibility, Ward saw it as the only feasible device for turning evolution to the larger social good. "The action of society in inaugurating and carrying on a great educational system," he urged, "however defective we may consider that system to be, is undoubtedly the most promising form thus far taken by collective achievement. It means much even now, but for the future it means nothing less than the complete social appropriation of individual achievement which has civilized the world." [8]

Ward's work was marked by a brilliance quite comparable to Spencer's and Sumner's; and in moving education to the forefront of human affairs, he gave "scientific" expression to a theme that had flowed as part of the American mainstream from Jefferson through Mann and Harris to the generation of the eighties. But while Spencer and Sumner were widely read and discussed, Ward was massively ignored, known at best as a sociologist's sociologist. Had it not been for the eager discipleship of Albion Small at the University of Chicago, a whole generation of educators might well have missed his work.

An early graduate of Johns Hopkins, Small had gone to Chicago in 1892 to head the first department of sociology in the United States. There, through his own writings and later through the *American Journal of Sociology*, he soon became an acknowledged spokesman for the new discipline. A fascinating lecturer, possessed of a delightfully whimsical sense of humor, he was ever hospitable to new ideas, and in the work of Ward he found both inspiration and a solid base on which to build his own social theories. [9]

---

[8] Ward: *Pure Sociology*, p. 575.

[9] Although he was later one of Ward's severest critics, Small continually acknowledged his debt to his mentor, writing in 1913: "I have often said, and it remains my estimate, that, everything considered, I would rather have written *Dynamic Sociology* than any other book that has ever appeared in America." *American Journal of Sociology*, XIX (1913–14), 77. See also Bernhard J. Stern, ed.: "The Letters of Albion W. Small to Lester F. Ward," *Social Forces*, XII (1933–4), 163–73; XIII (1935–6), 323–40; and XV (1936–7), 174–86, 305–27.

Small's first major book was *An Introduction to the Study of Society*, published in 1894 in collaboration with George E. Vincent. His views on education there were essentially conservative; although he traced some of the ills of American society to poor teachers, faulty methods of instruction, and a conventional, unscientific curriculum, he was quite ready to limit the school to communicating humanity's wisdom to the young. Two years later, however, in an address to the National Educational Association in Buffalo, his views had changed markedly. Calling his speech "The Demands of Sociology upon Pedagogy," he now set the school in the vanguard of the movement to improve society. Education, he counseled, must place the upcoming generation in contact with the three great realities of modern life: interdependence, the realization that in the industrial world no man liveth unto himself; cooperation, the correlative of interdependence; and progress, the realization that new men and events forever necessitate new social arrangements. "Sociology knows no means for the amelioration or reform of society more radical than those of which teachers hold the leverage," Small concluded. "The teacher who realizes his social function will not be satisfied with passing children to the next grade. He will read his success only in the record of men and women who go from the school eager to explore wider and deeper these social relations, and zealous to do their part in making a better future. We are dupes of faulty analysis if we imagine that schools can do much to promote social progress until they are motivated by this insight and temper." [1]

By 1896 American educators could take their choice between Spencer and Sumner or Ward and Small, between what Eric Goldman has called Conservative Darwinism on the one hand or Reform Darwinism on the other. For what Ward and Small had done was to transform the harsh Spencerian doctrine of social Darwinism into a full-fledged philosophy of meliorism. For Small's younger colleague, John Dewey, the choice was not a difficult one at all. In 1897, when the editor of *The School Journal* asked him briefly to state his pedagogic

[1] National Educational Association; *Addresses and Proceedings*, 1896, p. 184.

creed, he declared that "education is the fundamental method of social progress and reform"; that "the teacher is engaged, not simply in the training of individuals, but in the formation of the proper social life"; and that "in this way the teacher always is the prophet of the true God and the usherer in of the true kingdom of God." [2] Little wonder that American educators came to view this quiet little man with the dark mustache as a Moses who would eventually lead them toward the pedagogic promised land!

I I I

The same era that saw the rise of social Darwinism—both the conservative and the reform varieties—also witnessed the birth of a new psychology dedicated to the scientific study of human behavior in general and the phenomena of mind in particular. As with correlative developments in sociology, European influences were critical, but they were always tempered by the distinctive demands of the American scene. Thus, Edwin Boring has noted that the paternity of American psychology was German, deriving from the work of Gustav Fechner, Hermann von Helmholtz, and Wilhelm Wundt; while the maternity was English, and is to be found in the work of Darwin, Francis Galton, and of course, Spencer.[3] The child, however, was much influenced by the environment in which it grew up; for the Americans, as usual, borrowed selectively, and ended up fashioning a psychology clearly designed to serve the practical needs of their own civilization.

Perhaps the most immediate effect of Darwinism on American psychology was to stimulate the erection of comprehensive systems explicitly evolutionary in character. One of the earliest

[2] *The School Journal*, LIV (1897), 77–80. Dewey's creed, reprinted in an 1897 pamphlet together with Small's NEA address, received wide circulation among teachers.

[3] Edwin G. Boring: "The Influence of Evolutionary Theory upon American Psychological Thought," in Persons: op. cit., p. 269; and Boring: A *History of Experimental Psychology*, 2nd ed. (New York, 1950), chs. xiv–xvi, xx.

of these—and it exerted profound effect on pedagogy—was the one developed by Granville Stanley Hall. Hall had earned Harvard's first doctorate in psychology in 1878 and had then gone on to study with three titans of German science: Helmholtz in physics, Ludwig in physiology, and Wundt in psychology. On his return from Germany he had assumed first a much-coveted professorship at Johns Hopkins—Dewey had been his student there—and then the presidency of Jonas Clark's new university in Worcester, Massachusetts. During the 1890's a steady stream of papers flowed from his prolific pen, and the decade saw his rise to prominence as one of the foremost figures in American psychology and education. By the turn of the century Hall was a man to be reckoned with, and his influence was already widely manifest among avant-garde teachers and professors of pedagogy.

An overzealous friend once introduced Hall to an audience as "the Darwin of the mind." Hall reports in his autobiography that the allusion gave him more inner satisfaction than any compliment ever paid him. "To contribute ever so little to introduce evolutionary concepts into psychology," he wrote, "and to advance the view that there were just as many rudiments and vestiges in our psychic activity and make-up as in our bodies and that the former was just as much a product of slow evolutionary tendencies as the latter, comprised about all my insights and ambitions." [4] He may well have been too modest, for in the extent to which he succeeded in the realm of psychology, he influenced pedagogy as well, and in a way that undoubtedly cut deeper and lasted longer.

Hall's basic thesis—the "general psychonomic law," which he borrowed from Haeckel and Spencer—was that ontogeny, the development of the individual organism, recapitulates phylogeny, the evolution of the race. The thesis assumes that psychical life and individual behavior develop through a series of stages that correspond more or less to the stages through which the race is supposed to have passed from presavagery to civiliza-

[4] G. Stanley Hall: *Life and Confessions of a Psychologist* (New York, 1923), p. 360.

tion.[5] Moreover, the normal growth of mind requires living through each of the stages, since the development of any one stage is the normal stimulus for the emergence of the next. Herein lies the link between Hall's general psychology and its application to pedagogy. For he was ready to judge a civilization by the way its children grew, and a school system by the way it adapted itself to the natural growth of individuals.[6] Nature was right, he insisted, particularly in the lives of children. To a nation about to celebrate "the century of the child," his doctrines had enormous appeal.

As early as 1882, when he established his laboratory at Johns Hopkins, Hall decided to concentrate his energies on the hitherto unexplored problem of child development.[7] When he assumed the presidency of Clark University in 1889, that institution quickly became a leading center for research and writing in that field. The establishment of *Pedagogical Seminary* magazine in 1891 did much to diffuse the materials gathered at Clark to a growing audience of parents and pedagogues.

Hall's first major contribution to receive widespread notice was "The Contents of Children's Minds" (1883), a monograph based on questionnaire data.[8] His explicit conclusion there was that with the coming of cities, and the consequent changes in the experience of childhood, schools could no longer assume that children brought with them the same concepts as in the older farm days. But beneath this conclusion lay notions much more radical than the argument that subject matter might be taught more effectively if the results of child

[5] Ibid., pp. 357–74; Hall: "A Glance at the Phyletic Background of Genetic Psychology," *American Journal of Psychology*, XIX (1908), 149–212; and Sara Carolyn Fisher: "The Psychological and Educational Work of Granville Stanley Hall," *American Journal of Psychology*, XXXVI (1925), 1–52. The doctrine of recapitulation was also central to contemporary Herbartianism, from which Hall borrowed extensively.

[6] G. Stanley Hall: "Child-Study and Its Relation to Education," *The Forum*, XXIX (1900), 700. Hall stated in the first issue of *Pedagogical Seminary*: "Every educational reform has been the direct result of closer personal acquaintance with children and youth, and deeper insight into their needs and life." I, (1891), 123.

[7] Hall was clearly influenced by German forerunners, especially Wilhelm Preyer. See *Die Seele des Kindes* (Leipzig, 1882).

[8] *The Princeton Review*, XI (1883), 249–72.

study were used. For Hall was really urging that the content of the curriculum could itself be determined from the data of child development.

That this is so becomes evident from an essay, "The Ideal School as Based on Child Study," published some years later in *The Forum*. One can assume that it reached a highly literate and influential audience, both lay and professional. Here his key concept concerned the difference between the *scholiocentric* and the *pedocentric* school. The former, the dominant ideal of Western education throughout its history, fitted the child to the school; the latter, in Hall's view the only defensible ideal for a republic, fitted the school to the child. "The guardians of the young," he argued, "should strive first of all to keep out of nature's way, and to prevent harm, and should merit the proud title of defenders of the happiness and rights of children. They should feel profoundly that childhood, as it comes fresh from the hand of God, is not corrupt, but illustrates the survival of the most consummate thing in the world; they should be convinced that there is nothing else so worthy of love, reverence, and service as the body and soul of the growing child." [9] Thus did Hall build upon the laissez-faire pedagogy first advanced in *Émile* the idea of a child-centered school whose curriculum would be tailored to a larger view of the nature, growth, and development of children.

Hall's position, particularly as it was bolstered by the four massive volumes of his *Adolescence* (1904) and *Educational Problems* (1911), paved the way for some fundamental changes in American pedagogical opinion. It helped shift the focus of teaching to the student, asserting that no education could be worthy, much less efficient, that persisted in ignoring his nature, his needs, and his development.[1] Moreover, it threw

[9] *The Forum*, XXXII (1901–2), 24–5.

[1] The Herbartians, with their interest in psychologizing the presentation of subject matter in the classroom, had already contributed much to the shift. See, for example, Charles A. McMurry: *The Elements of General Method* (Bloomington, 1892), p. 194. By 1895 the NEA's Committee of Fifteen observed: "Modern education emphasizes the opinion that the child, not the subject of study, is the guide to the teacher's efforts. To know the child is of paramount importance." National Educational Association: *Addresses and Proceedings*, 1895, p. 242.

new emphasis on the scientific study of feelings, dispositions, and attitudes as elements in which education has an undeniable stake. Most important, perhaps, it subtly shifted the burden of proof in the educational situation, and in so doing, the meaning of equal opportunity as well. Formerly, when the content and purposes of the school had been fairly well defined and commonly accepted, the burden of proof was on the student: he was told to perform up to standard or get out. Educational opportunity was the right of all who might profit from schooling to enjoy its benefits. Now, the "given" of the equation was no longer the school with its well-defined content and purposes, but the children with their particular backgrounds and needs. And educational opportunity had become the right of all who attended school to receive something of meaning and value.[2]

The shift was truly Copernican, its effects, legion. On the one hand, it hastened the acceptance of academic studies long barred from the school by reason of tradition, custom, or simple apathy. On the other hand, it opened the pedagogical floodgates to every manner of activity, trivial as well as useful, that seemed in some way to minister to "the needs of children." Reformers had a field day, as did sentimentalists, and American schools were never quite the same again!

Hall's influence would have been prodigious merely on the basis of his own voluminous writings. But Clark quickly became the headquarters for a larger child-study movement. Hall himself lectured indefatigably, and *Pedagogical Seminary* became a clearinghouse for data and doctrine. Students like Lewis M. Terman and Arnold Gesell carried the work to other university centers, while child-study associations sprang up in every corner of the globe.[3] By 1909, the year Hall brought

[2] Boring makes the interesting observation that although Hall came to psychology through philosophy, he ultimately "turned the tables by saying that psychology furnished the true approach to philosophy; that is to say, the psychoanalysis of men is the key to the significance of their opinions." A *History of Experimental Psychology*, p. 521.

[3] Wilbur Harvey Dutton: "The Child-Study Movement in America from Its Origin (1880) to the Organization of the Progressive Education Association (1920)," (Unpublished Doctoral Thesis, Stanford University, 1945).

Freud to America, the movement was in full stride; and joined
to the militant feminism of Ellen Key, it made ready converts
among reformist women's groups who began to see in the new
education one major step toward the larger goal of final female
emancipation.[4]

I V

Stanley Hall was known for many qualities, but modesty was
not one of them. Very early in his career the sense of Messi-
anism that later pervaded his *Life and Confessions* began to reveal itself in his addresses and articles. In the fall of 1895, for
example, he published in the *American Journal of Psychology*
a long list of people who had been associated with him either
at Johns Hopkins or at Clark, suggesting that these were really
the scholars who had brought scientific psychology to Harvard,
Yale, Columbia, Wisconsin, and other leading American universities. When William James read this editorial, he wrote
Hall a long letter that said, in part: "As an arm-chair professor,
I frankly admit my great inferiority as a laboratory-teacher and
investigator. But some little regard should be paid to the good
will with which I have tried to force my nature, and to the actual things I have done. One of them, for example, was inducting YOU into experimental investigation, with very naive
methods, it is true, but you may remember that there was no
other place but Harvard where during those years you could
get even that." [5]

James had a point! Well before Hall had taken his doctorate
in 1878, James had been at Harvard leading in the effort to establish psychology as a truly scientific discipline. He had lectured on the relations between physiology and psychology as
early as 1875, and had even set up arrangements for informal
laboratory work by students in the course of their studies. In

<hr />

[4] Ellen Key: *The Century of the Child* (New York, 1909) and Hall:
"Child-Study and Its Relation to Education," p. 688. Ellen Key addressed
herself to those in the women's rights movement who were seeking to
reform family life rather than to eschew it.

[5] The story is told in Ralph Barton Perry: *The Thought and Character
of William James* (2 vols., Boston, 1935), II, 7–10.

1878 he had contracted to prepare a general psychology text for Henry Holt's "American Science Series," thinking to finish in two years a book that eventually took him twelve. When the work finally appeared in 1890, it quickly established his reputation, proving a milestone not only in psychology but in American intellectual history as well.[6]

James proposed in the *Principles of Psychology* to apply the doctrines of evolution to the phenomena of mind. His enterprise, of course, was not original: Spencer had made the same effort, and Hall was working along the same line as a contemporary. But the difference between James and the others was crucial. For Spencer the life of the mind was one of continuing adaptation to environment; here, as with the social organism, the principle of adjustment to circumstances pertained. Hall took one aspect of Spencer, the recapitulation doctrine, and worked it into a more general theory of human development, the main pedagogical implication of which seemed to be that educators ought not to interfere with nature's inexorable processes.

For James this sort of naturalistic determinism was anathema. Referring to Darwin's own work, he insisted that while mind is obviously molded by environment, it also reacts upon environment in an actively creative way. The business of intelligence is not merely to adapt to circumstances, but to change them as well. The knower is more than a mirror passively reflecting the world he comes upon, James declared; the knower is an actor who helps transform the world of which he is part. Voluntarism, not determinism, is the crucial fact of human affairs.[7]

To peruse the *Principles* is to turn from the formalist systems of Wundt and his disciples to a new functional view of psychology.[8] Man is conceived as a biological creature whose behavior

[6] William James: *Principles of Psychology* (2 vols., New York, 1890).

[7] James was early attracted to Spencer, but gradually became disenchanted under the prodding of Chauncey Wright and Charles Peirce. He made these points as early as 1878 in an article in Harris's *Journal of Speculative Philosophy* entitled "Remarks on Spencer's Definition of Mind as Correspondence," XII (1878), 1–18.

[8] The contrast is illuminated by Edna Heidbreder in *Seven Psychologies* (New York, 1933), chs. iv–v.

is founded upon certain instinctive tendencies to react. Upon these tendencies rest both habitual and voluntary action. As a result of the repetition of acts, habits emerge, testifying to the plasticity and modifiability of the human nervous system. Once formed, they increasingly govern behavior until eventually they become the overwhelming determinants of social and personal character. Obviously, a central task of education is the early inculcation of as many good and useful habits as possible. "The hell to be endured hereafter, of which theology tells," James remarks, "is no worse than the hell we make for ourselves in this world by habitually fashioning our characters in the wrong way. Could the young but realize how soon they will become mere walking bundles of habits, they would give more heed to their conduct while in the plastic state. We are spinning our own fates, good or evil, and never to be undone." [9]

There is a paradox about habit, though, for the more the details of life are given over to it, the further the higher powers of mind are released to do their own proper work. Here James's key concept is consciousness, or "the stream of thought" as he called it. Insisting that life itself, rather than any formal notions of mind or soul, is the starting point of psychology, James pictured consciousness as an intensely active phenomenon continually engaged in attending, emphasizing, ignoring, and interpreting the raw data of immediately felt experience. Mind is ever the "theatre of simultaneous possibilities," he observed, and it is the fate of each individual to be constantly choosing— what he perceives, what he knows, and ultimately, which of many possible selves he will become. Once again the knower is an actor whose very act of knowing helps transform the world.

In 1892, two years after the publication of the *Principles*, the Harvard Corporation invited James to deliver a series of lectures to the teachers of Cambridge, thereby affording him opportunity to extend his formulations more directly into the field of pedagogy. The result, characteristically literate, appeared seven years later in a little book entitled *Talks to Teach-*

[9] *Principles of Psychology*, I, 127.

ers on Psychology: and to Students on Some of Life's Ideals.
From beginning to end, the temper of the *Talks* is activist. The
child is presented as a behaving organism, whose mind is given
to aid him in adapting to this world's life. Hence, the purpose
of education is to organize his powers of conduct so as to fit
him for his social and physical milieu. Interests must be awakened and broadened as the natural starting points of instruction. The will must be trained to sustain the proper attention
for productive thought and ethical action. The right sorts of
habits must be early inculcated to free the child for his role as
an intelligent being, and his ideas must be put wherever possible to the practical test. In the end, the job of the teacher is to
turn the "sensitive, impulsive, associative, and reactive organism" that is the child into a purposeful, thinking adult who will
use his talents to the fullest in the struggle for a better life.[1]

With the completion of the *Principles,* James turned increasingly to the philosophical problems that had occupied him intermittently since 1878. The result was the emergence over the
next twenty years of a full-blown system of ideas that Ralph
Barton Perry has called "the most perfect philosophical expression of American individualism." [2] In 1897 a volume of essays called *The Will to Believe* gave forceful statement to
James's deep-seated voluntarism, his faith in a society of moral
individuals, each courageously staking his life on hopes, possibilities, and goals in which he deeply believed. A series of articles written in 1904–5, posthumously published as *Essays in
Radical Empiricism,* set forth a metaphysical notion of "pure
experience" that rejected ancient dualisms between thought
and object, knower and known, in favor of a unitary view in
which "the parts of experience hold together from next to next
by relations that are themselves parts of experience." [3] And

---

[1] In view of subsequent developments, it is interesting to note James's
recurring concern with possible charges of "softness" against his pedagogy.
See *Talks to Teachers on Psychology: and to Students on Some of Life's
Ideals* (New York, 1899), pp. 54, 109, and *passim.*

[2] Ralph Barton Perry: *Characteristically American* (New York, 1949),
p. 70.

[3] The quotation is from James's own summary of radical empiricism
in *The Meaning of Truth* (New York, 1909), pp. xii–xiii.

finally, the essays on *Pragmatism* in 1907 and on *The Meaning of Truth* in 1909 elaborated the now famous thesis: "The truth of an idea is not a stagnant property inherent in it. Truth *happens* to an idea. It *becomes* true, is *made* true by events. Its verity *is* in fact an event, a process: the process namely of its verifying itself, its veri-*fication*." [4] That such a philosophy would have deep appeal to James's countrymen is patent and has been commented upon at length. It was humane, adventurous, essentially democratic, and always optimistic. Like other Americans, James's younger colleague, George Santayana, once remarked, "James felt the call of the future and the assurance that it could be made far better, totally other, than the past." [5]

James's later philosophical writings could not but strengthen the cause of progressives who saw in education a device for aiding people to a new and better world.[6] And as might be expected, those seeking to turn the school to narrow utilitarian goals made ready capital of Jamesian catch phrases about the "cash value" of ideas. Yet in the end, it was the *Principles* and the *Talks* that most directly and radically influenced pedagogy. They cast aside older notions of faculty psychology in favor of an essentially behaviorist outlook; and they asked the teacher to help educate heroic individuals who would project daring visions of the future and work courageously to realize them. In a society of such individuals James saw man's best hope for human dignity and progress.

[4] William James: *Pragmatism* (New York, 1907), p. 201. For the European and American sources of James's philosophy, see Perry: op. cit., II, Part VI; and Philip P. Wiener: *Evolution and the Founders of Pragmatism* (Cambridge, 1949).

[5] George Santayana: *Character & Opinion in the United States* (New York, 1921), p. 88.

[6] Benjamin Gruenberg estimated in 1910 that probably nine tenths of the teachers who studied any psychology at all before the close of the century studied it from James's *Principles*. His estimate is probably high, but the sense of his judgment is undoubtedly correct. *Scientific American*, CIII (1910), 198. See also Bird T. Baldwin: "William James' Contributions to Education," *Journal of Educational Psychology*, II (1911), 369–82; and John Wesley Humphreys: "The Educational Philosophy of William James" (Unpublished Doctoral Thesis, University of Cincinnati, 1928).

V

Edward L. Thorndike reports in an autobiographical sketch that he had no memory of having heard or seen the word *psychology* until his junior year at Wesleyan University (1893–94), when he took a required course in the subject. As a literature major, he was not particularly stimulated either by the instructor or by the textbook. In connection with a prize examination, however, he was asked to read certain chapters in James's *Principles*. The event apparently marked a turning point in his life, for these chapters *were* stimulating, "more so than any book that I had read before, and possibly more so than any read since." During his first year at Harvard Thorndike eagerly registered for a course with James, and by the fall of 1897 he had dropped literature in favor of psychology as his major subject for the Ph.D.[7]

It was at Harvard that Thorndike undertook his first work with animal learning, a course of experimentation destined profoundly to influence the American school. He began investigating instinctive and intelligent behavior in chickens, a line of research so novel that he was refused space to experiment at the University and had to undertake his research in the basement of the James house in Cambridge. ("The nuisance to Mrs. James," he wrote, "was, I hope, somewhat mitigated by the entertainment to the two youngest children.") A fellowship from Columbia brought Thorndike to New York to study with James McKeen Cattell, another scientist trained in Wundt's laboratory, and with the anthropologist Franz Boas, from whom he derived a lifelong interest in the quantitative treatment of psychological data. He continued the experiments he had begun at Harvard, and in 1898 produced a dissertation on *Animal Intelligence* which stands as a landmark in the history of psychology.[8]

[7] Edward L. Thorndike: *Selected Writings from a Connectionist's Psychology* (New York, 1949), pp. 1–2. See also Robert S. Woodworth: *Biographical Memoir of Edward Lee Thorndike, 1874–1949* (Washington, 1952).
[8] Edward L. Thorndike: *Animal Intelligence* (New York, 1898).

What was the nature of the experiments? Basically, they involved an animal in a problem box, a situation in which a specific behavior, like pressing down a lever, was rewarded with escape from the box and a bit of food. The animal was placed in the box, and after a period of random activity, it pressed the lever and received the reward. In subsequent trials the period between the animal's being introduced into the situation and the pressing of the lever decreased, to a point at which introduction into the box occasioned a lunge at the lever and the conclusion of the experiment.

Thorndike called the process by which the animals tended to repeat ever more efficiently and economically behaviors which were rewarded *learning*, and out of his experiment came a new theory of learning and a new "law" founded on that theory. The theory maintained that learning involves the wedding of a specific response to a specific stimulus through a physiological bond in the neural system, so that the stimulus regularly calls forth the response. In Thorndike's words, the *bond* between S and R is "stamped in" by being continually rewarded. And from this follows what Thorndike called the "law of effect"—namely, that a satisfactory outcome of any response tends to "stamp in" its connection with a given situation, and conversely, that an unsatisfactory outcome tends to stamp out the bond or connection. Whereas previous theories had emphasized practice, or repetition, Thorndike gave equal weight to outcomes—to success or failure, reward or punishment, satisfaction or annoyance to the learner.

Now there is a great deal here of impressive originality. To begin, Thorndike's experiment inaugurated the laboratory study of animal learning, assuming that a demonstration of the conditions of animal behavior under laboratory conditions could help solve the general problems of psychology. The assumption, of course, represents a synthesis of scientific method and evolutionary doctrine, since in the absence of the latter animal learning would hardly have been considered a suitable topic for a psychologist. Equally important, perhaps, Thorndike's new law implied a new theory of mind. Building on the idea of the reflex arc, which connected the brain and neural tissue with the total behavior of the organism, he ended the search for mind by eliminating it as a separate entity. Mind appeared in the total response of the organism to its environment.

As Thorndike later pointed out in his classic three-volume work *Educational Psychology*, this conception does more than render psychology a science by making it the study of observable, measurable human behavior. In one fell swoop, it discards the Biblical view that man's nature is essentially sinful and hence untrustworthy; the Rousseauan view that man's nature is essentially good and hence always right; and the Lockean view that man's nature is ultimately plastic and hence completely modifiable. Human nature, Thorndike maintained, is simply a mass of "original tendencies" that can be exploited for good or bad, depending on what learning takes place.[9]

Thorndike believed his dissertation had a contribution to offer to pedagogical science, and he made this contribution explicit toward the end. "Now every observant teacher," he wrote, "realizes how often the cleverest explanation and the best models for imitation fail. Yet often, in such cases, a pupil, if somehow enticed to do the thing, even without comprehension of what it means, even without any real knowledge of what he is doing, will finally get hold of it. . . . The best way with children may often be, in the pompous words of an animal trainer, 'to arrange everything in connection with the trick so that the animal will be compelled by the laws of his own nature to perform it.' "[1]

This much would have been startling enough for the pedagogues, but Thorndike proceeded to a sharp critique of the conservative Darwinism of G. Stanley Hall. "This does not at all imply that I think, as a present school of scientists seem to, that because a certain thing *has been* in phylogeny we ought to repeat it in ontogeny. Heaven knows that Dame Nature herself in ontogeny abbreviates and skips and distorts the order of the appearance of organs and functions, and for the best of

[9] Edward L. Thorndike: *Educational Psychology* (3 vols., New York, 1913–14), I, ch. xvii.
[1] *Animal Intelligence*, pp. 104–5.

reasons. We ought to make an effort, as she does, to omit the useless and antiquated and get to the best and most useful as soon as possible; we ought to change what *is* to what *ought to be*, as far as we can." [2] Thus did Thorndike, within the context of evolutionary theory, refute Hall's pedagogy in much the same way as Ward had refuted Sumner's. Following James in the belief that even though habit ruled the world, mind could still remake it in consonance with human purposes, Thorndike from the beginning proclaimed that men could be changed, and for the better. Indeed, he modestly offered the results of his experiment to pedagogues, even if they did nothing more than justify themselves in making the business of education more efficient, more economical, and more effective.

Having completed his doctorate, Thorndike went on to Western Reserve University to continue his work on animal learning. There, prodded by James McKeen Cattell, the imaginative young James Earl Russell found him, and assuming that a student who had made a study of monkeys was worth trying out on humans, brought him to the new Teachers College at Columbia.[3] In a brilliant career spanning forty years Thorndike instructed a whole generation of educators in the now familiar doctrines of connectionism. His influence during this period was both prodigious and various. His studies with Robert S. Woodworth on the transfer of training, stemming from James's assertions about the specificity of habit, shattered time-honored assumptions about the "disciplinary" value of certain studies and thereby accelerated utilitarian tendencies already gaining in the schools.[4] His detailed investigations into

[2] Ibid., p. 105.
[3] James Earl Russell: *Founding Teachers College* (New York, 1937) p. 53.
[4] E. L. Thorndike and R. S. Woodworth: "The Influence of Improvement in One Mental Function upon the Efficiency of Other Functions," *Psychological Review*, VIII (1901), 247–61, 384–95, 553–64. While Thorndike himself was not willing to move from a completely general to a completely particular position on transfer, some of his readers were; as early as 1913 he criticized certain "careless thinkers" for rushing "from the belief in totally general training to the belief that training is totally specialized." *Educational Psychology*, II, 365. The attack on transfer provided too much ammunition to practicalists for qualifications to

heredity led him early to the problem of individual differences, and from there it was but a short step to correlative work on intelligence, mental testing, classroom grouping, and retardation.[5] And needless to say, his studies on learning itself produced a plethora of material on the actual business of instruction. His *Principles of Teaching* (1906), richly illustrated by examples, dealt with such matters as interest, attention, reasoning, feeling, and moral training, calling to mind the character of *Talks to Teachers* if not its literary charm. Subsequent work dealt more specifically with the design and choice of teaching materials, the organization of instruction, ways of adjusting to individual differences in the classroom, and methods of judging student progress. Certainly no aspect of public-school teaching during the first quarter of the twentieth century remained unaffected by his influence.

Ultimately, Thorndike's goal was a comprehensive science of pedagogy on which all education could be based. His faith in quantified methods was unbounded, and he was quoted ad nauseam to the effect that everything that exists exists in quantity and can be measured.[6] Beginning with the notion that the methods of education could be vastly improved by science, he came slowly to the conviction that the aims, too, might well be scientifically determined.[7] He deeply believed

---

prevail, however, and even Thorndike's strictures were ignored. See Pedro Tamesis Orata: *The Theory of Identical Elements* (Columbus, 1928); H. Gordon Hullfish: *Aspects of Thorndike's Psychology in Their Relation to Educational Theory and Practice* (Columbus, 1926); and Walter B. Kolesnik: *Mental Discipline in Modern Education* (Madison, 1958).

[5] Edward Lee Thorndike: *Notes on Child Study* (New York, 1901); and "Number in Honor of Edward Lee Thorndike," *Teachers College Record*, XXVII (1925–6), 458–586.

[6] It is generally maintained that Thorndike coined the first part of the phrase and that William A. McCall added the latter part. Thorndike himself in a 1918 essay, said: "Whatever exists at all exists in some amount. To know it thoroughly involves knowing its quantity as well as its quality." National Society for the Study of Education, *Seventeenth Yearbook* (Bloomington, 1918), Part II, p. 16. McCall's statement is: "Anything that exists in amount can be measured." *How to Measure in Education* (New York, 1923), pp. 3–4.

[7] Compare *Principles of Teaching* (New York, 1906), p. 2, with "Education for Initiative and Originality," *Teachers College Record*, XVII (1916–17), 415.

that with the training of a sufficient number of educational experts, many of the gnawing controversies that had plagued educators since the beginning of time would disappear.

Like James, he placed his hopes for civilization on free, scientifically educated individuals.[8] His studies of genius convinced him that the proper schooling of the gifted is at least as important as mass education, yet he never turned his back on mass education. His reputation has been eclipsed in recent years by that of John Dewey, partly because his social views were more conservative than Dewey's and partly because his psychology seemed less adequate than Dewey's in explaining higher mental functions.[9] But he stands as a seminal figure in the history of education, and must be reckoned with in any discussion of the early twentieth century transformation of the American school.

V I

Like Thorndike, John Dewey read James's *Principles* at a critical point in his own intellectual development. A close student of Kant and Hegel, Dewey had gone to the University of Michigan in 1884 following upon graduate work at the new Johns Hopkins University. Once in the West, he began almost immediately to discard the metaphysical baggage he had carried with him. An examination of his works during the later eighties, especially *Applied Psychology*, which he wrote with James Alexander McLellan, reveals a patent effort to embody the newer science into his ethical and philosophical thinking. Coming when it did in Dewey's intellectual Odyssey, the *Principles* contributed much of "new direction and quality" to his thinking. Particularly did he take from the work its idea of an

[8] Because of his emphasis on the limiting role of heredity, Thorndike has been attacked as a conservative Darwinist by a number of progressives. But his reform Darwinism was early in evidence. See, for example, his 1909 essay: "Darwin's Contributions to Psychology," *Selected Writings from a Connectionist's Psychology*, pp. 349–63.

[9] For Dewey's criticism of reflex-arc psychology, see his pioneering essay: "The Reflex Arc Concept in Psychology," *The Psychological Review*, III (1896), 357–70.

objective psychological theory firmly rooted in evolutionary biology. Of this assumption Dewey later wrote: "It worked its way more and more into all my ideas and acted as a ferment to transform old beliefs." [1] When William Rainey Harper brought him to Chicago in 1894 to head the departments of philosophy, psychology, and pedagogy, ideas that had already germinated came rapidly to fruition.

Many years later, at a seventieth birthday celebration, Dewey told a story designed modestly to describe his place in the history of American life and thought. It was about "a man who was somewhat sensitive to the movements of things about him. He had a certain appreciation of what things were passing away and dying and of what things were being born and growing. And on the strength of that response he foretold some of the things that were going to happen in the future. When he was seventy years old the people gave him a birthday party and they gave him credit for bringing to pass the things he had foreseen might come to pass." [2] His story was overly humble, to be sure; yet there was a measure of truth to it.

Consider his early role in the progressive education movement. All about him, a cacophony of voices was demanding educational reforms of every sort and variety. Businessmen and labor unions were insisting that the school assume the classical functions of apprenticeship. Settlement workers and municipal reformers were vigorously urging instruction in hygiene, domestic science, manual arts, and child care. Patriots of every stripe were calling for Americanization programs. And agrarian pub-

---

[1] John Dewey: "From Absolutism to Experimentalism," in George P. Adams and W. Pepperel Montague, eds.: *Contemporary American Philosophy* (2 vols., New York, 1930), II, 24. See also Jane M. Dewey, ed.: "Biography of John Dewey," in Paul Arthur Schilpp: *The Philosophy of John Dewey* (New York, 1939), pp. 3–45; Lewis S. Feuer: "John Dewey and the Back to the People Movement in American Thought," *Journal of the History of Ideas*, XX (1959), 545–68; Morton G. White: *The Origin of Dewey's Instrumentalism* (New York, 1943); and Willinda Savage: "The Evolution of John Dewey's Philosophy of Experimentalism as Developed at the University of Michigan" (Unpublished Doctoral Thesis, University of Michigan, 1950).

[2] John Dewey: *The Man and His Philosophy* (Cambridge, 1930), p. 174.

licists were pressing for a new sort of training for country life that would give youngsters a sense of the joys and possibilities of farming—and incidentally, keep them from moving to the city. Now note the common implication running through these proposals: educational functions traditionally carried on by family, neighborhood, or shop are no longer being performed; somehow they must get done; like it or not, the school must take them on.

It remained for Dewey to give classic statement to this notion of the school as a *legatee* institution. In 1899, in response to criticism of the Laboratory School he and his wife had founded three years before, Dewey delivered a series of three lectures to parents and patrons of the School. Published as a little tract called *The School and Society*, the talks were an immediate best-seller, going through seven printings in the next ten years. Surveying the pedagogical scene and attempting to make sense of it to his audience, Dewey laid the blame for the ferment in education squarely at the feet of industrialism. Society, he contended in Platonic terms, educates. Behind the older agrarian society lay the time-honored education of the agrarian household and neighborhood, where every youngster shared in meaningful work and where the entire industrial process stood revealed to any observant child. "We cannot overlook the factors of discipline and of character-building involved in this . . . ," Dewey contended; "we cannot overlook the importance for educational purposes of the close and intimate acquaintance got with nature at first hand, with real things and materials, with the actual processes of their manipulation, and the knowledge of their social necessities and uses." [3]

But social life, Dewey continued, had undergone a thorough and radical change under the impact of industrialism. "If our education is to have any meaning for life, it must pass through an equally complete transformation." And what would be the nature of this transformation? The school would have to assume all of the educative aspects of traditional agrarian life.

[3] John Dewey: *The School and Society* (Chicago, 1899), pp. 23–4.

"It remains but to organize all these factors," Dewey concluded, "to appreciate them in their fullness of meaning, and to put the ideas and ideals involved into complete, uncompromising possession of our school system. To do this means to make each one of our schools an embryonic community life, active with types of occupations that reflect the life of the larger society, and permeated throughout with the spirit of art, history, and science. When the school introduces and trains each child of society into membership within such a little community, saturating him with the spirit of service, and providing him with the instruments of effective self-direction, we shall have the deepest and best guarantee of a larger society which is worthy, lovely, and harmonious." [4]

There is more here, of course, than the simple demand that the school broaden its offering; more, too, than what Morton White has accurately perceived as a "revolt against formalism." Dewey's passage really provides the key to what was progressive about progressive education. Recall that Dewey's "embryonic community" was to *reflect* the life of the larger society, thereby removing the curse he saw in traditional education, isolation from reality. But even more important, Dewey's "embryonic community" was to *improve* the larger society by making it more "worthy, lovely, and harmonious." Once again, the school is cast as a lever of social change; for as soon as "worthy, lovely, and harmonious" are defined, educational theory—once more in Platonic terms—becomes political theory, and the educator is inevitably cast into the struggle for social reform.

Dewey made other telling points in his lectures. He bitterly condemned "the old school" for the passivity of its methods and the uniformity of its curriculum. The educational center of gravity had too long been "in the teacher, the text-book, anywhere and everywhere you please except in the immediate instincts and activities of the child himself." [5] The essence of the new education, Dewey observed, was to shift this center of gravity back to the child. His natural impulses to conversation, to inquiry, to construction, and to expression were now seen

[4] Ibid., pp. 43–4.   [5] Ibid., p. 51.

as natural resources, as "the uninvested capital" of the educative process. The business of the school was to begin with these, to lay hold upon them and so control their expression "as not only to facilitate and enrich the growth of the individual child, but also to supply the same results, and far more, of technical information and discipline that have been the ideas of education in the past." [6]

The School and Society is replete with good common sense about education. There are illustrations galore of first-rate teaching in the Laboratory School, and there are cogent observations about the preparation of teachers that have refused to become anachronistic. (There are also the usual contemporary homilies about instincts and recapitulation!) But, in the last analysis, the key to what was new in Dewey's analysis is his social reformism. The school is recalled from isolation to the center of the struggle for a better life. Dewey realized that a new society was coming into being, and he had a vision of a new kind of education that might spell the difference between the success or failure of that society measured in human terms. Once again the classical idea of education as cultural aspiration is called to mind, though in the very formulation of his ideal Dewey transformed the meaning of culture.

Seventeen years separate *The School and Society* from Dewey's magnum opus, *Democracy and Education*. During that time Dewey's stature as philosopher, educator, and social commentator rose steadily. He left the University of Chicago in 1904 after a series of wrangles with President Harper, and went on to an extraordinarily productive career at Columbia, publishing the *Ethics* with James H. Tufts in 1908, *Moral Principles in Education* in 1909, *How We Think* in 1910, *Interest and Effort in Education* in 1913, and *Schools of To-Morrow* with his daughter, Evelyn, in 1915. Although he was never a man to cultivate disciples, he inevitably attracted them; and with the launching of *The New Republic* in 1914, Dewey began to be known to the larger progressive public through the

[6] Ibid., p. 70.

vigorous discipleship of the gifted young writer Randolph Bourne.[7] By 1916 Dewey had come to be widely regarded as a leading spokesman of progressivism, and whatever he wrote was guaranteed a large and interested audience. It is not surprising that when *Democracy and Education* appeared, it was immediately hailed in some quarters as the most notable contribution to pedagogy since Rousseau's *Émile*.[8]

Dewey set out in the volume to explore the educational meanings of democracy, science, evolution, and industrialism. He ended by writing the clearest, most comprehensive statement of the progressive education movement. The ideas of the work are legion, and no systematic exposition will here be attempted.[9] There are illuminating critical discussions of Plato, Aristotle, Locke, Rousseau, Kant, Fichte, Hegel, Herbart, and Froebel (Dewey, unlike some of his disciples, had studied the history of philosophy) and there is a patent awareness of contemporary developments in psychology, sociology, and pedagogy. Much in the volume, of course, had been foreshadowed in earlier writings and bore a familiar ring.[1] Like any classic,

[7] Louis Filler: *Randolph Bourne* (Washington, 1943), chs. iv, vi. Max Lerner has argued that Dewey's public reputation derives in no small measure from Bourne's ardent discipleship. "Randolph Bourne and Two Generations," *Twice a Year*, V–VI (1940–1), 65.

[8] See, for example, Thomas Percival Beyer's review in *The Dial*, LXI (1916), 103. Walter Lippmann described the book in *The New Republic* as "the mature wisdom of the finest and most powerful intellect devoted to the future of American civilization." VII (1916), 231.

[9] Dewey himself summarized the seven leading ideas of the volume as: "the biological continuity of human impulses and instincts with natural energies; the dependence of the growth of mind upon participation in conjoint activities having a common purpose; the influence of the physical environment through the uses made of it in the social medium; the necessity of utilization of individual variations in desire and thinking for a progressively developing society; the essential unity of method and subject matter; the intrinsic continuity of ends and means; and the recognition of mind as thinking which perceives and tests the meaning of behavior." *Democracy and Education* (New York, 1916), p. 377. Extracts reprinted by permission of The Macmillan Company.

[1] The theory of motivation had been sketched in "Interest as Related to the Training of Will" (1896), and the conception of morality in "Ethical Principles Underlying Education" (1897). The pedagogy and the social philosophy had been advanced in *My Pedagogic Creed* (1897) and *The School and Society* (1899). The relation of the child's experience to organized knowledge had been dealt with in *The Child and the*

the work was both a reflection and a criticism of its age. It orchestrated the many diverse strands of pedagogical progressivism into a single inclusive theory and gave them unity and direction. Its very existence lent new vigor to the drive for educational reform.

Dewey's definition of democracy was cut from the stuff of the American experience. Democracy prevails as there are more, and more varied, points of shared common interest among the multifarious groups that go to make up society, and as there is ever freer interaction and mutual adjustment among these groups. A democratic society is thus committed to change, organized as intelligently and as scientifically as possible; it is, in Dewey's words, "intentionally progressive." [2] What more suitable theory for a society in flux, a society of immigrant groups engaged in a dramatic reshuffling of customs and allegiances, a society whose intellectuals sense a loss of community and a driving need to rebuild it? Democracy becomes the persistent quest for the "more perfect union," a kind of continuing social process of *e pluribus unum*. Hearken back to Dewey's 1899 vision of a new society "more worthy, lovely, and harmonious," and it is democracy incarnate.

Dewey saw in his conception of democracy a compelling demand on education; and in a passage that has since become famous he stated the theme of his work:

> The devotion of democracy to education is a familiar fact. The superficial explanation is that a government resting upon popular suffrage cannot be successful unless those who elect and who obey their governors are educated. Since a democratic society repudiates the principle of ex-

---

Curriculum (1902), while the theory of community had been implicit in "The School as a Social Center" (1902) and "Democracy in Education" (1903). It is significant that so much of Dewey's pedagogy had been formulated during the Chicago period; it was a decade during which he was in daily contact with the problems of the Laboratory School. For the pedagogy, see Melvin C. Baker: *Foundations of John Dewey's Educational Theory* (New York, 1955); for the social context, see Ray Ginger: *Altgeld's America* (New York, 1958) and Robert L. McCaul: "Dewey's Chicago," *The School Review*, LXVII (1959), 258–80.

[2] *Democracy and Education*, ch. vii and p. 375.

ternal authority, it must find a substitute in voluntary disposition and interest; these can be created only by education. But there is a deeper explanation. A democracy is more than a form of government; it is primarily a mode of associated living, of conjoint communicated experience. The extension in space of the number of individuals who participate in an interest so that each has to refer his own action to that of others, and to consider the action of others to give point and direction to his own, is equivalent to the breaking down of those barriers of class, race, and national territory which kept men from perceiving the full import of their activity. These more numerous and more varied points of contact denote a greater diversity of stimuli to which an individual has to respond; they consequently put a premium on variation in his action. They secure a liberation of powers which remain suppressed as long as the incitations to action are partial, as they must be in a group which in its exclusiveness shuts out many interests. . . . A society which is mobile, which is full of channels for the distribution of a change occurring anywhere, must see to it that its members are educated to personal initiative and adaptability. Otherwise, they will be overwhelmed by the changes in which they are caught and whose significance or connections they do not perceive.[3]

Dewey formulated the aim of education in social terms, but he was convinced that education would read its successes ultimately in the changed behaviors, perceptions, and insights of individual human beings. He defined education as "that reconstruction or reorganization of experience which adds to the meaning of experience, and which increases ability to direct the course of subsequent experience." [4] The quotation holds the key to his notion of *growth*, the central term in the much abused Deweyism that education is growth and subordinate to no end beyond itself. It was his way of saying that the aim of education is not merely to make citizens, or workers, or

[3] Ibid., pp: 101–2.   [4] Ibid., pp. 89–90.

fathers, or mothers, but ultimately to make human beings who will live life to the fullest—that is, who will continuously add to the meaning of their experience and to their ability to direct subsequent experience.

Ultimately, it is the conception of growth that ties Dewey's theory of the individual to progressivism writ large. He wanted education constantly to expand the range of social situations in which individuals perceived issues and made and acted upon choices. He wanted schools to inculcate habits that would enable individuals to control their surroundings rather than merely adapt to them.[5] And he wanted each generation to go beyond its predecessors in the quality of behavior it sought to nurture in its children. Progressive societies, he counseled, "endeavor to shape the experiences of the young so that instead of reproducing current habits, better habits shall be formed, and thus the future adult society be an improvement on their own. . . . We are doubtless far from realizing the potential efficacy of education as a constructive agency of improving society, from realizing that it represents not only a development of children and youth but also of the future society of which they will be the constituents."[6]

Having thus stated a general relationship between democracy and education, Dewey proceeded to pedagogical specifics, insisting that a new unifying spirit suffuse every aspect of teaching and learning. An avowed enemy of dualism—recall his early Hegelianism—he attacked the historic separation of labor and leisure, man and nature, thought and action, individuality and association, method and subject matter, mind and behavior. To reconcile these dualisms was to construct a philosophy "which sees intelligence to be the purposive reorganization, through action, of the material of experience."[7] Only such a philosophy could serve the interests of an "intentionally progressive" society.

[5] In discussing the adjustment of individual and environment, Dewey speaks of habits that facilitate *accommodation to* the environment and habits that facilitate *control over* it. Education is concerned with both, but more importantly with the latter. Savages adapt to the environment, he counseled, civilized men transform it. Ibid., pp. 55–7.

[6] Ibid., p. 92.   [7] Ibid., p. 377.

Of all the dualisms Dewey attacked, none was more crucial to his view of progressivism than the ancient divorce between culture and vocation. Like his contemporary Thorstein Veblen, Dewey was deeply concerned with the historic association of culture and class. For centuries culture had meant the possession of certain kinds of knowledge marking the knower as a member of a superior social group. From the time of the Greeks it had been associated with wealth as opposed to poverty, with leisure as opposed to labor, with theory as opposed to practice. And in the school curriculum it had come to imply an emphasis on certain literary and historical studies, the knowledge of particular classical works, and the mastery of particular foreign languages. For Dewey this notion of culture inevitably emphasized the differences among classes rather than their commonalities, exclusiveness rather than association. Moreover, while it was thoroughly utilitarian for some social groups—statesmen, professionals, intellectuals—it was equally irrelevant for others. On two counts, then—that of exclusiveness and that of inequity—the historic view of culture was blatantly aristocratic.[8]

Dewey believed that democracy necessitated a reconstitution of culture, and with it the curriculum, that would conceive of scientific and industrial studies as instruments for making the great body of the people more aware of the life about them. This meant introducing vocational subjects not merely to build utilitarian skills, but as points of departure for increasingly intellectualized ventures into the life and meaning of industrial society. "The problem of the educator," he maintained, "is to engage pupils in these activities in such ways that while manual skill and technical efficiency are gained and immediate satisfaction found in the work, together with preparation for later usefulness, these things shall be subordinated to *education*—that is, to intellectual results and the forming of

[8] For Dewey's theory of culture, see also "Culture and Industry in Education," *Educational Bi-Monthly*, I (1906), 1–9, and "Culture and Cultural Values," in Paul Monroe, ed.: A *Cyclopedia of Education* (5 vols., New York, 1911–13), II, 238–40. For the nineteenth-century discussion of culture, see Raymond Williams: *Culture and Society* (London, 1958).

a socialized disposition." [9] Growth meant beginning with present experience and adding meaning to it. If industrialism was the central problem of the time, why not begin with it as the key to all other problems?

Following this line of argument, Dewey concluded that there were no studies intrinsically endowed with liberating or cultural powers per se, that any subject could be cultural in the degree to which it was apprehended in its widest possible range of meanings. There is perhaps no better definition of culture, he wrote, "than that it is the capacity for constantly expanding the range and accuracy of one's perception of meanings." [1] As such, culture could embrace a much wider sphere of studies than had ever been the case, including the sciences and trades if properly taught with the goal of growth in mind.

How, then, would Dewey reply to Spencer's query: "What knowledge is of most worth?" The criterion he advanced was social. In planning curricula, he counseled, essentials must be placed first, refinements second. "The things which are socially most fundamental, that is, which have to do with experience in which the widest groups share, are the essentials. The things which represent the needs of specialized groups and technical pursuits are secondary." [2] A democracy cannot flourish where there is narrowly utilitarian education for one class and broadly liberal education for another. It demands a universal education in the problems of living together, one broadly humane in outlook, "calculated to enhance social insight and interest."

Whether Dewey really resolves the problem of priorities remains, of course, an open question, for his criterion is so vague as to be of little aid in judging curricular proposals. The history of American education is replete with instances of special groups pushing favorite schemes of educational reform "in the broader public interest." Calvin Woodward quickly moved from the position that manual training would be good for technical students at Washington University to the position

[9] *Democracy and Education*, p. 231.
[1] Ibid., p. 145.   [2] Ibid., p. 225.

that it would be good for everyone. Liberty Hyde Bailey made the same leap with nature study. After all, it is an old rule of democratic politics that everything be done in the name of the people! Then, too, there are the deeper difficulties inherent in social worth as a criterion, difficulties that were sharply noted by one reviewer who cautioned that "in the Deweyan social system there is no room for any individual who wishes to lead his own life in the privacy of reflective self-consciousness. Privacy is to be regarded as a sinful luxury. Individuals are to remember that, after all, they are only 'agencies for revising and transforming previously accepted beliefs.' In sum, one is driven to the belief that, in spite of Mr. Dewey's fine defence of individualism, his moral ideal is really that of the 'good mixer.' " [3]

Granted these difficulties, which stem after all from currents deep within progressivism itself, Dewey's formulations must be seen as essentially continuous with Horace Mann's. Dewey saw in universal schooling a crucial first step in the larger process of democratization, but one that would be robbed of social meaning without a concomitant transformation in the nature of schooling itself. The crux of this transformation would be a new view of culture extending beyond traditional preoccupation with language and literature to an inclusive concern with the whole vast panorama of human affairs.[4] Like Mann, Dewey recognized that education is a matter of individual growth and development; but like Mann too, his emphasis was ever on the social, the common, the public aspects of experience. Ultimately, Dewey believed that democracy would be achieved only as schooling was popularized in character as well as clientele. And hence, in the reform of education he saw the first and foremost work of an "intentionally progressive" society.

[3] *The Nation,* CII (1916), 480–1.
[4] *Democracy and Education,* pp. 300–1.

⊰⊹⊱ 5 ⊰⊹⊱

Pedagogical Pioneers

MASSACHUSETTS passed the first state-wide compulsory-attendance law in 1852; Mississippi was the last of the states to pass one, in 1918. During the interim educational reformers learned some painful facts of political life. They discovered, among other things, that passing a law does not necessarily get children to school; that in the absence of proper statistical records there is no way of knowing in the first place whether or not children are attending; that without effective enforcement procedures the very children the law is designed to coerce escape its beneficent influence; and that without correlative measures regulating child labor and employment a compulsory attendance law is a sham, unenforceable and ultimately meaningless.[1]

Granted this, compulsory school attendance marked a new era in the history of American education. The crippled, the blind, the deaf, the sick, the slow-witted, and the needy arrived in growing numbers. Thousands of recalcitrants and incorrigibles who in former times might have dropped out of school now became public charges for a minimum period. And as the school-leaving age moved progressively upward, every

[1] Forest Chester Ensign: *Compulsory School Attendance and Child Labor* (Iowa City, 1921).

problem was aggravated as youngsters became bigger, stronger, and more resourceful. The dreams of democratic idealists may have resided in compulsory-attendance laws, but so did the makings of the blackboard jungle.

Had there never been a progressive movement, had there been no social settlements, municipal reform associations, country life commissions, or immigrant aid societies, no William James, Stanley Hall, Edward Thorndike, or John Dewey, the mere fact of compulsory attendance would have changed the American school. What might have happened instead of what did is not, of course, the immediate concern of the historian. But that the situation was ripe for something to happen is. Compulsory schooling provided both the problem and the opportunity of the progressives; its very existence inexorably conditioned every attempt at educational innovation during the decades preceding World War I.

Like the pedagogical protests of the era, the pedagogical experiments were marked by a striking diversity. Some, like Francis W. Parker's at Quincy, were undertaken in public-school systems; others, like Dewey's at Chicago, were privately sponsored. Some, like Marietta Johnson's at Fairhope, were built on the artful insights of practitioners and only later received systematic statement; others, like Dewey's, were initiated to test theories that had already been formulated. Some reforms went forward under professional impetus, others under lay impetus. Some reformers were familiar with contemporary pedagogical developments in Europe and America; others were almost entirely ignorant of them. Diversity of purpose, program, and sponsorship was the theme. It was a diversity destined to leave its ineradicable mark on the progressive education movement.[2]

I I

"If I should tell you any secret of my life," Francis W. Parker once wrote in a reminiscence, "it is the intense desire I have to .

[2] See W. H. Page *et al.*: *The School of Tomorrow* (New York, 1911); and John Dewey and Evelyn Dewey: *Schools of To-Morrow* (New York, 1915).

see growth and improvement in human beings. I think that is the whole secret of my enthusiasm and study, if there be any secret to it,—my intense desire to see mind and soul grow." [3]

Dewey once referred to Parker as the "father of progressive education"; certainly he was the first home-grown hero of the progressive education movement. Born in New Hampshire in the fall of 1837, he had embarked at the age of sixteen on a career as a country schoolmaster, interrupting it in 1862 to serve in the Union Army (whence the title "Colonel," which he retained for the rest of his days). On his return from service, he found himself increasingly troubled with the ordinary school practices of his time, and during a period of teaching in Dayton, Ohio, he began avidly to read the works of contemporary educational theorists. When an aunt died and left him a small legacy, he decided to follow Horace Mann's example and spend a period of study in Europe. In his two and a half years abroad, he not only attended lectures at the University of King William in Berlin, but traveled widely through Holland, Switzerland, Italy, France, and Germany, eagerly observing the leading pedagogical innovations of the day. On his return to the United States, Parker was determined to sponsor similar changes in American education.

His opportunity was not long in coming. In 1873 the school board of Quincy, Massachusetts, sensing that all was not right with the system, decided to conduct the annual school examinations in person. The results were disastrous. While the youngsters knew their rules of grammar thoroughly, they could not write an ordinary English letter. While they could read with facility from their textbooks, they were utterly confused by similar material from unfamiliar sources. And while they spelled speedily through the required word lists, the orthography of their letters was atrocious. The board left determined to make some changes, and after a canvass of likely candidates, elected Parker to the Quincy superintendency of schools.

Things soon began to happen. The set curriculum was abandoned, and with it the speller, the reader, the grammar, and

[3] William M. Giffin: *School Days in the Fifties* (Chicago, 1906), p. 133.

the copybook. Children were started on simple words and sentences, rather than the alphabet learned by rote. In place of time-honored texts, magazines, newspapers, and materials devised by the teachers themselves were introduced into the classroom. Arithmetic was approached inductively, through objects rather than rules, while geography began with a series of trips over the local countryside. Drawing was added to encourage manual dexterity and individual expression. The emphasis throughout was on observing, describing, and understanding, and only when these abilities had begun to manifest themselves—among the faculty as well as the students— were more conventional studies introduced.[4]

The program was an immediate success and attracted national attention as the "Quincy System." Teachers, school superintendents, and newspapermen descended on the schools in such numbers as to require restrictions to prevent interference with the daily work. Interestingly enough, Parker himself decried the fuss, protesting that there was nothing at all novel about the Quincy approach. "I repeat," he wrote in his report of 1879, "that I am simply trying to apply well established principles of teaching, principles derived directly from the laws of the mind. The methods springing from them are found in the development of every child. They are used everywhere except in school. I have introduced no new principle, method, or detail. No experiments have been tried, and there is no peculiar 'Quincy System.' "[5]

Despite its warm reception, the program did not lack for critics, and almost from the beginning the board had a running battle just to keep it alive. Parker's disclaimers notwith-

[4] Charles F. Adams, Jr.: *The New Departure in the Common Schools of Quincy* (Boston, 1879); Lelia E. Patridge: *The "Quincy Methods" Illustrated* (New York, 1889); and A. D. Mayo: "The New Education and Col. Parker," *Journal of Education*, XVIII (1883), 84–5.

[5] *Report of the School Committee of the Town of Quincy for the School Year 1878–79* (Boston, n.d.), p. 15. For Parker's continued disclaimers, see F. W. Parker to Edwin C. Hewitt, December 13, 1879, *New England Journal of Education*, XI (1880), 164; and Francis W. Parker: "The Quincy Method," in United States Bureau of Education: *Report of the Commissioner of Education for the Year 1902*, pp. 239–40.

standing, there were continuing charges in professional circles that the Quincy plan was falsely grounded, unoriginal, and extravagant in its claims. And in the community itself there were constant complaints that education was being subverted and the fundamentals ignored. When an independent survey by an inspector from the Massachusetts State Board of Education revealed that Quincy's youngsters excelled at reading, writing, and spelling and stood fourth in their county in arithmetic, the survey was simply dismissed by critics as biased and unfair.[6] In the end, the program seemed to thrive on this sort of turmoil, and a decade later Joseph Mayer Rice reported that the town's most pressing problem was to hold its teachers in the face of lavish offers from the larger urban school systems.[7]

Parker left Quincy in 1880, and after a brief interlude as a school supervisor in Boston, went on to the principalship of the Cook County Normal School in Chicago. There the work begun in 1875 reached a kind of dramatic culmination. It was in the professional training classes at Cook County that Parker formulated his educational theories; and it was in the practice school of that institution, which became the local public school for its neighborhood shortly after Parker's arrival, that he worked his pedagogical techniques into final form.

There are innumerable accounts of what went on in the practice school, most of them by enthusiastic disciples who tend to wax eloquent about programs and outcomes.[8] Parker himself maintained that his effort was twofold: to move the child to the center of the educative process and to interrelate the several subjects of the curriculum in such a way as to enhance their meaning for the child.

[6] Charles Francis Adams, Jr.: "Scientific Common-School Education," *Harper's New Monthly Magazine*, LXI (1880), 934–42.
[7] Dr. J. M. Rice: *The Public-School System of the United States* (New York, 1893), p. 212.
[8] The standard source is Ida Cassa Heffron: *Francis Wayland Parker* (Los Angeles, 1934). See also Francis W. Parker: "An Account of the Cook County and Chicago Normal School from 1883 to 1899," *The Elementary School Teacher and the Course of Study*, II (1901–2), 752–80; and Wilbur S. Jackman: "Francis Wayland Parker," Ibid., 743–51.

To begin, the school was organized as "a model home, a complete community and embryonic democracy." [9] The large assembly hall became the common meeting ground of children and adults alike. Its exercises were conducted with the utmost informality, the emphasis being on sharing and self-expression. "It is the family altar of the school," wrote one of the teachers, "to which each brings his offerings—the fruits of his observations and studies, or the music, literature and art that delight him. . . ." [1] Colonel Parker himself presided each morning, assuming the posture of an amiable autocrat, benevolently paternalistic about children, faculty, and school. He was a large man of average height, his mouth shaded by a heavy mustache which he often fingered while in thought. Now he was reading a favorite passage from the Bible; now he was inviting a child to relate experiences of the day before; now he was insisting that a young faculty member lead a class in exercises worked out the day before. For all his autocracy, he was well loved by children and colleagues alike. "Mama," one of the children is supposed to have said on her return from school one day, "Colonel Parker put his hand on my head today. I think he blesses children just as Jesus did." [2]

From the morning assembly the youngsters passed to their classrooms, where the same techniques of informality prevailed. For reading and writing, the children created their own stories, and these, in the form of "Reading Leaflets" printed at the school, quickly replaced primers and textbooks. Spelling, reading, penmanship, and grammar were all thus combined as elements of communication, to be studied within the context of actual conversation and writing. Drill was recognized as a necessity, but always in the context of more immediate student interests.

At a time when drawing was first appearing on the American pedagogical scene, Parker made art a central enterprise of the practice school, arguing that modeling, painting, and draw-

---

[9] Francis W. Parker: *Talks on Pedagogics* (New York, 1894), p. 450.
[1] Martha Fleming: "Purposes and Values of the Morning Exercise," *Francis W. Parker School Year Book*, II (1913), 11.
[2] Heffron: op. cit., p. 60.

ing were modes of expression, "three great steps in the evolution of man." Science was begun in the form of nature study, and under the brilliant leadership of Wilbur Jackman, the children conducted trips through neighboring fields and along the lake shore. They made observations, drawings, and descriptions, thus correlating their work in science with their studies in language and art. They later carried certain of their investigations into the classroom, thereby beginning elementary laboratory work in physics and biology. Mathematics was frequently introduced in connection with this laboratory work, as well as with the occupations of the manual-training rooms. There youngsters actually made the equipment they needed for their studies in science, nature study, the drama, along with the ubiquitous bookends and samplers. Geography, too, began with first-hand knowledge of the surrounding countryside; and insofar as geography was conceived as a study of the world as the home of man, elementary economics and history were likewise introduced. So it was also with music, the drama, hygiene, and physical education: all were seen as vehicles for child expression; all began with what had meaning to the children themselves. The job of the teachers was to start where the children were and subtly lead them, through language and pictures, into the several fields of knowledge, extending meanings and sensitivities all along the way. It was an exciting experience to teach at the school, as testified by many of the faculty who served with Parker. There was an enthusiasm about the work that quickly passed to newcomers, and to the children themselves. Innumerable visitors came from far and wide and also caught the thrill of what was going on.[3]

[3] Joseph Mayer Rice was lyrical about the work, calling the faculty "one of the most enthusiastic, earnest, progressive, and thoughtful corps of teachers that may be found anywhere." Op. cit., p. 211. On the other hand, there was sharp and insistent opposition, particularly from Charles S. Thornton, a member of the Cook County Board of Education. After an examination of the school in the fall of 1891, Thornton wrote: "It is with great regret that I must report that the results indicate desultory work and careless, inattentive, and idle habits." Chicago Tribune, November 22, 1891, p. 3. Parker countered vehemently that Thornton was ill-informed, and ill-qualified to judge, thereby setting off a flurry of charges, countercharges, reports, and rejoinders that made continuing copy

Parker was essentially an artist rather than a theorist. What writings we do have from his pen derived mostly from lectures he gave to groups of teachers, and from materials he actually prepared in the course of his school duties. In 1883 he published *Talks on Teaching*, and in 1894 *Talks on Pedagogics*, probably the first American treatise on pedagogy to gain international repute. Borrowing heavily from Pestalozzi, Froebel, and Herbart—Pestalozzi for method, Froebel for his view of the child, and Herbart for the doctrine of concentration— Parker produced a synthesis that marked a transition from early American transcendentalism to a newer scientific pedagogy, and from dependence on European formulations to a more indigenous effort.[4] While both works talk about a science of education, neither really takes account of Darwinism. And while both works discuss the differences between aristocratic and democratic education, the differences are stated essentially in the terms of Horace Mann.

Moreover, granted Parker's acute social sensitivity, and his deep concern with a democratic community life, his philosophy ends up more Rousseauan than anything else. "The spontaneous tendencies of the child are the records of inborn divin-

---

for the Chicago newspapers during the remainder of the decade. For more scholarly critiques of Parker's work, see William T. Harris's articles in *Education*, XVI (1895), 132–4 and *Journal of Education*, LI (1900), 355–6.

[4] Parker, of course, had studied Pestalozzi, Froebel, and Herbart first-hand in Europe. But the nineteenth-century renaissance had early created stirrings in the United States. Pestalozzian ideas had appeared in educational journals, textbooks, and even a few school programs during the years after 1805, and had enjoyed considerable currency among the New England intelligentsia of Horace Mann's generation. Later, during the 1860's, they had received strong impetus from the work of Edward A. Sheldon at the Oswego (N.Y.) State Normal School. Meanwhile, the first American kindergarten had been organized in 1857, and the subsequent development of kindergarten associations in the major cities had done much to popularize Froebel's mystical idealism. And finally, in the last decades of the century, Herbartian ideas had come into their own, particularly among university professors seeking to develop a scientific approach to pedagogy. See Will S. Monroe: *History of the Pestalozzian Movement in the United States* (Syracuse, 1907); Nina C. Vandewalker: *The Kindergarten in American Education* (New York, 1923); and Charles De Garmo: *Herbart and the Herbartians* (New York, 1896).

ity," he wrote, paraphrasing Froebel: "we are here, my fellow-teachers, for one purpose, and that purpose is to understand these tendencies and continue them in all these directions, following nature." [5] His words instilled a Messianic ardor in the teachers who heard them and endeared him to a gencration of progressives. G. Stanley Hall used to visit Cook County annually, "to set my educational watch" as he once wrote Parker.[6]

I I I

When the Deweys first moved to Chicago in 1894, Professor Dewey visited the practice school of Cook County Normal and obviously liked what he saw. That year (1894–5) his son Fred was in Miss Flora Cooke's first grade at the school, and the following year his daughter Evelyn followed in her brother's footsteps. There is every reason to believe the children would have continued, had the Deweys not decided to establish their own school early in 1896.[7] Called the "Laboratory School" to emphasize its experimental character, the new institution was designed specifically to test Dr. Dewey's theories and their sociological implications. Beginning with sixteen pupils and two teachers, it grew by 1902 to an enterprise involving 140 children, twenty-three instructors, and ten assistants. Dr. Dewey served as director, Mrs. Dewey as principal, and Ella Flagg Young, later to be Chicago's first woman superintendent of schools, as supervisor of instruction.[8] By the

[5] Parker: *Talks on Pedagogics*, pp. 23–4.

[6] The letter, undated, is among the papers of Mrs. Emmons Blaine at the Wisconsin State Historical Society; see also Heffron: *Francis Wayland Parker*, p. 39. In 1890 Mrs. Blaine gave Parker a million dollars to endow a private teacher-training school to be called the Chicago Institute. The Institute subsequently became part of the new School of Education of the University of Chicago. A second gift of a million dollars launched the Francis W. Parker School with Flora J. Cooke as principal.

[7] These data are taken from a conversation between Flora Cooke and A. Gordon Melvin reported in Melvin: *Education: A History* (New York, 1946), p. 323.

[8] Jane Dewey reported in her 1939 biographical sketch that her father regarded Mrs. Young "as the wisest person in school matters with whom he has come in contact in any way." It was she who suggested the name *Laboratory School*, and it was she who helped crystallize Dewey's ideas

time Dewey left Chicago for Columbia in 1904, the school had become the most interesting experimental venture in American education; indeed, there are those who insist that there has been nothing since to match it in excitement, quality, and contribution.

Whereas Parker had begun in the realm of practice and only later moved to theory, Dewey began with a set of leading ideas—hypotheses, he called them—and devised methods and curricula to test them. The purpose of the Laboratory School, in Dewey's words, was "to discover in administration, selection of subject-matter, methods of learning, teaching, and discipline, how a school could become a cooperative community while developing in individuals their own capacities and satisfying their own needs." [9] The initial hypotheses, later elaborated in *The School and Society*, were that life itself, especially those occupations and associations that serve man's social needs, should furnish the ground experience of education; that learning can be in large measure a by-product of social activity; that the main test of learning is the ability of individuals to meet new social situations with habits of considered action; and that schooling committed to cooperative effort on the one hand and scientific methods on the other can be a beneficial influence on the course of social progress.[1]

Katherine Camp Mayhew and Anna Camp Edwards, two sisters who actually taught at the school during its early years,

into practice. See her own interpretation of the theory of the Laboratory School in *Isolation in the School* (Chicago, 1900), a doctoral dissertation done at Chicago. Mrs. Dewey's role in the founding of the school is told by Max Eastman in "John Dewey: My Teacher and Friend, II," *The New Leader*, April 6, 1959, pp. 22–3. She herself wrote in an unpublished sketch: "The trustees of the University had felt the need of a laboratory of Psychology, but they were suspicious of a laboratory of Education. It so happened that in Octo. of 1895 a sum of one thousand dollars had been appropriated for a Psychological laboratory. As no room or other facility for utilizing that fund could be provided, it was likely to revert. Influence upon the president at that moment brought him to consent to its use for Education, thus officially sanctioning the Educational phase of the new department."

[9] Katherine Camp Mayhew and Anna Camp Edwards: *The Dewey School* (New York, 1936), pp. xv–xvi.

[1] *University Record*, I (1896), 417–22; and The University of Chicago School: *School Record, Notes, and Plan*, October 23, 1896.

have written a detailed and engrossing account of the venture between 1896 and 1903. Generally, as with Parker's school, the work of the youngest children—four- and five-year-olds— was seen as an extension of the activities of the home. The watchword was "continuity," the effort to avoid breaks in the child's experience that might "retard, hamper, or frustrate the spontaneous expression of his intellectual life—his thought in action." Thus, a normal day might consist of conversations, constructive work, stories, songs, and games, all representing an attempt to begin with the familiar and steadily enlarge its meaning. Mayhew and Edwards report the activities of one group of four- and five-year-olds as follows:

. . . the child's many kinds of food, articles of clothing, and large and complicated house required many ques- tions. Many of the answers to the latter seemed to open paths into one main avenue which led back to the farm. They made a trip to a farm and saw the orchards, the har- vesting of the fruit, and the fields with their shocks of corn. This visit was the beginning of many activities which varied, of course, with teacher, children, and circum- stances. Part of the group played grocery store and sold fruit and sugar for the jelly-making of the others. Some were clerks, some delivery boys, others mothers, and some made the grocery wagons. The clerks were given measur- ing cups with which to measure the sugar and cranberries and paper to wrap the packages to take home. This led under guidance into a discussion of the large storehouse. It was considered as a roomy place where a great deal of fruit could be kept. From time to time it supplied the grocery store which held only enough for a few days. A wholesale house was constructed out of a big box. Eleva- tors would be necessary, a child volunteered, for store- houses have so many floors; and these were made from long narrow corset boxes, a familiar wrapping in every household of that day.[2]

[2] From Mayhew and Edwards: op. cit., pp. 64–5. Copyright 1936 by D. Appleton-Century Co., Inc. Reprinted by permission of Appleton- Century-Crofts, Inc.

For the staff such activities were pregnant with possibilities for learning. The children began, however naively, to grasp the connection between their homes and the productive and commercial activities of the wider community, and hence to perceive the essential interdependence of an industrial society. Moreover, in conversation lay the seeds of reading, writing, and correct speaking; in the farm trips lay the sources of physics, biology, chemistry, and geography; and in the construction of the "wholesale house" lay the beginnings not only of manual training but of measuring, counting, and more general number work. For the resourceful teacher, all activities and occupations had an instrumental as well as an intrinsic value; they afforded opportunity for social and intellectual growth as well as more immediate satisfaction to the children.

But there is a point to be made here, one that Dewey argued for the rest of his career but never fully communicated to some who thought themselves his disciples. A teacher cannot know which opportunities to use, which impulses to encourage, or which social attitudes to cultivate without a clear sense of what is to come later. With respect to character, this implies a conception of the kind of individual who is to issue from the school; and with respect to intellect, this implies a thorough acquaintance with organized knowledge as represented in the disciplines. To recognize opportunities for early mathematical learning, one must know mathematics; to recognize opportunities for elementary scientific learning, one must know physics, chemistry, biology, and geology; and so on down the list of fields of knowledge. In short, the demand on the teacher is twofold: thorough knowledge of the disciplines and an awareness of those common experiences of childhood that can be utilized to lead children toward the understandings represented by this knowledge. As Dewey himself pointed out, the demand is weighty indeed, and easily side-stepped. For simple as it is to discard traditional curricula in response to cries for reform, it is even simpler to substitute for them a succession of chaotic activities that not only fail to facilitate growth but actually end up miseducative in quality and character.

The principles governing the work of the subprimary group pertained throughout the work of the school.[3] The six-year-olds —or "sixes" as they were called—moved on to "occupations serving the household." After constructing a model farm in their classroom, they actually planted and raised some winter wheat in the school yard, following its progress from seed to bread, which, of course, they baked themselves. The "sevens" concentrated on "progress through invention and discovery," working with a science teacher on the historical development of fundamental occupations in the preliterate period. The "eights," building on the theme of "progress through exploration and discovery," moved from the trading activities of the Phoenicians to the larger topic of world exploration and commerce. The "nines" emphasized American history, concentrating on the settlement and early growth of Chicago. The "tens" took "colonial history and the revolution" as their theme, while the "elevens" emphasized the "European backgrounds of the colonists."

Along with these theme activities, specific work in languages, mathematics, the fine and industrial arts, science, music, history, and geography progressed in well-planned fashion, and always with the social motive in mind. History became a vivid picture of why and how men have come to their successes and failures; foreign languages were introduced easily and appropriately along with the study of European cultures; while literature was used as a record of the hopes and aspirations of men living under specific social circumstances. Indeed, as the

[3] The published records of the school are more voluminous and detailed than for any similar venture of the time. See especially the nine monographs published monthly through 1900 as *The Elementary School Record* and successive issues of *The Elementary School Teacher and the Course of Study* for 1901 and 1902. The June, 1903, issue of *The Elementary School Teacher* was devoted in its entirety to the Laboratory School. Mayhew and Edwards have done an admirable job of preparing a readable account from this mass of data. All of the manuscript material they used, including mimeographed syllabi, typewritten reports, letters from former teachers and students, photographs, examples of student work, and comments by Dr. Dewey, is in the possession of the Teachers College Library through the courtesy of Mrs. Mayhew and Professor William Heard Kilpatrick.

youngsters reached early adolescence, the faculty noted that their viewpoint gradually shifted "from the psychological approach of the learner or mere observer of facts to the logical one of the adult, who observes to an end and classifies what he has observed with the purpose of its further use." [4] Hence, the twelve- and thirteen-year-olds were encouraged to devote themselves to specialized projects in one or another of the academic disciplines instead of giving the burden of their time to some cooperative year-long problem.

By the conclusion of the thirteenth year the children had amassed a wide range of knowledge; they had developed a multitude of skills and sensitivities, manual and social as well as intellectual. They had learned to work both cooperatively and independently and could express themselves clearly and concisely. They had on countless occasions put new-found knowledge to the test, and they had made a clear beginning in all of the major fields of knowledge. In short, they were ready for secondary education, which Dewey and his colleagues defined as that phase of schooling marked by the dominance of distinctively intellectual interests organized along logically systematic lines.

Actually, there were few dramatic changes in Dewey's pedagogical theory as a result of the Laboratory School. Rather, he was able to state his initial hypotheses with ever greater confidence and specificity. In 1901, for example, he summarized his findings on the elementary-school curriculum as a whole in an article for the new *Manual Training Magazine*. In his view, three fundamental types of subject matter had emerged: active pursuits or occupations, such as carpentry, sewing, or cooking; those studies dealing with the background of social life, such as history and geography; and finally, those studies that provide command of the forms and methods of intellectual communication and inquiry, such as reading, grammar, and arithmetic. "Looking along the line of these three groups," Dewey concluded, "we see a movement away from direct personal and social interest to its indirect and remote forms. The first group presents to the child the same sort of activities that

[4] Mayhew and Edwards: op. cit., p. 223.

occupy him directly in his daily life, and re-present to him modes of social occupation with which he is thoroughly familiar in his everyday surroundings. The second group is still social, but gives the background rather than the direct reality of associated life. The third is social, but rather in its ultimate motives and effects—in maintaining the intellectual continuity of civilization—than in itself or in any of its more immediate suggestions and associations." [5] In an ordered progression from the first through the second to the third, Dewey saw the main line of a curriculum that was scientific in its view of the child and progressive in its effect on society. It was a view that he generalized the following year in *The Child and the Curriculum*, and subsequently embodied into *Democracy and Education*.

One cannot peruse the records of the Laboratory School—the published accounts, the teacher diaries, the scrapbooks, the few extant examples of student work, and such photographs as remain—without sensing that here was a first-rate school run by a first-rate staff.[6] True, in the ordered progression of theme activities from preliterate man to modern Chicago there were patent vestiges of the very recapitulation theory Dewey had attacked before the National Herbart Society.[7] And there was

[5] John Dewey: "The Place of Manual Training in the Elementary Course of Study," *Manual Training Magazine*, II (1901), 193–4.

[6] In addition to the excellent full-time staff, there was a distinguished group of consultants from the University. Thus, Mayhew and Edwards point out: "At that time Thomas C. Chamberlain was elaborating his planetesimal theory of the origin of the solar system and came to talk about it to the children. John M. Coulter planned and guided the experiments on plant relations. Others who cooperated were Charles O. Whitman in zoology, Jacques Loeb in physiology, W. I. Thomas and George Vincent in sociology, Frederick Starr in anthropology, Rollin D. Salisbury in geography, Albert Michelson in physics, Alexander Smith in chemistry, and Henry C. Cowles in ecology. The school was indebted to numerous persons in other departments of the University especially to Mr. and Mrs. William D. MacClintock, to G. E. Hale, Wallace Atwood, and to the members of Mr. Dewey's departments for continuous cooperation particularly to George H. Mead, James H. Tufts, and James R. Angell." Op. cit., p. 10.

[7] See John Dewey: "Interpretation of Savage Mind," *Psychological Review*, IX (1902), 217–30, and "Interpretation of the Culture-Epoch Theory," *Public School Journal*, XV (1895–6), 233–6.

undoubtedly an overemphasis on liberty in the early years—
Dewey himself remarked that the school was overweighted on
the "individualistic" side in consequence of the fact that in
order to get data, "it was necessary to give too much liberty of
action rather than to impose too much restriction." [8] But there
is ample evidence that most of the children learned and
learned well. More importantly, perhaps, Dewey sought to
substitute for the older curriculum he so roundly criticized a
new program that was better planned, better designed, better
organized. Convinced that his own innovations were far from
final, he saw the continuing quest for further improvement as
the central task of a science of education. He was destined for
disappointment; and a quarter-century later he pronounced
progressive education a failure, a movement that had destroyed
well but too soon abandoned the more difficult task of building something better to replace what had been done away with.

I V

In 1903 Walter Hines Page, sensing that a series on education
might do for *The World's Work* what Joseph Mayer Rice's
series had done for *The Forum* a decade before, launched a
politically astute young journalist named Adele Marie Shaw
on a muckraking expedition through the schools. Her articles,
which appeared intermittently through 1903 and 1904, stirred
little circulation and even less controversy; but they did testify
eloquently to the persistence of conditions that Rice had
earlier exposed. In New York she discovered a system overwhelmed by professional incompetence and political intransigence. In Philadelphia the schools were ruled "by the politician
for the politician." In Indiana she noted a stubborn unwillingness to make any adaptations to rural needs. And in the
suburbs she came upon Rip-Van-Winkle teachers plying their
ancient methods under appallingly unhygienic conditions.
After a year of study and observation, Miss Shaw concluded

[8] Mayhew and Edwards: op. cit., pp. 467–8.

that the schools were failing miserably in their responsibility to provide decent education to America's millions of children.[9]

A few bright spots shone on the journey, however, and one of them was her visit to Menomonie, in Dunn County, Wisconsin. It was only a little town of 5,600 people, she noted, and yet it was living proof of what the public school system of the United States could be made to do under proper management. "It contains within a few hundred acres the most varied, most complete object-lesson [Miss Shaw had learned her jargon well] in public education that exists anywhere today."[1] Here was lavish praise indeed for a venture in pedagogical pioneering that had begun just a little over a decade before.[2]

In 1889 James Huff Stout, a wealthy lumberman who had acquainted himself with Calvin Woodward's work at the St. Louis Manual Training School, had put the following proposal to the Menomonie Board of Education: "I will place upon the school-grounds, in a place to be designated by the Board of Education, a building of proper kind and size, furnished with all equipment necessary for the instruction of classes of boys and girls in the subjects included in the first year of a course in manual training. I will also pay the salaries of the necessary teachers, the cost of all necessary materials and supplies, and all the contingent expenses for three terms, or for a time equivalent to three school terms, except such a part thereof as shall be paid by five hundred dollars, which is to be provided by the Board of Education."[3] The Board hastened to accept the offer and at the end of the probationary period adopted the school. The action marked the beginning of two decades of active educational philanthropy by Stout; and by

[9] *The World's Work*, VII (1903–4), 4204–21, 4460–6, 4540–53; VIII (1904), 4795–8, 4883–94, 4996–5004, 5244–54, 5405–14; IX (1904–5), 5480–5.

[1] Adele Marie Shaw: "The Ideal Schools of Menomonie," Ibid., VII (1903–4), 4540.

[2] The story is told in its entirety in Ann M. Keppel and James I. Clark: "James H. Stout and the Menomonie Schools," *Wisconsin Magazine of History*, XLII (1959), 200–10.

[3] Shaw: op. cit., p. 4540. For a biography of Stout, see William T. Bawden: *Leaders in Industrial Education* (Milwaukee, 1950), ch. vii.

the turn of the century, Menomonie, like Quincy before it, had become a Mecca for admiring educators from all over the nation.

The manual-training building quickly became the center of a new school program dedicated to the principle of "learning by doing." For boys there was opportunity to work in the carpentry shop, the iron-working rooms, or the foundry, where objects appropriate to the seasons were constructed—sleds and skis in the winter, kites in the spring. And for girls there were the manifold studies associated with the home. They worked with fabrics and foods and were frequently assigned the task of preparing a meal on a given budget. Such meals were actually served to invited guests, mostly fathers and mothers ever ready to sacrifice digestion in the cause of pedagogic progress.

The emphasis of the manual-training building gradually radiated out to the whole system. The kindergartners stitched. The primary youngsters painted, sketched, wove baskets, and darned socks. The sixth graders began a systematic program in the use of tools that followed the principles of Della Vos. And capping the whole system was a special class for the preparation of manual-training teachers. "They need no truant officer in Menomonie," announced the editor of the *Wisconsin State Journal*, a sentiment later echoed by Miss Shaw. Boys who might have become disciplinary problems elsewhere actually remained in school after hours to work in the machine and carpentry shops.[4]

The activity emphasis was also furthered by a $75,000 gymnasium and swimming pool that Stout gave the schools, maintenance included. Boys and girls were given equal opportunity for physical training, an uncommon policy at the turn of the century, and the physical education program as a whole was closely tied to instruction in personal hygiene. Finally, the athletic staff concerned itself with all pupils, rather than merely with the talented. The clumsier the boy, Miss Shaw noted, the greater the determination of the physical education instructors to keep him at his tasks.

[4] *Dunn County News*, December 2, 1904.

Stout's philanthropy soon extended beyond Menomonie to the Dunn County rural schools as well. He placed a complete set of tools in every schoolhouse in the hope that country children might have similar opportunities to those in Menomonie. He offered free reproductions of great paintings to local boards of education as incentives to clean up classrooms and beautify school exteriors. He endowed traveling libraries for the county, insisting only that localities provide custodians for the books and funds to mail them. When teachers, postmasters, and farmers' wives volunteered to assist, Stout established librarians' institutes to help prepare them for their duties.[5] Thus, his philanthropy gradually extended well beyond Menomonie, and to adults as well as children. One older resident, speaking of the traveling library, wrote: "It helps to occupy our spar thime in a useful manner give us Purer thought less thime to think ill of our neighbours makes us better citizens. I would mis it badly." [6]

Dunn County was also one of the first in Wisconsin to take advantage of a state law offering to assist in the establishment and maintenance of county normal schools, and shortly there-after the county also availed itself of legislation to encourage local agricultural high schools.[7] The agricultural school quickly became a source for new and improved farming techniques in the county at large. The normal school, meanwhile, was instrumental over the years in providing Dunn County with a well-trained staff of teachers knowledgeable in rural ways and well equipped not only to teach agriculture, nature study, and manual training, but to relate traditional studies to the daily life of the students.

Although much of the pioneering in Menomonie stemmed directly from Stout's philanthropy, he proved a master at involving the public in his various enterprises. Indeed, Meno-

[5] Ibid., December 4, 1896; March 19, 1897; November 12, 1897; October 27, 1899.

[6] Shaw: op. cit., p. 4545.

[7] Stout, a La Follette Republican, served as Chairman of the State Senate Education Committee from 1896 until his death in 1910. In 1901 he urged the calling of a special meeting of the county board to establish a county agricultural school. *Dunn County News*, November 15, 1901.

monie's schools soon became the sort of social centers later envisioned by Roosevelt's Country Life Commission. Anyone could bathe or shower in the new gym for no more than fifteen cents. Businessmen's groups met regularly for exercise and swimming, while sewing and cooking circles were organized for the local ladies. The annual exhibits of student work attracted literally hundreds of admirers. At a Froebel celebration in 1899 the local newspaper reported a "thoroughly cosmopolitan" group representing "people from all walks of life and all ages from a six months old babe in arms to a gray haired septuagenarian." [8] The city Commercial Club made the school its headquarters, and visitors to the city banqueted there, served by students in the cooking classes. A carpenter who wanted to build a house came to the school, received instruction, constructed a model, and then erected the house from plans he himself had drawn. In the very best sense, the people of Menomonie felt the schools were theirs, a spirit encouraged in no small measure by Stout's unwillingness to seek or allow personal publicity.

As news of the work spread, Menomonie inevitably attracted the usual stream of visiting dignitaries. Remarkably enough, those who came were impressed not by a narrow vocationalism but rather by the "artistic and intellectual" atmosphere that seemed to pervade the system.[9] James Robertson, Canada's Deputy Commissioner of Agriculture, sought practical suggestions in Menomonie for Canada's rural schools, while representatives of the General Education Board, the Peabody Fund, and the Southern Education Board included Menomonie in their tour of significant northern educational experiments. Francis W. Parker addressed the assembled student body when he and Henry Belfield of the Chicago Manual Training School visited the city, and Liberty Hyde Bailey came to view with enthusiasm the experiments in agricultural education and teacher training. When the NEA met in Minneapolis in 1902, busloads of teachers from Indiana, Ohio, Kansas, and Utah

[8] Ibid., April 28, 1899.
[9] The description was by A. C. Winship, editor of the *New England Journal of Education*, in the *Dunn County News*, November 8, 1901.

traveled to Dunn County for a full day's tour.[1] No wonder
Miss Shaw entitled her article, "The Ideal Schools of Menomonie," and concluded that "measured by this actual demonstration of what the public schools can do, most other public-
school work is dead and ineffectual."[2]

V

By all the usual canons of the nineties, Marietta Pierce Johnson
was a first-rate teacher. Born and educated in Minnesota, she
had dreamed of teaching since the time she was ten. She had
taught every grade in the elementary school, had had some
high-school experience, and was working enthusiastically as a
"critic teacher" in the state normal school at Mankato, observing student teachers, giving them special instruction in
pedagogical methods, and often demonstrating her preachments by taking classes herself. Mrs. Johnson always got "results." She delighted the parents of her youngsters; she thrilled
her student teachers. In short, she was a success.[3]

Then one day, as she recounts it, her superintendent handed
her Nathan Oppenheim's book, *The Development of the
Child*, with the comment, "Unless education takes this direction, there is no incentive for a young man to enter the profession." Mrs. Johnson duly went home and read it, and apparently underwent a conversion experience. Oppenheim's
novel strictures, regarding the ways in which society and the
schools frequently work against the interests of the child by
following his unwholesome whims at certain times and by
inflicting unwholesome adult whims at others, became the inspiration for a whole new pedagogical approach on her part.
"*The Development of the Child* became my educational
Bible," she wrote years later, "and its frequent perusal has been

[1] Ibid., September 23, 1904; November 10, 1899; October 28, 1909;
August 18, 1902.
[2] Shaw: op. cit., p. 4552.
[3] See the *Golden Anniversary* publication of the School of Organic
Education (1957); *The Organic School* (Fairhope, n.d.); and Marietta
Johnson: "Thirty Years with an Idea" (Unpublished manuscript,
Teachers College, Columbia University, 1939).

a marvelous stimulation and support through many years of experimental work." [4]

Mrs. Johnson read other works that helped in formulating her ideas, among them *Education and the Larger Life* by C. Hanford Henderson, the scientist-headmaster of Pratt Institute in New York, and some of the early pamphlets of John Dewey. The principle that "the adult's supreme responsibility is to supply the right conditions of growth" and the notion of a practical program of activities that would be "life-giving to body, mind, and spirit," combined to form a new vision of education. "This idea took possession of me and I could not rest until I had started a school." [5] At first, Mrs. Johnson began experimenting with her own child and other children of her neighborhood. But then, several years later, there came the opportunity she had been waiting for.

During the winter of 1903, Mrs. Johnson and her husband decided to spend the winter in Fairhope, Alabama, a small resort town on the east coast of Mobile Bay founded about a decade earlier by single-tax disciples of Henry George. That year she did some public school teaching, organized a number of parents' meetings, and expounded some of her ideas before a teachers institute. The next year, when the Johnsons decided to settle on a pecan farm near Meridian, Mississippi, Mrs. Johnson had opportunity to return intermittently to Fairhope for other institutes and summer schools. And then, in the summer of 1907, Mr. and Mrs. H. S. Comings of Fairhope invited her to settle permanently in the community and conduct a free school, offering to contribute twenty-five dollars a month toward the enterprise. "There is a saying," Mrs. Johnson wrote later in a memoir, "that any one who visits Fairhope long enough to get Baldwin County sand in his shoes must eventually return. I was fully committed to the idea of starting a school and gladly embraced this opportunity. I was so anxious to 'try out' the idea that I should have been willing to pay children to come and let me experiment. So I accepted the

[4] Marietta Johnson: "Thirty Years with an Idea," p. 8.
[5] Ibid., p. 12.

twenty-five dollars per month, renting a cottage for fifteen, leaving ten dollars per month for salary and supplies! Six children came the first day. I did not know what to do. There was nothing in·my previous experience as a teacher to throw light upon my path. I had always had a course of study to follow and my main problem had been to find the best way to administer the curriculum. I had not been trained to look for 'results' in eagerness of attack, in spontaneous activity, in the growth of initiative—bright eyes, healthy satisfactions." [6]

Despite these disclaimers, Mrs. Johnson had soon worked out a curriculum that would have warmed the heart of G. Stanley Hall. The aim of the school was to "minister to the health of the body, develop the finest mental grasp, and preserve the sincerity and unselfconsciousness of the emotional life." [7] Mrs. Johnson called such an education "organic"—a term she undoubtedly borrowed from Henderson—and hence, her school was known as the Organic School. "We must constantly bear in mind that we are dealing with a unit organism," she counseled. "As Henderson says, it is impossible to have good health in one part of the organism and ill health in another! It is either good or ill for the entire organism always!" [8]

A studied informality pervaded the organization and life of the Organic School. Achievement groupings of all sorts were abandoned in favor of a simple classification based on age. Children were never compared; they were judged only in terms of their own abilities. And all extrinsic rewards were eliminated in favor of the inner satisfaction that is supposed to derive from "wholehearted disinterested service." Furthermore, formal studies of every sort were delayed as long as possible. "The prolonging of childhood," Mrs. Johnson maintained, "is the hope of the race—the longer the time from birth to maturity, the higher the organism." [9] Initially it was her hope to defer all

[6] Ibid., p. 14.

[7] Marietta Johnson: "What Is Organic Education?" in the *Golden Anniversary* publication of the School of Organic Education.

[8] Marietta Johnson: "Thirty Years with an Idea," p. 52.

[9] Marietta Johnson: *Youth in a World of Men* (New York, 1929). For the theory and practice of the school see also Marietta Johnson: *The*

systematic work in reading and writing until the age of ten, but in the face of parental insistence, she relented and reduced the age to eight. Even so, there were strict caveats against any pressures on the children. Spontaneity, initiative, interest, and sincerity were to guide their lives both inside and outside the classroom.

The school itself was organized into six divisions: a kindergarten for children under six, a first life class for children six and seven, a second life class for children eight and nine, a third life class for children ten and eleven, a junior high school for children twelve and thirteen, and a high school for children fourteen to eighteen. Mrs. Johnson conceived of the program as an articulated whole, borrowing Dewey's idea that more formal studies should grow out of activities and occupations intrinsically interesting to young children. In the kindergarten there were daily singing and dancing, stories selected for narrative interest and substantive content, trips over the surrounding countryside with subsequent conversations about the flora and fauna, creative handwork, and spontaneous, imaginative dramatization. These activities continued through the three life classes with the gradual addition of more systematic work in reading, writing, spelling, arithmetic, arts and crafts, and music.

The junior high school marked the real shift to more formal subjects. Arithmetic books were used for the first time. Nature study became elementary science, and literature, history, and geography were approached through more conventional readings. In the high school the youngsters traversed the conventional fields of study, but with an emphasis that discarded tests, grades, and formal requirements in favor of continuing encouragement for each child to develop his own purposes, use his own abilities to the fullest, and create his own standards for judging the results. "It is very thrilling to contemplate what society might be in a few years if our educational system could

---

Fairhope Idea in Education (New York, n.d.) and "The Educational Principles of the School of Organic Education, Fairhope, Alabama," National Society for the Study of Education: *Twenty-Sixth Yearbook* (Bloomington, 1926), Part I, ch. xxv.

accept and apply this point of view," Mrs. Johnson wrote. "No examinations, no tests, no failures, no rewards, no self-consciousness; the development of sincerity, the freedom of children to live their lives straight out, no double motives, children never subjected to the temptation to cheat, even to appear to know when they do not know; the development of fundamental sincerity, which is the basis of all morality." [1] Here was a pedagogical utopia entirely worthy of a single-tax community!

For all its radical innovation, the Fairhope experiment remained relatively unsung until 1915, when John Dewey decided to discuss it at length in *Schools of To-Morrow* as a living embodiment of Rousseauan pedagogical principles. Having visited the school in person, he was unqualified in his praise. He thought the manual training was on the whole the best he had seen, and he was much taken with the robust health of the students and their patent enthusiasm for books and studies. The program, he concluded, "has demonstrated that it is possible for children to lead the same natural lives in school that they lead in good homes outside of school hours; to progress bodily, mentally, and morally in school without factitious pressure, rewards, examinations, grades, or promotions, while they acquire sufficient control of the conventional tools of learning and of study of books—reading, writing, and figuring—to be able to use them independently." [2] Needless to say, such comments were of inestimable value in the perennial drive for funds. [3]

[1] Marietta Johnson: "Thirty Years with an Idea," p. 120. The quotation indicates a point Mrs. Johnson made frequently throughout her life: that the principles of the Fairhope experiment were entirely applicable to the public-school system.

[2] John Dewey and Evelyn Dewey: *Schools of To-Morrow* (New York, 1915), p. 40.

[3] Like most ventures of its kind, the Organic School was constantly in financial difficulty. Fairhope children attended free, and except for a few boarding students who paid their own way, the school depended almost entirely on Mrs. Johnson. For thirty years she lectured, wrote, cajoled, and implored in behalf of her cause. In 1908 Joseph Fels visited Fairhope out of interest in the single tax, and having seen the school, made contributions totaling $11,000. Mrs. Johnson's chance acquaintance with a Connecticut businessman named W. J. Hoggson brought another substantial grant, and later resulted in the establishment of an annual

One can accept Dewey's estimate at face value—although he visited the school only briefly over a Christmas holiday during which it was held in session—and still raise other questions. Mrs. Johnson's, after all, was easily the most child-centered of the early experimental schools. Like her mentors, Oppenheim and Henderson, she believed that the development of the child held the key to good education, and she sought constantly to build her program around pupil needs and interests. Yet in answer to charges that hers was a "do-as-you-please" school, she angrily insisted that quite the contrary was true. "Children do not know what is best for them," she maintained. "They have no basis for judgment. They need guidance, control, but this must really be for their good, not merely for the convenience of the adult! Every effort is made to have this conformity merge into and become obedience. That is, to have the child's *will* to act in harmony with the adult will." [4]

Now the real question, of course, is whether Mrs. Johnson was not attempting to have her pedagogical cake and eat it too. Her outlook retained the essential vigor and equalitarianism of Rousseau's—as Dewey correctly noted—but it presented all the difficulties as well. For to talk of control for the child's good, of conformity merging into obedience, and of wills acting in harmony, is to beg all of the very same questions Rousseau begged in the laissez-faire pedagogy of *Émile*. The school is supposed to honor spontaneity while it molds good habits, and to follow nature assuming that reason will emerge in its own good time; all children must constantly succeed, and yet realistic discipline and intelligence are among the goals. Granted the method may have produced results in the hands of an artful teacher like Mrs. Johnson, one still shudders at the thought of what it becomes under less capable sponsorship. Ultimately, such theoretical unclarities might have mattered little had they confined themselves to Fairhope, but they were

---

summer school in Greenwich and of a Fairhope League to support both the Organic School and the summer venture. Subsequently, a second Organic School opened in Greenwich, and Mrs. Johnson divided her energies between Alabama and New England.

[4] Marietta Johnson: "Thirty Years with an Idea," p. 87, and *The Fairhope Idea in Education*, p. 5.

destined to take on incalculable significance when Mrs. Johnson became the guiding spirit behind the Progressive Education Association in the years immediately after World War I.

V I

The Organic School was only one of many that John and Evelyn Dewey portrayed in *Schools of To-Morrow*. Indeed, no other volume documents more eloquently the richness and diversity of the early progressive-education movement. The reader is treated to an exciting collection of glimpses—into Junius Meriam's experimental school at the University of Missouri, the Francis Parker School in Chicago, Caroline Pratt's Play School in New York, the Kindergarten at Teachers College, Columbia University, and certain public schools of Gary, Chicago, and Indianapolis. In each instance the guiding theory is given and the techniques by which the theory is put into practice are described. The approach is essentially journalistic, the effort is to elucidate rather than to praise or criticize.

Merely as a record of what progressive education actually was and what it meant *circa* 1915, the book is invaluable. The text abounds in vivid descriptions of the physical education, the nature studies, the manual work, the industrial training, and the innumerable "socialized activities" in the schools of tomorrow. There is exciting talk of freedom for children, of greater attention to individual growth and development, of a new unity between education and life, of a more meaningful school curriculum, of a vast democratizing of culture and learning. Nowhere is the faith and optimism of the progressive movement more dramatically conveyed.

The Deweys' insistence throughout the volume is that the principles of good education are time-honored and that there is no one royal road to reform. Yet as the reader proceeds from chapter to chapter, he derives a subtle but unmistakable sense that all the systems expounded are not of equal worth. Mrs. Johnson's Rousseauan pedagogy, which comes first in order, is not allowed to stand alone but is soon incorporated into a larger social reformism that bears the earmarks of Dewey's own philosophy. Moreover, while each of the individual schools is supposed to exemplify one or another of the central principles of progressivism, the further one reads in the volume, the more comprehensive the example. It is not without significance, then, that the schools of Gary, Indiana, come last, and are treated most fully; nor is it an accident that the final chapter bears the fateful title, "Democracy and Education."

Dewey had argued in *The School and Society* that progressive education was essentially an effort to adapt the school to the circumstances, needs, and opportunities of industrial civilization. Certainly no city symbolized these conditions more dramatically than Gary. Before 1906, when the United States Steel Corporation began to erect a mammoth plant there, Gary had been a wasteland along the southern shore of Lake Michigan some twenty-seven miles southeast of Chicago. The decision to locate the plant had for all intents and purposes created the city. It enjoyed a mushroom growth, complicated by all the social and political problems of an industrial boomtown. By 1910 the population exceeded 12,000, mostly working-class people of immigrant origins.

In 1907 the school board of Gary decided to bring as superintendent a thirty-three-year-old educator named William Wirt. Wirt, who had once been an admiring student of Dewey at the University of Chicago, had begun in Bluffton, Indiana, to work out a plan whereby the local schools remained in session twelve months a year in an effort to further as much flexibility as possible in program and organization. At Gary he had the opportunity to design a school system from the bottom up; and he began almost immediately to put his ideas into practice. Within five years his innovations had generated sufficient interest to occasion a visit and report by the chief of the division of school administration of the United States Bureau of Education.[5] The publicity continued to mount, and by 1916

---

[5] William Paxton Burris: *The Public School System of Gary, Ind.* (United States Bureau of Education, Bulletin, 1914, No. 18), p. 5. The published survey by Burris, Dean of the College for Teachers of the University of Cincinnati, came two years later, and was based in part on Dr. Updegraff's 1912 report.

it seems fair to say that most progressives, if asked to cite the leading example of progressive education, would probably have mentioned Gary. "Those who follow Professor Dewey's philosophy," wrote the brilliant young journalist Randolph Bourne, "find in the Gary schools—as Professor Dewey does himself—the most complete and admirable application yet attempted, a synthesis of the best aspects of the progressive 'schools of to-morrow.' " [6]

What actually was the so-called Gary Plan? Essentially, it represented an effort to apply to an urban school system Dewey's idea of education as an "embryonic community life, active with types of occupations that reflect the life of the larger society and permeated throughout with the spirit of art, history, and science." Wirt's notion was not only to afford each child vastly extended educational opportunity—in playgrounds, gardens, libraries, gymnasiums and swimming pools, art and music rooms, science laboratories, machine shops, and assembly halls—but to make the school the true center of the artistic and intellectual life of the neighborhood. Open all day, twelve months a year, and to all age groups, the Wirt school would be the heart of all effort toward long-range community improvement, ultimately the most important single lever of social progress.

Administratively, Wirt tied these ideas to a unique system of organization that attracted nationwide attention because of its alleged economies. Instead of following the usual plan of assigning each child to a permanent desk, forty desks to a classroom, Wirt conceived of shop, laboratory, playground, and auditorium as fully used parts of any school. If half the children at any time could be using these facilities, then only half as many regular classrooms would be needed for a given number of children. The plan became widely known as the "platoon system" and commended itself to city boards across the country as a device for being progressive and saving money at the same time. And though controversy raged for years over whether or not the need for elaborate new auditoriums and

[6] Randolph S. Bourne: *The Gary Schools* (Boston, 1916), p. 144.

gymnasiums did not actually cancel the supposed saving on classrooms, many a board hastily adopted the plan after little or no investigation.[7]

Each school within the Gary system was organized as a miniature community. Elementary and high-school students remained in the same building, emphasizing the continuity of education as well as the heterogeneity of the typical social situation. The auditorium became the forum for discussion of common problems. The school shops, staffed by workmen chosen for character, intellect, and teaching ability, actually handled the upkeep and maintenance of the plant; the domestic science laboratories serviced the cafeteria; and the commercial science laboratories handled school records. The theory was straight from Dewey: whereas formerly the child participated in the industrial activities of the household, he now participated in the industrial activities of the school, with artisans, nurses, gardeners, lunchroom supervisors, and accountants taking the place of father, mother, and older siblings in the older agrarian home.

The Gary curriculum generally followed the Indiana course of study, though within individual subjects there was the typical attempt to relate content to individual and social needs. Grammar, spelling, reading, writing, and speaking were combined into a unified English program closely tied to the group activities of the auditorium. Geography and history often came together in topics like "The City: A Healthful Place in Which to Live." Science began with the usual trips and occupations and progressed to more systematic material. And trade training went beyond mere mechanical skill to a more general survey of industrial production, though how penetrating a survey remains a matter of conjecture.

Unlike most elementary programs, primary studies at Gary were departmentalized. Within each of the standard subjects students were classified as rapid, normal, or slow learners, and on the basis of tests and interviews each youngster was assigned

[7] Charles L. Spain: *The Platoon School* (New York, 1925); and Roscoe David Case: *The Platoon School in America* (Stanford, 1931).

his own individual program. There were voluntary Saturday
coaching sessions in each of the major fields, and students were
free to pursue extra work in any subject during play, shop, or
auditorium hours, or even to repeat work with another platoon.
The emphasis throughout was on flexibility, and students were
given a considerable measure of freedom to work at the pace
that best suited them.

There is no doubt that Dewey's extensive discussion in
Schools of To-Morrow would have evoked nationwide interest in the Gary Plan. In the end, however, it was Randolph
Bourne's rhapsodic praise in *The New Republic* that made
Gary the example par excellence of progressive education. In
the very first issue of the new journal the young critic had
inveighed against the artificiality and dullness of the American
schoolroom, and subsequent articles deploring "wasted years"
of "puzzle education" had done much to popularize educational protest among progressive intellectuals. Early in 1915,
having heard much of Wirt's innovations, possibly from Dewey
himself, Herbert Croly sent Bourne to Gary to do a series of
impressionistic pieces on the schools. The series that resulted
was undoubtedly the most lucid nonprofessional exposition of
educational reform of the decade, and won for Bourne an
enduring place in the progressive-education movement.[8]

So far as Bourne was concerned, he had seen the pedagogical future and it worked. The Gary Plan had solved the problem of industrial education, avoiding "that sinister caste-feeling
which seems to be creeping into the vocational movement." It
had provided a large measure of individual instruction, and it
exemplified "the educational truth that learning can come only
through doing." It was capable of reproduction generally in
American towns and cities; indeed, its mere "prosaic business
economy" recommended it for adoption. "Its philosophy is
American," Bourne concluded, "its democratic organization
is American. It is one of the institutions that our American
'Kultur' should be proudest of. Perhaps professional educators,

[8] *The New Republic*, II (1915), 198–9, 233–4, 259–61, 302–3,
326–8.

accustomed to other concepts and military methods and administrative illusions, will not welcome this kind of school. But teachers hampered by drill and routine will want it, and so will parents and children." [9] Less than a year later, Bourne's book, *The Gary Schools*, appeared, setting these impressions in a larger sociological context and arguing them as exemplifications of Dewey's pedagogical creed. It was generally well reviewed, and enjoyed excellent circulation. At a time when the Gary idea was spreading for good reasons and bad, Bourne put the stamp of progressive authenticity all over it.

The popularity—or notoriety—of the Gary Plan engendered a good deal of controversy during the war years. Indeed, in New York, where Wirt served as a consultant to preside over the installation of his system, it quickly turned into a political football and became one of the central issues of the mayoralty campaign of 1917.[1] As a consequence, Wirt and his board invited the General Education Board to conduct an impartial survey of the Gary schools and report on its findings. Carried out under the leadership of Abraham Flexner and Frank P. Bachman, the survey actually undertook the first systematic evaluation of Wirt's innovations using the best achievement tests then available; and insofar as Gary had become the most popular large-scale manifestation of progressive education, it provides some fascinating contemporary insights into the early successes and shortcomings of the movement.[2]

[9] Ibid., II (1915), 328.

[1] Criticism of Wirt appeared almost immediately after news of his New York appointment. *School and Society*, II (1915), 528–30. In the campaign itself, John Purroy Mitchel, the reform incumbent, supported the Gary Plan, while John F. Hylan, the Tammany candidate who won the election, attacked it. Hylan charged that the Plan represented an attempt to economize on the education of slum children rather than a genuine pedagogical advance. And inasmuch as Wirt had introduced released-time religious instruction in Gary, the religious issue also reared its head. The campaign is dealt with at length in two doctoral studies now in progress at Columbia: Edwin Lewinson's on Mitchel and Sol Cohen's on the Public Education Association of New York City. Finally, the Gary Plan is discussed as the quintessence of "Taylorism"—or business efficiency imposed on the schools—in a recent manuscript by Raymond Callahan of Washington University.

[2] Abraham Flexner and Frank P. Bachman: *The Gary Schools* (New York, 1918). The general account by Flexner and Bachman was based on

Flexner and Bachman found much of merit in the Gary Plan. Instead of playing it safe with commonplace education, the city had "adopted the progressive, modern conception of school function, formulated its conception in clear terms and with all possible expedition provided facilities adequate to the conception." [3] There had been notable advances in school organization, and genuine progress in applying democratic principles to school conduct and discipline. The plan had been bold and courageous, liberal and imaginative, pioneering and experimental.

But granted this, and granted the transitional and novel character of the program, there were questions to be raised. [4] The two-platoon plan had not always worked out in practice. Some of the activities in the auditorium had been perfunctory and wasteful; some of those in the gymnasium and park had been good fun but not particularly educative. Moreover, "that patient and close attention to details by which alone good work can be obtained was far too irregular to be effective." School records kept by the students were sloppy; poor spelling, arithmetical inaccuracies, and grave omissions passed unchallenged. Not only was the immediate educative effect lost, but children were fast becoming "habituated to inferior performance."

There were problems with the formal subjects too. The science survey, for example, found that while formalism had been effectively attacked, the new concrete activities did not necessarily lead to better learning. Indeed, in the absence of sound principles of organization, science was tending to become "a transient diversion rather than a profoundly formative and disciplinary influence in the child's development." Of the reading heard in the upper grades, some was good, but most ranged from ordinary to poor. In the main, classroom instruction in history, geography, mathematics, and the lan-

---

a series of special studies by authorities such as George Strayer, Charles Richards, Otis Caldwell, and Stuart Courtis; in its entirety the survey report ran to eight volumes.

[3] Flexner and Bachman: op. cit., p. 196.
[4] Ibid., ch. xvi.

guage arts was found to be meager and formal. It is one thing to propose a new philosophy, the survey suggested, but quite another to find teachers who are first committed to it and then able to carry it through. For all its novelty and pioneering, the Gary program left much to be desired; and complaints about shoddiness that have since become endemic with activity programs seemed already in order.

Flexner reported in his autobiography years later that the general effect of the survey was disastrous to the exploitation of the Gary system. "Education," he observed, "is far too complicated a process to be advertised on the basis of inadequate supervision and without definite accounting—mental, moral, and financial. With the publication of the report the school world was relieved, and the Gary system ceased to be an object of excitement. It disappeared from discussion as suddenly as it had arisen." [5] Flexner was only partly correct: the report did take the wind out of the raging discussion, but the system continued to spread. By 1929 over 200 cities in forty-one states had adopted it in part or in whole, and few other communities remained totally unaffected by its innovations.[6]

Flexner himself seems to have been as deeply affected by the survey as the fortunes of the system; and the Gary experience may well mark a major step in the evolution of his own position from the moderate progressivism of *A Modern School* (1915) to the unrelenting antiprogressivism of the 1920's. Thus, he also noted in his autobiography: "The Gary and other surveys taught me something that I have had to learn and relearn. On May 10, 1916, I wrote to my wife, 'There is something queer about the genus "educator"; the loftiest are not immune. I think the cause must lie in their isolation from the rough and tumble contacts with all manner of men. They lose their sense of reality.' From time to time from that day to this I have had a repetition of precisely the same impression." [7]

---

[5] Abraham Flexner: *I Remember* (New York, 1940), p. 255.
[6] Case: op. cit., pp. 29–30.
[7] Ibid., pp. 255–6. From the tone of Flexner's comments, it may well be that he actually set out to puncture the Gary bubble in the survey.

VII

However much Progressivism has come to be associated almost
exclusively with the reform of elementary and secondary education, the fact remains that it deeply affected the universities as
well. Particularly in those midwestern states which had modeled their school systems along Jeffersonian lines, public higher
education quickened during the Progressive era to many of the
very same influences that were transforming the lower schools.[8]
The leading example, of course, is Wisconsin during the La
Follette period. There, under the vigorous presidency of
Charles Van Hise, the university quickly became the pivotal
element in that larger program of reform commonly referred
to as "the Wisconsin idea."

Van Hise's inaugural address of 1904 has often been cited
as the classic Progressivist statement of the role of higher education in a democracy. Its theme from beginning to end is service to the state. A public university can only succeed when its
doors are open to all of sufficient intellect, when the financial
terms are manageable for the "industrious poor," and when
student sentiment is such that each stands upon equal footing
with his colleagues. Combining the best of the English residential college and the German research seminar, it must remain hospitable to every form of creative endeavor in the
humanities, the natural and social sciences, and the practical
arts, sending into the community a steady stream of dedicated
citizens who will lead the way to constructive advance in every
realm. "Be the choice of the sons and daughters of the state,
language, literature, history, political economy, pure science,
agriculture, engineering, architecture, sculpture, painting, or
music, they should find at the state university ample opportunity for the pursuit of the chosen subject, even until they

[8] See Frederick Jackson Turner's 1910 address: "Pioneer Ideals and
the State University," reprinted in *The Frontier in American History*
(New York, 1920), pp. 269–89. The standard source on the Progressive
movement in American higher education, itself written from a Progressive
point of view, is R. Freeman Butts: *The College Charts Its Course* (New
York, 1939).

become creators in it. Nothing short of such opportunity is just, for each has an equal right to find at the state university the advanced intellectual life adapted to his need. Any narrower view is indefensible." [9] Here again was the transformed view of schooling at the heart of the Progressive ideal. Is it any wonder that La Follette himself observed on the occasion of Van Hise's address that the university had "continued to lead and reflect the progressive thought of the state," and had "liberalized culture for the people." [1]

As Van Hise's administration progressed, it became apparent that "service to the state" would take two complementary directions: the provision of expert leadership in a great variety of spheres and the extension of new knowledge gained in the university's research programs to as large a segment of the population as possible. Neither activity was entirely new; both had flourished under the aegis of Van Hise's predecessors, John Bascom, Thomas Chamberlin, and Charles Kendall Adams. But Van Hise, acting in concert with the La Follette administration, brought them to a pinnacle. Cooperation between university and capitol, between the two ends of State Street in Madison, became the heart of the Wisconsin experiment in progressivism.

It was probably in the realm of agriculture that the ideal of service to the state had earliest taken form. At Wisconsin an Agricultural Experiment Station had been established in 1883 and had subsequently become part of the newly created College of Agriculture in 1889. Spurred on by William A. Henry, first director of the station and dean of the college, the university embarked on an ambitious program of grass-roots practicalism that soon won enthusiastic support among farmers. The station pioneered in more nutritious livestock feeds, in superior methods of curing cheese, and in the fight against animal tuberculosis. The station horticulturist, Emmett S. Goff, carried on thousands of investigations designed to produce salable

[9] *Inaugural Address of President Charles Richard Van Hise of the University of Wisconsin* (Madison, 1904), p. 28.
[1] *The Jubilee of the University of Wisconsin* (Madison, 1905), p. 69.

fruit and vegetable crops for the state; while Stephen M. Babcock's butterfat test gave farmers a reliable device for determining fair payment for their milk and gained the university international repute as well. Indeed, the Department of Agriculture in 1900 estimated that the test alone had saved the state some $800,000 a year, twice the annual operating budget of the whole university. In 1907 a group of younger professors in the agriculture school, among them Edwin B. Hart, George C. Humphrey, and Harry Steenbock, initiated the dramatic series of nutrition experiments subsequently described in Paul de Kruif's *Hunger Fighters*.[2]

It was this fruitful union of academic and practical studies that Van Hise sought to extend throughout the university, and his efforts in the social sciences provide the clearest evidence of affinity with the larger progressive movement. Although there had been notable work in history at Wisconsin during the eighties, under William F. Allen and his student Frederick Jackson Turner, the founding of the School of Economics, Political Science, and History in 1892 probably marks the real beginning of sustained scholarship in the social sciences. The idea for such a school was not original: Herbert Baxter Adams had early developed a social-science research program at Johns Hopkins; while Columbia in 1880 had organized a Faculty of Political Science under the leadership of John W. Burgess. But the founding of Wisconsin's school under Richard T. Ely, one of the distinguished economists of the time, did focus attention on the university. As Curti and Carstensen have pointed out, it meant that the public would be served not merely in the preparation of lawyers, engineers, teachers, and agriculturists, but in the schooling of public administrators as well.[3]

Trained in the newer German research methods, Ely came to Wisconsin convinced that economics was not a harsh Spen-

[2] See Merle Curti and Vernon Carstensen: *The University of Wisconsin: A History 1848–1925*, II, ch. xi; and W. H. Glover: *Farm and College* (Madison, 1952).

[3] Curti and Carstensen: op. cit., I, 631–2. The authors contend that Ely's coming "marked a new chapter in the study of the social sciences in the Middle West." I, 619.

cerian science of inexorable natural laws, but rather a humane study that could assist the social growth of mankind.[4] His text, *An Introduction to Political Economy* (1889), had become a standard work even before he came to the Midwest; and his *Monopolies and Trusts* (1900) and *Studies in the Evolution of Industrial Society* (1903), in their opposition to child labor, their support of unions, and their advocacy of public control of resources, did much to advance the notion of an ethically grounded, socially responsible, reformist economics.

Ely brought a sparkling group of young men to work with him at the university, among them Paul Reinsch and Samuel Sparling in public administration, Jerome Raymond in sociology, and William A. Scott and Edward David Jones in economics. His outstanding appointment was the young labor economist John R. Commons, who came to Wisconsin as Ely's assistant in 1904. As much at home in political science and sociology as in economics, Commons made brilliantly practical as well as theoretical contributions to progressivism. He directed the work on the monumental *Documentary History of American Industrial Society* (1910–11), a cooperative venture that deeply influenced the course of American economics; he pioneered in the use of the expert commission as a device for uncovering public needs and formulating solutions to meet them.[5]

As Russel Nye has pointed out in *Midwestern Progressive Politics*, it was men of the Ely-Commons stamp that gave La Follette and other midwestern progressives the "scientific ballast" that the early Grangers and Populists had lacked.[6] In Wisconsin professors of the university increasingly became advisers to the state administration, in the sciences, engineering, finance, education, and agriculture. Charles McCarthy, chief

---

[4] Richard T. Ely: "Fundamental Beliefs in My Social Philosophy," *The Forum* (1894–5), 173–83, and *Ground Under Our Feet* (New York, 1938).

[5] See the bibliography and the biographical sketch by Selig Perlman in John R. Commons: *The Economics of Collective Action* (New York, 1950).

[6] Russel B. Nye: *Midwestern Progressive Politics* (East Lansing, 1959) pp. 141–2.

of the Wisconsin Legislative Reference Department, listed in
1912 some forty-six men who were jointly serving both state
and university. Some, like Dean E. A. Birge of the College of
Letters and Science, held multiple memberships on the Forestry Commission, the Conservation Commission, and the Fish
Commission, and drew salaries from both the university and
the state. Others, like Van Hise, served in official positions but
without additional compensation from the state; while still
others, like Commons and Reinsch, served unofficially in all
respects. McCarthy, on the other hand, drew his salary from
the state, but taught gratis at the university.[7] This network of
formal and informal associations had become so extensive by
1912 that Charles P. Cary, Wisconsin's Superintendent of
Public Instruction, felt constrained to warn that unless the
university were checked in its scramble for power, the people
would have "a university state instead of a state university."
His sentiments were loudly echoed by leading editors and
businessmen who excoriated Professor McCarthy's "bill-fac-
tory" in Bascom Hall. Van Hise kept his fences well mended,
however, and the university rose to the criticism.[8]

However significant these direct contributions to the machinery of government, Van Hise saw the real service of the
university to the people at large. "I shall never be content until
the beneficent influence of the University reaches every family
in the state," he declared in 1905. "This is my ideal of a state
university." [9] Here, as with other aspects of Van Hise's program, there had been important beginnings under his predecessors. As early as 1885 the Regents had established the Short
Course, an academic device whereby persons lacking formal
preparation were encouraged to attend the university for
limited periods of time to undertake specific practical studies,
and the legislature provided that same year for institutes to
deal with the "theory and practice" of farming. There were
modest beginnings along both lines, and then in 1891 President Chamberlin obtained Regents authorization for a general

[7] Charles McCarthy: *The Wisconsin Idea* (New York, 1912), pp.
313–17.
[8] Curti and Carstensen: op. cit., II, 101–2.   [9] Ibid., II, 88–9.

program of University Extension following the English plan.[1] The costs were to be borne by those who attended; the professors were to receive honoraria for their labor; and certificates were authorized for those who attended the lectures and satisfactorily completed the examinations. There was a great deal of popular interest in the new program, and Chamberlin indicated in his first report that fifty courses, ranging all the way from Scandinavian literature to landscape geology, had been offered, with an estimated average attendance of 170.

As at other institutions, the extension work at Wisconsin tended to die out during the later nineties, and Van Hise's commitment to enlarge it meant virtually starting anew. Directly influenced by Lester Frank Ward, Van Hise was convinced that the true way to democracy lay in the widespread extension of available knowledge. He wanted no "mute, inglorious Milton" in the state to have suffered from an inability to get to Madison. Under Louis E. Reber, whom he brought to Wisconsin in 1907 from Pennsylvania State College, the work was enthusiastically pushed under four general departments: correspondence study, instruction by lectures, debating and public discussion, and general information and welfare. "It should be understood," Reber wrote in his first annual report, "that it is the desire of the university to reach not only those who feel the need of assistance but also those who, not realizing a need, may upon learning the possibilities for self-improvement open to them through the several departments of extension be led to avail themselves of the opportunities thus offered." [2]

[1] For the English backgrounds, see Albert Mansbridge: *University Tutorial Classes* (London, 1913); William H. Draper: *University Extension: A Survey of Fifty Years, 1873–1923* (Cambridge, 1923); and C. Hartley Grattan: *In Quest of Knowledge* (New York, 1955). With respect to adult education in general, it is interesting to ponder Grattan's observation (p. 175) that the Chautauqua movement, the most popular of the adult programs, was an important vehicle for disseminating the kind of thinking that supported the careers of Wilson and the two Roosevelts. For a general account of the Wisconsin program, see Frederick M. Rossentreter: *The Boundaries of the Campus: A History of the University of Wisconsin Extension Division, 1885–1945* (Madison, 1957).

[2] University of Wisconsin: *Biennial Report of the Board of Regents, 1907–8*, p. 194.

Under Reber's enthusiastic direction, the extension department engaged in a host of activities. Several hundred courses were prepared during the early years, varying from regular university work to elementary school lessons, from liberal learning to trade training. Special textbooks and pamphlets were issued for correspondence students, and a lending library of books and periodicals was compiled for the use of debaters. The department organized special institutes for bakers, assembled educational slides for circulation, prepared a milk exhibit, held a conference on criminal law, and developed a community music bureau. "Right or wrong," explained Reber to the first National University Extension Conference in 1915, "you find here a type of University Extension that does not disdain the simplest form of service. Literally carrying the University to the homes of the people, it attempts to give them what they need—be it the last word in expert advice; courses of study carrying University credit; or easy lessons in cooking and sewing." [3] Here in the extreme was the transformed view of the university inherent in Van Hise's idea of service.

Needless to say, Van Hise's program elicited widespread and enthusiastic comment in the popular press. A 1907 article in *The Outlook* referred to the university as "a kind of 'consulting engineer' in the public life of the State of Wisconsin." [4] When Charles W. Eliot conferred an honorary degree on Van Hise in 1908, he called Wisconsin America's leading state university. And Lincoln Steffens wrote in the *American Magazine:* "In Wisconsin the university is as close to the intelligent farmer as his pig-pen or his tool-house; the university laboratories are part of the alert manufacturer's plant; to the worker, the university is drawing nearer than the school around the corner and is as much his as his union is his or his favorite saloon. Creeping into the minds of students with pure seed, into the debate of youth with pure facts, into the opinions of

[3] Louis E. Reber: "The Scope of University Extension and Its Organization and Subdivision," in National University Extension Association: *Proceedings,* 1915, p. 25.

[4] William Hard: "A University in Public Life," *The Outlook,* LXXXVI (1907), 667.

voters with impersonal, expert knowledge, the state university is coming to be a part of the citizen's own mind, just as the state is becoming a part of his will. And that's what this whole story means: the University of Wisconsin is a highly conscious lobe of the common community's mind of the state of the people of Wisconsin." [5]

Other universities sent delegations to Madison to study the extension division, the role of the university experts in state commissions, and the organization and support of research. In 1904 forty Georgians, including the chancellor and trustees of the university, the governor, newspaper editors, and members of the legislature, visited Madison to study those features which made the University of Wisconsin "a model northern state university." The General Education Board sent the governor of Arkansas to Madison, wiring Van Hise that "we are all looking to you for counsel." Representatives from Ohio, Kansas, Texas, and Pennsylvania also came to study the "Wisconsin Idea." [6] "In no other State in the Union," wrote Theodore Roosevelt, "has any university done the same work for the community that has been done in Wisconsin by the University of Wisconsin." [7] He spoke for an enthusiastic public that saw in the Wisconsin idea the true union of politics and education that was the crux of the larger Progressive movement.

V I I I

From the beginning, progressivism cast the teacher in an almost impossible role: he was to be an artist of consummate skill, properly knowledgeable in his field, meticulously trained in the science of pedagogy, and thoroughly imbued with a burning zeal for social improvement. It need hardly be said that here as elsewhere on the pedagogical scene of the nineties, the gap between real and ideal was appalling. True, a

[5] Lincoln Steffens: "Sending a State to College," *The American Magazine*, LXVII (1909), 364.
[6] Curti and Carstensen: op. cit., II, 109–11.
[7] Theodore Roosevelt: "Wisconsin: An Object-Lesson for the Rest of the Union," *The Outlook*, XCVIII (1911), 144.

number of private and public normal schools had for several
decades been purporting to prepare genuinely professional
teachers. But their offerings were meager at best, and confined
largely to the methods and mechanics of the classroom. They
varied tremendously in character and quality, with some, especially in the poorer regions of the country, purveying one-year
courses at the secondary level strongly reminiscent of New England's first efforts during the years before the Civil War.[8] "The
office of teacher in the average American school," observed
Joseph Mayer Rice in 1893, "is perhaps the only one in the
world that can be retained indefinitely in spite of the grossest
negligence and incompetency." [9] He was writing an exposé, to
be sure, but what he said was much more truth than exaggera-
tion.

Yet it should also be noted that Rice's own remedy for America's educational ills—adequate professional preparation for
teachers—was itself being widely trumpeted during the nineties, and with notable effect on teacher-training institutions.
Beginning in 1890 with the reorganization of the state normal
school at Albany into the New York State Normal College, a
number of the better normal schools across the country began
to design regular four-year baccalaureate courses, thereby con-
verting themselves into collegiate institutions. Liberal arts colleges and universities also responded to sharpening demands
for secondary school teachers by creating normal departments
or regular chairs of pedagogy, so that by 1900 fully a fourth of
all institutions of higher learning were offering formal professional work in education. Then too, with the consequent increase of enrollments in teacher-training courses, the content
of pedagogy as a subject of study also broadened. Building
initially on the work of their European counterparts, especially
in Germany, Henry Barnard, William H. Payne, and Elmer
Ellsworth Brown were writing the first native treatises in the

[8] Lawrence A. Cremin: "The Heritage of American Teacher Education," *The Journal of Teacher Education*, IV (1953), 163–70.

[9] Rice: *The Public-School System of the United States*, p. 15. It is
interesting that both Rice and Jacob Riis saw teachers generally resistant
to school reform. See Riis: *The Battle with the Slum* (New York, 1902),
pp. 369–70.

history and philosophy of education, while William T. Harris, B. A. Hinsdale, Charles De Garmo, and G. Stanley Hall were opening up the formal study of educational psychology. Others, like Rice himself, were devising the first systematic investigations into the actual products of classroom teaching. Applying the latest scholarly techniques to the study of pedagogy, these men were destined to be extraordinarily influential in shaping the course of American teacher education.[1]

This general quickening of professional education manifested itself in all parts of the country, particularly the great university centers at Chicago, Michigan, and Stanford; but no one institution symbolized it more dramatically than the new Teachers College at Columbia University. Interestingly enough, the very founding of the college in 1887 reflected a union of the professionalism of Nicholas Murray Butler and the progressivism of Grace Hoadley Dodge.[2] The eldest daughter of William E. Dodge, one of New York's wealthiest merchants, Grace Dodge was typical of the energetic reformist ladies of her generation. After some early activities with the Children's Aid Society, the State Charities Aid Association, and the Association of Working Girls Societies, she turned her attention in 1880 to the Kitchen Garden Association, a new organization dedicated to the amelioration of slum living through education for household management. The organization soon broadened, and in 1884 it reorganized as the Industrial Education Association and extended its lobbying to include all forms of industrial education. The Association succeeded in generating a good deal of public interest but rapidly discovered that its efforts would come to naught without sufficient numbers of properly qualified instructors. Normal classes were improvised, but it became apparent that strong professional leadership was needed. The story goes that Grace Dodge told George W. Vanderbilt that more than anything the Asso-

[1] See Merle L. Borrowman: *The Liberal and Technical in Teacher Education* (New York, 1956); and Walter S. Monroe: *Teacher-Learning Theory and Teacher Education, 1890 to 1950* (Urbana, 1952).

[2] Lawrence A. Cremin, David A. Shannon, and Mary Evelyn Townsend: *A History of Teachers College, Columbia University* (New York, 1954), chs. i–ii.

ciation required brains. The next morning she had his check for $10,000 with the accompanying note: "Here is your 'brain money' for one or two years, now find your brains."

Fortunately, the brains were readily available, and in February, 1887, Nicholas Murray Butler, Associate Professor of Philosophy in Columbia College, assumed the presidency of the Association as "a strong advocate of its principles and a man who had already made his mark as an educator." Butler had been early attracted to the study of education by President Frederick A. P. Barnard and had spent several years of reading and travel systematically preparing himself for work in that field. Repeated efforts to introduce pedagogy into the Columbia curriculum had failed, however, and Butler and Barnard had decided to "build up a teacher's college outside the University, and to bring it later into organic relations with the University." It is no surprise, therefore, that the young philosopher saw a pregnant opportunity in the work of the Association and readily accepted its leadership. Two months after he assumed office, the Association established the New York College for the Training of Teachers, with Butler as President and principal professor.[3]

Once founded, the College made rapid headway. Its first *Circular of Information* proudly announced that here was no ordinary normal school but a full-fledged professional school whose students were expected to be at least eighteen years of age and to have completed a good secondary education. The institution received a provisional charter from the New York Regents in 1889, and a permanent charter under the name Teachers College in 1892. The following year it entered into a fateful alliance with Columbia, under which it became for all intents and purposes the pedagogy department of the University. Meanwhile, Butler resigned in 1891 to accept the headship of Columbia's Department of Philosophy, Ethics, and Psychology, and was succeeded by Walter Hervey, who ap-

---

[3] There is much new material on Butler in a dissertation in progress at Columbia by Richard Whittemore entitled "Nicholas Murray Butler and Public Education." See also Nicholas Murray Butler: *Across the Busy Years* (2 vols., New York, 1939–40), I, chs. iv–viii.

parently shared Butler's dreams about professional education but not his energy for promoting it. By 1897 Hervey too had resigned, leaving the college beset with internal strife and financial growing pains. The stage was set for James Earl Russell, the organizing genius who would transform the struggling professional school into a world-renowned center of pedagogy.

An early rebel against pedagogical formalism, Russell had joined the stream of students to Germany in 1893 "to see if there was not some better way." [4] He had studied Herbartianism with Wilhelm Rein at Jena—where incidentally he had come to know Joseph Mayer Rice—and had gone on to work with Wundt at Leipzig, returning in 1895 with a Leipzig Ph.D. and a vision of a science of education that would transform teaching from an ordinary craft into the highest professional art. A professorship of philosophy and pedagogy at Colorado had provided opportunity to put his theories to the test; and then in 1897 he had accepted an invitation to Teachers College, assuming he would serve under his long-time friend Benjamin Ide Wheeler. He arrived in New York in October, only to discover that Wheeler had decided not to come on; two months later Russell found himself Dean-Elect of Teachers College.

Russell's genius revealed itself in an uncanny ability to find talent, attract it, and encourage it to fruition. By the beginning of World War I he had brought to the college a truly dazzling collection of pedagogical luminaries. There was Paul Monroe, whose pioneering researches literally opened up the field of American educational history, and Edward L. Thorndike, whose rigorous experimental work not only dominated the field of educational psychology, but extended into innumerable other fields as well. John Dewey, though formally attached to the university Department of Philosophy, served by virtue of that position as a member of the Teachers Col-

[4] Likewise, there is new material on Russell in another dissertation in progress at Columbia by Kenneth H. Toepfer entitled "James Earl Russell: Pioneer of Professional Education." See also James Earl Russell: *Founding Teachers College* (New York, 1937).

lege faculty; and he not only lectured at the college but also took a warm interest in its affairs. His disciple, William Heard Kilpatrick, joined the faculty in 1913 and expounded Deweyan ideas to a generation of teachers.

Frank McMurry came in 1898, and having moved away from his earlier Herbartianism, built a completely new approach to curriculum and teaching on the basis of functional psychology. Patty Smith Hill, a sometime student of Parker, Dewey, and Hall, came in 1906 to fight a thirty-year war on formalism in the kindergarten. Mary Adelaide Nutting served as the first professor of nursing education anywhere in the world. Julius Sachs not only opened up the field of secondary education, but ran one of the most prominent private preparatory schools in New York City. And specialists like David Eugene Smith in mathematics, Gonzalez Lodge in Latin, Henry Johnson in history, and Arthur Wesley Dow in fine arts made distinguished contributions not only to their respective subject fields but to the techniques of teaching these fields as well. It is no wonder that the enrollment climbed during the first two decades of Russell's administration from 450 to 2500 and soon came to include students from every corner of the globe.

As early as 1899 Russell laid down the basic conception of professional education that would guide the college during its formative years.[5] There would be four goals: general culture, special scholarship, professional knowledge, and technical skill. By general culture he meant the commonly accepted end of a liberal education that would "enable the student to see the relationships everywhere in the various fields of knowledge, even the unity of all knowledge." By specialized scholarship he implied concentration on the materials the student was preparing to teach. "Let no one derogate the scholarship essential in professional education," he warned in a passage that retains its relevance. "Selection of appropriate materials from any field, presupposes a knowledge of the field that is both

[5] Teachers College: *Dean's Report*, 1900, pp. 13–15; and James Earl Russell: "The Function of the University in Training Teachers," *Columbia University Quarterly*, I (1898–9), 323–42.

comprehensive and evaluated." No amount of professional training could compensate for a teacher's ignorance of his field.

By "professional knowledge" Russell referred to the need to know more about the learner and learning (educational psychology and child study), about past achievement and present educational practice at home and abroad (history of education and comparative education), and about school administration and its relation to teacher, student, and society. To this end he envisioned students trained in the theories underlying educational practices as well as the practices themselves, and for Russell this meant applying in education the same union of systematic research and controlled observation that was coming to mark professional work in medicine and engineering. Finally, by technical training, Russell alluded to formal preparation in pedagogical skills and procedures, those techniques of the teaching art without which the wisest and most learned scholar is destined to failure in the classroom. In a balanced synthesis of culture, theory, and art Russell saw the makings of a truly professional education for teachers.

Closely related to these ideas on teacher preparation were Russell's views on the nature of education itself. Having observed a wide variety of German secondary schools during his period of study abroad, he had returned to the United States with a compelling sense that democracy demands a very special sort of education, one closely linked in every possible way with the common life of the people.[6] Thus, he early advocated the extension of the college's interest beyond the realm of public schooling alone to every legitimate form of educational effort. There was need for trained teachers and competent leaders in private schools, reform schools, hospitals, settlements, houses of refuge, and other philanthropic institutions, and it was the job of Teachers College to provide them.

Moreover, Russell never doubted for a moment education's responsibility ultimately to serve the common good. He took an active interest in southern reconstruction, cooperating

[6] See James Earl Russell: *German Higher Schools* (New York, 1899), pp. 421–2.

with the General Education Board in selecting able young
men and women to be trained at Teachers College; and time
and again he joined Robert Ogden, Russell Sage, and Frank
Chambers in first-hand tours of southern schools and colleges.
In New York he early sought to establish an experimental
school that would serve as a pilot neighborhood center spe-
cializing in industrial and domestic education; indeed, he even
went so far as to suggest the possibility of expanding such a
school into "an Experimental College Settlement, with the
further purpose of promoting intelligent study of all forms of
public education and social service." [7]

Thus did Russell merge the professionalism and progressivism that had been instrumental in the founding of the college
into a full-fledged reformist philosophy of teacher preparation.
It was a merger of prodigious significance for American education. For in progressivism teachers soon found that they had
an ideology that dignified in the noblest terms their own quest
for status, while in professionalism progressives had the key to
their demand for scientifically trained pedagogues who could
bring into being a new society "more worthy, lovely, and harmonious." [8] The merger colored the whole subsequent history
of progressive education, and goes far in explaining Teachers
College's meteoric rise to pre-eminence during the years of
Russell's administration.

None of this is meant to imply that Teachers College was
ever the one-idea institution portrayed in some caricatures;
indeed, there is truth to the statement that the faculty has
always been "one big unhappy family." But there is no denying that its hospitality to all of the major streams of progressivism in education quickly made it the intellectual crossroads

[7] Teachers College: *President's Report*, 1899, p. 14. The experiment
became the Speyer School.

[8] The merger may well have been a factor in the substantial rise in the
real and relative wages of teachers between 1890 and 1915. See W.
Randolph Burgess: *Trends of School Costs* (New York, 1920); and Paul
H. Douglas: *Real Wages in the United States, 1890–1926* (Boston,
1930). Douglas attributes the rise to the lengthening of the school year,
the improvement of teacher quality, and increasingly effective teacher
organizations.

of the movement. Recall that it was Charles R. Richards, one of the first professors ever appointed at Teachers College, who founded the National Society for the Promotion of Industrial Education; that it was Mabel Carney who published the earliest best-seller for rural teachers based on the Report of the Country Life Commission; that Dewey and Thorndike were senior professors almost from the beginning; and that Patty Smith Hill's kindergarten was one of the "schools of tomorrow" sketched by the Deweys; and the crucial role of the college in advancing progressive education becomes abundantly clear.

A final point also bears comment: it concerns the historical accident of the college's autonomy. Despite the long-time alliance with Columbia, it was an autonomy that, joined to the particular professionalism of Russell, proved both a boon and a bane to the college, and to progressivism as well. It afforded the political and financial freedom to pioneer in every conceivable realm of pedagogical theory and practice. But it also led to an inexorable divorce from the arts and sciences that tore asunder the teacher-preparing function of the university and increasingly insulated the work of the pedagogical faculty.[9] Such insulation undoubtedly served the ideological cause of Progressivism by allowing it free and unrestricted growth, but it deprived the movement of valuable criticism—and indeed, valuable political allies—it would one day discover it could ill afford to lose.

[9] For a discussion of the split as a general phenomenon in American higher education, see Howard M. Jones, Francis Keppel, and Robert Ulich: "On the Conflict Between the 'Liberal Arts' and the 'Schools of Education,'" *The ACLS Newsletter*, V (1954), 17–38; and Eugene Charles Auerbach: "The Opposition to Schools of Education by Professors of the Liberal Arts—A Historical Analysis" (Unpublished Doctoral Thesis, University of Southern California, 1957). The unfortunate consequences of the split for one field, the history of education, are brilliantly discussed by Bernard Bailyn in *Education in the Forming of American Society* (Chapel Hill, 1960).

PART · II

The Progressive Era

in Education

1917–1957

6

Scientists, Sentimentalists, and Radicals

For many reasons, World War I marks a great divide in the history of progressive education. Merely the founding of the Progressive Education Association in 1919 would have changed the movement significantly, since what had formerly been a rather loosely joined revolt against pedagogical formalism now gained a vigorous organizational voice. But there were deeper changes, in the image of Progressivism itself, that were bound to influence the course and meaning of educational reform.

Many of these changes, as Henry F. May has persuasively argued in *The End of American Innocence*, were already in the making well before the war. Freud had first lectured at Clark University in 1909. Harriet Monroe had founded *Poetry* magazine and Max Eastman had taken over *The Masses* in 1912. The year 1913 had witnessed the introduction of modern art to over 100,000 New Yorkers at the now legendary

Armory Show. By 1914 the brilliant young journalist Walter Lippmann had already published A *Preface to Politics* and *Drift and Mastery,* and in 1915 Van Wyck Brooks had proclaimed a new declaration of literary independence in *America's Coming-of-Age.* Each of these in its own way symbolized a break with the past, a revolt not only against the traditional verities of conservatives, but against the moralizing of progressives as well.

The war itself only hastened the change. Progressives split sharply on the issue of pacifism, some following Dewey in his pragmatic support of Wilson, others sharing Randolph Bourne's bitter disenchantment with pragmatism in its ready acceptance of the conflict. For two years reform at home was eclipsed by the larger crusade to make the world safe for democracy; and then, when the armistice finally came, Progressivism seemed strangely fragmented and lacking in appeal. The younger generation wanted nothing to do with "middle-class values"—Theodore Roosevelt's or anyone else's. As Lloyd Morris later remarked of them, they were tired of moral indignation and wanted only to be amused.[1]

Education was inevitably affected. Progressives had gone into the war convinced that it would afford a unique opportunity to advance their cause. Soon after the declaration Dewey himself had assured a group of vocational educators that wars throughout history had aided the forces of "educational readjustment," [2] while Arthur Dean, Professor of Vocational Education at Teachers College, published a 1918 volume detailing wartime opportunities for extending progressive practices in the schools.[3] In the end, however, such hopes were

[1] Lloyd Morris: *Postscript to Yesterday* (New York, 1947), p. 149. Eric F. Goldman reports in *Rendezvous with Destiny* (New York, 1952), p. 288: "As the new era opened, so the story goes, Herbert Croly went home and refused to see anyone for three days. On the fourth day he summoned his editors to his office and told them that progressivism was finished. 'From now on we must work for the redemption of the individual.'"

[2] John Dewey: *Vocational Education in the Light of the World War* (Chicago, 1918).

[3] Arthur D. Dean: *Our Schools in War Time—and After* (Boston, 1918).

only partly realized. Vocational education did advance, and specific programs in school gardening and physical training did make temporary headlines. But the war also brought a substantial decline in teacher salaries and a wave of encroachments on the social science curriculum that hardly seemed to herald any new era of pedagogical freedom.[4]

With the cessation of hostilities, progressive education again quickened amidst Wilsonian promises of a new and better world. But somehow the movement, like Progressivism writ large, had changed. During the twenties, as the intellectual avant garde became fascinated with the arts in general and Freud in particular, social reformism was virtually eclipsed by the rhetoric of child-centered pedagogy. During the thirties, when influential groups within the profession sought to tie progressive education more closely to political Progressivism, the movement was racked by a paralyzing partisanship from which it never fully recovered. After World War II the added curse of inertness cast its pall over the enterprise. By the 1950's the enthusiasm, the vitality, and the drive were gone; all that remained were the slogans.

Certainly if any single career symbolizes the constantly changing image of progressive education during the decades after World War I, it was Harold Rugg's. A New Englander originally trained at Dartmouth in civil engineering, Rugg had gone on to graduate study in psychology, sociology, and education at the University of Illinois, taking the Ph.D. in 1915. The shift from engineering to education was a painless one, he once noted, since both fields in that era were consumed with a passion for precise measurement. "We lived in one long orgy of tabulation," he wrote of the work at Illinois. "Mountains of facts were piled up, condensed, summarized and interpreted by the new quantitative technique. The air was full of normal curves, standard deviations, coefficients of correlation, regression equations." [5]

[4] Howard Ralph Weisz: "Progressive Education and the First World War" (Unpublished Master's Thesis, Columbia University, 1960).

[5] Harold Rugg: *That Men May Understand* (New York, 1941), p. 182.

Having completed his studies at Illinois, Rugg went on to teaching and research with Charles Judd at the University of Chicago. There he published *Statistical Methods Applied to Education* (1917), a volume which proclaimed the need for a "clear, scientific, and complete statement" of the statistical and graphic methods that schoolmen would need "to determine the present status of school practice and to direct scientifically the course of its development." [6] It was no doubt on the basis of this work that the young educationist was invited to serve during the war with the army's Committee on the Classification of Personnel and to participate with Thorndike, Yerkes, and others in the first mass use of aptitude and intelligence tests in history.

The high point of the war years for Rugg was his warm and stimulating friendship with Arthur Upham Pope, who introduced him to Van Wyck Brooks's *America's Coming-of-Age* and to the social critics writing for *The New Republic* and *Seven Arts*. These new materials, at first confusing, were destined to mark a turning point in Rugg's career. He returned briefly to Chicago after the armistice and then went on to Teachers College as Director of Research for the newly established Lincoln School. Immersing himself in the invigorating life of Greenwich Village, he resumed the education Pope had begun, joining the group of artists and literati that clustered around Alfred Stieglitz and drinking the heady wine of bohemian protest against puritanism, Babbittry, and machine culture. [7]

At Lincoln he began work on the series of social science texts that made him famous in some quarters, infamous in others—a massive effort to combine the resources of history, geography, sociology, economics, and political science into a sweeping interpretation of modern industrial civilization. His professorship at Teachers College, his spirited participation in the Progressive Education Association, and his own personal associations with the leading lights of Greenwich Village put

---

[6] Harold O. Rugg: *Statistical Methods Applied to Education* (Boston, 1917), p. 4.

[7] See Harold Rugg: "The Artist and the Great Transition," in Waldo Frank *et. al.*: *America and Alfred Stieglitz* (New York, 1934), pp. 179–98.

him in touch with every conceivable aspect of educational reform; and in 1928 he published with Ann Shumaker what was
destined to become the characteristic progressivist work of the
twenties, *The Child-Centered School.* Like *Schools of To-
Morrow* before it, the volume was an interpretive survey of
pedagogical innovations across the country. And it also sought
to relate these innovations to the broader stream of Progressivism. But whereas the Deweys had seen the crux of progressive
education in its connection with social reformism, Rugg and
Shumaker found their insight in its tie with the historic battle
of the artist against the superficiality and commercialism of
industrial civilization. The key to the modern creative revolution, they argued, was the triumph of self-expression, in education as well as in art; hence in creative self-expression they
found the quintessential meaning of the progressive education
movement.

As with so many of his contemporaries, the Depression
shifted the emphases in Rugg's thinking, though it was less in
the nature of any pendulum swing from Rousseauism back to
social reconstructionism than a subtle realignment of elements
that had long been present in his work. *Culture and Education in America* (1931) set forth a theory of the school as a
conscious agent in the progressive improvement of the social
order. *The Great Technology* (1933) elaborated the interpretation of industrial civilization at the heart of the social science
texts, arguing that man's creative potential could be liberated
only as scientific method was applied to government and social relations as well as to industrial production. And *American
Life and the School Curriculum* (1936) projected an education in which every community agency—family, neighborhood,
press, church, government, and industry—would become the
adjunct of a new "school of living" that would lead in
the business of intelligent social change. Rugg envisioned the
three volumes as a trilogy; and indeed, one finds in *American
Life and the School Curriculum* the first effort to synthesize
his concerns with science, art, and social reconstruction into
the over-all view ultimately set forth in *Foundations for American Education* (1947).

The *Foundations* was clearly Rugg's magnum opus: a Herculean attempt to weave the disparate elements of a progressive education movement that was now falling apart into a single comprehensive program. But interest in progressivism was clearly on the wane, and the book found its market almost exclusively as a required textbook in professional education courses across the country. Rugg's enthusiasm never flagged, though, and as late as 1959 he was projecting a two-volume semi-autobiographical work in which he hoped to distill from his own experience the quintessential meaning of a half-century of pedagogical reform. He died before he ever began it, full of faith in the ultimate regenerative powers of education, relentless in his opposition to the "forces of educational reaction," and bitterly disappointed in the teaching profession which had clothed itself in the mantle of progressivism only to allow that mantle to be torn to shreds before its very eyes.

Rugg's career instructs us on much more than the shifting meaning of progressive education after 1917, for the fact of his professorship at Teachers College is itself a crucial clue to the changing character of the movement. As professionalism moved inexorably forward, fewer men and women like Jane Addams, Jacob Riis, Theodore Roosevelt, and Walter Hines Page concerned themselves directly with educational reform; and wedded as it was to professionalism, pedagogical progressivism found itself increasingly cut off from its sources in the broader Progressive movement. The system of ideas that for a moment in history seemed to converge in *Schools of To-Morrow* and *Democracy and Education* fragmented; and what had appeared as minor inconsistencies in the earlier movement now loomed overwhelmingly large as different segments of the profession pushed different aspects of progressive education to their logical—if sometimes ridiculous—conclusions. Thus, Thorndike's early interest in the precise study of education blossomed into a vigorous scientism which fed on the voracious demand of the profession for esoteric knowledge that would set it apart from the layman. Similarly, Hall's early concern with child-study, now heavily overlaid with Freudianism, became a virulent sentimentalism in the hands of the Greenwich Village intelligentsia. And the reformism that had impelled Jacob Riis and Jane Addams became ever more radical in the social blueprinting of George Counts and his *Social Frontier* colleagues during the 1930's.

There is no denying, of course, that professional espousal of progressivism gave the movement enormous thrust in its drive to transform American education. But the price was tremendous, for professionalism ultimately divorced the movement from the lay power necessary to sustain it in the schools. When public sentiment began to shift during the early 1940's, the movement seemed frozen and unable to respond, and the more perceptive within the fold quickly realized that the end was only a matter of time. Had the Russian Sputnik never illuminated the Western pedagogical skies, the movement would have died of its own internal contradictions. Sputnik may well have dramatized the end; but even so, there were few mourners at the funeral.

I I

"Whatever exists at all exists in some amount," Thorndike wrote in 1918. "To know it thoroughly involves knowing its quantity as well as its quality. Education is concerned with changes in human beings; a change is a difference between two conditions; each of these conditions is known to us only by the products produced by it—things made, words spoken, acts performed, and the like. To measure any of these products means to define its amount in some way so that competent persons will know how large it is, better than they would without measurement. To measure a product well means so to define its amount that competent persons will know how large it is, with some precision, and that this knowledge may be recorded and used. This is the general *Credo* of those who, in the last decade, have been busy trying to extend and improve measurements of educational products." [8]

It had been an exciting decade indeed for those who shared

[8] Edward L. Thorndike: "The Nature, Purposes, and General Methods of Measurements of Educational Products," in National Society for the Study of Education: *Seventeenth Yearbook* (Bloomington, 1918), Part II, p. 16.

Thorndike's dream of a genuine science of pedagogy, and the key to the ferment had been the rapid development of intelligence and aptitude tests for use in the schools. Tests themselves, of course, had long been known to European and American psychologists: Francis Galton had experimented with them during the interval between *Hereditary Genius* (1869) and *Inquiries into Human Faculty* (1883), and James McKeen Cattell, following Galton, had apparently used them in his laboratory at the University of Pennsylvania as early as 1885. But the real breakthrough for education had come during the years between 1905 and 1908, when the French psychologists Alfred Binet and Théodore Simon conceived the idea of an intelligence *scale*, a series of problems of graded difficulty, each one corresponding to the *norm* of a different mental level. Once Binet's work had been translated—by H. H. Goddard, a student of Hall—American educators quickly recognized that the *scale* idea could be applied not only to intelligence but to achievement as well. There followed a phenomenally creative period during which testmakers developed instruments for appraising virtually every aspect of educational practice.[9]

There were numerous adaptations and refinements of the Binet scale, the most important of which was the so-called Stanford Revision described by Lewis Terman in *The Measurement of Intelligence* (1916). It was Terman, by the way, who popularized the idea of the Intelligence Quotient, a number expressing the relation of an individual's mental age to his chronological age. Meanwhile, Thorndike and his students developed scales for measuring achievement in arithmetic (1908), handwriting (1910), spelling (1913), drawing (1913), reading (1914), and language ability (1916).[1] The work was

[9] Joseph Peterson: *Early Conceptions and Tests of Intelligence* (Yonkers, 1925), chs. v–x.

[1] See Walter W. Cook's article and bibliography on achievement tests in Walter S. Monroe, ed.: *Encyclopedia of Educational Research* (New York, 1941), pp. 1283–1301. The measurement effort also extended into school administration; the pioneer study here was Leonard P. Ayres's analysis of retardation and elimination in city school systems: *Laggards in Our Schools* (New York, 1909).

quickly taken up at other universities, particularly at Chicago under Charles H. Judd. By 1918, when the National Society for the Study of Education published its yearbook on *The Measurement of Educational Products*, Walter S. Monroe described over a hundred standardized tests designed to measure achievement in the principal elementary- and secondary-school subjects, and these represented his culling of the best.

All this feverish activity—which Rugg described as the "orgy of tabulation"—would undoubtedly have remained very much a professional phenomenon had it not been for the historical intervention of World War I. Following the declaration in 1917 the American Psychological Association through its president, Robert Yerkes, tendered its services to the United States Army, specifically offering to construct group intelligence tests for army recruits. The Army took Yerkes up on the offer and invited him to organize a team of psychologists in Washington to devise the tests and administer them on a mass basis. Under Yerkes's direction, a number of instruments were developed, the most famous of which were the army Scale Alpha, a group test for recruits who could read and comprehend English, and the army Scale Beta, a group test consisting largely of pictures and diagrams, with directions in pantomime, for recruits unable to comprehend English. The results of the Alpha were ranged on a scale running from 0 to 212, with letter ratings assigned as follows: [2]

Test score	0–14	15–24	25–44	45–74	75–104	105–134	135–212
Letter rating	E or D–	D	C–	C	C+	B	A
Per cent of 128,747 literate white draftees achieving these scores	7.38	14.38	21.86	26.78	16.69	8.82	4.09

The tests were administered to hundreds of thousands of recruits, and while they were initially devised to weed out the

[2] Clarence S. Yoakum and Robert M. Yerkes: *Army Mental Tests* (New York, 1920), p. 134; and Robert M. Yerkes, ed.: *Psychological Examining in the United States Army* (Washington, 1921), pp. 421–2.

grossly incompetent and to cream off the exceptional for officer training, they were ultimately used for a much greater
variety of classificatory purposes.

Yerkes and his colleagues made it abundantly clear that
their tests made no judgment of character, and were quite
unable to appraise "loyalty, bravery, power to command, or
the emotional traits that make a man 'carry on.' " But they
did commit the error of attempting to assign mental ages to
the several letter ratings on the Scale Alpha. They did this
by administering to a carefully selected group of men both the
Scale Alpha and the Stanford-Binet and then assigning mental
ages derived from the latter to scores achieved on the former.
The results of this procedure, which assumed that scales derived from schoolchildren who took the Stanford-Binet could
be used to judge the mental ages of adults long out of school,
were disastrous, as indicated below: [3]

Letter rating	E & D—	D	C—	C	C+	B	A
Mental age on Stanford-Binet	0–9.4	9.5–10.9	11–12.9	13–14.9	15–16.4	16.5–17.9	18–19.5

Nonetheless, the results were supposedly scientific and quickly
triggered one of the major social controversies of the twenties.

It began with a number of writers citing the Yerkes data
in support of the contention that the average mental age of
Americans was fourteen, and hence that most Americans were
uneducable beyond the high school.[4] President George B. Cutten of Colgate University made headlines in 1922, for example, by arguing that only fifteen per cent of the population
had the intelligence to get into college and profit from it.[5]
The next year Henry S. Pritchett of the Carnegie Foundation
went on record with the observation that too many children
were going to school, and that tests indicated that most were

[3] Yoakum and Yerkes: op. cit., p. 134.
[4] One of the earliest was Lothrop Stoddard in *The Revolt Against
Civilization* (New York, 1922).
[5] George B. Cutten: "The Reconstruction of Democracy," *School and
Society,* XVI (1922), 477–89.

not prepared to profit from too much schooling.[6] A report from the University of Michigan in 1927 urged that the lower twenty per cent of the class might well have been refused admission with no loss to the college;[7] while Dean Christian Gauss of Princeton wrote in the October, 1927, *Scribner's* that fully one sixth of the college population had no business in college.[8] A year later Max McConn, the peppery dean at Lehigh University, published a popular book called *College or Kindergarten?* in which he argued that only a fixed percentage of the population could be educated with any reasonable personal and social benefit.[9]

Progressive intellectuals were of two minds about the controversy, if the columns of *The New Republic* give any indication of their attitudes. An editorial on October 4, 1922, came out squarely in favor of limiting college enrollments, taking the opportunity to rebuke the colleges as "social clubs for the aristocracy." Colleges were failing to teach students to think, the editorial inveighed, partly because they were inundated with thousands of flighty youths who had no serious business there to begin with.[1] Here was the side of Progressivism impatient with the archaic formalism of the colleges, with their control by the business interests, with the waste of time involved in student spectacles and quasi-professional athletics. "Education remains the dominant superstition of our time," wrote Robert Morss Lovett in *Civilization in the United States* (1922). It aimed not at truth but conformity. In grade

[6] Henry S. Pritchett: "Are Our Universities Overpopulated?" *Scribner's Magazine*, LXXIII (1923), 556–60.

[7] II. W. Miller: "Segregation on the Basis of Ability," *School and Society*, XXVI (1927), 84–8, 114–20. The study was also reported in *Time* for August 1, 1927.

[8] Christian Gauss: "Should Johnny Go to College," *Scribner's Magazine*, LXXXII (1927), 411–16.

[9] Max McConn: *College or Kindergarten?* (New York, 1928), ch. iii–iv. For Alexander Meiklejohn's rebuttal to McConn, see *The New Republic*, LVII (1929), 238–41. It should be noted that the elitist argument was itself an ancient one; the significance of the articles cited here is that they used the tests as one further justification of elitism. For a discussion of the historic elitist position, see R. Freeman Butts: *The College Charts Its Course* (New York, 1939), ch. xviii.

[1] *The New Republic*, XXXII (1922), 137–8.

schools it regimented the mind; in the universities it was a
servant of the interests. As a national institution, it was "the
propaganda department of the state and the existing social
system." [2] On the other hand, there was an inherent elitism
here that deeply disturbed the editors; hence an editorial entitled "Fundamentals in Education" sharply criticized Pritchett's statement that too many Americans were going to school.
What the nation needed, the editors contended, was better individualized schooling for the children of all social and intellectual strata.[3]

More important, perhaps, were a number of fascinating
articles the journal sponsored during the height of the controversy in 1922 and 1923. A series by Walter Lippmann
ripped into the new restrictionism based on test data, remind-
ing readers that the Army Alpha had been designed as an instrument to aid classification, not to measure intelligence.[4]
Tests in general were a useful device for fitting individuals
into their proper places in the educational program, he granted;
but it was stupid and contemptible to stamp a sense of inferiority on any person by classifying him uneducable. "The
claim that we have learned how to *measure hereditary intelligence* has no scientific foundation," he concluded; by
recognizing this, psychologists could "save themselves from
the humiliation of having furnished doped evidence to the ex-
ponents of the New Snobbery." [5]

As if to press the point, *The New Republic* brought up the
august guns of John Dewey. In an article slamming into President Cutten, he too pointed out that the tests were a helpful
classificatory device, but that their use beyond classification
had reprehensible social overtones. The IQ, Dewey argued,
"is an indication of risks and probabilities. Its practical value
lies in the stimulus it gives to more intimate and intensive
inquiry into individualized abilities and disabilities." Barring

[2] Harold E. Stearns, ed.: *Civilization in the United States* (New
York, 1922), pp. 88–9.
[3] *The New Republic*, XXXIV (1923), 57–9.
[4] Ibid., XXXII (1922), 213–15, 246–8, 275–7, 297–8, 328–30;
XXXIII (1922–3), 9–11; XXXIV (1923), 263–4, 322–3.
[5] Ibid., XXXIII (1922), 10.

complete imbecility, he continued, even the most limited member of the citizenry had potentialities that could be enhanced by a genuine education for individuality. "Democracy will not be democracy until education makes it its chief concern to release distinctive aptitudes in art, thought, and companionship." Insofar as tests assisted this goal, they could serve the cause of progress; insofar as they tended in the name of science to sink individuals into numerical classes, they were essentially antithetical to democratic social policy.[6]

Probably the most systematic attack on educational restrictionism during the 1920's came in a collection of essays by William Chandler Bagley of Teachers College entitled *Determinism in Education*.[7] Interestingly enough, Bagley considered himself an archopponent of progressive education; yet he ended up the outstanding exponent of progressivism in the testing controversy. His title, of course, located the problem within the classic argument over social Darwinism, with Bagley taking a vehemently reformist position. The IQ rightly interpreted spoke with compelling force not for restriction but for expansion, Bagley concluded. For there was no limit to the educational opportunity a democracy might provide—for the superintelligent and for everyone else as well. The only function of the tests was to tell the educator where he began; it was the educator's vision—and society's—that ultimately set the goals.

The testing controversy continued to blow hot and cold during the next two decades, though it never again commanded the burning headlines of the twenties. For a while it raged around the question of race differences, undoubtedly fanned by the winds of Nazi doctrine;[8] and it again burst to

[6] John Dewey: "Mediocrity and Individuality," *Ibid.*, XXXIII (1922), 35–7. See also Dewey: "Individuality, Equality and Superiority," *Ibid.*, XXXIII (1922), 61–3; and Dewey's review of *The Theory of Education in the United States* by Albert J. Nock in *The New Republic*, LXX (1932), 242–4.

[7] William C. Bagley: *Determinism in Education* (Baltimore, 1925).

[8] One of the earliest systematic arguments in favor of "racial explanations" for differences in intelligence was Carl C. Brigham: *A Study of American Intelligence* (Princeton, 1923). Brigham later recanted in the *Psychological Review*, XXXVII (1930), 164. For the continuing con-

the fore after World War II as part of the national controversy over school segregation.[9] As late as 1939 Lewis Terman and George Stoddard debated before the National Education Association whether the IQ remains constant or varies with environment and education, with no apparent resolution of the problem.[1] Twenty years later educators were still arguing over what the tests actually measured and how they should be used, while the most tested generation of youngsters in history rabidly competed for places in the nation's hard-pressed schools and colleges.[2]

I I I

If science promised nothing else, it promised efficiency; this ultimately was the plum the educational scientist dangled before the taxpaying public. The promise itself was not new, for the National Education Association had been talking about efficiency at least since Charles W. Eliot had delivered his notable speech, "Can School Programs Be Shortened and Enriched?" to the Department of Superintendence in 1888.[3]

---

troversy see Otto Klineberg: *Race Differences* (New York, 1935), Part II; and Klineberg, ed.: *Characteristics of the American Negro* (New York, 1944), Part II.

[9] See Frank McGurk: "A Scientist's Report on Race Differences," *U.S. News & World Report*, September 21, 1956, pp. 92–6; William M. McCord and Nicholas J. Demerath III: "Negro Versus White Intelligence: A Continuing Controversy," *Harvard Educational Review*, XXVIII (1958), 120–35; and Frank C. J. McGurk: " 'Negro vs. White Intelligence'—An Answer," *Harvard Educational Review*, XXIX (1959), 54–62.

[1] National Education Association: *Addresses and Proceedings*, 1939, pp. 89–90; and *Time*, July 17, 1939, p. 65. See also the extended discussions of the question in the *Twenty-Seventh* and *Thirty-Ninth Yearbooks* of the National Society for the Study of Education, and George D. Stoddard: *The Meaning of Intelligence* (New York, 1943).

[2] See, for example, Fred M. Hechinger's report in *The New York Times* for June 27, 1960, of an experiment by Dr. Albert Upton of Whittier College in which it was claimed that a "special method" of working with a group of 280 freshmen raised their IQ's by an average of 10.5 points in eight months. See also John Hersey's trenchant commentary on the use and misuse of the tests in *Intelligence: Choice and Consent* (New York, 1959) and *The Child Buyer* (New York, 1960).

[3] Charles W. Eliot: *Educational Reform* (New York, 1898), pp. 51–76.

But there was a heightening sense after 1908 that educational measurement had ushered in a new era in which the promise of efficiency could at last be scientifically fulfilled. It was no surprise, then, when the NEA's Department of Superintendence in 1911 appointed a Committee on Economy of Time in Education, charging it with formulating recommendations for the systematic removal of waste from the school curriculum.[4]

The Committee made four major reports between 1915 and 1919, all of which were carefully read and pondered in professional education courses across the country.[5] Economy of time, the Committee maintained, could be achieved in at least three ways: by eliminating nonessentials, by improving teaching methods, and by organizing courses of study to conform more closely to the realities of child development. Of the three it was the first at which the Committee labored most assiduously, and the first that posed the most gnawing difficulties. After all, men had been arguing for a long, long time over what knowledge was of most worth!

The Committee reasoned as follows: The purpose of education is to insure the acquisition of "those habits, skills, knowledges, ideals, and prejudices which must be made the common property of all, that each may be an efficient member of a progressive democratic society, possessing the power of self-support and self-direction, the capacity and disposition for co-operative effort, and, if possible, the ability to direct others in positions of responsibility requiring administrative capacity."

[4] The concern of the Department of Superintendence grew out of the work of an earlier Committee on Economy of Time in Education appointed in 1908 by the National Council of Education. See the *Report of the Committee of the National Council of Education on Economy of Time in Education* (United States Bureau of Education, Bulletin, 1913, No. 38). It is interesting to note the composition of the 1911 Committee: three superintendents of schools, three professors of education, and the president of a state normal school. The absence of academic scholars or college presidents—a relatively new phenomenon in educational policy-making in 1911—further documents the developing schism between professional educationists and arts and science professors alluded to on pp. 175–176.

[5] The reports were published as *Yearbooks* of the National Society for the Study of Education in 1915, 1917, 1918, and 1919.

Granted this, the content and emphasis in each subject should be determined with reference to common social needs, while the organization of this content and the methods of teaching it must be worked out in accordance with the abilities and interests of the children to be taught. From here it was but a short step to the Committee's fundamental criteria of selection: whatever is included for children of any age must be readily comprehensible by a majority of normal children that age, and whatever is included must minister to the social needs common to ordinary American children.

Having arrived at this point, though, the Committee still faced the nasty business of determining what knowledge would best minister to the needs of American children. Their decision here was portentous. "If it is impossible to discover from educational theory the fundamental tests for exclusion or inclusion," they argued, "we are driven to the method of determining minimum essentials on the basis of the best current practices and experimentation which give satisfactory results. Those results are satisfactory which meet adequately the common needs of life in society."[6] Such reasoning, circular at best, could become meaningful only as terms like *best, satisfactory,* and *adequately* were defined. Unfortunately, the Committee never really defined them, with the result that while its reports provided an extraordinary amount of new and useful information, its recommendations were fraught with theoretical difficulties that ultimately went unresolved.

The Committee began in 1915 with a detailed survey of existing conditions in representative city school systems. The effort was not merely to discover what was actually being taught—itself a revealing enterprise—but also to determine how much students were really learning, as a basis for building norms of performance in each of the subject fields. Needless to say, the best of the recently developed achievement scales were applied wherever possible, and the results reported in an impressive array of charts, graphs, and tables that lent an unmistakable aura of precision to the undertaking.

[6] National Society for the Study of Education: *Fourteenth Yearbook* (Chicago, 1915), Part I, p. 16.

Having made its survey of what was actually going on, the Committee proceeded to the business of working out the "minimum essentials" of a good education. Since it had defined satisfactory educational results as those "which meet adequately the common needs of life in society," the indicated next step was to specify those needs. The Committee therefore embarked upon a vast Spencerian attempt to describe what people actually do in the course of "life in society" and to derive from this analysis the content of the school curriculum. The effort in the field of mathematics furnishes an excellent illustration. In the Committee's report for 1917 Walter S. Monroe of the Kansas State Normal School at Emporia contributed "A Preliminary Report of an Investigation of the Economy of Time in Arithmetic." [7] Monroe assumed that the primary purpose of elementary-school arithmetic was "to equip the pupil (1) with the knowledge of facts, principles, and relationships existing between quantities, etc., which is needed to decide what arithmetical operations are to be performed in solving valuable practical problems and (2) with the skills which are necessary to perform these operations." Defining a practical problem as any occurring within the course of human activity, Monroe set out to survey the typical activities that a person might confront in his vocational, domestic, and personal affairs. The result, not surprisingly, was a long, detailed, and somewhat indiscriminate list of activities, which Monroe then used as a yardstick to appraise the content of four widely used elementary arithmetic texts.

The section on arithmetic in the Committee's 1918 report followed along many of these same lines.[8] H. Edwin Mitchell of Minnesota's State Normal School at Moorhead tabulated data from four typical sources—a standard cookbook, a number of factory payrolls, representative advertisements, and a general hardware catalogue—and then proceeded to draw inferences for the design of an arithmetic syllabus, assuming that his data were the "concrete stuff out of which arise the arithmetical problems of housewives, wage earners, consumers,

[7] Ibid.: *Sixteenth Yearbook* (Bloomington, 1917), Part I, pp. 111–27.
[8] Ibid.: *Seventeenth Yearbook* (Bloomington, 1918), Part I, pp. 7–17.

and retail hardware dealers. . . ." It was such reasoning, he argued, that would have to form the basis for the ultimate determination of the elementary-school arithmetic program.

What Monroe and Mitchell did for arithmetic, others did for English, geography, history, civics, literature, and physical education. Brought together in the Committee's reports of 1917 and 1918, these analyses added up to a formidable criticism of conventional syllabi and textbooks, and their immediate thrust was overwhelmingly reformist. After all, merely to inquire systematically into what was going on was itself a novelty; while to add the question, "Why?" was already to begin the process of brushing away cobwebs. Yet there were difficulties in the Committee's theoretical position destined to dog curriculum makers for at least a generation. For in the particular method it had chosen to determine "minimum essentials"—however precise and scientific it may have appeared—the Committee had ended by defining the goals of education in terms of life as it was, and hence by proposing a curriculum that would accommodate youngsters to existing conditions with little emphasis on improving them. This was hardly the progressive or the Deweyan ideal, however much it was construed as such in some circles. It was utilitarian and antiformalist, to be sure, but with conservative overtones that ultimately set it far apart from its sources in the earlier progressive movement.

The Committee's final report, prepared under the chairmanship of Ernest Horn of Iowa State University, presented "in simple, direct language" the best available scientific findings to guide the pedagogy of each subject.[9] "Both forearms should rest on the desk for approximately three quarters of their length," cautioned the handwriting expert; statistical evidence had indicated that when one elbow went unsupported, spinal curvature was often the result. "The first step in economy of time in learning to spell is to see that the pupil learns those words which he needs to and no others," counseled the spelling expert. "A preliminary practice of five minutes at the beginning of the recitation serves as a 'mental tonic,'" advised the

[9] Ibid.: *Eighteenth Yearbook* (Bloomington, 1919), Part II.

mathematics expert. Here the pedagogical scientists were in their element, stating their findings as maxims that any classroom teacher could follow in her quest for professionalization. Needless to say, this part of the Committee's report enjoyed the widest circulation of the four.

Both the strengths and the difficulties in the work of the Committee on Economy of Time were patently reflected in the two major streams of curricular reform that flowed from the scientific movement during the interbellum period. The first of these represented the effort to use the findings of educational science to do a better job of teaching traditional subject matter. Partisans of this approach were really the spiritual heirs of Charles W. Eliot and were seeking less to revamp the curriculum in any radical way than to recharge it with new vigor and vitality. Consider Eugene Randolph Smith as an outstanding example. A graduate of Syracuse University in mathematics, Smith had taught in the public schools of Montclair, New Jersey, and at Brooklyn Polytechnic High School before being asked to Baltimore in 1912 to organize the Park School; he went on during the 1920's to head the Beaver Country Day School in Massachusetts. An organizer of the Progressive Education Association and one of its early presidents, Smith typified the progressive faith in science as an instrument of educational reform. He was aware of Binet's work, he had participated in Stuart Courtis's early experiments with arithmetic tests in Montclair, and he had subsequently worked out a "syllabus method" of teaching plane and solid geometry without the usual textbooks that was rapidly adopted in the Montclair system.

Smith's magnum opus, *Education Moves Ahead* (1926), provides a superb example of one school of progressive educational thought during the twenties. It is generally a tough-minded book, responsive to the need for reform, but deeply concerned with preserving the values of traditional education. Smith's aims were eclectic: he spoke of health and vocation as concerns of the school along with training in initiative, originality, imagination, leadership, intellectual power, and aesthetic sensibility. But he was convinced that teaching was a difficult professional undertaking and that scientific knowledge was essential to its satisfactory conduct. He favored the use of intelligence and achievement scales and even urged the construction of tests to assess the development of character. He stressed the need for more and better motivation, "not to make work easy, but to secure the driving force that accomplishes even the most difficult undertakings." In all of this Smith was very much the Deweyan. The school must never be isolated from life, the child must always be an active participant in the learning process, teaching must never be dull and external, and the professional educator must use all of the scientific tools at his disposal to advance these ends.

But given all this, Smith was ready to abandon neither college-entrance requirements nor hard intellectual work in the school. One has the sense of the old humane standards in Eugene Randolph Smith, extended and informed by the needs of a scientific, democratic society. No radical to begin with, he was already reacting against the excesses of some progressives. "Education has been building for thousands of years," he wrote in the peroration to his volume. "It carries on its back loads of useless traditions and outgrown theories, but there is too much vigor in it to warrant too drastic treatment. We may cut away a useless part here and there, or recast one part or another, but it should be done with reverence, if without fear. And in making our changes, let us not become obsessed with any one method or system. The limitations of any system, or of the thought of any one man or woman or any group of men and women, are too narrow for the education of the race." [1]

A second stream of curriculum reform during the twenties was more radical in its antiformalism and more conservative in its ultimate social impact. This was the work of those professors of education who followed in the footsteps of the Committee on Economy of Time. Accepting without reservation the Committee's social utilitarianism, this group proceeded

[1] Eugene Randolph Smith: *Education Moves Ahead* (Boston, 1924), p. 143. The book, appropriately, carries an introduction by Charles W. Eliot.

with the analysis of contemporary society as the criterion of priority in the curriculum. The two notable leaders of the group were Professors Franklin Bobbitt of the University of Chicago and Werrett Wallace Charters of the Carnegie Institute of Technology; of the two, Bobbitt, who had originally worked with the Committee, serves as the quintessential example.[2]

In 1924 Bobbitt published a major work called *How to Make a Curriculum* in which he carried the theory and procedures of the Committee to their logical outcome.[3] Likening the curriculum-maker to a "great engineer"—the phrase was common during the twenties among those with an unqualified faith in science—he set the goal of educational science as a general educational blueprint based on "a broad over-view of the entire field of man's life." Education, he contended, was preparation for adulthood; hence the job of the curriculum-maker was to classify and detail the full range of human experience with a view to building a curriculum that would prepare for it.[4] "At all stages of the analysis," Bobbitt cautioned, "attention should be fixed upon the actual activities of mankind."

Here again was the identification of the actual with the desirable that had earlier marked the work of the Committee. And it was an identification closely tied to the quest for a science of education. For in the ongoing life of the community, Bobbitt had something eminently visible, measurable, and classifiable, something on which he could use all the paraphernalia of quantification. True, there was a gross criterion of value in his mind; after all, he made no analysis of criminal life or social disorganization. But ultimately, Bobbitt fell vic-

[2] Charters served subsequently as the University of Pittsburgh (1923–5), the University of Chicago (1925–8), and Ohio State University (1928–42). See his volume: *Curriculum Construction* (New York, 1923).

[3] Franklin Bobbitt: *How to Make a Curriculum* (Boston, 1924). See also Bobbitt's earlier work: *The Curriculum* (Boston, 1918).

[4] The long lists of detailed curriculum aims that ensued were undoubtedly supported by the popular Watsonian behaviorism of the twenties. See Lucille Birnbaum: "Behaviorism in the 1920's," *American Quarterly*, VII (1955), 15–30.

tim to his own techniques. Abandoning the world of hazy ideals, of ineffable human qualities, and of tiresome philosophical debate, he ended by measuring what could be measured. His results may well have sparkled with precision, but in the process he had given up the progressive quest for the better life through education.[5] In Bobbitt's scientism lay the seeds of the life-adjustment theory that proved the final manifestation of progressive education in the years after World War II.

The scientific movement exerted its greatest influence on education at a time when the study of education was making rapid headway as a university discipline. One need only check the dissertation lists at Columbia, Chicago, and Stanford after World War I to see the vast enthusiasm for scientific topics. Here was no dabbling with the tricks of the trade that had been the earmarks of the normal school; here was *Wissenschaft* with a vengeance. Little wonder that professors of education, ever under attack for having no real content to teach, saw in science the great panacea for their field. And in the schools themselves science gave classroom teachers the rules and maxims they needed to make mass education work at the same time it set them apart from the lay public as professional personnel worthy of appropriate status and compensation. More to the point perhaps, it enabled them to be "progressive" without incurring the stigma of radicalism, an opportunity that must have been appealing in an era when the average board of education was a group of businessmen, lawyers, and farmers little interested in schemes to reform society, however moderate, gradual, or utopian they might have been.[6]

[5] Bobbitt wrote in the *Twenty-Sixth Yearbook* of the National Society for the Study of Education: "The school is not an agency of social reform. Its responsibility is to help the growing individual .continuously and consistently to hold to the type of living which is the best practical one for him."

[6] I have obviously made no attempt here to portray the whole scientific movement in education, but rather to discuss those aspects which bear on progressivism. For the larger scientific movement, see Part II of the *Thirty-Seventh Yearbook* of the National Society for the Study of Education. In connection with the criticisms I have advanced, it is interesting to note the editor's conclusions. The movement, he suggested, had gone about as far as it could in improving the schools; what was needed was a

I V

Malcolm Cowley, in his delightful reminiscence *Exile's Return*, sketches a fascinating account of what happened to Progressivism after World War I that goes far in explaining the subsequent history of progressive education. Intellectual protest in prewar years, Cowley suggests, had mingled two quite different sorts of revolt: bohemianism and radicalism. The one was essentially an individual revolt against puritan restraint; the other, primarily a social revolt against the evils of capitalism. World War I, he argues, brought a parting of the ways. People were suddenly forced to decide what kind of rebels they were. If they were merely rebels against puritanism, they could exist safely in Mr. Wilson's world; if they were radicals, they had no place in it.[7]

Cowley's analysis provides a key to one of the important intellectual shifts of the twenties. With the end of the war, radicalism seemed no longer fashionable among the avant garde, particularly the artists and literati who flocked to the Greenwich Villages of New York, Chicago, and San Francisco. It did not die; it was merely eclipsed by a polyglot system of ideas that combined the doctrines of self-expression, liberty, and psychological adjustment into a confident, iconoclastic individualism that fought the constraints of Babbittry and the discipline of social reform as well. And just as prewar Progressivism had given rise to a new educational outlook, one that cast the school as a lever of social reform, so this postwar pro-

---

rediscovery of the basic values that underlie education. "Science has shot its bolt," he concluded. "It remains for philosophy to take the field." National Society for the Study of Education: *Thirty-Seventh Yearbook* (Bloomington, 1938), Part II, p. 488. For a general exegesis of scientism as progressivism, see Charles H. Judd: *Introduction to the Scientific Study of Education* (Boston, 1918) and *Education and Social Progress* (New York, 1934). See also Norman Woelfel: *Molders of the American Mind* (New York, 1933), pp. 81–118. For the social attitudes of school-board members, see George G. Struble: "A Study of School Board Personnel," *American School Board Journal*, LXV (1922), 48–9, 137–8; George S. Counts: *The Social Composition of Boards of Education* (Chicago, 1927); and Claude E. Arnett: *Social Beliefs and Attitudes of American School Board Members* (Emporia, Kansas, 1932).

[7] Malcolm Cowley: *Exile's Return* (New York, 1934), ch. ii.

test developed its own characteristic pedagogical argument: the notion that each individual has uniquely creative potentialities and that a school in which children are encouraged freely to develop these potentialities is the best guarantee of a larger society truly devoted to human worth and excellence.

Now those who had read their Dewey must certainly have recognized this essentially Rousseauan stance; it had been at the heart of several of the experiments enthusiastically described in *Schools of To-Morrow*. Yet readers who had troubled to follow that book to the end, and who had accepted Dewey's analysis incorporating Rousseau's insights into a larger social reformism, must have noted a curious difference in emphasis here. For just as radicalism seemed eclipsed in some of the broader protests of the twenties, so it seemed to disappear from the progressive pedagogy of the decade.[8] For all intents and purposes, the avant-garde pedagogues expanded one part of what progressive education had formerly meant into its total meaning, and in so doing they wrought a caricature that was quickly taken up as the ultimate meaning of the movement itself.

Nowhere is the transformation as readily apparent as in the life and work of Caroline Pratt.[9] Born at Fayetteville, New York, in 1867, Miss Pratt had taught in the Fayetteville schools for several years before a scholarship brought her to Teachers College in 1892 for courses in kindergarten methods and industrial arts. Having won her diploma in 1894, she went on to teach manual training in the Normal School for Girls in Philadelphia, where she plied her trade with the deepening conviction that she was "helping to perpetuate a system which had no real educational value." A summer trip to Sweden to study *slöjd* did little good, and she returned to the normal school convinced that something else was needed to replace the graded exercises that had come down from the days of Della Vos and Woodward. It was at this point that Caroline

---

[8] Radicalism even tended to disappear from the pedagogical formulations of many political radicals. See, for example, Agnes de Lima: *Our Enemy the Child* (New York, 1925), ch. xii.

[9] Caroline Pratt: *I Learn from Children* (New York, 1948).

Pratt found her "guide"—a reform-minded Quaker librarian named Helen Marot.

Miss Marot, later to be known for her work in organizing the Women's Trade Union League, for her books on American trade unions, and for her editorial services to *The Dial*, had made her library a center of liberal thought in Philadelphia. Socialists, philosophical anarchists, Single-Taxers, protestors of every shade and variety, gathered there to sample the stimulating conversation and the unusual selection of books and pamphlets. For the young normal school instructor it was a revelation. She was soon drawn into Helen Marot's investigations of working and living conditions in the Philadelphia slums, and found herself dreaming ever more vividly of a new sort of education that would provide real opportunities to the tenement children who so badly needed them.

The Normal School now proved more constraining than ever, and Caroline Pratt decided to resign and go to New York. There she found three teaching positions, one in a small private school and two in settlement houses. Freed of curriculum rules and restrictions, she determined to put her students to work not at the carefully graded exercises of the manual-training syllabus, but at any constructive activity they chose. The results were dramatic: there were some discipline problems at first, but along with them came the rewards of freedom; her shops literally hummed with activity as the children reveled in the joys of "purposeful effort."

Then one day Caroline Pratt—in the fashion of so many of the leading progressive educators—had her conversion experience. It occurred during a visit with a friend whose son, an inventive six-year old, was at play in his nursery. Miss Pratt describes the situation as follows: "On this occasion I found the floor covered with a miniature railroad system. He was building with blocks, toys, odd paper boxes, and any material he could find. Some of it was obviously salvaged from the wastepaper basket. As I watched him push his freight train onto a siding while a fast express roared by to stop at a station where lines of passengers and automobiles were waiting, as I listened to the unceasing accompaniment of happy noises in realistic imitation of train whistles and bells and automobile horns—it seemed to me that this child had discovered an activity more satisfying to him than anything I had ever seen offered to children." [1] In this youngster's extraordinarily creative use of materials, in his imaginative way of learning about the world in which he lived, Miss Pratt saw the vision of a new school: a child-sized community in which the inhabitants, through play, might grasp the essential truths of the universe. Then and there, the idea of the Play School was born.

The school was actually opened in the autumn of 1914 in a three-room apartment at the corner of Fourth and Twelfth Streets in Greenwich Village. [2] Miss Pratt reports in her autobiography that the choice of locale was entirely fortuitous; she knew little about the Village and simply assumed that she would be dealing with the children of tradesmen, laborers, and white-collar workers. When the school moved to a small house on Thirteenth Street, however, and expanded to include older children, she found difficulty in recruiting students; parents who had gladly placed preschool children in her care balked at forsaking public education for a "play school." What she discovered, however, was that the artists and writers who were moving into the Village in increasing numbers were more than willing to take a chance. What had begun as an effort to build a richer life for slum children was slowly transformed into a classless experiment in creative education.

The whole subsequent history of the Play School—later known as the City and Country School—was colored by this fortuitous association of Caroline Pratt and the Greenwich

[1] Ibid., p. 23.
[2] For the work of the Play School—later the City and Country School —see John Dewey and Evelyn Dewey: *Schools of To-Morrow* (New York, 1915), ch. v; Caroline Pratt, ed.: *Experimental Practice in the City and Country School* (New York, 1924); Caroline Pratt and Jessie Stanton: *Before Books* (New York, 1926); and Bureau of Educational Experiments: *Bulletin No. 3* (New York, 1917). The Bureau of Educational Experiments was founded in 1916 by Lucy Sprague Mitchell in an attempt to unify the movement to found experimental schools with the movement to build a science of education; the Bureau subsequently became the Bank Street College of Education. See Lucy Sprague Mitchell: *Two Lives* (New York, 1953).

Village intelligentsia. Her effort from the beginning was to afford the children as rich a variety of first-hand experiences as possible—trips to parks, stores, zoos, the harbor, etc.—and then to provide them with play materials—blocks, clay, paints, boxes, toys, and the like—through which they might imaginatively portray what they had experienced. The usual ingredients of an elementary education were there; reading, writing, arithmetic, history, geography, the arts, and physical education were present; but the teaching situations themselves remained unstructured and unpatterned. She saw the children as artists, each with an intense desire to express or externalize what he had seen, heard, felt, each with his own personal perception of reality. An artist starts out with an idea, she once wrote, but he clarifies it through his method of dealing with it. "He is dominated by a desire to clarify this idea for *himself*. It is incidental to his purpose to clarify it for others." [3]

Such reasoning must have been both welcome and familiar to the artists and literati who patronized the school.[4] For theirs was the generation that had heard the clarion call of *The Seven Arts* magazine in the brief period of its existence during World War I. Founded in 1916 by James Oppenheim, Waldo Frank, Paul Rosenfeld, and Van Wyck Brooks, it had lasted less than a year, but long enough to hand down a bitter indictment of American culture and to proclaim a doctrine of salvation through the arts that was destined profoundly to influence the twenties. "It is our faith and the faith of many," wrote Oppenheim in a statement of purpose, "that we are living in the first days of a renascent period, a time which means for America the coming of that national self-consciousness which is the beginning of greatness. In all such epochs

[3] Pratt and Stanton: op. cit., pp. 2–3. See also the illuminating discussions by Robert Holmes Beck in "American Progressive Education, 1875–1930" (Unpublished Doctoral Thesis, Yale University, 1942), ch. vi; and "Progressive Education and American Progressivism: Caroline Pratt," *Teachers College Record*, LX (1958–9), 129–37.

[4] For the ideology of the Greenwich Village intelligentsia during the twenties, see Caroline Ware: *Greenwich Village, 1920–30* (New York, 1935), ch. viii. Miss Ware advances the intriguing observation that the pedagogy of the progressive schools in the Village was a response to the changing character of the urban intellectual family.

the arts cease to be private matters; they become not only the expression of the national life but a means to its enhancement. . . . It is the aim of *The Seven Arts* to become a channel for the flow of these new tendencies; an expression of our American life." [5] Subsequent issues had spoken in dithyrambic phrases of a revival in literature, painting, music, and architecture that would ultimately overcome the bleakness and spiritual aridity of contemporary industrial civilization.

The Seven Arts ceased publication in the autumn of 1917, after its vehement anti-war stand had caused its sponsor, Mrs. A. K. Rankine, to withdraw her financial support. But the intoxicating idea of artist-leaders who would unleash the true spiritual forces in American life persisted, adding tremendous vitality to an expressionism that was already pervading every realm of aesthetic discussion. These were the years when Isadora Duncan and Martha Graham were attempting to develop an expressionist dance, Max Weber and John Marin, an expressionist painting, Charles Ives, an expressionist music, Alfred Stieglitz, an expressionist photography, and William Zorach, an expressionist sculpture. However different their individual perceptions of the creative act, these men and women were one in their revolt against the shallow aestheticism of formal Victorian art, and one, too, in their determination to express in new and imaginative forms intuitive truths about the world.[6]

When Caroline Pratt spoke of the child as artist, she was really propounding a pedagogical version of the expressionist credo.[7] And when this credo was applied to education on a broad scale—particularly by artist-teachers like Hughes Mearns and Satis Coleman of the Lincoln School, Lucy Sprague Mitchell and Willy Levin of the City and Country School,

[5] *The Seven Arts*, I (1916–7), 52–3. The story of *The Seven Arts* and its influence on educational theory is told in Mark Phillips: "*The Seven Arts* and Harold Rugg: A Study in Intellectual History" (Unpublished Master's Thesis, Columbia University, 1961).

[6] The standard work in expressionist aesthetics remains Sheldon Cheney: *Expressionism in Art* (New York, 1934). See also Harold Rugg: *Foundations for American Education* (Yonkers, 1947), Part IV.

[7] Probably the most fulsome version of the credo was propounded in Floyd Dell's novel: *Were You Ever a Child?* (New York, 1919).

and Florence Cane of the Walden School—it seemed to release an extraordinary flow of genuinely first-rate student art. One need only examine the poems, the music, the painting and sculpture, and the theater sets that fill the pages of *Progressive Education* during the twenties to sense the elation progressives themselves must have felt.[8] And when the artist-teachers were asked the clue to their success, they answered as if in chorus: Take the lid off youth! "The creative impulse is within the child himself," proclaimed Rugg and Shumaker in *The Child-Centered School*. "No educational discovery of our generation has had such far-reaching implications. It has a twofold significance: first, that every child is born with the power to create; second, that the task of the school is to surround the child with an environment which will draw out this creative power." [9] Once the creative power had been released in a generation of American children, the authors held little fear of the future.

Granted these superb results, though, the doctrine of creative self-expression raised the same problems in education as it raised elsewhere.[1] Taken up as a fad, it elicited not only first-rate art, but every manner of shoddiness and self-deception as well. In too many classrooms license began to pass for liberty, planlessness for spontaneity, recalcitrance for individuality, obfuscation for art, and chaos for education—all justified in the rhetoric of expressionism. And thus was born at least one of the several caricatures of progressive education in which humorists reveled—quite understandably—for at least a generation.

V

Expressionism was one of two major intellectual streams that converged to form the child-centered pedagogy of the twenties;

---

[8] See Gertrude Hartman and Ann Shumaker, ed.: *Creative Expression* (New York, 1932).

[9] Rugg and Shumaker: op. cit., pp. 228–9.

[1] Many of these problems are portrayed with photographic accuracy in Rachel Crothers's delightful satire *Expressing Willie* (1923), reprinted in Richard A. Cordell: *Representative Modern Plays* (New York, 1930).

the other, of course, was Freudianism. Freud himself had given a general exegesis of psychoanalytical theory at Clark University as early as 1909, dealing with the phenomenon of neurosis, the unconscious and its mechanisms, the problem of sexuality, and the interpretation of dreams; and notices of his lectures had been carried in a number of influential medical and lay journals.[2] But it was really through the efforts of Dr. A. A. Brill, who had first come upon Freud's work at Jung's clinic in Zurich, that Freudian ideas were slowly disseminated to the larger American public. During the years after 1909, Brill worked indefatigably not only at the business of translating Freud's voluminous writings, but also at publicizing them among the intelligentsia.[3] A welcome visitor at Mabel Dodge's famous Greenwich Village salon, he frequently discussed "the new psychology" and its revolutionary implications for social thought with the brilliant coterie that gathered there. Walter Lippmann took account of these discussions in his *Preface to Politics* (1914) and later wrote some of them up for *The New Republic* (1915). In the summer of 1915 Max Eastman published a rather thorough popular account in *Everybody's Magazine,* and that same year Edwin Holt published *The Freudian Wish and Its Place in Ethics,* exploring the impact of Freudianism on philosophy. By the time of the war psychoanalysis was a popular topic of conversation around the Village; Floyd Dell, whom Frederick Hoffman has called "the great apostle of psychoanalysis in Greenwich Village," reported that the jargon was already common, and intellectuals were using it to justify a revolt against traditional social and moral standards.[4]

[2] The lectures are discussed in Ernest Jones: *The Life and Work of Sigmund Freud* (3 vols., New York, 1953–7), II, 56–66, 211–4 and reprinted in James Strachey, ed.: *The Standard Edition of the Complete Psychological Works of Sigmund Freud* (24 vols., London, 1953–   ), XI, 7–55.

[3] For Brill's role in the dissemination of Freudian ideas, see C. P. Oberndorf: A *History of Psychoanalysis in America* (New York, 1953); and Frederick J. Hoffman: *Freudianism and the Literary Mind,* 2nd ed. (Baton Rouge, 1957), ch. ii.

[4] Hoffman: op. cit., p. 58. For the role of psychoanalysis in the ideology of the intelligentsia, see Caroline Ware: op. cit., ch. viii; and John C.

While the Freudians had dealt indirectly with education from the beginning—after all, psychoanalysis is itself an effort at re-education—it was not until after the armistice that books began to appear specifically applying Freudian doctrine to pedagogy. The year 1919 saw the publication of *The Mental Hygiene of Childhood* by William A. White, Superintendent of St. Elizabeth's Hospital, and *The Child's Unconscious Mind* by Wilfrid Lay, a secondary school teacher who had taken a Columbia doctorate at the same time as Thorndike. That same year Brill delivered a series of lectures at New York University "primarily intended for those who are occupying themselves with problems of education and psychology." 1922 brought *Psycho-Analysis in the Service of Education* by the Swiss Freudian Oskar Pfister, *The New Psychology and the Teacher* by H. Crichton-Miller, an English psychiatrist, and *Psychoanalysis in the Classroom* by George H. Green, carrying a friendly introduction by William McDougall of Harvard. During the next few years there was a spate of articles, reviews, and commentaries in popular and professional journals, and a whole generation of teachers and laymen was educated in the language and thought of Freudian pedagogy.

As might be expected, certain psychoanalytical concepts in particular dominated the discussion. Teachers were urged to recognize the *unconscious* as the real source of motivation and behavior in themselves and their students. The essential task of education was seen as one of *sublimating* the child's *repressed* emotions into socially useful channels. "A pedagogy informed by Psycho-analysis will make use of sublimation wherever possible . . . ," wrote Sandor Ferenczi. "The pedagogue of the future will not leave this development to chance, but on the basis of a knowledge of the instincts and the possibilities of their conversion will himself create the situations necessary for development, and thereby guide character formation into proper channels." [5] The real function of the teacher

---

Burnham: "Psychiatry, Psychology, and the Progressive Movement," *American Quarterly*, XII (1960), 457–65.

[5] Sandor Ferenczi: *Further Contributions to the Theory and Technique of Psycho-Analysis*, translated by Jane Isabel Suttie and others

was to provide as many opportunities as possible for successful sublimation during the child's formative years. Here, rather than in communicating specific bodies of information or rules of behavior, was the most important work of the school.

The Freudians were fond of pointing out that the classroom was inevitably an emotionally charged situation which only psychoanalytically sophisticated teachers could really comprehend. "In school," wrote Isador H. Coriat, an early president of the American Psycho-Analytical Association, "the teacher becomes a substitute for the father or mother of the child and in the emotional tie which exists between teacher and pupil, the earlier parent-child relationship is re-lived and re-animated. Teachers must understand their own unconscious, for if they fail to do so, they will never realize *why* they are acting in a certain manner towards the pupil or the effects of their daily contacts." Were teachers to comprehend the phenomena of *transference* and *identification*, the whole disciplinary pattern of the classroom would change drastically as "repressive authority" gave way to the effort to free pupils from earlier childhood *fixations* so that they might undergo normal development.[6]

Like Freud himself, some Freudians used these notions to try to develop more effective bases for rational behavior. Thus, Coriat argued that the real aim of education should be an understanding of the instincts, interests, and tendencies, "for through this knowledge, early fixations may be minimized, thus removing the chief obstacles to intellectual achievement." For others, however, Freudianism seemed to shift the focus of the school almost entirely to nonintellectual, or indeed, anti-intellectual, concerns. For these people preoccupation with repression became a denial of authority, preoccupation with the emotions, a denial of rationality. Once again license began to pass for liberty, and once again the cartoonists had a field day.

However much the analysts themselves may have influenced

(New York, 1953), p. 428. The statement was quoted in Barbara Low: *Psycho-Analysis and Education* (New York, 1928), p. 142 .

[6] Isador H. Coriat: "The Psycho-Analytic Approach to Education," *Progressive Education*, III (1926), 21.

pedagogy, it was probably the pedagogues who sought to borrow what they could from Freudianism who exerted the greatest influence on the progressive education movement. Chief among these was Margaret Naumburg, who founded the Children's School in 1915 and directed it through its formative years.[7] A graduate of Barnard College, where she had been an enthusiastic student of Dewey and President of the Socialist Club, Miss Naumburg had gone to Europe just before the war to study first with the Webbs at the London School of Economics and then, somewhat disillusioned with socialism, with Maria Montessori at the famous Case dei Bambini in Italy. Although the two ladies apparently did not get on too well, Miss Naumburg thought enough of Mme. Montessori's pedagogy to manage a Montessori kindergarten at the Henry Street Settlement on her return to New York. The Montessori Method proved dull and unimaginative, however, and in 1914, after a summer session under Marietta Johnson, she determined to open a school of her own in which the emotional side of education would have parity with the intellectual. The year 1914 also marked the beginning of a three-year period of analysis under the Jungian psychiatrists Beatrice Hinkle and A. A. Brill.

The name of the Children's School—it later became the Walden School—provides the key to its effort: to provide a curriculum built on the "apparently unlimited desire and interest of children to know and to do and to be." [8] The tension and stiff posture of the formal school was unconditionally rejected. "For to us," Miss Naumburg wrote in *The Child and the World*, "all prohibitions that lead to nerve strain and repression of normal energy are contrary to the most recent findings of biology, psychology, and education. We have got to

[7] For biographical data on Margaret Naumburg, see Robert Holmes Beck: "American Progressive Education, 1875–1930," ch. vii, and "Progressive Education and American Progressivism: Margaret Naumburg," *Teachers College Record*, LX (1958–9), 198–208.

[8] For the work of the Children's School, see Margaret Naumburg: *The Child and the World* (New York, 1928); Agnes de Lima: op. cit., ch. xi; and Bureau of Educational Experiments: *Bulletin No. 4* (New York, 1917).

discover ways of redirecting and harnessing this vital force of childhood in constructive and creative work." [9] So far as she was concerned, this meant abandoning a "false dependence on the blind authority of teacher or textbook," and seeking instead to nurture in children an indomitable "independence of feeling, thought, and action."

By applying the principles of analytical psychology, Miss Naumburg was convinced she could go beyond the constriction, the repression, and the misdirection of the group-minded mass methods of Mann and Dewey to a pedagogy that would preserve the vitality of each fresh crop of children entering the school.[1] Above all, she rejected social panaceas; they had died with the war. "Any possibility of an immediate social or economic escape from the impasse of our civilization," she wrote in 1928, "has become quite remote and rather absurd to me now. I've lived to see that whether people fought to save democracy or imperialism does not make the profound difference I had once hoped. I've wakened to a complete realization that all social and economic groups have identical methods of acting and reasoning, according to whether they are in or out of power." [2] One could do nothing with social groups as they then existed, she reasoned, but one could do something with individuals, who would later reform the groups they joined. The answer, then, lay not in social action but in individual transformation; hence individual transformation became the goal of the Children's School.

An enthusiastic journalist reported in 1925 that the school

[9] Naumburg: op. cit., p. 14.

[1] In view of the widespread assumption among intellectuals that public schools inevitably nurtured "group-mindedness," it is interesting to note the comment of one Italian resident of Greenwich Village concerning a local "progressive" experiment: "The program of that school is suited to the children of well-to-do homes, not to our children. We send our children to school for what we cannot give them ourselves, grammar and drill. The Fifth Avenue children learn to speak well in their homes. We do not send our children to school for group activity; they get plenty of that in the street. But the Fifth Avenue children are lonely. I can see how group experience is an important form of education to them." See Caroline Ware: op. cit., p. 343.

[2] Naumburg: op. cit., p. 40.

was really accomplishing its purpose. The Walden School, wrote Agnes de Lima in *Our Enemy the Child*, "has dared to create a child's world and then for the most part to stand aside and watch the children grow in it under the conditions of real freedom." [3] The staff made no attempt to define syllabi for given age levels; the effort instead was to provide a rich variety of resources in people and materials and let the children do the rest. For a time Lewis Mumford taught English, Hendrik Van Loon, history, and Ernest Bloch, music. During 1924 and 1925 the twelve-year olds studied anthropology with Alexander Goldenweiser of the New School for Social Research. Even with such men, however, the youngsters took the lead. Thus, Miss De Lima described enthusiastically the work in a science room where the students worked individually with the teacher off in a corner, his back to the room. Addressed by his first name, the teacher readily responded to student queries, but otherwise left the youngsters to their own devices. When Miss De Lima asked if he were the teacher, he responded: "Well, you can call me that; at least I'm here." [4]

In searching for a curriculum that would really nurture independence of thought and spirit, the faculty—at least half of whom had undergone analysis at the urging of Miss Naumburg—tended to emphasize the arts, arguing that artistic creations serve to bring into conscious life the buried material of the child's emotional problems. [5] In dramatics, in creative writing, and especially in painting the school really excelled. Under the leadership of Florence Cane, Miss Naumburg's sister, art became the great vehicle of self-expression, the crux of the student's search for self. Guided by her reading of Jung and by her own analysis under Dr. Hinkle, Mrs. Cane urged the children to paint exactly what they felt impelled to paint. "I never suggest a subject," she wrote in *Progressive Education*; "it is always the children's choice. If one says occasionally she doesn't know what to paint I talk with her until I draw

[3] De Lima: op. cit., p. 203.   [4] Ibid., p. 206.
[5] In a way, the union of psychoanalysis and expressionism was symbolized by Miss Naumburg's marriage for a time to Waldo Frank.

out of her a hidden wish for something she wanted to do but was afraid she couldn't." [6] Whatever doubts one might have about the soundness of the theory, the results were impressive.

If the school's art program was an acknowledged success, its attempt to provide enlightened sex education raised the expected questions. Here the faculty's effort was to respond as simply, as directly, and as accurately as possible to the "natural curiosity" of the children, starting with nature-study and progressing to frank discussions of the biological, physiological, and ethical aspects of the sex act. A 1929 essay by C. Elizabeth Goldsmith, one of the two codirectors who succeeded Margaret Naumburg, described the program in some detail, including reports of parent-teacher conferences, transcripts of conversations in the nature-study laboratory, case studies of disturbed children, and one characteristic story of a four-year-old who stayed overlong in the lavatory, and when offered assistance by one of the teachers, replied: "Oh Terry, I was so long because I'm getting so interested in my underneath!" [7] One assumes that Walden's parents applauded such efforts, though Miss Naumburg implies that some of them needed constant reassurance. In any case, the caricaturists once again had a field day.

In the end, Freudianism made a direct impact upon a relatively limited circle of educators. However much the Greenwich Village intelligentsia may have enthused over "the new psychology," most teachers remained ignorant of its technicalities, having been educated in the doctrines of connectionism. The really pervasive influence of Freudianism on pedagogy came rather indirectly through gradual public acceptance of the psychoanalytical image of the child. It is more than symbolic that G. Stanley Hall was the man who first brought Freud to the United States to lecture, for the immediate effect of Freudianism was to accelerate changes in the emotional climate and authority pattern of the classroom that the child-

[6] Florence Cane: "Art in the Life of the Child," *Progressive Education*, III (1926), 159.

[7] C. Elizabeth Goldsmith: "Sex Consciousness in the Child," in V. F. Calverton and S. D. Schmalhausen, ed.: *Sex in Civilization* (New York, 1929), pp. 621–40.

study movement had already set in motion. Ultimately, it is here, rather than in any effort to build explicitly Freudian schools, that we must locate the real pedagogical significance of Freudianism during the interbellum period.

V I

Social reformism may well have disappeared from the child-centered rhetoric of the twenties, but it certainly did not die. Rather, it manifested itself in a variety of pedagogical theories, the most influential of which contended that social change had so accelerated under the conditions of industrialism that teachers could no longer be certain of the problems their students would ultimately confront, and hence, that they could best serve the cause of reform by teaching a method of thinking generally applicable to all social problems. The method, of course, was problem-solving, as outlined by Dewey in *How We Think* (1910) and *Democracy and Education* (1916).

Of the leading progressives of the twenties, none was so closely associated with this position as William Heard Kilpatrick of Teachers College. More than any other, he has been acclaimed over the years as the great interpreter and popularizer of Dewey's theories during the time when Dewey himself had moved on to the concerns reflected in *Human Nature and Conduct* (1922), *Experience and Nature* (1925), and *The Public and Its Problems* (1927). Kilpatrick's first encounter with Dewey had come in a course at the University of Chicago in 1898, and he reminisces, interestingly enough, that he failed to find there the leadership he had hoped for.[8] Nine years later, however, as a graduate student at Columbia, he once again enrolled for work under Dewey, and this time there resulted a dramatic reorientation in his outlook. "Prof. Dewey has made a great difference in my thinking," he

[8] Samuel Tenenbaum has written an authorized but completely uncritical biography: *William Heard Kilpatrick* (New York, 1951). For a friendly, though not uncritical, assessment of Kilpatrick's contribution, see John L. Childs: *American Pragmatism and Education* (New York, 1956), ch. vii.

wrote in his diary during the spring of 1909. "I came here wishing to do for education what I conceived Caird had done for religion; I leave having given up the whole attitude of desire of a closed universe." [9] Dewey, in turn, is said to have written to John A. MacVannel, Kilpatrick's major professor: "He's the best I ever had." [1]

A native Georgian, Kilpatrick had come to Columbia in the hope of returning eventually to the South. However, a part-time position teaching the history of education at Teachers College in 1909 marked the beginning of a lifelong association with that institution. His first published works were essentially critical. Thus, *The Dutch Schools of New Netherland and Colonial New York* (1912), his doctoral dissertation, was a useful rearguing of the controversy over whether New York or Massachusetts had established the first North American school. Likewise, *The Montessori System Examined* (1914) and *Froebel's Kindergarten Principles Critically Examined* (1916) were critical estimates of pedagogical theories that had commanded widespread interest in the United States. Kilpatrick himself remained dissatisfied with these early efforts. "My success is much better as a teacher and student than as an investigator or original thinker," he noted in 1914. "While I hope to become well known as a teacher and a writer, I have no reason for hoping to make specific contributions to thought. . . . Occasionally, I have an additional insight following Dewey or others; and I am able to organize perhaps above most; so that I am a little hopeful of what I may do." [2]

In the spring of 1918 Kilpatrick set out to prepare an essay called "The Project Method," a theoretical analysis setting "the purposeful act" at the heart of the educative process. He suffered the tortures of the damned in drafting it, finding that in addition to his usual difficulties in writing, he was consumed with discouragement and doubt about his enterprise. The article appeared the following September in the *Teachers College Record* and literally catapulted him to national and

[9] Kilpatrick Diary, May 14, 1909.
[1] Ibid., May 19, 1909.   [2] Ibid., January 1, 1914.

international fame. Over 60,000 reprints were destined to circulate during the next twenty-five years.

Kilpatrick's effort in his celebrated essay was to present "wholehearted purposeful activity proceeding in a social environment"—his formal definition of the project—as a pedagogical principle capable of reconciling Thorndike's connectionism with the Deweyan view of education. By emphasizing *purposeful activity*, activity consonant with the child's own goals, he sought to take maximum account of Thorndike's law of effect, thereby enhancing both direct and concomitant learning. And by locating this activity in a *social environment* he believed he could facilitate certain ethical outcomes, since moral character was for him "the disposition to determine one's conduct and attitudes with reference to the welfare of the group." In a curriculum reorganized as a succession of projects he saw the best guarantee of sharpened intellectual acumen and enhanced moral judgment. "The regime of purposeful activity," he concluded, "offers . . . a wider variety of educative moral experiences more nearly typical of life itself than does our usual school procedure, lends itself better to the educative evaluation of these, and provides better for the fixing of all as permanent acquisitions in the intelligent moral character." [3]

Kilpatrick's major work of the twenties, *Foundations of Method* (1925), is for all intents and purposes an elaboration of "The Project Method." Proceeding from Dewey's notion of the school as a refined social environment, Kilpatrick was sharply critical of traditional education. "As I see it," he wrote, "our schools have in the past chosen from the whole of life certain intellectualistic tools (skills and knowledges), have arranged these under the heads of reading, arithmetic, geography, and so on, and have taught these separately as if they would, when once acquired, recombine into the worthy life. This now seems to me to be very far from sufficient. Not only do these things not make up the whole of life; but we

[3] William H. Kilpatrick: "The Project Method," *Teachers College Record*, XIX (1918), 330 .

have so fixed attention upon the separate teaching of these as at times to starve the weightier matters of life and character. The only way to learn to live well is to practice living well." [4] The problem of method, then, was to design an education as "life-like" as possible, one that would militate for the better life by actually teaching the business of living.

Once again, Kilpatrick set "wholehearted purposeful activity" at the heart of the new education. Such activity, he explained, always proceeds through four steps: purposing, planning, executing, and judging. The important thing in education is to insure that the purposes and plans are those of the learners, not the teachers.

"Don't you think that the teacher should often supply the plan," asks one of the participants in Kilpatrick's dialogue. "Take a boy planting corn, for example; think of the waste of land and fertilizer and effort. Science has worked out better plans than a boy can make." Kilpatrick answers, "I think it depends on what you seek. If you wish corn, give the boy the plan. But if you wish boy rather than corn, that is, if you wish to educate the boy to think and plan for himself, then let him make his own plan." [5] Although Kilpatrick steadfastly refused to countenance any dichotomy between "teaching subjects" and "teaching children," time and again in *Foundations of Method* he ends up choosing "boy" over "corn," with the result that his method, willy-nilly, inevitably favors the child-centered approach.

This tendency is clearly strengthened by his trenchant attacks on what he called extrinsic subject matter, or subject matter "fixed-in-advance." Thus, for example, Kilpatrick reiterates Dewey's contention that the sweeping economic and social changes set in motion by scientific and industrial advance necessitate a complete transformation of the school.

"As long as people looked on the world as fixed and static [one of Kilpatrick's discussants explains], they had children mainly memorize answers to the questions they

[4] William Heard Kilpatrick: *Foundations of Method* (New York, 1925), pp. 108–9.
[5] Ibid., p. 212.

might expect to meet. Memorization and adjustment to a fixed order, habituation I mean; that's the kind of school we should expect, and that's the kind they did have. . . ."

"Yes [Kilpatrick responds], and if people face a rapidly shifting and changing world, changing in unexpected ways and in unexpected directions, then what?"

"Why, their education would stress thinking and methods of attack and principles of action rather than merely what to do. Yes, I see it. Such a school would try to make self-reliant and adaptable people; and are not the better of our newer schools working just exactly along these lines?" [6]

Although there was bound to be continuity, one could never be certain of where changes would occur. And so in morality, in taste, and in action intelligence was the only guide. Schools would have to teach methods of investigating and confirming truth rather than the truth itself, or, as the slogan developed, they would have to teach children *how* to think, not *what* to think. Hence the subject matter of the curriculum could never be set in advance; it would have to be that knowledge called to the fore by the students in pursuing the activities they themselves had purposed and planned.

Now, however unmistakable the Deweyan cast about these formulations, there are differences with Dewey that become crucial. Dewey too talked about problem-solving as central to education, and Dewey was deeply concerned with the interests and purposes of children.[7] But Dewey's enterprise in tho

---

[6] Ibid., pp. 266–7. The argument as advanced here is the crux of Kilpatrick's other major work of the twenties: *Education for a Changing Civilization* (New York, 1926). There he contended: "While we cannot be sure of the precise details of future social problems—and for real education it is better so—we can within limits foretell that certain unsolved problems will press for solution. These with proper care for age and interest will furnish excellent subject-matter for the kind of study demanded . . . for the unknown future. Here methods of attack upon that shifting future can be worked out and learned. That teachers do not know the answers to the problems will help, not hurt, the work." p. 110.

[7] Dewey also spoke approvingly of the project method in *The Way out of Educational Confusion* (Cambridge, 1931), though he did warn

Laboratory School was to develop a new curriculum to take the place of the old—a new body of subject matter, better ordered and better designed, that would begin with the experience of the learners and culminate with the organized subjects that represented the cumulative experience of the race. Kilpatrick, on the other hand, in his emphasis on future uncertainty and in his unrelenting attack on subject matter "fixed-in-advance," ultimately discredits the organized subjects and hence inevitably shifts the balance of Dewey's pedagogical paradigm toward the child. The resultant child-centered emphasis calls to mind the very position Dewey himself rejected, first in *The Child and the Curriculum* (1902) and later in *Experience and Education* (1938).

There are those who contend that whatever the significance of Kilpatrick's writings, it was ultimately as teacher and lecturer that he exerted his greatest influence. He was by all reports a master at working with classes numbering in the hundreds, managing to engage individuals to the point where both their ideas and their teaching techniques changed radically. And however much he personally detested indoctrination, he seems to have been extraordinarily effective in making disciples. In all he taught some 35,000 students from every state in the Union at a time when Teachers College was training a substantial percentage of the articulate leaders of American education. Any competent teacher occupying the senior chair of philosophy of education at the College between 1918 and 1938 would have exerted a prodigious influence on educational theory and practice. In the hands of the dedicated, compelling Kilpatrick, the chair became an extraordinarily strategic rostrum for the dissemination of a particular version of progressive education that still remains the dominant image of the movement within the American teaching profession.

Kilpatrick's emphasis on method as the quintessential element in progressive education was paralleled in the work of Boyd Henry Bode at Ohio State University. For almost a

---

that this was not the only alternative to the traditional curriculum and that too many projects were already so trivial as to be miseducative.

quarter-century, between 1921 and 1944, Bode made Columbus a center of graduate studies in philosophy of education
that clearly rivaled New York in quality and importance. But
his work never had the influence of Kilpatrick's in his own lifetime. The reasons are partly personal, partly institutional, and
partly accidental. Bode considered himself a contemporary of
Dewey, a man who was indebted to Dewey but who
had arrived at many of Dewey's insights independently
through a "lifelong process of personal reconstruction"; [8] Kilpatrick was unabashedly the disciple, the interpreter of Dewey.
Bode spent his lifetime as a progressive critic of progressive
education; Kilpatrick was far more the exponent who entered
the pedagogical lists bearing his own particular theories, methods, and techniques. In the last analysis, it may well be that
Bode's work more closely resembled the spirit and temper of
Dewey's, while Kilpatrick's, in seeking to make Dewey's ideas
manageable for mass consumption by the teaching profession,
ended by transforming them into versions quite different from
the originals.

Bode published three principal works during the 1920's:
Fundamentals of Education (1921), *Modern Educational
Theories* (1927), and *Conflicting Psychologies of Learning*
(1929). The *Fundamentals* is frankly Deweyan in orientation
—"I have been under constant and very extensive obligation to
the writings of Professor John Dewey"—and reads like an exe-
gis of *Democracy and Education* for normal school students.
But it already sounds some of the critical themes destined to be
central in Bode's work. If education is to have a part in the

___

[8] Bode wrote John L. Childs of his own education in 1951: "Educa-
tionally speaking, what ails the modern man chiefly is, I think, the fact
that his cultural heritage is a gosh awful mess of which he is unaware.
This is what ailed me, and I think I am in this respect fairly representative. I got myself straightened out pretty well—I think so anyway—because I had extraordinary advantages. One was light teaching schedules
in high-grade universities. Another was that I could take years and years
to 'reconstruct' myself, which is an unbelievably slow process when a
person does it on his own. I'll never forgive my teachers for letting me
flounder without the help to which I was entitled." Childs: op. cit.,
p. 249. For an assessment of Bode's contribution, see ch. ix of the Childs
volume.

building of a better world, he notes, it must have a clear and definite sense of direction, and no amount of statistical manipulation can take the place of hard philosophical thought in determining this direction. "Unless we know where we are going there is not much comfort in being assured that we are on the way and traveling fast. The result is likely to be that much of our progress is but seeming. We do not escape the bondage of the past merely by issuing an Emancipation Proclamation. The old contrast between the cultural and the practical has tended to persist, with little appreciation of the fact that the cultural could be practical or that the practical could be cultural. Vocational subjects on the one hand, and literature and science on the other, are still left too much without a significant social context; and to the extent that this is the case, the aims of culture are defeated and the idea of democracy is left to take care of itself. If education is to discharge its rightful function of leadership, it must clarify its guiding ideals." [9]

Modern Educational Theories is a brilliant critique of progressive pedagogy in the twenties; it was too little read in its time and is virtually forgotten today. A searching, thoughtful, humane volume, it comes as close as any to what Dewey might have written had he continued to concentrate on pedagogy in the interbellum era. After criticizing the Bobbitt-Charters school of scientific curriculum-making, pegging it for the conservative theory it was, Bode goes on to discuss the project method. Insofar as the emphasis on wholehearted purposeful activity is antiformalistic—insofar as it militates against perfunctory, mechanical, and meaningless schoolwork—Bode is all for it. But to use the project method as a guide to curriculum-making is another matter, for Bode is convinced that "the emphasis on initiative and purposeful activity frequently suggests a mystic faith in a process of 'inner development' which requires nothing from the environment except to be let alone." [1] And this sort of pedagogical naturalism he rejects out

[9] Boyd H. Bode: *Fundamentals of Education* (New York, 1921), pp. 241–2.

[1] Boyd H. Bode: *Modern Educational Theories* (New York, 1927), p. 163.

of hand as a naive belief in spontaneous intellectual germination that misconstrues the real nature of thought.

Bode goes on from these criticisms to his own view of education; his emphasis, not surprisingly, is on the cultivation of intelligence. Education must fit the individual to reorganize his world. Science, literature, art, vocation, all can serve as means to this end. Culture, he argues with Dewey, means "the capacity for constantly expanding in range and accuracy one's perception of meanings." And it is the business of the school to turn people toward culture, toward that kind of life in which powers, sensitivities, perceptions, and appreciations continually expand. When all people are encouraged to live such a life, and when conditions make that life universally possible, the ideal democracy will have come into being.

Having thus restated the Deweyan view of education, Bode was far less specific than Kilpatrick as to how method and curriculum might be adjusted to meet new demands on the school. But he wrote *Conflicting Psychologies of Learning* to clarify the issues, contending insightfully that in matters of educational practice there is no such thing as psychology, but only psychologies. Like Dewey, he was convinced that any new pedagogy would have to make the individual pupil the point of departure; moreover, to emphasize individual creativity in the classroom, older social ideals of conformity would have to change. The teacher would need as equipment "not only the quality of sympathy and discernment to understand individual pupils and the ability to understand the ends that are to be attained, but also the further quality of resourcefulness, which will enable him to keep his methods or procedures flexible so as to suit the needs of the occasion." [2]

And here Bode departed in a very significant way from Kilpatrick. For he believed no one general method could incorporate all the findings of the new psychology. Sensitive to the fact that even projects could become formalized—as indeed they did—he argued that methods and procedures would have to vary in terms of the content and the children to be taught.

[2] Boyd H. Bode: *Conflicting Psychologies of Learning* (New York, 1929), p. 284.

They would be sometimes free and informal, sometimes controlled and regulated, but never stereotyped. Quoting from V. T. Thayer, Bode analogized to the scoutmaster, "who leads his group into a country familiar to himself but filled with adventure and wonderful opportunities for the moral and intellectual development of his followers." Once again, one cannot help but call to mind the phraseologies of Dewey in *The Child and the Curriculum.*

With the differences between Bode and Kilpatrick thus stated, perhaps it is well to re-emphasize that on the larger spectrum of progressive opinion they were closer than most. They disagreed initially in their interpretation of connectionism, but Kilpatrick gracefully acknowledged in 1948 that he was instructed in this matter by Bode.[3] And they disagreed significantly in those elements within the progressive tradition each sought to emphasize. But they were one with Dewey in the contention that education is a continuing reconstruction of experience, one in the faith that the supreme task of education is the development of a civilization dedicated to the progressive liberation of intelligence, and one in the belief that schools could never accomplish this task without a thoroughgoing transformation in spirit as well as practice. Certainly these similarities are at least as important as any differences in estimating the wider significance of Bode and Kilpatrick in the progressive education movement.

V I I

What Malcolm Cowley called radicalism—the protest against the evils of capitalism—also flourished in the pedagogical milieu of the twenties, though in a decidedly minor key. Thorstein Veblen's trenchant critique of business domination of the

[3] William Heard Kilpatrick: "Bode's Philosophic Position," *Teachers College Record*, XLIX (1947–8), 271. Kilpatrick's acknowledgment came in an address on November 10, 1947, marking the award to Bode of the William H. Kilpatrick Award for Distinguished Service in Philosophy of Education.

universities, *The Higher Learning in America* (1918), was widely read, as were Upton Sinclair's two polemics *The Goose-Step* (1923) and *The Goslings* (1924), and John Kirkpatrick's more objective study, *The American College and Its Rulers* (1926). Harold Stearns's sardonic symposium, *Civilization in the United States* (1922), tore into the schools and colleges for borrowing mass-production methods, as did the several education supplements of *The New Republic* that appeared during the decade. The theme of all these works was essentially the same: that until the dead hand of the businessman was removed from the schools and the control of education placed with the teachers, where it belonged, it was folly to talk about liberating intelligence or reforming the curriculum.

No one advanced this Veblenian critique of American education more insistently or more insightfully than George S. Counts.[4] A midwesterner trained under Albion Small and Charles Judd at the University of Chicago—his doctoral dissertation reflected work with arithmetic scales on the 1915 survey of the Cleveland schools—Counts early abandoned the science of education for a career of social analysis and criticism. In 1922 he published a study of high-school dropouts called *The Selective Character of American Secondary Education* in which he demonstrated beyond the shadow of a doubt that despite ideals to the contrary, high schools were perpetuating glaring inequalities along race, class, and ethnic lines. "At the present time," Counts maintained, "the public high school is attended quite largely by the children of the more well-to-do classes. This affords us the spectacle of a privilege being extended at public expense to those very classes that already occupy the privileged positions in modern society. The poor are contributing to provide secondary education for the children of the rich, but are either too poor or too ignorant to avail themselves of the opportunities which they help to provide."[5] What was called for was a transformation of the spirit and the program of the public high school that would make of

---

[4] Counts's life and work are discussed in. Childs: op. cit., ch. viii.

[5] George Sylvester Counts: *The Selective Character of American Secondary Education* (Chicago, 1922), pp. 151–2.

it truly a people's institution; pedagogical traditions and administrative conveniences would have to adapt themselves to the conditions of life if the cause of democracy was to be truly served.

In 1927 Counts published *The Social Composition of Boards of Education*, and a year later, *School and Society in Chicago*; both represented pioneering inquiries into the politics of American education. The first was a scathing critique of class bias in American school board membership—the domination of local boards by merchants, lawyers, physicians, manufacturers, and bankers—coupled with a plea for franker recognition of political and social conflict in the making of educational policy. The second was an analysis of the political controversy that had resulted in the dismissal of William McAndrew as Chicago's superintendent of schools in 1927. Here Counts pilloried the notion that education should be "above politics," contending that the real need was rather to devise machinery to make the school more responsive to politics. "Let the employing groups, the working-classes, the women's clubs, the more important religious sects, and other groups have their representatives on the board," he advised. "Recourse to the methods of indirection would then be unnecessary, and genuine differences would be brought out into the clear sunlight of discussion." [6] In addition, he lashed out against unintelligent, untrained teachers, calling for a superior, well-organized profession that could speak clearly and authoritatively on matters of educational policy. In the absence of a powerful profession, he warned, even the most representative control in the world could not save the schools from the demoralizing buffeting of partisan popular passions. [7]

[6] George S. Counts: *School and Society in Chicago* (New York, 1928), p. 357.

[7] Counts tied together here the two political thrusts of the progressive education movement: a more effective populism reflected in a more representative board, and a more effective professionalism reflected in a well-organized, scientifically trained teaching group. The two themes have too rarely come together in writings on the politics of American education. Thus, more recently, James Bryant Conant in *The Child, the Parent, and the State* (Cambridge, 1959) argues that the road to educational improvement is ultimately through citizen activity, while Myron

Finally, in 1929 Counts synthesized these various criticisms into the general position that was to mark his work for the next three decades. The ultimate problem, he argued in a slender volume called *Secondary Education and Industrialism*, was that educational reform in the United States had never really come to terms with the realities of industrial civilization, and until it did it would continue to be a piecemeal process that dealt at best with superficialities. "A school cannot become socially progressive by mere resolve," Counts insisted. "Unless it reaches down into the substratum of society and taps the deep-flowing currents of social life, it can only be another pedagogical experiment, of interest to the academician but destined for an early grave. The founding of a progressive educational movement is as difficult as the founding of a progressive political party, and for much the same reasons. If it is not rooted in some profound social movement or trend, it can be but an instrument of deception. In spite of all of the well-intentioned efforts of intellectuals, society stubbornly chooses its own roads to salvation." [8] Schools could never be the prime movers of an industrial civilization, but they could, by remaining close to society, become the cultural instruments for humanizing it. Here was an educational opportunity unparalleled in history; did teachers dare to take up the challenge? [9]

Certainly Counts's writings were among the outstanding progressivist statements of the twenties; yet few thought of them as progressive education. Attention was too exclusively focused on the child-centered schools that Rugg and Shumaker celebrated in their 1928 volume. With the onset of the depression, though, radicalism no longer seemed passé, in politics or in pedagogy; indeed, it was bohemianism that appeared a little out of date. Socially conscious notions of progressive education, disparaged by the avant garde of the twenties as conform-

Lieberman in *The Future of Public Education* (Chicago, 1959) contends that professionalism is the only answer. See my review in *The Progressive* for April, 1960.

[8] George S. Counts: *Secondary Education and Industrialism* (Cambridge 1929), p. 68.

[9] The dare was reiterated in much bolder form in Counts's pamphlet, *Dare the School Build a New Social Order?* (New York, 1932).

ist moralizing, now seemed very much to the point. Gradually, the reformist emphasis that had been central in Dewey's earlier writings came once again to the fore.[1]

Although this new emphasis appeared fairly generally in the pedagogical formulations of the 1930's, particularly in the work of the National Education Association's Educational Policies Commission, the American Historical Association's Commission on the Social Studies, and the American Youth Commission of the American Council on Education, it has been commonly—and quite properly—associated with Teachers College. The origins of this association lie in a small informal discussion group that seems to have gathered around Kilpatrick in 1927. Harold Rugg reminisces that although he and Kilpatrick had begun in the early twenties to discuss systematically the reconstruction of the American school, they were very much alone in the enterprise. Then, one by one, other like-minded progressives began to join the Teachers College faculty: George S. Counts, John L. Childs, R. Bruce Raup, Goodwin Watson, Edmund deS. Brunner, Jesse Newlon, Harold F. Clark, and F. Ernest Johnson. Regularly from 1927 to 1934, intermittently from 1934 to 1938, and then regularly again for several years, this group—joined by Dewey and others for varying periods of time—carried on bimonthly discussions under the chairmanship of Kilpatrick.

"Not only was the sky the limit—," Rugg recounts, "the uttermost reaches of man's changing culture of industrialism were too, and every new angle in the scholars' researches and interpretations in the sciences and the arts. We all revolutionized our personal understandings and our theories of society and the culture and of the bio-psychology of the 'Whole Person,' and got glimpses of the meaning of the concepts of the new field-relativity physics." By 1932 the group had achieved an

[1] Oscar Cargill's intriguing observation in *Intellectual America* (New York, 1941) that the leading spirits of the twenties were "iconoclasts" while the leading spirits of the thirties were "shapers" is relevant here, as is his caution against allowing October 29, 1929, to mark too sharp a break in American intellectual history. See also Leo Gurko: *Angry Decade* (New York, 1947) and Cowley's Epilogue in the 1951 reissue of *Exile's Return*.

extraordinary measure of intellectual cohesion, taking its stand "for the general conception of a welfare state, agreeing fairly closely on the constituents of the democratic principle." Interestingly enough, Rugg adds: "All but two of us [probably Counts and Childs] avoided membership or participation in political organizations, confining our efforts to studying and critically appraising platforms, creeds, programs, and strategies. This was practicing what we preached—vigorous adult education." [2]

The first major formulation of this new "frontier" position as it came to be called came in a book entitled *The Educational Frontier* (1933). The work did not emanate directly from the Teachers College group, but rather from the lugubrious process by which professional yearbooks are born into the world. In 1932 the National Society of College Teachers of Education appointed a committee consisting of Kilpatrick (chairman), Bode, Dewey, Childs, Raup, H. Gordon Hullfish, and V. T. Thayer to produce a statement of philosophy of education appropriate to the contemporary "socio-economic situation." All of the authors were of the Deweyan persuasion; four of the seven were members of the Kilpatrick group. It is no surprise that the volume which emerged is for all intents and purposes a restatement of Dewey's philosophy appropriate to depression America.

The thesis of *The Educational Frontier* is that given the vast social transformation wrought by science and technology, it becomes the task of education "to prepare individuals to take part intelligently in the management of conditions under which they will live, to bring them to an understanding of the forces which are moving, [and] to equip them with the intel-

---

[2] Rugg: *Foundations for American Education*, pp. 578–82 and *The Teacher of Teachers*, p. 225. The Kilpatrick Group also provided the nucleus of the John Dewey Society for the Study of Education and Culture, organized in 1935. The Society published a number of significant yearbooks, among them William H. Kilpatrick, ed.: *The Teacher and Society* (New York, 1937); Harold B. Alberty and Boyd H. Bode, ed.: *Educational Freedom and Democracy* (New York, 1938); Harold Rugg, ed.: *Democracy and the Curriculum* (New York, 1939); and George E. Axtelle and William W. Wattenberg, eds.: *Teachers for Democracy* (New York, 1940).

lectual and practical tools by which they can themselves enter into direction of these forces." [3] The key to obtaining such an education is threefold: a massive adult program that will build political and educational support for a radically revised school curriculum by creating an education-conscious public wise in the realities of industrial civilization; a completely reoriented professional education, heavily emphasizing history and the social sciences, that will alert teachers to the pressing social issues of the day; and a drastically altered administrative system under which teachers and students can play a much more central role in the actual management of the schools.

Two chapters, jointly conceived by Dewey and Childs and written by Dewey, state the underlying philosophy of education. The plea is for a school program conceived in the broadest terms, one which has "definite reference to the needs and issues which mark and divide our domestic, economic, and political life in the generation of which we are part." [4] As with Dewey's educational outlook from the beginning, the call is for a school close to life, one that will send into society people able to understand it, to live intelligently as part of it, and to change it to suit their visions of the better life. Once again, he sees changes through education as "correlative and interactive" with changes through politics. "No social modification, slight or revolutionary," he warns, "can endure except as it enters into the action of a people through their desires and purposes. This introduction and perpetuation are effected by education." [5] How reminiscent of Dewey's 1897 credo that "education is the fundamental method of social progress and reform."

Like *The Child-Centered School* before it, *The Educational Frontier* is the characteristic progressivist statement of its decade. And of all the major postwar versions of progressive education, it is far and away the most hardheaded and realistic. Yet one puts the volume down with an uneasy sense that for all its sophistication, it is curiously naive in matters of program. It is not merely that teachers—hardly the most courageous segment

[3] William H. Kilpatrick, ed.: *The Educational Frontier* (New York, 1933), p. 71.
[4] Ibid., p. 36.   [5] Ibid., p. 318.

of the population—are asked to assume Herculean responsibilities. It is rather that for all the talk about reform, there are pitifully few specific leads regarding curriculum, methods, and
organization, the day-by-day concerns that so condition the life
of any school. Despite constant preachments about practical-
ity, the volume stops short at the very point of what to do.
And so a generation of teachers found themselves reading the
Kilpatrick of *The Educational Frontier* to guide their social
outlook, and the Kilpatrick of *Foundations of Method* to guide
their practice, however much the two Kilpatricks may have
differed. It was a problem that the reformist pedagogues of the
thirties never really solved, however vehement their criticism
of their predecessors' softheadedness.

If *The Educational Frontier* was the characteristic progressive statement of the decade, *The Social Frontier* was the characteristic progressive journal. The plan for a magazine that
would afford the reformist group a vehicle of public discussion
was initially advanced by two graduate students at Teachers
College, Mordecai Grossman and Norman Woelfel, and subsequently taken up by the Kilpatrick group. The eventual list
of twenty-seven directors read like a progressive *Who's Who* of
the thirties: Kilpatrick was chairman, and Counts was selected
as editor, though Grossman and Woelfel did much of the work
as associate editors during the early, and most vigorous, years.

The first issue of October, 1934, carried a policy statement
pointing to the death of laissez-faire individualism and the
concomitant rise of collective planning and control and urging
frank exploration of the meaning of these changes for social
and educational reconstruction. As one might expect, the view
of education was exceedingly broad: "THE SOCIAL FRON-
TIER acknowledges allegiance to no narrow conception of
education. . . . On the contrary, it includes within its field of
interest all of those formative influences and agencies which
serve to induct the individual—whether old or young—into the
life and culture of the group. It regards education as an aspect
of culture in process of evolution. It therefore has no desire to
promote a restricted and technical professionalism. Rather does
it address itself to the task of considering the broad role of edu-

cation in advancing the welfare and interests of the great masses of the people who do the work of society—those who labor on farms and ships and in the mines, shops, and factories of the world." [6]

The magazine remained remarkably faithful to its self-image, particularly during its early years. It attracted to its pages some of the leading progressives of the era, and achieved a level of polemical journalism that frequently rivaled *The Nation* and *The New Republic*. Dewey, and later Kilpatrick, contributed regular articles; Charles Beard, Lewis Mumford, William F. Ogburn, Henry Pratt Fairchild, Bruce Bliven, Robert M. Hutchins, Harry Gideonse, and Merle Curti were sometime contributors. The January, 1935, issue carried a splendid discussion of indoctrination by Lawrence Dennis, F. J. Sheed, Earl Browder, George Coe, Boyd Bode, Harry Gideonse, and George Counts; the March issue two months later included a penetrating symposium by Dewey, Beard, Rugg, Newlon, and Childs on the political role of the school administrator. Indeed, throughout the thirties, *The Social Frontier* remained the only journal specifically addressed to teachers that openly and forthrightly discussed the ideological problems of an ideological age.

Counts, Grossman, and Woelfel continued to edit the journal until 1937. Under their leadership circulation rose rapidly, standing for several years at around 5,000. But expenses outran income, and there were continued deficits that had to be met by the sponsoring group. George Hartmann of Teachers College assumed the editorship in 1937, and during his three-year tenure there were repeated overtures to the Progressive Education Association to take over the journal and publish it as an official organ. In 1939, after a succession of refusals, the PEA accepted, stipulating that the name be changed to *Frontiers of Democracy* and that a new Board of Editors be constituted

---

[6] *The Social Frontier*, I (1934–5), 4–5. Woelfel wrote to *The New Republic*, LXXX (1934), 217, that the new journal "represents a crystalization of so-called left-wing thinking upon social and economic matters within the educational profession."

to remove the taint of radicalism. These conditions met, a new magazine emerged, edited from 1939 to 1943 by Kilpatrick and James L. Hymes, Jr., an official of the PEA, and then for a few final issues by Harold Rugg before the PEA's governing board killed the journal in executive session. By that time, though, the magazine had lost much of its function as a sounding board for reformist elements within the profession; the worst of the depression was over, and World War II was already overshadowing issues with which the journal had traditionally dealt.

To look back on *The Social Frontier* is to contemplate a fascinating episode in the history of American reform. It was without a doubt one of the authentic progressive voices of the thirties; and while its excellence was not consistent, its vitality was. Indeed, there is an urgency about its formulations that quickly calls to mind the grim years during which it came into being. Yet for all the fear of a "pedagogic party, through which Columbia University would control the United States," [7] the journal, like *The Educational Frontier* before it, proved curiously ineffective in changing practice. Those who have studied the evolution of New Deal educational policy, for example, report no influence from *The Social Frontier*; if the National Education Association had little effect on Roosevelt's policies, *The Social Frontier* had less.[8] And except in the realm of the social studies, classroom procedures too remained relatively untouched. The gulf between theorist and practitioner was already widening in the educational profession, and the brilliant polemicists of *The Social Frontier* were simply finessed by less imaginative men with more specific pedagogical nostrums to purvey. In the end, the journal left one more image of progressive education in the public mind, the caricature of the radical pedagogue using the school to subvert the American way of life—a sardonic commentary on a group that spent the

[7] *Time*, July 17, 1935, pp. 48–9.
[8] Harry Zeitlin: "Federal Relations in American Education, 1933–1944: A Study of New Deal Efforts and Innovations" (Unpublished Doctoral Thesis, Columbia University, 1958).

best of its energies seeking to preserve that way of life amidst the chaos of the depression.[9]

VIII

Though Dewey himself turned to other concerns during the interbellum era, he remained deeply interested in educational reform, as his numerous essays attest.[1] Yet as the twenties progressed, he became less the interpreter and synthesizer of the progressive education movement, and increasingly its critic. As early as 1926, for example, he attacked the studied lack of adult guidance in the child-centered schools with a sharpness uncommon in his writing. "Such a method," he observed, "is really stupid. For it attempts the impossible, which is always stupid; and it misconceives the conditions of independent thinking." Freedom, he counseled, is not something given at birth, nor is it bred of planlessness. It is something to be achieved, to be systematically wrought out in cooperation with experienced teachers, knowledgeable in their own traditions. Baby, Dewey insisted, does not know best! [2]

Two years later, the same year *The Child-Centered School* appeared, Dewey used the occasion of a major address before the Progressive Education Association to reiterate his point. "Progressive schools," he noted, "set store by individuality, and sometimes it seems to be thought that orderly organization of subject-matter is hostile to the needs of students in their individual character. But individuality is something developing

[9] In view of the common—if somewhat ridiculous—charge that *The Social Frontier* was subject to communist influence, it is interesting to report Robert W. Iversen's observation in *The Communists and the Schools* (New York, 1959) that some communist educational theorists in the United States actually borrowed from Counts and *The Social Frontier* group the very un-Marxian idea that schools could play a crucial role in changing the social order. The idea never became too popular, though, and the run-of-the-mill proletarian novels of the thirties generally pilloried the American *via sacra* of education.

[1] Many of them are reprinted in John Dewey: *Education Today* (New York, 1940).

[2] His essay, originally published in the *Journal of the Barnes Foundation*, is reprinted in John Dewey *et al.*: *Art and Education*, 2nd ed. (Merion, Pennsylvania, 1947), pp. 32–40.

and to be continuously attained, not something given all at once and ready-made." Far from being hostile to the principle of individuality, he continued, some systematic organization of activities and subject matter is the only means for achieving individuality; and teachers, by virtue of their richer and fuller experience, have not only the right but the high obligation to assist students in the enterprise.[3]

In 1929, in a trenchant little treatise called *The Sources of a Science of Education*, Dewey similarly questioned the scientism that had come to dominate some versions of progressive education. Education, he counseled, is ultimately an art rather than a science; it becomes scientific only as teachers attempt to be more intelligent about the goals they seek to serve and the practices they devise to attain these goals. "The sources of educational science," he pointed out, "are any portions of ascertained knowledge that enter into the heart, head and hands of educators, and which, by entering in, render the performance of the educational function more enlightened, more humane, more truly educational than it was before. But there is no way to discover what *is* 'more truly educational' except by the continuation of the educational act itself. The discovery is never made; it is always making. It may conduce to immediate ease or momentary efficiency to seek an answer for questions outside of education, in some material which already has scientific prestige. But such a seeking is an abdication, a surrender. In the end, it only lessens the chances that education in actual operation will provide the materials for an improved science." [4] Continuing to view philosophy as a generalized theory of education, Dewey contended that education was itself a more inclusive category than science and hence that education could never become a science in the common meaning of that term.

In reacting to the radicalism of the thirties, Dewey also remained remarkably faithful to his earlier formulations. R. Bruce Raup remarks that Dewey once told him that the dif-

[3] John Dewey: "Progressive Education and the Science of Education," *Progressive Education*, V (1928), 197–204. See also "How Much Freedom in New Schools?" *The New Republic*, LXIII (1930), 204–6.

[4] John Dewey: *The Sources of a Science of Education* (New York, 1929), pp. 76–7.

ference between his earlier and his later pedagogical writings was that the former dealt with society in general while the latter dealt with a particular society at a particular time. Even so, Dewey's call in the thirties was still for an education that would produce intelligent men and women sensitive to social issues and able to act on them. To George Counts's dare that teachers build a new social order, Dewey replied that in an industrial society with its multiplicity of political and educative agencies the school could never be the main determinant of political, intellectual, or moral change. "Nevertheless," he continued, "while the school is not a sufficient condition, it is a necessary condition of forming the understanding and the dispositions that are required to maintain a genuinely changed social order." [5] It would be revolution enough, Dewey once told the National Education Association, were educators to begin to recognize the fact of social change and to act upon that recognition in the schools.[6]

Dewey steadfastly opposed the teaching of fixed social beliefs. But he did contend that for schools to be progressive, teachers would have to select the scientific, technological, and cultural forces producing changes in the old order, estimate their outcomes, and see what could be done to make the schools their ally.[7] To some, of course, this was as crass a form of indoctrination as any; and Dewey was criticized on the one hand by conservatives who insisted that his notions would cast the school into an indefensible presentism and on the other by progressives who maintained that any adult guidance was an unwarranted imposition on children.

Dewey replied to both groups in what was destined to be his most important pedagogical work of the thirties, *Experience and Education* (1938). The volume is really a restatement of

[5] John Dewey: "Education and Social Change," *The Social Frontier* III (1937–8), 237, and "Can Education Share in Social Reconstruction?" Ibid., I (1934–5), 11–12.
[6] John Dewey: "Education for a Changing Social Order," in National Education Association: *Addresses and Proceedings, 1934*, pp. 744–52.
[7] John Dewey: "Education and Social Change," op. cit., and "Education, Democracy, and Socialized Economy," *The Social Frontier*, V (1938–9), 71–2.

aspects of his educational outlook in the context of the criticisms, distortions, and misunderstandings that had grown up over two decades. There is little fundamentally new, except perhaps the poignant tone. Progressive education, he suggests, should begin to think "in terms of Education itself rather than in terms of some 'ism about education, even such an 'ism as 'progressivism.' For in spite of itself any movement that thinks and acts in terms of an 'ism becomes so involved in reaction against other 'isms that it is unwittingly controlled by them. For it then forms its principles by reaction against them instead of by a comprehensive constructive survey of actual needs, problems, and possibilities."[8] By 1938, always the sensitive observer, Dewey could already perceive the ideological fragmentation that was destined to paralyze the movement.

Granted these successive clarifications of his position—they continued, by the way, right up to his death in 1952—one wonders at the incredible distortions that have marked contemporary assessments of Dewey's role in the development of progressive education. His writings are available for all to see. Some of his books have been translated into a dozen or more languages; many are still in print. Yet the grossest caricatures of his work have come from otherwise intelligent commentators in the United States and abroad. One is led to wonder why.

A number of explanations have been advanced. There is, for example, the frequently discussed problem of Dewey's style, described by Irwin Edman as "lumbering and bumbling," by Justice Oliver Wendell Holmes as "inarticulate," and by William James as "damnable; you might even say God-damnable."[9] In his war against dualism Dewey frequently construed words like "experience," or "growth," or "inquiry," or "inter-

---

[8] John Dewey: *Experience and Education* (New York, 1938), pp. vi–vii. The poignancy of the 1938 volume also runs through Dewey's last published essay on education, his Introduction to Elsie Ripley Clapp: *The Use of Resources in Education* (New York, 1952).

[9] See Irwin Edman: *John Dewey: His Contribution to the American Tradition* (Indianapolis, 1955), p. 23; Mark DeWolfe Howe, ed.: *Holmes-Pollock Letters* (2 vols., Cambridge, 1941), II, 287; and Harold A. Larrabee: "John Dewey as Teacher," *School and Society*, LXXXVII (1959), 379. Larrabee reports James's comment as part of a conversation with the late Edward G. Spaulding of Princeton.

est" to connote so much that they could be used by others to mean anything and everything. One need only follow the pedagogical wars over his statement that education is growth and that "there is nothing to which growth is relative save more growth" to establish the point. True, if one reads on in *Democracy and Education*, one can gain a fairly clear notion of what Dewey meant by growth. The difficulty is too many of those who quoted him did not read on, if, indeed, they read him at all. Yet the distortions of Dewey cannot be traced to language alone; for granted the semieducated among his proponents and detractors alike, there has been intelligent exegesis and intelligent criticism over the years, and despite Dewey's turgid prose, his arguments are, in the last analysis, comprehensible.

The problem of language, of course, is compounded by the problem of discipleship; and here Dewey suffers a fate common to all major thinkers. For almost by definition, influential ideas lend themselves to widespread appropriation, and the historian immediately faces the difficult task of allocating responsibility for the inevitable distortions. For example, to what extent were William Heard Kilpatrick's 35,000 graduate students actually influenced by Dewey? Or conversely, to what extent should Dewey be held responsible for the "project method" which Kilpatrick formulated and preached for four decades as the pedagogical extension of Dewey's philosophy? What was Dewey's responsibility within the movement for pointedly clarifying his differences with Kilpatrick? And in the absence of such clarification—Dewey was a gentle man—is Dewey responsible for whatever distortions of his thought Kilpatrick might have introduced? Now, if the same questions are raised with a host of other disciples once, twice, and thrice removed, the difficulties of assessing Dewey's significance become enormous. The problem cannot be solved merely by recourse to what Dewey actually said, though this may often clear the air. For a man's influence frequently exceeds his intentions, and sometimes in quite unexpected directions.

Finally, and perhaps most importantly, there is the problem of anachronism, a problem intensified by Dewey's own notion of philosophy as social criticism. Dewey, after all, was steeped in the thought of early twentieth-century urban Progressivism, and his writings on education must be seen as of a genre with those of Thorstein Veblen, Jane Addams, and Jacob Riis. Statements of educational aim, he once wrote, are matters of emphasis at a given time. "And we do not emphasize things which do not require emphasis. . . . We frame our explicit aims in terms of some alteration to be brought about." [1] In an era of excessive formalism Dewey wrote of bringing the school closer to life; in an age of educational inequity he talked of democratizing culture; at a time of unbridled economic indi- vidualism he called for a new "socialized education" that would further a spirit of social responsibility. The timeliness of his criticism was its greatest strength, and it should be no sur prise that a newly self-conscious teaching profession adopted him as its first major prophet.

Yet this very same timeliness has raised some of the greatest difficulties confronting present-day commentators. For though Dewey's "social spirit" was never meant to produce William Whyte's "organization man," in today's corporate age it seems to many to justify him; and however tortuous the intellectual line from *Democracy and Education* to the pronouncements of the Commission on Life Adjustment Education, that line can be drawn. The reviewer who wrote in 1916 that "in spite of Mr. Dewey's fine defence of individualism, his moral ideal is that of the 'good mixer'" was sounding a minority view at best; his criticism is more in fashion today. And however scan- dalous the charge that Dewey idealized organization men, or indeed, that their abundance can be traced to his influence on American education, the charge is not downed merely by quot- ing from the master's books. Rather there is need for further systematic study of Dewey's work and the context in which it proceeded, so that the changes he wrought can be distin- guished from the changes he explained—or indeed, criticized. In the absence of such study, Dewey will remain little more than a symbol of the educational hopes and despairs of the American people at any given moment in their history.

[1] John Dewey: *Democracy and Education* (New York, 1916), p. 130.

❧ 7 ❧

The Organization
of Dissent

THE year 1919 brought the progressive education movement an association. A young man named Stanwood Cobb had become interested in educational reform and had taken the lead, along with a number of like-minded Washington ladies, in forming an organization to advance the cause. We are told they cast about for a name, rejecting "The Association for the Advancement of Experimental Schools" and "The Association for the Advancement of the New Schools" in favor of "The Association for the Advancement of Progressive Education." [1] The winter of 1918–19 was given to drafting a statement of principles (e.g., "The aim of Progressive Education is the freest and

[1] Stanwood Cobb: "The Founding and Early Organization of the Progressive Education Association" (Unpublished Manuscript, Teachers College Library). The early history of the Association is told in Robert Holmes Beck: "American Progressive Education, 1875–1930" (Unpublished Doctoral Thesis, Yale University, 1942); and Berdine Jackman Bovard: "A History of the Progressive Education Association, 1919–1939" (Unpublished Doctoral Thesis, University of California at Berkeley, 1941). Of the two the Beck study is by far superior. Patricia A. Graham is currently writing a new history of the Association as a doctoral study at Columbia.

fullest development of the individual, based upon the scientific study of his mental, physical, spiritual, and social characteristics and needs") and a plan of organization. Charles W. Eliot accepted the honorary presidency, something of a coup for Cobb.[2] And on April 4, 1919, in the hall of the Washington Public Library, "upward of a hundred people" launched the new association on its historic career.[3] The participants left with the fires of reform burning brightly; and from that time forward—for better or worse, as the preachers say—the cause of progressive education was inextricably wedded to the fortunes of the Progressive Education Association.

"Our aim from the very beginning had in it little of modesty," Cobb reminisced in 1929. "We aimed at nothing short of reforming the entire school system of America."[4] The goal had apparently burned long and brightly in the mind of Stanwood Cobb. As a student at the Newton (Mass.) High School at the turn of the century, he had been "extremely bored by the recitation system, especially in the languages." But there was one English teacher, Andrew George by name, whose classes were "always on fire." "Under his tutelage were we ever bored with futile recitations? Not at all! Disposing of the question of marks by a ten-minute written quiz at the beginning of the lesson, he devoted the rest of the period to free discussion —a discussion which roved from the central theme of English literature out to any subject under the sun." Later on, when Cobb taught at Newton High, he did his best to imitate Andrew George's methods, and to strike similar fire. It is not surprising that when he found himself teaching English at the United States Naval Academy in 1917—"the acme of educational bureaucracy and Prussianism"—he chafed under the old order and yearned to found a school of his own.[5]

[2] Cobb's cousin, Ernest Cobb, describes the invitation to Eliot in *One Foot on the Ground* (New York, 1934), pp. 9–10, as does Stanwood Cobb in "The Romance of Beginnings," *Progressive Education*, VI (1929), 71–2.
[3] Baltimore *Sun*, June 1, 1919, p. A–14.
[4] Cobb: "The Romance of Beginnings," p. 68.
[5] Stanwood Cobb: "Biographical Notes" (Unpublished Manuscript, Teachers College Library).

Cobb began to inquire in educational circles. He visited an Organic School fashioned on the principles of Marietta Johnson by a Massachusetts acquaintance of his, Mrs. Milan V. Ayers, and "was fascinated with the atmosphere of freedom and self-direction on the part of the children." Shortly thereafter he heard Marietta Johnson herself at a lecture in Baltimore, and also met there the youthful headmaster of the newly organized Park School, Eugene Randolph Smith. Cobb further reports that he read *Schools of To-Morrow* and was delighted to learn of other schools carrying on experimental programs.

Mrs. Johnson, always the crusader, asked Cobb to form an educational association to back her work, and gave him a list of people in the Washington vicinity who might be interested in assisting, among them Mrs. Laura C. Williams, organizer and sponsor of the Washington Little Forum, who was destined to become an early supporter of the Progressive Education Association. For a while Cobb toyed with the notion of forming such an association, and perhaps an Organic School of his own; but he dropped the idea in favor of a broader sort of conference in which various experimental educators and parent groups might gather to exchange ideas. When he returned to Annapolis in the autumn of 1918, he outlined plans for this new association to Smith, envisioning an organization that would tap lay as well as professional interests. "I had a vision of the vast number of mothers, heartily dissatisfied with the present methods of education, reaching out for new and better methods—a splendid potential material upon which to found an educational reform movement." [6] Smith was enthusiastic, and the two men decided to go ahead with the idea.

During the winter of 1918–19 a small group began to meet regularly at the home of Mrs. Williams to lay plans for a new association that would furnish "a focus to the then scattered and ununified attempts at educational reform going on in different parts of the country." Cobb, Smith, and Anne E. George, directress of the Washington Montessori Schools, were regular participants. They were occasionally joined by Marietta Johnson; Hans Froelicher, professor at nearby Goucher Col-

[6] Cobb: "The Founding and Early Organization. . . ."

lege, May Libbey, a local kindergarten teacher; Mrs. A. J. Parsons, a Washington philanthropist; and Cobb's friend Mrs. Ayers. The group's main task, in addition to choosing a name and working out organizational paraphernalia, was to formulate a platform to guide the venture. The following statement of principles, clearly a synthesis of Smith's and Mrs. Johnson's ideas, emerged: [7]

1. *Freedom to Develop Naturally*

The conduct of the pupil should be self-governed according to the social needs of his community, rather than by arbitrary laws. This does not mean that liberty should be allowed to become license, or that the teacher should not exercise authority when it proves necessary. Full opportunity for initiative and self-expression should be provided, together with an environment rich in interesting material that is available for the free use of every pupil.

2. *Interest the Motive of All Work*

Interest should be satisfied and developed through: (1) Direct and indirect contact with the world and its activities, and use of the experience thus gained. (2) Application of knowledge gained, and correlation between different subjects. (3) The consciousness of achievement.

3. *The Teacher a Guide, Not a Task-Master*

It is essential that teachers believe in the aims and general principles of Progressive Education. They should be thoroughly prepared for the profession of teaching, and should have latitude for the development of initiative and originality. They should be possessed of personality and character; and should be as much at home in all the activities of the school, such as the pupils' play, their dramatic productions, and their social gatherings, as they are in the class-room. Ideal teaching conditions demand that classes be small, especially in the elementary school years.

[7] *Association for the Advancement of Progressive Education* (Washington, n.d.).

Progressive teachers will encourage the use of all the senses, training the pupils in both observation and judgment; and instead of hearing recitations only, will spend most of the time teaching how to use various sources of information, including life activities as well as books; how to reason about the information thus acquired; and how to express forcefully and logically the conclusions reached. Teachers will inspire a desire for knowledge, and will serve as guides in the investigations undertaken, rather than task-masters.

To be a proper inspiration to their pupils, teachers must have ample opportunity and encouragement for self-improvement and for the development of broad interests.

4. *Scientific Study of Pupil Development*

School records should not be confined to the marks given by the teachers to show the advancement of the pupils in their study of subjects, but should also include both objective and subjective reports on those physical, mental, moral, and social characteristics which affect both school and adult life, and which can be influenced by the school and the home.

Such records should be used as a guide for the treatment of each pupil, and should also serve to focus the attention of the teacher on the all-important work of development, rather than on simply teaching subject matter.

5. *Greater Attention to All That Affects the Child's Physical Development*

One of the first considerations of Progressive Education is the health of the pupils. Much more room in which to move about, better light and air, clean and well ventilated buildings, easier access to the out of doors and greater use of it, are all necessary. There should be frequent use of adequate playgrounds.

The teachers should observe closely the physical condition of each pupil, in co-operation with a school physician who should examine the children at stated intervals.

6. Co-operation Between School and Home to Meet the Needs of Child-Life

The school should provide, with the home, as much as is possible of all that the natural interests and activities of the child demand, especially during the elementary school years. It should give opportunity for manual experience for both boys and girls, for home-making, and for healthful recreation of various kinds. Most, if not all, of a child's studying should be done at the school and such extra-curriculum studies as a child may take should be at the school or home, so that there will be no unnecessary dissipation of energy.

These conditions can come about only through intelligent co-operation between parents and teachers. It is the duty of the parents to know what the school is doing and why; and to find out the most effective way to co-operate. It is the duty of the school to help the parents to a broader outlook on education and to make available all the resources of the school that can give information or help to the home.

7. The Progressive School a Leader in Educational Movements

The Progressive School should be a leader in educational movements. It should be a laboratory where new ideas if worthy meet encouragement; where tradition alone does not rule, but the best of the past is leavened with the discoveries of today, and the result is freely added to the sum of educational knowledge.

Given these guiding principles, the new organization was conceived as "primarily an association of parents and others who are interested in education as it affects the community and the nation." The planners were careful to indicate that though teachers would be eligible for membership the organization would *not* be professional in character. The initial executive committee and advisory council—the latter largely window dressing—included well-known authors like H. G. Wells, Herbert Quick, and Floyd Dell along with numbers of private-school representatives, a few professors of education, and several public-school men of the stature of Angelo Patri and William McAndrew. The organization was to serve as an exchange bureau and a propaganda agency; members were promised information via lectures, newspaper and magazine articles, and ultimately, a periodical. And finally, there were assurances that the association was not committed, and never would be, to any particular method or system of education. "In regard to such matters it is simply a medium through which improvements and developments worked out by various agencies can be presented to the public." [8]

Eighty-five members were enrolled at the organizational meeting on April 4, 1919, and their dues ($85), along with a gift of several hundred dollars from Mrs. Williams, provided the shoestring on which the work was launched. "We who organized the Progressive Education Association," Cobb reminisced years later, "were, for the most part, a handful of nobodies, educationally speaking. We had no appreciation or respect from the standard educational field, including the schools of education and the universities; nor did we greatly care about this—our support came from the lay public and a few outstanding liberals in education." [9] His view is essentially correct. The organization began on the fringes of the progressive education movement, with little sense of its traditions or accomplishments to date.[1] Of the leading progressives during the quarter-century before 1919, only Marietta Johnson played a central role at the founding. Dewey refused to join, and only later, after the death of Eliot, accepted the honorary presidency. The

[8] Ibid.

[9] Cobb: "The Founding and Early Organization. . . ."

[1] See, for example, Cobb's article, "A New Movement in Education," in the *Atlantic Monthly* for February, 1921 (CXXVII (1921), 227–34), in which he contends: "The term 'progressive,' as applied to a special and definite type of education, was first used two years ago, in Washington, D.C., by a group of people then organizing the 'Progressive Education Association'—an association which is bringing together educators working along certain new lines, and laymen interested in this kind of education."

early leaders paid a kind of spiritual obeisance to Pestalozzi, Froebel, and Parker, and they were aware of contemporary pedagogical protest in Europe. But their initial platform was at best a partial expression of progressive education circa 1919. Indeed, it may well be that only a fortuitous choice of name coupled with a large measure of enthusiasm made the Association the principal voice of the movement during the period between the wars.

There was plenty of enthusiasm in the early years; indeed, something of a religious fervor suffused the Association's activities that goes far in explaining its meteoric rise to prominence. Its annual conventions were well run and managed to attract some notable speakers. Angelo Patri was featured at the first in 1920; Charles Kettering, who had helped found the Moraine Park School in Detroit, addressed the second in 1921; Adolf Meyer, Professor of Psychiatry at Johns Hopkins, lectured the third. In addition, the practice was early introduced of having brief reports from the floor of promising progressive innovations in public and private schools, a device that inevitably heightened interest among the participants.[2]

In 1924 *Progressive Education* was founded with a large contribution from Mrs. Avery Coonley, a Washington philanthropist long interested in political affairs. No single activity during the Association's first decade proved so effective in attracting public interest and acclaim. Under the able editorship of Gertrude Hartman, the journal appeared first three times a year and then quarterly. Richly illustrated and extraordinarily attractive in format, it presented news of progressive experiments in the United States and in Western Europe. The most significant issues of the early years were those devoted to "creative expression" through art, literature, music, and dramatics, appearing in 1926, 1927, 1928, and 1931, respectively. Throwing their emphasis on "the child's own modes of self-expression through all of the creative arts, as opposed to more adult standards of finish and perfection," these numbers were quickly

[2] The proceedings of these conventions are reported in *Bulletins* No. 2, 6, 7, 8, 9, 13, and 14 of the Association.

snapped up as standard reference works and had much to do with creating a particular image of progressive education in the public mind.

From the beginning, the PEA was conscious of being part of an international movement, and it early sought ties with its counterparts abroad. One of the first *Bulletins* described the work of the International Bureau of New Schools, calling particular attention to Cecil Reddie's work at Abbotsholme, to Edmond Demolins's *École des Roches*, and to Hermann Lietz's *Landerziehungsheime*; while the initial issue of *Progressive Education* carried accounts of experiments with the Dalton Plan in England and with the Decroly Plan in Belgium. It was virtually inevitable that efforts would be made to develop some sort of tie with the New Education Fellowship in England, and the first feelers came in 1925 when Gertrude Hartman and Marietta Johnson attended an NEF conference in Edinburgh as representatives of the Association. But the PEA's Board balked at formal affiliation later that year, probably fearing the taint of pedagogical and political radicalism that attached to the NEF.[3] Nonetheless, a good deal of cooperation did ensue: some 200 American delegates attended the NEF conference at Elsinore, Denmark, in the summer of 1929, and in 1932 the PEA actually became the American section of the NEF.

An organization passes a turning point in its life when it takes on full-time executive personnel. Like many infant ventures, the PEA had drawn liberally upon its founders for administrative and clerical services. Cobb himself had served as Executive Secretary for the first two years with Mrs. Ayers's assistance, and others had contributed on an intermittent basis thereafter. Then, in the autumn of 1926, the Association found itself able to employ a professional Director to plan and supervise its multifarious activities. The first person to occupy the new post was Morton Snyder, an Amherst alumnus who had served successively as principal of the Scarborough School, the

[3] Progressive Education Association: Executive Committee Minutes, April 23–5, 1925, October 24, 1925 (Unpublished Manuscript, Teachers College Library).

Newark Academy, and the University of Chicago High School. Snyder's background in private education was quite represent-ative of the Association's leadership in the twenties, as was the background of his successor, J. Milnor Dorey. Needless to say, his coming enabled the Association to advance its activities at a pace that would have been prohibitive to his part-time prede-cessors.

In 1926, when Eliot died, the PEA was obliged to search for a new Honorary President. After some discussion the Executive Committee decided to invite John Dewey, writing him in 1927: "More than any other person you represent the philo-sophic ideals for which our Association stands." [4] Dewey ac-cepted and occupied the office until his death in 1952. Though he never became active in the Association, and was indeed sharply critical of its outlook in his presidential address of 1928,[5] his willingness to serve is undoubtedly indicative of how far the PEA had come during its first decade. Membership had risen to 6,000 by 1928, and the annual budget to $35,000. More importantly, perhaps, the Association had been enormously successful in advancing the cause of progressivism and the im-age of itself as the font of progressive education. Thus, Mar-garet Naumburg wrote of the 1928 convention: "Anything less than 'progressive education' is now quite out of date in Amer-ica. No one wishes any longer to be called conservative. Every shade, therefore, of radical, progressive, and mildly conserva-tive educator, from public as well as private schools, was to be found at the Eighth Conference on Progressive Educa-tion. . . ."[6]

Yet granted this, the leadership remained much as it had been at the founding, a small coterie of educators and laymen associated with a particular kind of private progressive school. Arthur E. Morgan of Antioch College, who had helped organ-ize Detroit's Moraine Park School, was the first President. He

[4] Ibid., April 30, 1927.
[5] John Dewey: "Progressive Education and the Science of Education," *Progressive Education*, V (1928), 197–204.
[6] Margaret Naumburg: "Progressive Education," *The Nation*, CXXVI (1928), 344.

was succeeded by Eugene Randolph Smith, and Smith in turn by Cobb, who was by that time headmaster of the Chevy Chase School. While the Executive Committee seemed more representative, the inner circle of the organization remained for all intents and purposes Cobb and the founders. Needless to say, the image of progressive education they proffered was intimately associated with the kind of school they represented. One need only peruse Smith's *Education Moves Ahead* (1924) or Cobb's *The New Leaven* (1928) to find it: it is the image of an eastern private preparatory school attempting to infuse vigor into its traditional studies at the same time as it broadens them to include a good deal of work in the creative arts. Once again, though, one looks in vain for the reformism that had been the leitmotif of the movement before 1919.

I I

I once asked Stanwood Cobb what happened to the Association after he gave up the Presidency in 1930. He replied: "They took it away from us." I asked him: "Who were *they?*" And he responded: "The people at Teachers College, Columbia University." Cobb's comment, the bitter reminiscence of all who found organizations and then find themselves displaced as the organizations expand in membership and purpose, is only partly true. He himself was succeeded in the Presidency by Burton P. Fowler, head of the Tower Hill School in Wilmington, and Fowler in turn was succeeded by Willard W. Beatty, Superintendent of Schools in Bronxville, New York. There were few people from Teachers College on the Executive Board at that time, or indeed, at any time. Yet Cobb's visceral sense that *something* happened to the PEA toward the end of the twenties is indeed accurate. The Association had done its work so well that the same profession that had refused to notice it in its infancy was now literally forced to pay heed. What had started as an association of parents in which teachers were "also eligible for membership" was slowly but surely transformed as professionals eager to identify themselves with the latest thinking in their field flocked to its standards.

The origins of the transformation probably lie in the Executive Board's growing conviction circa 1929–30 that the time had come to concentrate more heavily on extending and diffusing progressive education, and hence, to emphasize "action techniques" like commissions and committees.[7] During the course of the decade the Association created a Commission on Educational Resources, which worked closely with the National Education Association; a Commission on Educational Freedom, which concerned itself—though never very effectively —with the academic rights of classroom teachers; a Commission on Secondary School Curriculum; and a Commission on Human Relations. (The John Dewey Society also became a Commission in 1939.) At one time or another there were also Committees on Social and Economic Problems, Rural Schools, Home-School Relationships, Adult Education, Experimental Schools, Intercultural Education, Teacher Education, and Radio Education. Composed principally of educational experts, all of these agencies were more or less effective in carrying the Association's message to the profession; none, however, exerted anything approaching the influence of the Commission on the Relation of School and College. Long after the other efforts of the PEA have faded into history, its work may well remain as the Association's abiding contribution to the development of American education.

The Commission—and its celebrated Eight-Year Study— grew out of a discussion at the 1930 convention on how the high school might improve its services to American youth, or, put more bluntly, on how progressive education might be extended more effectively to the secondary level. We are told that suggestions were plentiful, but that apparently one difficulty lurked in the minds of all: the problem of college entrance requirements. Therefore, it was suggested that the Executive Board appoint a committee "to explore the possibili-

[7] The conviction, voiced frequently in the Board's minutes, runs through J. Milnor Dorey: "The Present and Future of the Association," *Progressive Education*, VI (1929), 73–6; and Burton P. Fowler: "President's Message," Ibid., VII (1930), 159. See also Fowler: "Progressive Education Enters a Second Phase," Ibid., IX (1932), 3–6.

ties of better co-ordination of school and college work and to seek an agreement which would provide freedom for secondary schools to attempt fundamental reconstruction." [8]

The Board responded the following October by naming a Commission on the Relation of School and College. Wilford M. Aikin, Director of the John Burroughs School, was chairman; Walter Agard, the Wisconsin classicist, Bruce Bliven of *The New Republic*, William S. Learned of the Carnegie Foundation, President Robert D. Leigh of Bennington, President Raymond Walters of the University of Cincinnati, and Professors Rugg and Watson of Teachers College were among the prominent members.[9] The group set to work immediately, and after a year of study came up with a report sharply indicting American high schools on a number of familiar counts: they had failed to convey a sincere appreciation of the American heritage; they did not prepare adequately for citizenship; they seldom challenged gifted students to the limit of their abilities; they neither guided nor motivated their pupils effectively; and their curricula were a hodgepodge of lifeless material unrelated to the real concerns of young people.

Based on its analysis, the Commission proposed an experiment in which some twenty leading secondary schools, public and private, would be invited to redesign their offerings with a view to achieving (1) greater mastery in learning, (2) more continuity of learning, (3) the release of the creative energies of students, (4) a clearer understanding of the problems of contemporary civilization, (5) better individual guidance of students, and (6) better teaching materials and more effective teaching. "We wish to work toward a type of secondary education which will be flexible, responsive to changing needs, and clearly based upon an understanding of young people as well as an understanding of the qualities needed in adult life," the

[8] Wilford M. Aikin: *The Story of the Eight-Year Study* (New York, 1942), p. 2. That Aikin, the chairman of the discussion, was primed for the occasion is manifest from his essay "The Prospect in Secondary Education," *Progressive Education*, VII (1930), 28–33. See also Aikin's account in *Progressive Education*, VIII (1931), 318–19.

[9] The Commission was originally named The Committee on College Entrance and Secondary Schools.

Commission declared. "We are trying to develop students who regard education as an enduring quest for meanings rather than credit accumulation; who desire to investigate, to follow the leadings of a subject, to explore new fields of thought; knowing how to budget time, to read well, to use sources of knowledge effectively and who are experienced in fulfilling obligations which come with membership in the school or college community." [1]

The proposal engendered a good deal of interest, and by 1932 an experiment had been projected along the lines suggested. Thirty secondary schools were invited to participate (one, Pelham Manor, later withdrew with the consent of the Commission) and over 300 colleges agreed to take part by waiving their formal admissions requirements for recommended graduates of these schools during the term of the experiment. As Director Aikin later recalled: "To some teachers even in the participating schools the Study was an unnecessary and dangerous innovation; to some college professors 'Progressive Education now had enough rope to hang itself'; and to some parents the Study was a source of uneasiness and dissatisfaction. But to most of the teachers in the Thirty Schools and to thousands of educators and parents throughout the nation, it held great promise for the future." [2]

The story of the experiment, which ran to 1940, hence the name Eight-Year Study, has been told fully and dramatically in five volumes issued in 1942.[3] It is a pity they appeared in the

[1] By permission from *The Story of the Eight-Year Study*, by Wilford M. Aikin, p. 144. Copyright, 1942. McGraw-Hill Book Company, Inc. The Commission's "Proposal for Better Co-ordination of School and College Work" is reprinted in Aikin: *The Story of the Eight-Year Study*, pp. 140–6.

[2] By permission from *The Story of the Eight-Year Study*, by Wilford M. Aikin, pp. 23–4. Copyright, 1942. McGraw-Hill Book Company, Inc.

[3] The series was entitled *Adventure in American Education*. Aikin's volume, *The Story of the Eight-Year Study*, summarized the enterprise; *Exploring the Curriculum*, by H. H. Giles *et al.*, summarized the work of the thirty schools; *Appraising and Recording Student Progress*, by Eugene R. Smith *et al.*, dealt with evaluation and records in the thirty schools; *Did They Succeed in College?* by Dean Chamberlin *et al.*, followed the graduates of the thirty schools through college, comparing

middle of a war, for they have never received the attention they deserve; even after two decades the challenge and excitement of the venture are apparent to the most casual reader. The schools approached the problem of curriculum revision in very different ways, conditioned, of course, by their varying circumstances. There were select private schools catering exclusively to culturally privileged children and slum schools enrolling an infinitely more diverse clientele. In some schools administrative leadership faltered; in others the faculty divided into warring cliques. In most the early efforts were clouded with uncertainty. As one teacher reminisced: "At the beginning of the Eight-Year Study all of us were rather frantic in our new undertaking. We wanted to do everything, omit nothing. That, of course, was wrong. We have learned so much from this fine experience that it makes one laugh sometimes at the way we started out."

Gradually, though, certain common reforms emerged. The standard subjects gained new vitality as teachers began to ask why certain traditional topics were being taught. Ancient barriers between departments crumbled as subject matter was reorganized around student interests and concerns. Many of the schools were extraordinarily successful in reaching out to their surrounding communities: the Winsor School made Boston "a kind of demonstration laboratory for elementary economics, civics, science and architecture"; students at Denver's East High School made motion pictures explaining the sources of the city's food supply; the Lincoln School sent classes to study the TVA and the industrial organization of the West Virginia coal fields. The excitement of the venture seemed to infuse the work of students and teachers alike. Student yearbooks spoke with self-conscious seriousness about the aims and ends of edu-

them with like graduates of other secondary schools; and *Thirty Schools Tell Their Story* presented an account by each of the schools of its participation in the study. In addition to these volumes, there are the printed reports of the Commission's annual conferences issued as supplements to *The Educational Record*, an occasional publication called the *Thirty Schools Bulletin*, and a mass of teacher reports, student publications, and sundry mimeographed materials from the thirty schools themselves.

cation, while teachers reported a heightened sense of participation in educational policymaking. Old lesson plans were scrapped, and new material introduced; there were conferences galore, to plan, to execute, to appraise. In short, there was all the thrill, the vigor, and the commotion that attaches to any reform enterprise—so much so that probably *anything* attempted would have succeeded better than what had come before.

The experiment might have been judged in many different ways; after all, the ultimate proof of an education is in the lives people lead when they have left the classroom. But the Commission was determined to test the results in terms of how well graduates of the thirty schools performed in college. Under the able leadership of Ralph W. Tyler of the University of Chicago, a team of measurement experts set out to compare these graduates with other college students of similar background and ability. The team's technique was to set up 1,475 pairs of college students, each consisting of a graduate of one of the thirty schools and a graduate of some other secondary school matched as closely as possible with respect to sex, age, race, scholastic aptitude scores, home and community background, and vocational and avocational interests.

In comparing the 1,475 matched pairs, the evaluation team found that graduates of the thirty schools (1) earned a slightly higher total grade average; (2) received slightly more academic honors in each of the four years; (3) seemed to possess a higher degree of intellectual curiosity and drive; (4) seemed to be more precise, systematic, and objective in their thinking; (5) seemed to have developed clearer ideas concerning the meaning of education; (6) more often demonstrated a high degree of resourcefulness in meeting new situations; (7) had about the same problems of adjustment as the comparison group but approached their solution with greater effectiveness; (8) participated more and more frequently in organized student groups; (9) earned a higher percentage of nonacademic honors; (10) had a somewhat better orientation toward choice of vocation; and (11) demonstrated a more active concern with national and world affairs.[4] Moreover, the graduates of the *more* experimental of the thirty schools showed even greater differences along these lines from the students with whom they were matched. In a summary report to the Association of American Colleges early in 1940 Dean Herbert E. Hawkes of Columbia College concluded: "The results of this Study seem to indicate that the pattern of preparatory school program which concentrates on a preparation for a fixed set of entrance requirements is not the only satisfactory means of fitting a boy or girl for making the most out of college experience. It looks as if the stimulus and the initiative which the less conventional approach to secondary school education affords sends on to college better human materials than we have obtained in the past."[5]

Much more might be written about the Eight-Year Study; suffice it here to say that its reports still bear careful study and analysis.[6] What is more to the point, perhaps, is the impact of the study on the Association itself. When the Commission was appointed in 1930, it represented only one among many diverse activities of the PEA. Very soon, however, the tail began to wag the proverbial dog as secondary education loomed ever larger in the life of the Association. The Commission on Secondary School Curriculum, created in 1933, was a direct outgrowth of the Commission on the Relation of School and College;[7] while the Commission on Human Relations was in

---

[4] Dean Chamberlin *et al.*: *Did They Succeed in College?*, pp. 207–8.

[5] By permission from *The Story of the Eight-Year Study*, by Wilford M. Aikin, p. 150. Copyright, 1942. McGraw-Hill Book Company, Inc. Dean Hawkes's report is reprinted in Aikin: *The Story of the Eight-Year Study*, pp. 147–50.

[6] Frederick L. Redefer, Executive Secretary of the PEA during the Eight-Year Study, reviewed the findings in 1950 in a study entitled: "The Eight-Year Study—Eight Years Later" (Unpublished Doctoral Thesis, Teachers College, Columbia University, 1952). Redefer visited each of the thirty schools and talked with its faculty; he reported that little remained of the experimental programs. See also Helmar G. Johnson: "Some Comments on the Eight-Year Study," *School and Society*, LXXII (1950), 337–9; Paul E. Diederich: "The Eight-Year Study: More Comments," Ibid., LXXIII (1951), 41–2; and Helmar G. Johnson: "Here We Go Again," Ibid., LXXIV (1951), 41–2.

[7] V. T. Thayer was Chairman of the Commission on Secondary School Curriculum; Caroline B. Zachry was Director of Research. The Commis-

turn an offshoot of the Commission on Secondary School Curriculum.[8] All three proved extraordinarily attractive to the foundations. The Carnegie Foundation made grants totaling $70,000 to the Eight-Year Study, while the General Education Board became interested in 1933 and contributed more than a million and a half dollars over the next eight years: $622,500 to aid the Commission on the Relation of School and College; $360,000 to aid the Commission on Secondary School Curriculum; $223,670 to aid the Commission on Human Relations; and $420,835 in support of the Association's research projects, summer institutes, and general administration.[9]

This torrent of money obviously strengthened the PEA—foundation funds had a way of sweetening programs then, as now—but it also accelerated its transformation into a professional organization. The PEA rapidly became the pedagogical bandwagon of the thirties as membership, which had fallen from 6,600 in 1929 to 5,400 in 1932 now climbed to 8,500 in 1937 and to a peak of 10,440 in 1938.[1] What the leadership failed to recognize, though, was that this apparent success would prove the Association's ultimate undoing. For the immediate effect of the foundation largesse was to make the Association almost completely dependent on outside aid; when that aid came to an abrupt halt in 1941, there was no financial program to take its place. More importantly, perhaps, the success of the Association in broadening its scope and thereby identifying itself as the authentic voice of progressive educa-

___

sion's principal publications were V. T. Thayer, Caroline B. Zachry, and Ruth Kotinsky: *Reorganizing Secondary Education* (New York, 1939); Caroline B. Zachry and Margaret Lighty: *Emotion and Conduct in Adolescence* (New York, 1940); and Peter Blos: *The Adolescent Personality* (New York, 1941).

[8] Alice V. Keliher was Chairman of the Commission on Human Relations. The Commission's principal publications were Alice V. Keliher: *Life and Growth* (New York, 1941); and Katherine Whiteside Taylor: *Do Adolescents Need Parents?* (New York, 1938). For a guide to the films it produced, see *The Human Relations Series of Films* (New York, 1939).

[9] The financial history of the Association to 1940 is told in Bovard: op. cit., ch. xv.

[1] Membership statistics fluctuated by as much as 2,500 during the course of a year as the files were culled, usually at the end of August.

tion inevitably attracted the same powerful elements in the profession that had initially shunned it. With them came the ideological conflicts that were racking the larger movement, the very conflicts the founders had so skillfully avoided during the twenties in their effort to create an organization genuinely receptive to all schools of pedagogical reform.

I I I

"Although our Association has never promulgated or approved anything like a program, either of principles or procedure," wrote President Burton Fowler in 1930, "we do endorse, by common consent, the obvious hypothesis that the child rather than what he studies should be the centre of all educational effort and that a scientific attitude toward new educational ideas is the best guarantee of progress." [2] For a decade the PEA had steadfastly maintained that progressive education could not be defined, that it was a "spirit," a "method," an "outlook," a "matter of emphasis." Indeed, so concerned were the leaders about being identified with any particular pedagogical position that in 1930 the statement of principles carried in each issue of *Progressive Education* was abandoned "lest any published doctrine be regarded as rigid or universal in an association that is actually fluid and progressive." [3] On the one hand, the Association refused to have a stated philosophy, because none was broad enough to encompass the "total spirit" of progressive education; on the other hand, the Association feared that any statement would freeze the continuing definition essential to progress. As Robert Beck has noted, some of the reformers may have been radicals, but the majority were inclined to make haste slowly.

[2] Burton P. Fowler: "President's Message," *Progressive Education,* VII (1930), 159.

[3] *Progressive Education,* VII (1930), 252. The seven principles of the founders appeared in *Progressive Education* from Volume I, Number 1, in April, 1924, through Volume VI, Number 1, in January, 1929. From Volume VI, Number 2, in April, 1929, through Volume VII, Number 1, in February, 1930, the journal carried a revised version of those principles referred to as "a statement of goals toward which the new education is tending."

This complacency might well have continued indefinitely had it not been rudely shattered by George S. Counts at the Association's 1932 convention. In an address entitled "Dare Progressive Education Be Progressive?" Counts attempted to turn the PEA to the reformism of the earlier progressive movement.[4] Progressive education to date, he granted, could boast some notable achievements: it had focused attention squarely on the child; it had recognized the fundamental importance of the interest of the learner; it had defended the thesis that activity lies at the root of all true education; it had conceived learning in terms of the growth of character; and it had championed the rights of the child as a free personality. All this was to the good, but it was not enough. The great weakness of the movement was that it had drifted into the hands of the upper middle class who had deliberately chosen to ignore the great transformation of society that had come in the wake of industrialism. "If Progressive Education is to be genuinely progressive," Counts warned, "it must emancipate itself from the influence of this class, face squarely and courageously every social issue, come to grips with life in all of its stark reality, establish an organic relation with the community, develop a realistic and comprehensive theory of welfare, fashion a compelling and challenging vision of human destiny, and become somewhat less frightened than it is today at the bogeys of *imposition* and *indoctrination*."

What would such a vision look like? Counts sketched it along lines partly Marxian, partly reminiscent of the traditional progressive critique of capitalist society. In the course of indus-

[4] George S. Counts: "Dare Progressive Education Be Progressive?" *Progressive Education*, IX (1932), 257–63. Counts combined the address with two others he delivered that year to form the pamphlet, *Dare the School Build a New Social Order?* (New York, 1932). Both the address and the pamphlet really accused the PEA of parochializing the progressive education movement. When Augusta Alpert, a New York psychologist, insisted in *The New Republic* "that the word *progressive* in progressive education never carried political or sociological implications or obligations; that it is descriptive only of educational techniques which *progress* in keeping with psychological and other relevant findings . . . ," Counts replied: "She's exactly what I'm talking about." *The New Republic*, LXXII (1932), 75.

trial transformation, capitalism had become cruel and inhuman, wasteful and inefficient; traditional ideals in economics, politics, morals, and religion had been rendered totally anachronistic. America had reached a point where competition would have to be replaced by cooperation, the urge for profits by careful planning, and private capitalism by some form of socialized economy. A new world was in the making in which the common man, for the first time in history, could rise above the meaninglessness of drudgery and toil.

The message for the PEA was clear. Unless the progressive education movement was ready, ostrich-like, to turn away from the burning problems of the age, unless it was ready to change its name to the "Contemplative Education Movement" or the "Goodwill Education Movement" or the "Hopeful Education Movement," it would have to contend with these new realities in a way hitherto eschewed by educators. It would have to "come to grips with the problem of creating a tradition that has roots in American soil, is in harmony with the spirit of the age, recognizes the facts of industrialism, appeals to the most profound impulse of our people, and takes into account the emergence of a world society." Teachers would have to use their collective intelligence to plan the best society possible, and then they would have to abandon their timid fear of indoctrination and forthrightly teach the vision of this new society in the schools. To refuse to do so, Counts concluded, would be to evade the most crucial, difficult, and important educational responsibility of the era.

The response to Counts's speech that evening in Baltimore was electric. Frederick Redefer reminisced years later: "There was a silence when he finished. A silence that speaks far more eloquently than applause. Dare the schools build a new social order? Many knew something had to be done. Many were willing to try. In hotel rooms and overflowing into corridors, teachers talked far into the morning. Dare the school? Dare teachers? More than any other speech ever given at an educational convention, this one stirred the minds of educators. The planned discussions of the next day were forgotten in the excitement. Even the Board of Directors called a special meeting to talk about this challenge." [5] Out of it all came a resolution presented at the annual business meeting two days later (February 20) by Nellie Seeds, Director of the Manumit School, Pawling, New York, and adopted by the delegates: "That we authorize and instruct the Chairman of the Board of Directors to provide for an Economics and Sociology Section or Committee within the organization, which shall promote within the schools and their affiliated bodies, thoughtful and systematic study of the economic and industrial problems confronting the world today." [6]

The Board of Directors and Advisory Board of the PEA met at Vassar College the following April and further discussed the problem. There was general agreement that the school of the future must be more than child-centered, that the development of individuality does not necessarily insure the development of social consciousness, and that the school "cannot build for social idealism and a living faith without coming to grips somewhere with the controversial issues perplexing our changing social order." One could sense the beginning of deep disagreements on just how these aims were to be served, but in the end a Committee on Social and Economic Problems was duly appointed with Counts as Chairman. [7]

Following the instructions of the membership, the Committee was charged with promoting within the schools and their affiliated agencies "thoughtful and systematic study of the economic and industrial problems confronting us today." The Directors must have known what they would get, for in addition to Counts, they appointed Merle E. Curti, John S. Gambs, Sidney Hook, Jesse H. Newlon, Willard Beatty,

[5] Frederick L. Redefer: "Resolutions, Reactions and Reminiscences," *Progressive Education*, XXVI (1948–9), 188. Augusta Alpert, on the other hand, noted that the address received "a cool reception." Loc. cit. Redefer's observation seems the more accurate in view of the emotionally charged responses to Counts's challenge reported in *Progressive Education* for April, 1932.

[6] *Progressive Education*, IX (1932), 289.

[7] Ibid., IX, 229–30. The Progressive Education Association incorporated in the District of Columbia on March 28, 1931, and in the incorporation the Executive Board became the Board of Directors. See Board of Directors Minutes, March 28, 1931.

Charles L. S. Easton, Goodwin Watson, and Frederick L.
Redefer to the Committee. Yet there was surprise, and a measure of consternation, when the Committee reported back to
the Board in March, 1933, and outlined a contemplated program. To begin, there was a long discussion of the relation of
national committees to the larger Association, one of those
interminable controversies in which academics revel in the
business of hairsplitting. Carleton Washburne questioned the
advisability of giving any committee's report the approval of
the Association, while Willard Beatty affirmed that no committee had the right to speak on behalf of the Association. A
motion was finally passed holding that committees functioned
"primarily for the purpose of furnishing to members of the Association channels of thought and action for the improvement
of education" and that "neither the Board of Directors nor the
Association is committed officially or as a whole to any philosophy, program or policy embodied in the report of any national
committee."

Having thus disavowed in advance the work of any of its committees, the Board heard the tentative oral report of Dr.
Counts. The reception was less than enthusiastic. One member
contended that the report was "too negative"; another thought
it was too socialistic and radical. Washburne reiterated his
point that the report would commit the Association to a philosophy and decried this, suggesting that teachers and superintendents who were members of the PEA were already under
heavy pressure and that their cause would not be advanced by
a report committing the schools to some new social utopia.
The inevitable resolution was proffered suggesting careful
study of the report when it was ready in final form, with provision for "further study and modification and possible ampli-
fication in the light of the various discussions at the Chicago
meeting of the Association and Board of Directors." [8] Apparently final approval of the Board and the Association was never
forthcoming, and in the spring of 1933 the report of the Committee on Social and Economic Problems was issued inde-

[8] Board of Directors Minutes, March 4, 1933.

pendently as a pamphlet entitled A *Call to the Teachers of the Nation*.[9]

It is no surprise that the report, written by Professor Counts, closely paralleled his earlier address. The scientific-industrial-technological revolution had transformed America, rendering older ideas of individualistic capitalism obsolete—indeed, positively harmful. To teach these ideas without the necessary reformulation was "extreme intellectual dishonesty," the Committee proclaimed. "It constitutes an attempt to educate the youth for life in a world that does not exist. Teachers therefore cannot evade the responsibility of participating actively in the task of reconstituting the democratic tradition and of thus working positively toward a new society. . . . They owe nothing to the present economic system except to improve it; they owe nothing to any privileged class except to strip it of its privileges."

The Committee also sketched the broad outlines of the new education. "It should aim to foster in boys and girls a profound devotion to the welfare of the masses, a deep aversion to the tyranny of privilege, a warm feeling of kinship with all the races of mankind, and a quick readiness to engage in bold social experimentation." It would have to aim at a "frank abandonment of the doctrines of *laissez-faire*, the administration for the common good of the means of production, and the wide adoption of the principle of social and economic planning." To achieve these ends, teachers would need to throw off the yoke of service to narrow social and class ideals and fight boldly for tenure, higher compensation, a voice in the formulation of educational policy, and a program of professional education that would equip them to accomplish these ends. And their instrument would have to be a powerful professional organization militantly devoted to social reconstruction.

[9] The pamphlet carried an introduction by President Beatty stating: "The publication of a report of such a Committee does not commit either the Board of Directors of the Association or the members of the Association, individually or as a whole, to any program or policy embodied in the report." The Committee of the Progressive Education Association on Social and Economic Problems: A *Call to the Teachers of the Nation* (New York, 1933), p. 5.

"In the defense of its members against the ignorance of the masses and the malevolence of the privileged, such an organization would have to be equipped with the material resources, the legal talent, and the trained intelligence necessary to wage successful warfare in the press, the courts, and the legislative chambers of the nation. To serve the teaching profession of the country in this way should be one of the major purposes of the Progressive Education Association."

It is difficult to assess the influence of the Counts Report. Redefer wrote years later that it caused little stir: teachers neither rose in revolt nor emancipated themselves from business control. Indeed, few of them read it in the first place.[1] The signers did find themselves listed in Elizabeth Dilling's *The Red Network*, along with Eleanor Roosevelt, John Dewey, Jane Addams, and other notables.[2] And here, probably, lies the clue to the Report's real effect: it branded the stigma of radicalism on the PEA, like it or not. It was a stigma destined to exert growing influence as the decade progressed.

Notwithstanding, the quest for a guiding philosophy continued, as the minutes of the Board of Directors testify *ad nauseam*. A typical discussion occurred in December, 1933, six months after the appearance of *A Call to the Teachers of the Nation*. President Willard Beatty led off with a plea for "a clearer understanding of the policies and purposes of the Association," a plea echoed in demands around the table for courageous leadership and for a clearer definition of the Association's responsibility in the realm of social action. There followed the usual cautions about "limiting the activities of the Association" and about becoming "so inclusive that we do not move but simply mill around"—both comments, by the way, from the same person—and about committing a large and diffuse membership to any single point of view. After several hours there was agreement that any new platform would require adequate financing, and that therefore new members would be needed. Having reached these conclusions,

[1] Redefer: loc. cit.
[2] Elizabeth Dilling: *The Red Network* (Kenilworth, Illinois, 1934), pp. 216–17. The Association itself was also listed.

the Board congratulated itself, taking due note that "a new chapter in the history of the Association" had begun. But, still, there was no philosophy.[3]

A special Committee on Educational Philosophy labored through a good part of 1936 in an effort to develop a statement of principles, but when W. Carson Ryan, Jr., later to be president of the Association, presented its report to the Board of Directors in September of that year, he declared that he "was not satisfied with the statement as it stood but confessed that he was puzzled as to the next steps." The Board after discussion unanimously recommended that "a study and statement of educational and social philosophy was urgent," and that therefore the matter should be taken up as a first order of business by the Association's regional advisory committees on policy.[4] These committees met in the spring of the following year, and as might have been expected, came no closer to conclusions than the Board itself.[5]

The effort to state a guiding philosophy in resolutions presented to the Association's annual conventions came to somewhat the same impasse. A typical set of resolutions, adopted unanimously in 1936, called for an extension of the Association's concern to all phases of education, for better articulation between the several levels of the school system, for more vigorous protection of academic freedom, for a clearer federal policy on youth affairs, and for facilitation of true democracy in the coming presidential campaign through the discussion of issues rather than personalities.[6] When the resolutions committee of 1938 sought to commit the PEA to "cooperate with all other organizations and movements whose objectives are

[3] "Meeting of the Executive and Advisory Boards of the Progressive Education Association, December 1–2, 1933" (Unpublished report bound with the Board of Directors Minutes).

[4] Board of Directors Minutes, September 26–7, 1936.

[5] "Report of the Board of Directors and the Advisory Board of the Mid-Western Policies Meeting of the Progressive Education Association, April 10–11, 1937" and "Report to the Board of Directors and the Advisory Board of the Western Policies Meeting of the Progressive Education Association, April 24–5, 1937" (Unpublished reports bound with the Board of Directors Minutes).

[6] Progressive Education, XIII (1936), 300–1.

likewise directed at the improvement of economic security through the use of our democratic institutions for controlling change" and to "cooperate with other groups in vigorously resisting the growth of authoritarianism and dictatorship in this country," [7] it could not even get the membership to approve such cooperation as "representing the general sense and mood of the members assembled this afternoon." [8]

Late in 1938 the Association appointed yet another Committee on Philosophy of Education, this one destined to produce the most fundamental statement of principles ever to issue from the PEA. Under the chairmanship first of Orville Brim, and later of Harold Alberty, both of Ohio State University, the Committee determined early to avoid both the extreme child-centered and the extreme social-reformist positions, attempting instead "to set a *direction* for education, the gradual realization of which may become the value by which education defines itself as progressive." The Committee's report, *Progressive Education: Its Philosophy and Challenge,*[9] is Deweyan from beginning to end. Insisting that any philosophy of education appropriate to the time needed both a clear view of human nature and a realistic understanding of the industrial crisis inherent in the depression, the Committee envisioned an education that would "make the culture aware of itself in order that its essential values may be made the more effective." The educated individual of this Report is Dewey's intelligent man, working cooperatively to solve the problems and reconstruct the values of the community to which he belongs. "We come, then, finally to the conclusion," the Committee affirmed, "that a reflective study of human nature, of natural forces, and of human experience, leads to the convic-

[7] "Report of the Resolutions Committee Presented to the Progressive Education Association at Its National Conference, 1938," *Progressive Education*, XV (1938), 275–83.

[8] "Minutes of the Meeting of the Members of the Progressive Education Association, held at the National Conference of the Association at the Hotel Pennsylvania, February 24, 1938" (Unpublished manuscript bound with the Board of Directors Minutes).

[9] Harold Alberty *et al.*: "Progressive Education: Its Philosophy and Challenge," *Progressive Education*, XVIII (1941), Special Supplement to the May Issue.

tion that *growth is the richest reward for the individual when, in concert with all others, he brings his intelligence and good will to the shared task of creating the values for which his culture is to strive.*"

Based on this general position, the Committee reiterated the usual homilies: "the school should be the exemplification of democratic living at its best"; "there should be greater recognition of and cooperation with other social agencies on the part of educators"; "education should deal directly with the values individuals hold as they enter educative experiences"; "those who teach should capture the dynamic character of individual behavior, not ignore it"; and finally, "if we are to entertain real hope for the progressive advancement of the democratic values, our present practices in the education of teachers must be reconceived and reconstructed."

The Committee's report was published in mimeographed form in May, 1940, and reprinted as a special supplement to the May, 1941, issue of *Progressive Education*. But, so far as can be determined, it was never formally adopted by the Association. Redefer recalls that on the one occasion when the Report was discussed by the membership in open session even the Committee could not agree on what it really meant. "The document was accepted for study," he noted poignantly, "but no one seriously considered adopting this or any other statement as the educational viewpoint of the Association." [1]

The persistent failure of the PEA to define a platform for itself and for the public had already begun to take a heavy toll by the end of the thirties. Criticism of progressive education was mounting; indeed, the year 1940 was something of an open season on progressive teachers, as national magazines, reacting to a decade of extremist pronouncements, lashed out against the movement as naively sentimental on the one hand, dangerously subversive on the other.[2] Moreover, reports flow-

[1] Redefer: loc. cit.
[2] See, for example, O. K. Armstrong: "Treason in the Textbooks," *The American Legion Magazine*, September, 1940, pp. 8–9, 51, 70–2; Ann L. Crockett: "Lollypops vs. Learning," *Saturday Evening Post*, March 16, 1940, pp. 29, 105–6; Ann L. Crockett: "Confessions of a Schoolteacher," *Catholic Digest*, November, 1940, pp. 14–17; Margaret

ing in from the field testified to growing opposition from teachers and administrators as well. Barely ten years after Stanwood Cobb had confidently charged his colleagues with extending "that splendid quality of education we call progressive" to every school and college in the land, the Association suddenly found itself in imminent danger of collapse. While members deserted in droves—a combination of war and dissatisfaction had shrunk the membership to a generous estimate of 6,500 by February, 1943 [3]—the leaders talked incessantly but took few significant actions.

"Has the Association accomplished what it set out to achieve?" "Should it continue as a separate organization?" These and similar questions of despair dominated Board discussions of the early 1940's. One group was frankly for closing up shop, contending that the time had come for participation as an active minority in larger and more powerful associations. Another argued that the only real need was for renewed vision and vigor. Still a third pressed for a united front of liberal organizations to resist the sharpening assault on progressive education. By the spring of 1944 the last position had prevailed, and the Board of Directors, sustained by a mail ballot of the membership, changed the name of the Association to American Education Fellowship,[4] contending: "We are proud of our tradition and our old name, but there is a new, broader job to be done that no other group is undertaking." [5] Regrettably, no reason was given as to why the new, broader job could not be undertaken under the old name.

Weymouth Jackson: "Has Your School Gone Fancy?" *Country Gentleman*, December, 1940, pp. 7–8, 54; B. G. Portwell: "Mumbo Jumbo in Education," *The American Mercury*, L (1940), 429–32; and Augustin G. Rudd: "Our Reconstructed Education System," *Nation's Business*, April, 1940, pp. 27–8, 93–4.

[3] Vinal H. Tibbetts: "Report to the Board of Directors of the Progressive Education Association, October 15, 1943" (Unpublished report bound with the Board of Directors Minutes).

[4] *Progressive Education*, XXI (1944), 201.

[5] Board of Directors Minutes, October 15–17, 1943. For a critical review of the motives and procedures involved in the change of name, see Archibald W. Anderson: "There Is Something in a Name," *Progressive Education*, XXXI (1953–4), 46–50.

In any case, the change had little real significance. The Association was by 1944 a shadow of its former self; indeed, there were so few members that for the first time in its history it adopted a formal policy statement.[6] The purpose of the American Education Fellowship, the statement proclaimed, "is first, to define good education; and then to enlist and direct the fighting interest of its parent, teacher, student and citizen membership to achieve this good education for all children and youth." And what was good education? "That process of learning and living by which the child becomes an understanding adult citizen with strong concern for the development of a world in which free men can and will act together, even fight if necessary, for the common good." Since good schools could only thrive in a good society, the statement continued, the AEF would be committed not only to educational reform, but to a broader program of social reform as well, one that would seek "adequate health services, recreation, good housing, a chance for assured employment, and democratic civic practices which will do away with religious and racial intolerance." After a quarter-century, the PEA finally had a creed; but few people cared, and even fewer read it.

The history of the Association from 1944 until its demise in 1955 is at best a footnote to all that had gone before, a rather sad tale of manifestos and revised manifestos, of little by way of program, of few members, of bedevilment with the same ideological issues that confronted all liberal organizations during the postwar decade, and of constant flirtation with bankruptcy.[7] A temporary resurgence followed a well-attended Thanksgiving conference in 1947, but it did not last.[8] There was a new statement of principles in 1948,[9] adopted by a small

[6] "Objectives and Program of the American Education Fellowship," Ibid., XXII (1944–5), 9–10.

[7] The Association was actually declared "insolvent" in an auditor's report of August 28, 1946; see "Meeting of New York Board Members, October 4, 1946" (Unpublished manuscript bound with Board of Directors Minutes).

[8] The Conference is reported in *Progressive Education* for January, 1948.

[9] See Theodore Brameld: "A New Policy for A.E.F.," Ibid., XXV (1946–7), 258–62, 269. President John J. DeBoer reported in the Jan-

mail vote of a small membership; this stood for three years until the Board of Directors established a committee on revision in 1951.[1] In 1953 the Board rescinded the 1948 statement and issued a new one to take its place.[2] But it was all much ado about nothing; the members, the money, and the vitality had long since vanished, and all that remained was a small coterie of academics arguing over creed. The group also changed its name back to Progressive Education Association that year, only to discover that the old name retained little of its former appeal. Finally in 1955 President H. Gordon Hullfish, realizing he was presiding over little more than a mailing list of institutional subscribers to *Progressive Education,* announced the end of the organization; two years later the journal too suspended publication. Except for the briefest items in newspapers of record, there is little evidence that the public or the profession concerned itself with either passing.

I V

To what extent did the Progressive Education Association incarnate the progressive education movement? To raise the question is to suggest the significant differences that distinguish social movements from the organizations that seek to advance them; it is to ponder what the church is to religion, what the party is to ideology.[3] There is no denying the im-

uary, 1948, issue of *Progressive Education* that the policy had been "unanimously" endorsed, but Carleton Washburne later indicated (Ibid., XXIX, 126) that in the mail ballot which "confirmed" the convention's action "relatively few votes were cast." That ideological considerations were central is clear from Washburne's comments, as from Roma Gans's in the same issue and from Isaac B. Berkson's and E. V. Sayers's in the January, 1953, issue. See also Lester B. Ball and Harold G. Shane: "The New A.E.F. Policy in Review," Ibid., XXV (1947–8), 110–12; and Willard B. Spalding: "The Stereotype of Progressive Education in the Profession and in the Public," Ibid., XXIX (1951–2), 42–50.

[1] Kenneth D. Benne: "Plan for Revising A.E.F. Policy Statement," *Progressive Education,* XXIX (1951–2), 50.

[2] Harold Rugg: "A Proposed Statement of Policy for Progressive Education," Ibid., XXXI (1953–4), 33–40, 43, and "A.E.F. Policy Statement Rescinded," Ibid., 57–8.

[3] Jerome Davis has argued: "Every social movement tends to traverse a cycle of change. First of all, there arises a tangible need, and some

measurable service the PEA performed in the cause of educational reform. It gave the movement structure, voice, and visible form; it infused the movement with vitality and enthusiasm; and it provided the movement with dedicated leadership. In pamphlets, books, conferences, conventions, committees, and institutes that touched the lives of thousands upon thousands of teachers, the Association spread the progressive word. And it measured its success in the changing character of the American schoolroom.

But these services, however valuable, came at the high cost of parochialism. The Association early committed itself to popularization, and popularization is rarely achieved by balanced, abstruse arguments. The popularizer seeks pungency and simplicity; the slogan soon replaces the extended discussion. Of course, the PEA could write John Dewey to the effect that he more than any other symbolized the philosophic ideals of progressive education. But Dewey's writings, however brilliant, are long and involved, and frequently ambiguous. Teachers were busy and parents were busier. Some shorter summing up, some statement of key ideas, was needed. And so, despite continuing protestations that progressive education was experimental and could not be defined, despite the persistent failure to agree on formal policy statements, the inevitable definition occurred.

Individual or group begins to voice this need more or less publicly. Second, propaganda and agitation result. Third, there follows a growing consciousness of this need in a small or large group. Fourth, they organize. Fifth, concerted action and strong leadership develop and new converts are won. Sixth, if the movement is successful it becomes institutionalized—becomes the pattern of the majority, and group control sets in. Any one who does not conform to the new pattern code is disciplined. Seventh, eventually bureaucracy, inflexibility, and reaction become dominant. When this occurs some one usually feels a new need and either the institution changes to meet that need or in time it is superseded." *Contemporary Social Movements*, pp. 8–9. Copyright 1930 by the Century Co. Reprinted by permission of Appleton-Century-Crofts, Inc. In terms of Davis's cycle, which the progressive education movement matches to a degree, the Association comes both fortuitously and late, and from the margins of the movement at best. See also Rudolf Heberle: *Social Movements* (New York, 1951), which is written almost entirely out of the European experience.

Even the sincerest leaders rarely see a movement whole, and as the work went forward, certain strands of the larger movement were gradually eclipsed. Thus, time and again after 1919, progressive causes arose that the Association simply refused to countenance. Upton Sinclair's *The Goose-Step* (1923) and *The Goslings* (1924) were ignored.[4] So was the Scopes trial (1925)—a veritable crisis of the soul in modern education. So was the much-publicized political attack on Superintendent McAndrew of Chicago (1927). So, too, were most of the reforms in the state universities, notably Lotus D. Coffman's at Minnesota. By the thirties the CCC and the NYA could touch the lives of millions and yet draw only passing comment from the PEA. They were progressivism to be sure; but they were not really "progressive education."

Berdine Jackman Bovard has spoken of the "waspish effect" of the PEA on traditional education, "stinging it out of its lethargy, its mechanized routine, forcing it to evaluate and justify its program and modernize its procedures."[5] There is truth to her observation, particularly during the Association's heyday in the thirties; certainly the sort of systematic inquiry and appraisal typified by the Eight-Year Study has been all too rare in the history of American education. And yet here too questions must be raised, for the fact remains that other organizations were much more effective in pressing for certain planks in the progressive program. Thus, for example, the National Education Association continued to sponsor vocational training, health education, improved rural schooling and extended student services throughout the twenties and thirties at a time when the so-called progressive schools catered to a much narrower segment of the population.[6] Likewise, the American Federation of Teachers, founded in 1916, was infinitely more vocal, and indeed more effective, in the defense of academic freedom and the campaign for adequate tenure laws in the

[4] Sinclair praised the Association in *The Goslings*, interestingly enough, in a chapter on "Workers' Education."

[5] Bovard: op. cit., p. 290.

[6] Edgar B. Wesley discusses the NEA's contribution to the progressive movement in *NEA: The First Hundred Years* (New York, 1957), ch. xvii.

several states. Finally, one need only examine the seventy-odd yearbooks of the National Society for the Study of Education between 1919 and 1955 to sense the richness and diversity of the problems the PEA might have dealt with in seeking to serve as a clearinghouse for progressive ideas and innovations.

None of these criticisms, however, touches the real failure of the Association—that is, in allowing itself to be transformed into a quasi-professional organization. In so doing it undoubtedly strengthened the movement momentarily by further cementing the long-standing marriage of professionalism and progressivism, but it weakened the movement in the long run by narrowing the base of its political support. For years the Child Study Association, the National Committee for Mental Hygiene, the National Congress of Parents and Teachers, and dozens of other special-interest groups—to say nothing of interested business, labor, farm, and civic organizations— worked side by side with the PEA in the cause of educational improvement, with never more than a halfhearted attempt at cooperation, usually in the form of joint conventions. The Association had committed itself from the beginning to unifying the forces of reform—this indeed had been the very reason the founders had scrupulously avoided any clear definition of its cause. Yet it failed miserably to do so; indeed, one need only compare its utter political naïveté with the sophisticated machinations of the National Society for the Promotion of Industrial Education between 1906 and 1917 to realize how miserable the failure really was.

Bemused by the ancient truism that as the teacher goes, so goes the school, the Association neglected the equally important dictum that he who pays the piper calls the tune. In its definition of the movement it so limited its scope as to cut itself off from many of the most progressive elements of the time, and in its persistent fear of radicalism it shunned the arduous business of marshaling the diverse political forces that might have supported its cause. In the end, the PEA's failure was neither financial nor philosophical, but ultimately political: it simply failed to comprehend the fundamental forces that move American education.

8

The Changing
Pedagogical Mainstream

AMERICAN education grew phenomenally during the quarter-century following World War I: each year more students studied in larger schools for longer periods of time at greater expense to the public. The depression may have occasioned a falling birthrate and a decline in local expenditures, but the most significant educational fact of the thirties remains the steady increase in the holding power of the schools: secondary enrollments rose from 4,800,000 in 1929–30 to 7,100,000 in 1939–40. As in the period before the war, an expanding and increasingly diverse clientele rendered the schools readily receptive to reform, and it was almost inevitable that the polyglot system of ideas, assumptions, and practices called progressive education would continue to exert profound influence.

Along with the steady rise in enrollments came a growing measure of centralization. School buses appeared for the first time in appreciable numbers during the twenties, and with them the beginning of a nationwide consolidation of school districts. There must have been some 200,000 local districts around 1920; and as the number declined, individual schools were able to afford infinitely richer programs, and hence to go along with many of the recommendations of the progressives. At the state level newly professionalized departments of education sponsored a plethora of publications—curricula, lesson plans, and instructional materials—as well as conferences, institutes, and seminars designed to put hitherto isolated teachers and administrators in touch with the latest pedagogical thought. Needless to say, progressive ideas and practices were widely disseminated, with state aid and favor as the reward for interested localities.

Then, too, there were the spirited—if limited—efforts of the United States Office of Education. Confined by law and tradition to diffusing information and statistics, it also became a prime propagator of progressivism. It administered the Smith-Hughes Act in such a way as to speed the adoption of vocational programs. It circulated pamphlets dealing with new curricular offerings and with new methods of teaching, grouping, testing, and the like. And it even published architectural plans of buildings that would enable districts to make wider use of new educational practices and procedures. The U.S. Office had little power except to persuade, but it used that power with extraordinary effectiveness in the cause of progressive education.

Finally, there was the centralization in professional affairs wrought by the National Education Association. NEA membership rose phenomenally in the postwar era, from around 10,000 in 1918 to over 210,000 in 1941.[1] And while the organization remained in many respects a loose confederation of state education associations, thereby reflecting the power structure of American education, it too became an influential proponent of reform. The NEA *Journal*, with a circulation in the hundreds of thousands, was pointedly written for classroom teachers, and widely read by them, while the Association's re-

[1] Edgar B. Wesley: *NEA: The First Hundred Years* (New York, 1957), p. 397.

search bulletins and technical publications carried a steady stream of information on "best practices" to school administrators across the nation. Like the U.S. Office, the Association had little power except to persuade, but it too chose to use that power in the cause of progressivism.

The continuing pressure of enrollments, then, combined with a growing measure of centralization after 1918 to accelerate the educational transformation begun in an earlier era. Not only did individual experiments continue on all sides, but schools generally began to be visibly affected. By 1937 the Progressive Education Association's Committee on Experimental Schools could write with optimism: "It is evident . . . that the tendency to be avowedly experimental is gaining ground. To 'experiment with children,' to 'experiment with taxpayers' money,' are not the crimes they used to be. 'Radical notions' may safely be incorporated in the instructions of a city superintendent to his corps of principals and teachers, or in the public pronouncement of a state commissioner concerning his plans for a drastic overhauling of the whole educational machinery of his state. In short, there is growing perception of the truth that a rapidly changing society demands a responsive effort on the part of education; there is a growing public which willingly supports such responses." [2] Progressive education, as Frederick Redefer remarked in *Time* a year later, was no longer a rebel movement; it had become respectable.[3]

I I

The view of the PEA's founders that progressive education began with them has long been joined to an equally popular misconception: that private schools and the educators associated with them have always been the real pioneers of educational reform. As late as 1947 Harold Rugg published a list of the three dozen leading progressive ventures between 1870 and 1930 in which he included only four public-school systems:

[2] Progressive Education Association, Committee on Experimental Schools: *What Schools Are Doing* (New York, 1937).

[3] *Time,* October 31, 1938, pp. 31 ff.

Quincy under Francis W. Parker in the 1870's, Winnetka (Ill.) under Carleton Washburne in the 1920's, and Bronxville (N.Y.) under Willard Beatty and Shaker Heights (Ohio) under Arthur K. Loomis during the 1930's.[4] The notion, of course, is as inaccurate as its limited view of progressive education on the one hand and public education on the other. Yet to point this out is in no way to deny that some of the most courageous and imaginative pedagogical experiments of the interbellum era did proceed under private auspices, and that these experiments did exert incalculable influence on the larger course of American education.

Lloyd Marcus has probed rather intensively into the origins of the leading private progressive schools, with the conclusion that few generalizations apply.[5] Apparently they stemmed from the most varied political and philosophical sources. Baltimore's Park School, for example, was founded in 1912 after a bitter controversy in the city board of education in which one faction —including Professor Hans Froelicher of Goucher—resigned and decided to establish a school of its own. Froelicher, who had read avidly in Comenius, Rousseau, Pestalozzi, and Froebel, had long cherished the idea of an education based on the genuine interests of youngsters. The group invited Eugene Randolph Smith as the first headmaster; and by 1918, when Stanwood Cobb conceived the idea of the PEA, the Park School was already known as a center of pedagogical innovation.

We have already seen the quite different origins of the Children's School, later the Walden School, and the Play School, later the City and Country School. Both of these institutions were started by individual teachers seeking to apply particular pedagogical theories. Margaret Naumburg attempted in the Children's School to build an education that would take proper account of psychoanalytical principles; likewise, Caro-

---

[4] Harold Rugg: *Foundations for American Education* (Yonkers, 1947), pp. 569–70.
[5] Lloyd Marcus: "The Founding of American Private Progressive Schools, 1912–1921" (Unpublished Honors Thesis, Department of Social Relations, Harvard University, 1948).

line Pratt undertook in the Play School to generalize the notion that children comprehend the world most vividly through their play activities. Both women actually went out and enlisted the parent clientele that would ultimately support their ventures.

The founding of the Shady Hill School in 1915 presents still another tale. Here the prime movers were Professor and Mrs. William Ernest Hocking. Mrs. Hocking, who had been a teacher before her marriage, was familiar with the "open-air" school movement in Europe; and when the Hockings became concerned over the persistent ill-health of their children in the cramped, overheated quarters of the public schools, they decided to found a school of their own. Shady Hill began as a cooperative endeavor catering mostly to the children of Professor Hocking's Harvard colleagues and a few Cambridge businessmen. Mrs. George Sarton later recounted that some of their neighbors considered them all "cranks."

And so the story varied from school to school. Oak Lane Country Day School grew in 1916 out of the efforts of a group of Philadelphia businessmen to apply John Dewey's educational theories. The Moraine Park School was begun that same year by Arthur E. Morgan, an engineer long bemused by Pestalozzi's *Leonard and Gertrude*. The Chevy Chase School was started by Stanwood Cobb in 1919 as a privately owned and operated venture. The Beaver Country Day School was founded in 1921 by two ladies who had come upon *Schools of To-Morrow* and liked what they read. The Manumit School was launched in 1924 as an experimental residential school primarily for workers' children, with A. J. Muste of the Brookwood Workers' College as chairman of the board.

In the case of the Play School, the Children's School, and the Chevy Chase School the educator went out and sought the parents; in the case of Park, Oak Lane Country Day, and Beaver Country Day the parents went out and sought the educator. No generalization suffices on the question of lay or professional sponsorship. But there is one phenomenon worth noting: except for Manumit and one or two other labor schools, the clientele was overwhelmingly upper middle class.

There was an occasional effort to enroll the children of blue-collar families, but Caroline Pratt's experience here is both typical and instructive: working-class parents were not as a rule willing to participate in radical pedagogical innovation. The charges of class bias leveled in the thirties by Counts and others were essentially well taken; the progressive private schools did depend for all intents and purposes on middle-class sponsorship and support.

Some of the founders were familiar with other ventures. Margaret Naumburg knew of Caroline Pratt's effort, and both knew of Marietta Johnson's school. The group that founded Beaver Country Day School went to Baltimore to counsel with Eugene Randolph Smith, as did those who started Oak Lane Country Day School. But in general there was no sense of a movement until after the organization of the Progressive Education Association. Indeed, one of the most common reminiscences of early members of the PEA was their surprise at learning that so much else was going on: thus, the format of the early conventions at which the participants themselves exchanged reports; and thus also the lack of any explicitly felt need for a "unifying philosophy."

The activities of these private progressive schools of the twenties are vividly described by Agnes de Lima in *Our Enemy the Child* (1926) and by Harold Rugg and Ann Shumaker in *The Child-Centered School* (1928). In general, the schools tended to organize subject matter in radically different ways, to take the life of the surrounding community more immediately into account in the business of instruction, and to enlist students more directly in the management and operation of school affairs. As a rule, classrooms were more cheerful and tended to be filled with a richer variety of equipment, books, teaching materials, artist supplies, and the like. More than De Lima, Rugg and Shumaker found elements to criticize: some of the schools lacked design in their curricula; some followed too slavishly the interests of individual children; some overemphasized one or another of the subjects; some took few pains to appraise results. But these criticisms were all but lost in the overwhelming flow of praise.

If any one institution symbolized the private progressive school of this era—and there are good reasons for insisting that none did—it was probably the Lincoln School. Nowhere did the several strands of postwar progressivism converge and intertwine so effectively. Nowhere was the rich diversity of the movement more dramatically documented. And certainly, no single progressive school exerted greater or more lasting influence on the subsequent history of American education.

Emerson once remarked that every revolution is first a thought in one man's mind. Insofar as the Lincoln School wrought a revolution, Abraham Flexner was the man. Flexner reports autobiographically that it was at a 1915 meeting of the General Education Board that he talked informally of his long-cherished notion of a model school that would do for general education what the Johns Hopkins Medical School had done for medical education. Charles W. Eliot, who was present, remarked: "I have long wanted some such experiment; now I should regard it as a calamity if we, having in our service the one man best fitted to organize such a school, should fail to give him and the country the chance." [6] Flexner was asked to frame a document for future consideration; the result was his celebrated essay "A Modern School." [7]

Read a half-century later, "A Modern School" is strikingly prophetic in content and tone. The purpose of Flexner's school was "to give children the knowledge they need, and to develop

[6] Abraham Flexner: *I Remember* (New York, 1940), pp. 250–1. Flexner in his 1939 commencement address at Lincoln insisted that President Eliot was the real founder of the Lincoln School, since it was Eliot who had initiated the conversation.

[7] Abraham Flexner: "A Modern School," *American Review of Reviews*, LIII (1916), 465–74; the essay was reprinted in Flexner: *A Modern College and A Modern School* (Garden City, N.Y., 1923). Reprinted by permission of Doubleday & Company, Inc. Asked many years later about the source of the ideas in the pamphlet, Flexner mentioned the influence of John Dewey and Charles W. Eliot. Lester Dix: *A Charter for Progressive Education* (New York, 1939), p. 1. But a close examination of his autobiography locates the principal source in his own teaching experience in the school he organized and conducted as a young man in Louisville, Kentucky. For a trenchant critique of "A Modern School," see Paul Shorey: *The Assault on Humanism* (Boston, 1917).

in them the power to handle themselves in our own world." All claims on school time would be judged according to this criterion. Even the so-called progressive schools, he believed, had been too timid in what they had eliminated; they had occasionally dropped or curtailed individual topics or subjects, but an unmistakable traditionalism continued to suffuse their work. Flexner's utilitarianism, on the other hand, was uncompromising: "modern education," he insisted, "will include nothing simply because tradition recommends it or because its inutility has not been conclusively established. It proceeds in precisely the opposite way: *it includes nothing for which an affirmative case cannot now be made out.*" [8]

Based on these principles, Flexner's school would organize its work around activities in four fundamental fields: science, industry, aesthetics, and civics. Greek and Latin would be dropped in favor of the modern European languages. Much of conventional mathematics would also go. As subjects were regrouped and reorganized, teachers would find it necessary to create new syllabi, new textbooks, and new pedagogical procedures, and hence the modern school would become a laboratory for the study of educational problems. And here Flexner saw its most radical and significant contribution, as a pacesetter in the search for scientific as opposed to dogmatic educational standards. "The scientific spirit is just beginning to creep into elementary and secondary schools," he wrote, "and progress is slow, because the conditions are unfavorable. The Modern School should be a laboratory from which would issue scientific studies of educational problems—a laboratory, first of all, which would test and evaluate critically the fundamental propositions on which it is itself based, and the results as they are obtained." [9]

Early in 1916 the General Education Board entered into discussion with the authorities at Teachers College, and by May the Board reported that the College was ready to cooperate in the establishment of the proposed modern school "as a laboratory for the working out of an elementary and

[8] Flexner: *A Modern College and a Modern School*, pp. 119–20.
[9] Ibid., p. 141.

secondary curriculum, which shall eliminate obsolete material and endeavor to work up in usable form material adapted to the needs of modern living." Flexner later recalled that he from the beginning had urged that the school be established independently of any existing institution, but apparently other counsels prevailed.[1] In an agreement dated January 1, 1917, the GEB agreed to meet the annual deficit incurred by such a school, and on September 24, 1917, Flexner's modern school came into existence as the Lincoln School of Teachers College.[2]

The story of the Lincoln School from that time until its demise thirty-one years later is one of the exciting chapters of the progressive education movement.[3] As Harold Rugg reminisced years later, the whole approach of the staff was summed up by the motto: "Try anything once and see if it works."[4] And while as in any experimental situation, some of what was tried did not work, the impressive fact about the Lincoln School is that so much did. Flexner had warned that teachers would be difficult to find, but the school managed to bring together an unusually imaginative faculty: Nell Curtis, Martha Groggel, Lula Wright, and Satis Coleman in the elementary division; Hughes Mearns, Harold Rugg, and John R. Clark in the secondary division. Flexner had warned that materials were not available; and so the staff proceeded to produce a commendable array of curriculum guides, texts, workbooks, teaching units, and achievement tests. Most important, perhaps, the staff ran a first-rate school: morale was high; classroom teaching was generally good, frequently excellent; and a pioneering

[1] Abraham Flexner: "Commencement Address, The Lincoln School of Teachers College, 1939" (Mimeographed, Teachers College Library).
[2] Lawrence A. Cremin, David A. Shannon, and Mary Evelyn Townsend: *A History of Teachers College, Columbia University* (New York, 1954), pp. 110–11.
[3] A history of the Lincoln School is badly needed. Its story is told sketchily in Agnes de Lima: *A School for the World of Tomorrow* (New York, 1939), *Democracy's High School* (New York, 1941), and *Lincoln School Comes of Age, 1917–1938* (New York, 1938). The February, 1936, issue of the *Teachers College Record* was given over entirely to the work at Lincoln.
[4] Rugg: *Foundations for American Education*, p. 563.

spirit pervaded the activities of teachers, students, and parents alike.

What the Lincoln School set out to do was to build a curriculum around "units of work" that would reorganize traditional subject matter into forms taking fuller account of the development of children and the changing needs of adult life.[5] Thus, for example, the first and second grades—six- and seven-year-olds—carried on a study of community life in which they actually built a play city. A third-grade project under Nell Curtis, growing out of the fascinating day-by-day life of the nearby Hudson River, turned into the most celebrated of the Lincoln School units, the one on boats: a study of boats, past and present, of their design, construction, and cargos, and of their place in the history of transportation. In the hands of Miss Curtis, boats became the entrée into history, geography, reading, writing, arithmetic, science, art, and literature. Even a hasty glance at the accompanying diagrams (pp. 284–5) will quickly reveal how one imaginative teacher used the normal interests of children in the life around them.

In similar fashion, the fourth grade worked on foods, the fifth on land transportation, and the sixth on books through the ages. Each of the units was broadly enough conceived so that different children could concentrate on different aspects depending on their own interests and the teacher's sense of their pedagogical needs; each of the units called for widely diverse student activities; and each of the units sought to deal in depth with some crucial aspect of contemporary civilization. To one familiar with the work of the Deweys' Laboratory School at the turn of the century, the continuities and similarities are striking.

The high school, conceived as a six-year program, was continuous with the elementary school.[6] The "general course" in the seventh grade dealt with "man and his environment"—

[5] The theory and practice of the units of work, as well as an extensive bibliography, are given in James S. Tippett et al.: *Curriculum Making in an Elementary School* (New York, 1927).

[6] A selected bibliography of materials dealing with the theory and practice of the high school program is included in De Lima: *Democracy's High School*, pp. 88–90.

A UNIT OF STUDY RELATED TO BOATS

THIRD GRADE

PROBLEMS-QUESTIONS

STIMULATION

In the spring of last year many of the boys of this group were interested in trains and other means of travel.

Many summer experiences with boats.

Wood in supply box cut in shapes suggestive of boats.

Bulletin prepared by the teacher.

Trip to see Half-Moon.

Trip to see boat models.

To construct boats that will look like a certain kind and with which children can play.

How do boats "go"?

Who first thought of making a sailboat?

How did people get the idea for different shapes for boats?

To know more about the people who traveled on the seas in early times.

To find out about the making of boats.

How many different kinds of boats do we have today and how is each kind used?

How did early people use their ships?

To find out about the different parts of a boat.

How do people know how much to put into a boat before it will sink?

SUBJECT MATTER CONTENT WHICH HELPED SOLVE THE PROBLEMS

INDUSTRIAL ARTS
Construction of boats: Making pattern, shaping hull, making sail, making keel, casting weight for keel, making rack for boat, and testing boat.
How boats developed from early times to the present day.
The difficulty involved in building a toy boat so it will balance in water.
Different kinds of sail boats.
The need for a keel on a boat.
Different methods of propelling a boat.
Modern inventions in connection with the propulsion of boats.
What makes boats float.
Different uses of boats today.

HISTORY
The Half-Moon directed interest to Hendrick Hudson and his ship.
Historic ships: Santa Maria, Mayflower.
Reference work, reading and discussions about:
Vikings: What color and kinds of clothing did they wear? What did they eat? What kind of houses did they have? What were their boats like? Did Vikings have stores? How did Viking writing look? Story of Lief Erickson. The gods of the Vikings. Their beliefs.
Phoenicians: Scenery, boats, people, trade, beliefs, clothing, cities, industries, etc.
Egyptians: Scenery, country, boats, beliefs, tools, writing, etc. Story of the building of Solomon's Temple.
Early Mediterranean peoples.

GEOGRAPHY
Pictures of boat from newspaper which interested children in world geography.
Geography related to countries studied.
Norway: Country, climate, people and occupations.
Phoenicia: Country, climate, people, trading routes, daily life of early people compared with that of today.
Egypt: Country, climate, trading, etc.
Map interest: Norway, showing ancient home of the Vikings.
The Mediterranean countries, showing cities of Phoenicia and routes on which King of Tyre sent materials for Solomon's Temple.
Plasticene map of Mediterranean Sea and surrounding countries on which children sailed card-board models of early boats.
Globe in frequent use to locate places mentioned.
Outline world map, locating countries.
Interest in determining distances (reading scales on map).
How far is it from Norway to Phoenicia?
How far is it from Norway to America?
Building Lower Manhattan on floor with blocks to exhibit boats.
Map was drawn on floor; buildings in New York City that helped most with sea travel.

ARITHMETIC
Measuring for boat patterns and measurements in boat making.
Figuring the number of board feet used by class in building boat racks.
Arithmetic problems in connection with science experiment of water displacement and floating objects.
What is a gram?
What is a cubit?
Dimensions of Solomon's Temple compared with dimensions of the Lincoln School.
Children saw a cubit measure at the Museum.

FINE ARTS
Sketching and painting pictures of Half-Moon.
Sketching and painting boat models.
Drawing blackboard frieze showing history of boats.
Ten easel pictures showing story of Lief Erickson.
Cut paper pictures of boats.
Painting Egyptian boats seen at Museum.
Painting Viking pictures showing clothing.
Painting modern boats.
Making clay tablet.

COMPOSITION—LITERATURE
Stories written about the trip to see Half-Moon.
Stories of other trips by individual children.
Original poems about boats and the sea.
Labels and invitations for boat exhibit.
Written and oral reports about boats, Vikings, Phoenicia and Egypt.
Stories for bulletin, room paper, council news, or absent class members, telling of class interest and study.

READING
Reference material pertaining to topics under discussion, found in school library or at home.
Children's reading material: Lief and Thorkle, Viking Stories, Early sea people, Boat Book prepared by other Third Grade, material prepared by student teachers.

SCIENCE
How can we tell if our boats will float and balance? Try out in delta table.
Three experiments: Why do some objects float and why do some sink?
How do people know how much to put into boat before it will sink?

DRAMATIZATION
Play-Story of Lief Erickson, spontaneously prepared by class.

MUSIC
Old Gaelic Lullaby. Volga Boat Song. Sail Bonnie Boat.

PROBABLE OUTCOMES

DESIRABLE HABITS AND SKILLS

Better skill in sketching.
Better skill in handling brush and paints.
A beginning of the development of how to sew.
Developing the habit of making a pattern before constructing an article.
Developing skill in shaping wood by means of plane and spokeshave.
Developing skill in using gouge and mallet.
Developing skill in reading distances on map.
Rapid growth in map drawing.
Developing habit of reading the newspaper.
Better skill in measuring.
Ability to gather information on a certain subject and reporting to class.
Increased ability in writing.

ATTITUDES AND APPRECIATIONS

Economic:

An appreciation of the use of weights and measures.
What it means to construct a real boat that will float and balance properly.
Appreciation of the change in the lives of the people caused by the discovery of iron and the use of sails.
Appreciation of paper as a writing material.
Appreciation of the modern inventions in connection with the propulsion of ships.

Social:

What the early people contributed to the world.
The number of people and industry it takes to supply materials for the construction of one building.
Comparison of the ideas of fairness of the early people with the present day.

Recreational:

Developing a joy in painting, sketching and drawing.
Growing interest in reading books about historical peoples, inventions or boats.
Playing with boats made.
Interest in the construction of a toy-boat.
Interest in the construction of a real boat.
The pleasure in making maps.
The pleasure of playing with maps.

Aesthetic:

Appreciation of the beauty in line and construction of boats.
The adventure of the ship.

INFORMATION

Knowledge of the development of the boat from raft to steamship.
Who Hendrick Hudson was.
General idea of historic ships.
An interesting acquaintance with Vikings, Phoenicians, and Egyptians.
General geographical knowledge of the world.
What a cubit measure is.
Knowledge of how to draw maps.
Some idea of what makes objects float.
Some idea of how to make boats balance in water.
Some idea of how to construct a toy-boat.
How the early people made their clay tablets.
How to make a clay tablet.
The need for molds in casting metals.
Some idea of how iron is made into different shapes.

TOTAL
PERSONALITY
AS
MODIFIED
BY THE
FOREGOING
EXPERIENCES

Interest in world geography and travel.
Maps and actual distances between given places.
The time it takes to get to certain places.

Interest in silk through answering the questions:
What kind of clothing did the Vikings wear?
How is velvet made?

Interest in what clay is:
How it is prepared for our use and how it was prepared by early people for making clay tablets.

Interest in the Egyptian and Phoenician alphabet and how our alphabet was developed from it.
The materials the Egyptians used for writing.

Interest in metals.
Interest in weight of different metals through casting of lead for keels.
How metals are shaped.

Interest in the construction of modern buildings through reading about Solomon's Temple and comparing it with the construction of the Lincoln School.

Interest in other phases of transportation.

really the study of human geography. The eighth grade, emphasizing the relationship between culture and environment, worked on "living in a power age," visiting factories and farms as far distant as Massachusetts. The tenth and eleventh grades followed a two-year sequence called "ancient and modern cultures," an effort to deepen historical understandings; while the twelfth grade concentrated on "living in contemporary America," a unit revolving around the social and economic problems of the thirties.

Grouped around these core projects was a fascinating array of required and elective activities available to the children. In the elementary school there was special work in music, in the fine and industrial arts, in the natural sciences, in home economics, and in physical education—the Lincoln School building, erected in 1921–22 on the corner of 123rd Street and Morningside Avenue, boasted an enclosed all-weather gymnasium on the roof. Similarly, the high school offered special studies in mathematics, English, biology, physics, social studies, the modern foreign languages, and again, in the fine and industrial arts, home economics, and physical education. Finally, the school afforded rich opportunities for ancillary travel, a fantastic variety of extracurricular activities, an excellent library, and a well-staffed testing and guidance program that assisted students from the day they entered until well after they left.

What kind of education did all this add up to? There are a number of bases for judgment. To begin, some of the work is still extant and readily available for appraisal. There are excellent selections of student prose and poetry in Hughes Mearns's *Creative Youth* (1925) and *Creative Power* (1929), as well as in the many volumes of *Lincoln Lore* and *Lorette,* the student literary magazines. Satis N. Coleman's book *A Children's Symphony* (1931) reproduces the orchestral score of Lincoln School Symphony No. 3—in four movements!— which was composed by the children and played by them largely on instruments of their own making. And the pages of *Creative Expression* (1932) by Gertrude Hartman and Ann Shumaker literally teem with illustrations of Lincoln painting and sculpture. A great deal of this work clearly stands the test of time; one has the sense that it would be enviable in any school anywhere.

Another sort of judgment derives from the innumerable tests administered to Lincoln students over the years. A 1934 compilation by L. Thomas Hopkins and James E. Mendenhall is useful in this respect.[7] The authors compared achievement at Lincoln with national norms in the various subject fields. In general, academic performance comfortably exceeded that of the general school population but was slightly inferior to achievement at a selected group of eastern independent schools. Likewise, Lincoln graduates tended to place above the general school population on the College Entrance Board Examinations, and they tended to do superior work in college. None of this, of course, is surprising. From the beginning, the typical Lincoln student came from a well-to-do family, he was college-bound, and his IQ ran considerably above 100. That his achievement exceeded national norms is hardly noteworthy. What may be important, though, is that the school was apparently able to serve its own distinctive pedagogical ends without any significant sacrifice of academic achievement—a phenomenon later confirmed by the more general findings of the Eight-Year Study.

Still another kind of appraisal came in 1930 when the presidents of Yale, Oberlin, and Iowa—James R. Angell, Ernest H. Wilkins, and Walter A. Jessup—surveyed all three of the Teachers College Schools: Lincoln, the Horace Mann Boys' School and the Horace Mann Girls' School.[8] The committee, certainly as distinguished as any that ever undertook a school survey, found the college records of alumni of all three schools

[7] L. Thomas Hopkins and James E. Mendenhall: *Achievement at Lincoln School* (New York, 1934). Toward the end of the thirties educators began to experiment much more systematically with instruments to assess nonacademic achievement in the progressive schools. See J. Wayne Wrightstone: *Appraisal of Newer Elementary School Practices* (New York, 1938); and G. Derwood Baker *et al.*: *New Methods vs. Old in American Education* (New York, 1941), pp. 34–56.

[8] "Summary Report, Survey Committee of the Affiliated Schools of Teachers College, June, 1930" (Unpublished manuscript in the files of the President of Teachers College).

hardly distinguishable from one another; nonetheless, they took pains to point out that Lincoln graduates scored a much higher percentage of A and B records in college grades than graduates of either of the other schools. Of the three, Lincoln was by far the most experimental.

Finally, there were the judgments of the students themselves who, while not quite as precocious as *New Yorker* cartoons made them out to be, were nonetheless quite sophisticated about their own educational experience. Generally the students were favorable, a reaction to be expected in view of their own deep involvement. The inquiring reporter of *Highlights*, the high school newspaper, asked on the twentieth anniversary of the school's opening: "In what way has Lincoln benefited you most?" Amidst the usual clowning, there were the serious phrases about Lincoln teaching leadership, bestowing a sense of responsibility, bringing out the individual, and indeed, teaching busy adolescents to get along on six hours of sleep a day. "At public school they jam facts into you," one student insisted. "Here you really learn something." [9] The verdict was not unanimous, however. Several alumni criticized the school quite severely, claiming that they had not learned to study, that they had wandered aimlessly through loosely planned activities, and that college life had been difficult to settle down to after years of progressive pedagogy.[1] Just as the praise was not surprising, neither was the criticism; one might certainly expect some graduates to experience difficulty in adjusting to more formal educational situations after protracted stays at Lincoln.

The convergence of the scientific, child-centered, and reformist strains of progressive theory at Lincoln during the interbellum era was a phenomenon worthy of comment. Apparently, for all but a few of the more logically minded, it caused little discomfort. At Lincoln one could find the very best of the testing movement in action: written records were kept for each child from the day he entered, and both teachers and guidance counselors made extensive use of the data. In-

[9] *Highlights*, May 10, 1938.
[1] See *Time*, May 16, 1938, p. 34; and Gertrude Hildreth: "Graduates of Lincoln School." *Teachers College Record*, XLIV (1942–3), 361–8.

deed, the very questions Flexner asked in "A Modern School" were strikingly similar to those raised by the Committee on Economy of Time. Likewise, as one looks at the plethora of student activities at Lincoln, both inside the classroom and out, one sees incarnate the new articles of pedagogical faith celebrated by Rugg and Shumaker in *The Child-Centered School*. And finally, there were few better manifestations of pedagogical reformism during the 1920's than the work of Rugg and his associates that eventuated in the so-called Rugg social science texts.[2]

Apparently, while progressive theorists found themselves less and less able to live with one another, their theories did somehow converge in the life of the schools. As Charlotte Winsor of the Bank Street College of Education noted in a recent conversation: "For purposes of analysis the theoretical streams are visible and can be separated; but for those of us working in the schools, it was easy to be scientific, to be concerned with individual growth and development, and to look to the reform of society at one and the same time. There was so much to be done that we didn't look for neat consistencies; the children were there to be educated, and they seemed more important than logical niceties." So it is frequently in the course of reform movements.

The Lincoln School came to an untimely end in 1948 after a bitter decade-long battle between the school's parent association and the Teachers College administration.[3] The College had decided in 1940 to merge Lincoln with its Horace Mann Schools in the interest of greater economy and administrative efficiency; and at the same time it had organized the Horace Mann-Lincoln Institute of School Experimentation and charged it with conducting and publicizing the experimental work of the new combined institution. Seeking to serve as a link with the public schools, the Institute soon ran

---

[2] The story of the Rugg texts and the bitter controversy they stirred in 1940–41 is told in Harold Rugg: *That Men May Understand* (New York, 1941).

[3] An account is given in Cremin *et al.*: *A History of Teachers College, Columbia University*, pp. 229–37.

into the age-old problem that much of what succeeded under laboratory conditions was not readily applicable in the schools at large.[4] This, coupled with continuing financial difficulties and the growing hostility of Lincoln's parents, who had fought the consolidation from the beginning, led the College to decide to close the school in 1946. There followed a two-year court battle in which a parent group contended that Teachers College was not within its power to close the school under the formal legal arrangements originally made with the General Education Board. Ultimately, the College won; the school was closed and its funds transferred to the Institute for further work in the public schools.

Only time will tell whether it was a Pyrrhic victory. Writing in his autobiography late in 1939, Flexner contemplated the impending merger in a passage that still conveys bitterness: "Unfortunately, as I write, the future of the Lincoln School is imperiled. Teachers College and its Horace Mann Schools are in financial difficulties. I am told that a consolidation is being considered, under which, of course, the endowment of the Lincoln School would be used to pull them out of the hole. I should regard as unethical any steps which utilized the income from the endowment of Lincoln School to finance a scheme of consolidation. The legal right Teachers College may or may not possess; of moral and scientific right it possesses not a vestige. The Lincoln School is the only elementary and secondary school in the world adequately endowed for research and experimentation in its field. Shall it be sacrificed? If it is sacrificed or impaired, who will ever endow another?"[5] Flex-

---

[4] Inasmuch as the Lincoln School had been established as a laboratory, certain remarks by Dewey during the early months of the University of Chicago's Laboratory School are relevant. "As it is not the primary function of a laboratory to devise ways and means that can at once be put to practical use," he wrote in 1896, "so it is not the primary purpose of this school to devise methods with reference to their direct application in the graded school system. It is the function of some schools to provide better teachers according to present standards; it is the function of others to create new standards and ideals and thus to lead to a gradual change in conditions." *University Record*, I (1896–7), 417–18.

[5] From *I Remember*, pp. 252–3. Copyright 1940 by Abraham Flexner. Reprinted by permission of Simon and Schuster, Inc. The passage, in-

ner's question continues to gnaw as one ponders the work of the school over three decades, and the subsequent history of American education.

I I I

Just as diversity characterized the private progressive schools of the interbellum era, so diversity marked the vast number of public-school experiments. The twenties and thirties were an age of reform in American education, as thousands of local districts adopted one or another of the elements in the progressive program. As might be expected, the movement proceeded at a vastly uneven pace, varying from region to region and from state to state. And as in earlier times, different aspects of progressivism were taken up by different communities, depending on circumstances and clientele. It would be pointless to try to catalogue this plethora of reform, since the job has already been done in some detail by the sundry publications of the National Society for the Study of Education and the Society for Curriculum Study.[6] But perhaps a few notable examples will suffice.

At the time of World War I there were some 200,000 one-teacher schools in the United States, attended by around five million children. One such institution was the Porter School in Adair County on the outskirts of Kirksville, Missouri. In 1912 the Porter district board invited Marie Turner Harvey to take over the school, with the guarantee of a free hand and

---

terestingly enough, is omitted from the 1960 reissue of the work. Flexner urged throughout the controversy that if Teachers College could no longer maintain the Lincoln School, it was morally obligated—despite the generous terms of the GEB grant—to relinquish control over the endowment, thereby allowing the school to continue independently.

[6] See, for example, National Society for the Study of Education: *Twenty-Sixth Yearbook* (Bloomington, 1926), Part I; and Henry Harap *et al.: The Changing Curriculum* (New York, 1937). A sense of the public image of public-school progressivism may be gleaned from a series of articles by Harold Cary, John Amid, and others in *Collier's* for October 6, November 10, 17, 24, December 1, 15, and 22, 1923, and January 26, February 9, 23, March 15, April 5, 19, 26, May 10, August 9, and October 25, 1924.

three years in which to demonstrate the practicability of a "socialized rural-school curriculum." Mrs. Harvey stayed more than a decade; and her innovations were so successful as to inspire Evelyn Dewey to write *New Schools for Old* (1919), a volume that went through four printings the year it was published and quickly made Porter the quintessential example of progressive education in a one-room country school.

Mrs. Harvey had come to Kirksville in 1908 as a critic-teacher at the State Normal School there.[7] An experienced and well-educated country schoolmistress, she was invited two years later to teach in the model rural schoolhouse President John R. Kirk had built on campus to demonstrate the possibilities of rural-school reform.[8] Mrs. Harvey also taught an undergraduate course called "rural life and problems," the syllabus for which, not surprisingly, read like the report of the Country Life Commission.[9] She was apparently a first-rate teacher, and her efforts were widely applauded. But she herself felt increasingly uneasy about the fact that for all its talk about educating for farm life, her demonstration rural school in the middle of Kirksville was actually drawing children away from neighboring farms. Hence she concluded in 1912 that her work might be better pursued in a typical rural school.

If the Porter School was nothing else when Mrs. Harvey arrived, it was typical. Built at the turn of the century at a total cost of $600, it had fallen into dreadful disrepair: the paint had peeled; the plaster had fallen; the clapboarding was off; the outhouses were filthy; and the usual pot-bellied stove even at red heat failed to warm the place. Since the district bordered on a railroad, the building for years had served as a hostel for tramps—the school board acquiesced so long as they

---

[7] Lucy Simmons: *History of Northeast Missouri State Teachers College* (Kirksville, 1927), pp. 25–6, 94.

[8] *Bulletin of the First District Normal School, Kirksville, Missouri*, X (1910), No. 1, p. 240; and Ferdinand Del Pizzo: *The Contributions of John R. Kirk to Teacher Education* (Ann Arbor, University Microfilms, Publication No. 12, 795).

[9] *Bulletin of the First District Normal School, Kirksville, Missouri*, X (1910), No. 3, Part 2, p. 10.

left the farmhouses alone. Needless to say, teachers came and went from semester to semester, and attendance was sparse at best, sometimes dwindling to half a dozen children.

Evelyn Dewey insists that Mrs. Harvey came to Porter "not with a ready-made plan for classroom lessons, and a schedule of clubs and social activities for the adults, but with a firm belief that in Porter there lay the possibilities for the development of a real social spirit which, when once awakened, would be powerful enough to build up for itself the methods of expression that were best suited to its needs."[1] Her observation is entirely correct insofar as it emphasizes Mrs. Harvey's continuing flexibility, but it is also true that Mrs. Harvey brought with her all of the intellectual paraphernalia of the country-life movement, and with them a larger plan to make of Porter a school that would regenerate the entire life of the surrounding locality.

She began by enlisting the aid of the parents in repairing the schoolhouse and providing a comfortable cottage for herself and her assistant, thereby ending the odious practice of boarding the teacher from family to family. The remodeled building became not only the pride and joy of the district, a project in which people had invested their own energy and enthusiasm, but a convenient center to which the citizenry repaired to discuss and act upon common problems. Soon there was a Farm Women's Club committed to unifying the community in a spirit of neighborly cooperation, and its inevitable concomitant, a Farmers' Club dedicated to the advancement of local agriculture. Both organizations maintained a continuing interest in the school, and in Mrs. Harvey's efforts to improve it.

The real transformation, of course, came in the curriculum. Here Mrs. Harvey's guiding principle was the familiar dictum that the everyday life of the community must furnish the main content of education. Not only did activities like gardening, cooking, and poultry and animal husbandry move to the center of the program, but the standard work in the three R's

[1] Evelyn Dewey: *New Schools for Old* (New York, 1919), p. 69.

was drastically revised. The youngsters wrote letters and kept notebooks in connection with their agricultural projects; they read the bulletins of the Department of Agriculture and the state experiment station along with the standard children's books in the traveling library; and they used arithmetic on the problems of farm accounts. Under Mrs. Harvey's imaginative guidance, interest soared, and with it learning.[2] New purpose was infused into the school, and it radiated out to the community in a thousand different ways. "Thru *cooperation*," she told the National Education Association in 1918, "this school has become more than a community center; it is in fact a *distributing center of efficiency*, social and economic, used every day in the week, twelve months of the year." Moreover, she proudly reported, not one boy or girl who had attended the reorganized school had subsequently left the community, with the exception of the few cases in which families had departed for business reasons.[3]

Mrs. Harvey remained at Porter until 1925, at which time she returned to the faculty of the normal school, now Northeast Missouri State Teachers College. Her work was carried forward, however, by an assistant whom she herself had trained. Meanwhile her effort, widely publicized by *New Schools for Old*, was repeated in countless rural districts across the nation. In 1930 Mrs. Harvey made what was probably one of her last major public addresses, to the NEA's Department of Rural Education. Reviewing the forces that continued to impede the advance of rural education, she took her hearers on an imaginary visit to Porter and pointed to the many reforms that had

[2] Ellsworth Collings discovered in an experimental rural school in McDonald County, Missouri, during the early twenties that children actually learned the 3 R's better under the sort of conditions Mrs. Harvey created. See Collings: *An Experiment with a Project Curriculum* (New York, 1923).

[3] Marie Turner Harvey: "Rural Schools in the War," in National Education Association: *Addresses and Proceedings, 1918*, p. 439. Like the Commission on Country Life and most progressives, Mrs. Harvey simply assumed that farm children should remain on the farm. The assumption, in view of the continuing mechanization of agriculture, was at best moot.

been accomplished. "I leave it to your judgment," she modestly concluded, "whether the situation can be labeled 'progressive' and is practicable in all such schools." [4]

In 1919, the very year Evelyn Dewey published *New Schools for Old*, a relatively different venture in public school progressivism began when the school board of Winnetka, Illinois invited Carleton Washburne of the San Francisco State Normal School to assume the superintendency of schools there.[5] Winnetka was a residential suburb of Chicago with a population around 10,000, most of them home-owning families with incomes that ran considerably above average. The district sent an unusually high percentage of its children on to college, and it boasted a long tradition of high-caliber, nonpolitical school government. Washburne's work there over the next quarter century typifies the particular brand of progressive education that developed in numbers of small, high-income suburban districts scattered across the country from Bronxville, New York, to Shaker Heights, Ohio, to Pasadena, California.

The San Francisco State Normal School from which Washburne came had become quite a center of educational reform in its own right during the years before World War I. President Frederic Burk had begun as early as 1912 to redesign the curriculum of the model elementary school to allow greater freedom for each of the 700 students to progress through his studies at his own particular pace. Each child was given a copy of the course of study for each subject on his program. Class recitations were abandoned, as were daily assignments. Provision was made for testing and promoting pupils as soon as the work outlined for any grade in any subject was completed. The

---

[4] Marie Turner Harvey: "Is Progressive Education Procedure Practicable in the Small Rural Schools?" in ibid., 1930, p. 448.

[5] The story of Winnetka's search for a superintendent is told by Carleton Washburne and Edward Yeomans, a member of the Winnetka board, in "The Inception of the Winnetka Technique," *Journal of the American Association of University Women*, XXIII (1930), 129–36. Yeomans, a Chicago pump manufacturer, became deeply interested in education and subsequently published *Shackled Youth* (Boston, 1921), a ringing critique of the "academic lockstep" in the public schools. He also founded the Ojai Valley School in California in 1923.

arrangement soon came to be known as the "Individual System." [6]

It was immediately apparent that new teaching materials would be needed if youngsters were to advance with minimum assistance from their teachers. And so the faculty set about producing textbooks to guide the work. After a good deal of trial and error, a series of self-instructive bulletins was published in the fields of arithmetic, geography, grammar, history, language, and phonics. Over 100,000 of these bulletins were sold without an iota of advertising—and with no profit to the authors. A 1916 ruling by the California attorney-general prohibiting further sale of the bulletins temporarily curtailed the continuing dissemination of the work, but the efforts of Burk's disciples subsequently broadcast it to the world. Three in particular left their mark: Willard W. Beatty, who joined Washburne at Winnetka and later went on to the superintendency of Bronxville; Helen Parkhurst, who introduced the "Individual System" into the high school at Dalton, Massachusetts and later carried it to England as the "Dalton Plan"; [7] and Washburne.

Washburne took over a system in which the board was composed of unusually intelligent and public-spirited citizens, in which the teachers were carefully selected and fairly well paid, and in which the students boasted a median IQ of 106.65 on the National Intelligence Test. He began by dividing the curriculum into two parts: the tool subjects or "common essentials"—the three R's, the sciences, and the social studies—and

[6] The work at San Francisco Normal School is described in National Society for the Study of Education: *Twenty-Fourth Yearbook* (Bloomington, 1925), Part II, pp. 59–77. Washburne contended that the intellectual forerunners of President Burk were William T. Harris and Preston W. Search, who had attempted to introduce individualized instruction in the public schools of Pueblo, Colorado, during the late 1880's. *Loc. cit.* See Search: *An Ideal School* (New York, 1901), a book dedicated to G. Stanley Hall and published in William T. Harris's "International Education Series." For a history of the effort to introduce administrative flexibility in the grouping of children, see National Society for the Study of Education: *Nineteenth Yearbook* (Bloomington, 1920), Part II, chs. i–ii.

[7] Helen Parkhurst: *Education on the Dalton Plan* (New York, 1922).

those subjects that provided for each child "self-expression and the opportunity to contribute to the group something of his own special interests and abilities." It was the "common essentials" that were "individualized" at Winnetka. Each of the subjects was marked out into parcels, and each child was encouraged to advance at his own pace. Instead of a whole class proceeding at the same rate and achieving varying quality, each student proceeded at his own rate, thereby varying time in place of quality. "The common essentials," wrote Washburne, "by definition, are those knowledges and skills needed by everyone; to allow many children, therefore, to pass through the school with hazy and inadequate grasp of them, as one must under the class lock-step scheme, is to fail in one of the functions of the school." [8]

Along with the common essentials, students pursued two other sorts of activity: self-expressive work, in which each child might differ from his neighbor in what he got from the school, and certain group projects revolving around the community life of the school—assemblies, dramatics, student self-government, and the like. Mornings and afternoons were divided into periods for individual work and periods for group activity. Teachers, freed of the age-old business of hearing recitations seriatim, were able to help, encourage, and supervise on an individual basis. As children completed the parcels of their individual work, they asked their teacher for a test; if successful, they went on, if unsuccessful, they labored at the weaknesses revealed by the test and then requested a retest. No child failed; no child skipped. In a standard fourth-grade room a visitor might discover one youngster beginning compound multiplication, another in the middle of long division, and still another beginning fractions. The same student who did

[8] Carleton W. Washburne: "Burk's Individual System as Developed at Winnetka," in National Society for the Study of Education: *Twenty-Fourth Yearbook*, Part II, p. 79. Washburne also describes the Winnetka Plan in "Winnetka," *School and Society*, XXIX (1929), 37–50, and in a subsequent volume entitled *Adjusting the School to the Child* (Yonkers, 1932). The extent to which Washburne saw Winnetka as the prototype of progressive education is evident in his book *What Is Progressive Education?* (New York, 1952).

fourth-grade arithmetic during one period might work at fifth-grade reading a few minutes later. During another part of the day all might labor together on the school grounds.

The usual questions arose early in Washburne's tenure: Did the children learn as well? Did teachers end up with intolerable burdens? Did costs become prohibitive? In 1926, under a subvention from the Commonwealth Fund, the University of Chicago's School of Education surveyed the system under the supervision of Dean William S. Gray. The results were quite favorable. Retardation had been all but eliminated, and in the fields of reading, language, and arithmetic, as measured on standardized tests, the efficiency of the teaching increased. Only in spelling did Winnetka's students lag behind. The burden on teachers did not seem unreasonable, and no additional costs were incurred; indeed, the elimination of retardation proved an economy. The survey left some questions unanswered; for example, as to whether Winnetka's schools actually nurtured greater initiative and self-reliance—there were simply no tests available to measure such traits. But in the large, Gray and his associates concluded, "Sufficient evidence has been adduced, not in Winnetka alone but in other schools and under differing conditions as well, to make it difficult to justify complacent adherence to traditional methods." [9]

The Winnetka schools continued along the lines laid down by Washburne throughout the next two decades, and were commonly cited as the example par excellence of individualized instruction. Many communities, finding it unwise or politically impossible to go quite so far, nonetheless introduced something of a compromise between the so-called Winnetka Plan and the traditional practice by which anywhere from twenty to sixty children proceeded through a year of work at essentially the same pace. Most frequently this took the form of dividing the students in each grade into sections of slow, average, and rapid learners on the basis of group intelligence tests. The practice is fraught with difficulty, since the aptitudes and achievement of any given child may vary considerably

[9] Carleton Washburne, Mabel Vogel, and William S. Gray: *A Survey of the Winnetka Public Schools* (Bloomington, 1926), p. 134.

from subject to subject.[1] It spread rapidly, however, particularly in larger communities, so that by the middle twenties the federal Bureau of Education could report that 247 cities with a population exceeding 10,000 were already employing some form of ability grouping in their elementary schools.[2]

Yet another instance of public-school progressivism during the period between the wars—this one in a city with a population exceeding 250,000—was the celebrated Denver program of curriculum revision. Like the reforms at Porter and Winnetka, Denver's effort stemmed largely from the vision of one gifted educator—in this case Superintendent Jesse II. Newlon. And like those reforms, too, Denver's effort was quickly taken up by school systems across the country as a kind of prototypical example of progressive innovation at its best.

Two principles were at the heart of the Denver program: an abiding commitment to universal education and a profound faith in the average classroom teacher. Jesse Newlon shared unreservedly the standard progressive belief that it was the responsibility of the public schools to serve all comers, and that to do so required drastic curricular adjustments in terms of changing social circumstances. Here there was little new in his thinking. Rather, his originality lay in his notion of how these adjustments might be accomplished. "No program of studies will operate that has not evolved to some extent out of the thinking of the teachers who are to apply it," he wrote his Board in 1923.[3] Hence the need was not for more committees of administrators, supervisors, and college professors to pro-

---

[1] Alice V. Keliher discusses the difficulties in *A Critical Study of Homogeneous Grouping* (New York, 1931).

[2] *Cities Reporting the Use of Homogeneous Grouping and of the Winnetka Technique and the Dalton Plan* (United States Bureau of Education, City School Leaflet No. 22, December, 1926).

[3] *The Denver Program of Curriculum Revision* (Denver, 1927), p. 12. See also Jesse H. Newlon: "Practical Curriculum Revision in the High Schools," *The North Central Association Quarterly*, I (1926), 254–63; and Jesse H. Newlon and A. L. Threlkeld: "The Denver Curriculum-Revision Program," in National Society for the Study of Education: *Twenty-Sixth Yearbook*, Part I, ch. xii. That Newlon retained his confidence in classroom teachers is evident from his later writings, especially *Education for Democracy in Our Time* (New York, 1939).

nounce on what the schools ought to do, but rather for some new device by which teachers themselves could participate in the business of curriculum making. In effect, what Newlon wanted was a way of democratizing the experience of the Committee on Economy of Time. And it was to this end that he introduced the Denver program of curriculum revision.

The effort began in 1922 with the creation of a series of system-wide curriculum committees, one for each of the school subjects at each of the school levels, elementary, junior high, and senior high. Composed almost exclusively of classroom teachers, these committees were requested to study and discuss the available literature in their professional fields with a view eventually to reworking courses of study. No official principles were laid down, and no time limit was set. The teachers were simply asked to read widely and to think as deeply as possible in the pursuit of their enterprise.

The initial phase seemed to go well, and in the spring of 1923 Newlon made three proposals to the Board: (1) that the curriculum committees meet during regular school hours and that substitutes be provided for teachers engaged in committee work, (2) that curriculum specialists from the education faculties of Colorado State Teachers College at Greeley and the University of Colorado at Boulder be employed to meet with the committees and coordinate their efforts,[4] and (3) that a variety of specialists in education and in the subject fields be called in as consultants and critics of the enterprise. The cost of these arrangements, Newlon assured, would be more than offset by the savings to taxpayers once "nonessentials and misplaced materials" had been culled from the curriculum. The Board readily acquiesced, appropriating $35,500 in support of the program.

Thus encouraged, the teachers redoubled their efforts. Following the pattern of the Committee on Economy of Time,

---

[4] These specialists were among the earliest of what Franklin Bobbitt later referred to as "educational generalists," the prototype of the modern system-wide curriculum-maker as well as the modern professor of curriculum. See National Society for the Study of Education: *Twenty-Sixth Yearbook*, Part II, ch. iii.

the Denver committees first worked out long lists of objectives
—drawn, of course, from "life situations"—and then determined the subject matter and activities that would most effectively achieve these objectives. The committees on home economics made a detailed survey of the home activities of junior
and senior high school girls. The committee on language in
the elementary school drew "a complete picture of the life
situations in which language is used by adults." The committee on mathematics in the junior high school spoke of the need
for citizens who understand modern business practices, the
expenditure of public money, and the world's commerce and
industries. Newlon himself was delighted that as time passed
goals were stated more and more "from the pupil point of
view." Once objectives had been determined, the committees
worked out not only courses of study but tests to measure student progress. To assist them in their work Newlon brought a
host of pedagogical luminaries from the leading teachers colleges and public-school systems of the country.

Gradually, revised syllabi began to appear, published as
successive numbers of the Denver Research Monograph Series.
Not surprisingly, they were snapped up by the thousands for
use in other school systems, not only in the United States
but abroad. So far as Newlon was concerned, however, the
publication of a course of study marked not a conclusion, but
merely a new beginning; for social change went inexorably
forward, necessitating continuous curricular readjustment.
Moreover, as committee personnel rotated—Newlon's effort
was to involve as many teachers as possible—new ideas came
to the fore, and with them the need for further reworking.

By the time Newlon left the superintendency in 1927 to assume the directorship of the Lincoln School at Teachers College, most courses of study at Denver had already gone through
at least one revision. Archie L. Threlkeld, Newlon's deputy
who succeeded him, commenced his administration with an
appraisal of the five-year effort—by the teachers themselves, of
course. The results were mixed: while teachers judged the revised courses satisfactory for the superior students, they were
disappointed in the provision for students of average or limited

ability.[5] Threlkeld, however, was little concerned, for he, like Newlon, considered the courses of study themselves the least important of the outcomes.[6] Far more significant were the long-range gains in teacher growth, enthusiasm, and morale. "Give every member of our profession a chance to do his best for it and the results need not be feared," Threlkeld told an NEA audience. "This is the challenge of curriculum making to every community." [7]

The Denver program continued unabated in the years after Newlon's departure, and spread rapidly to other urban communities.[8] Its great strength remained its supreme confidence in the classroom teacher; contending that professionals must have professional responsibilities, Newlon moved teachers to the very center of the business of curriculum making. Yet there were weaknesses too that soon became apparent as the program diffused: the weaknesses inherent in any enterprise that so stresses procedure as to subordinate substantive considerations. Newlon may have had a point when he contended that a revised course of study was the least important outcome of the process he set in motion; the procedure itself was the thing. And yet, as so often happens with reform movements, in less capable hands curriculum revision became procedure and little else. In too many school systems that fell heir to the Denver approach the rigorous wrestling with ideas that Newlon saw at the heart of the process was somehow lost, and instead teachers met and talked incessantly, seemingly to no end except further meeting and further talk. It all became a

[5] A. K. Loomis: "Recent Developments in Curriculum-Making in Denver," *Progressive Education*, VI (1929), 262–4; and *Denver Public Schools Bulletin*, II (1928), Nos. 1–2.

[6] Jesse H. Newlon: "Outcomes of Our Curriculum Program," in National Education Association: *Addresses and Proceedings*, 1925, p. 803.

[7] A. L. Threlkeld: "Curriculum Revision: How a Particular City May Attack the Problem," Ibid., p. 833.

[8] See Hollis L. Caswell *et al.*: *Curriculum Improvement in Public School Systems* (New York, 1950), ch. vii, "Curriculum Development in the Denver Public Schools" (Unpublished Mimeographed Statement, October 10, 1958, Denver Public Schools), and *Review of Four-Year Period, August, 1923 to July, 1927: A Part of the Forthcoming Twenty-Fourth Annual Report of the Denver Board of Education* (Denver, 1927), p. 24.

game in which the curriculum itself was subordinated to the techniques by which it would be revised—a sorry fate for the subject William T. Harris often referred to as "the most important question which the educator has before him."

If the Porter, Winnetka, and Denver reforms represent versions of progressive education in something of its pure form, contemporary developments in Muncie, Indiana, as portrayed by Robert and Helen Lynd in their classic *Middletown* studies, are perhaps more typical of what happened in the average American community—though even Muncie, by virtue of the location of Ball State Teachers College there, was somewhat atypical.

The Lynds in 1925 found a school system that had changed subtly but substantially during the preceding thirty years. The school of the nineties had been something of a "casual adjunct of the main business of 'bringing up' that went on day by day in the home"; the school of the twenties, on the other hand, was relied upon to carry "a more direct, if at most points still vaguely defined, responsibility." There had been a perceptible trend toward greater utility in subject matter and approach, but changes generally had been peripheral rather than central; Middletown's school, like its factory, remained a thoroughly regimented world:

> Immovable seats in orderly rows fix the sphere of activity of each child. For all, from the timid six-year-old entering for the first time to the most assured high school senior, the general routine is much the same. Bells divide the day into periods. For the six-year-olds the periods are short (fifteen to twenty-five minutes) and varied; in some they leave their seats, play games, and act out make-believe stories, although in "recitation periods" all movement is prohibited. As they grow older the taboo upon physical activity becomes stricter, until by the third or fourth year practically all movement is forbidden except the marching from one set of seats to another between periods, a brief interval of prescribed exercise daily, and periods of manual training or home economics once or

twice a week. There are "study-periods" in which children learn "lessons" from "text-books" prescribed by the state and "recitation-periods" in which they tell an adult teacher what the book has said. . . . With high school come some differences; more "vocational" and "laboratory" work varies the periods. But here again the lesson-textbook-recitation method is the chief characteristic of education. For nearly an hour a teacher asks questions and pupils answer, then a bell rings, on the instant books bang, powder and mirrors come out, there is a buzz of talk and laughter as all the urgent business of living resumes momentarily for the children, notes and "dates" are exchanged, five minutes pass, another bell, gradual sliding into seats, a final giggle, a last vanity case snapped shut, "In our last lesson we had just finished"—and another class is begun.[9]

When the Lynds returned in 1935, they found Middletown emotionally ready for changes of a "conservatively progressive" sort in its schools. As in the nation at large, the curse of bigness was spreading its pall: as the student body became larger and increasingly unselective, routinized procedures seemed more and more necessary. The same sort of mechanical bureaucracy that Rice had decried in New York, Boston, and Philadelphia in the nineties was now infecting Muncie. Thus the Lynds noted: "Middletown's school system, in step with those of other cities, has been becoming thoroughly 'modernized' and 'efficient' in its administrative techniques—to the dismay of some of the city's able teachers as they have watched the administrative horse gallop off with the educational cart. Some teachers regard it as characteristic of the trend toward administrative dominance that in one recent year eight administra-

[9] From *Middletown* by Robert S. Lynd and Helen Merrell Lynd, p. 188, copyright 1929, by Harcourt, Brace & World, Inc.; renewed, 1957, by Robert S. Lynd and Helen Merrell Lynd. Reprinted by permission of the publishers. Shortly before *Middletown* appeared, the noted German educator Erich Hylla published *Die Schule der Demokratie* (Berlin, 1928), in which he commented upon the widespread interest in progressive education in the United States, but the equally widespread prevalence of traditional methods of instruction.

tors and no teachers had their expenses paid to the National Education Association convention." [1]

Amidst all of this bureaucratization, there was much fine rhetoric about individual differences and their meaning for democracy. The philosophy of education of the Muncie schools, one major document proclaimed, "advocates that the aim of education should be to enable every child to become a useful citizen, to develop his individual powers to the fullest extent of which he is capable, while at the same time engaged in useful and lifelike activities." [2] Here, the Lynds were careful to point out, was not the voice of the businessmen, who dominated the school board, but rather that of the professional educators. Out of a concern for individual differences there did grow a guidance program to channel youngsters through the labyrinth of the high school into careers in Muncie and elsewhere. But that concern extended only to the point where it might challenge cherished community values. " 'Education for individual differences,' " the Lynds concluded, "will continue to mean tolerance as to the poet one reads, if any, and 'majoring' in literature or science, but it may mean in the years that lie ahead, less than at any time in the history of the city, the right to be 'different' as regards the broadening area of issues and activities which Middletown regards as central to its group welfare." [3]

The point should not be overgeneralized, but in many ways Muncie's conservative progressivism typifies the influence of progressive education on the pedagogical mainstream during the interbellum era. On the one hand, there were the shining examples like Winnetka; on the other hand, there were schools that must have taught McGuffey and little else well into the

[1] From *Middletown in Transition* by Robert S. Lynd and Helen Merrell Lynd, p. 206, copyright, 1937, by Harcourt, Brace & World, Inc. and reprinted with their permission.

[2] Ibid., pp. 220–1. Italics removed.

[3] Ibid., p. 226. The Lynd analysis must itself be placed in historical perspective. See, for example, Joseph A. Kahl: *The American Class Structure* (New York, 1957), ch. iii; Milton M. Gordon: *Social Class in American Sociology* (Durham, 1958); and Maurice R. Stein: *The Eclipse of Community* (Princeton, 1960), ch. ii.

thirties. Yet granted this, progressivism did leave its unmistakable imprint at a number of points: [4]

1. There was a steady extension of educational opportunity, downward as well as upward. A greater percentage of the population continued into the high schools, while kindergartens and nursery schools also flourished as the number of working women rose.

2. Numbers of school systems shifted from an eight-year elementary school followed by a four-year high school to a six-year elementary school followed by a three-year junior high school and then a three-year senior high school, partly to give greater attention to the special requirements of pubescent children.[5]

3. There was a continuing expansion and reorganization of the curriculum at all levels, and frequently in directions advocated by the progressives. In the secondary schools in particular there were vastly extended opportunities for work in trades, agriculture, home economics, physical education, and the arts.[6]

4. Along with the proliferation and reorganization of the formal curriculum, there came a concomitant expansion of extracurricular—or as the progressives called them to emphasize their integral part in the school program, "cocurricular"—activities. The informal student clubs and activities that had been radical innovations at the turn of the century became established features of the American school.

5. There was infinitely more variation and flexibility in the grouping of students, most commonly on the basis of intelligence and achievement tests. In addition, as districts con-

[4] An excellent general picture is given in *Education in the United States of America* (United States Office of Education, Bulletin, 1939, Misc. Number 3, Washington, 1939).

[5] For a view of the junior high school as "obviously a child of the progressive education movement," see S. R. Logan: "The Junior High School and Its Relations," *Progressive Education*, VI (1929), 17–22. Logan was assistant superintendent of schools at Winnetka.

[6] *Offerings and Registrations in High-School Subjects, 1933–34* (United States Office of Education, Bulletin, 1938, No. 6, Washington, 1938); and John F. Latimer: *What's Happened to Our High Schools?* (Washington, 1958).

solidated and schools became larger, guidance programs developed in an effort to take account of the varying needs and concerns of individual youngsters.

6. The character of the classroom changed markedly, especially at the elementary level, as projects began to compete with recitations as standard pedagogical procedure. Students and teachers alike tended to be more active, more mobile, and more informal in their relationships with one another.[7]

7. The materials of instruction changed dramatically as those who prepared them sought to incorporate the latest research on learning and child development. Textbooks became more colorful and attractive, and supplementary devices like flash cards, workbooks, simulated newspapers, slides, filmstrips, and phonograph records were used in growing numbers. In addition there were innumerable attempts to employ indigenous materials, ranging from local flora and fauna to locally manufactured products, in the course of instruction.

8. School architecture was modified to take account of these new developments, thereby lending them a measure of permanence. Assembly rooms, gymnasiums, swimming pools, playgrounds, athletic fields, laboratories, shops, kitchens, cafeterias, and infirmaries; miniature tables and chairs; movable furniture and partitions, improved lighting and ventilation—all testified eloquently to the changing program and commitment of the school.

9. Teachers were better educated; and by virtue of state certification requirements, their programs of preparation—both preservice and inservice—increasingly included professional courses that tended to reflect one or another of the versions of progressive education.[8]

[7] The effectiveness of these new procedures is examined in G. Derwood Baker et al.: New Methods vs. Old in American Education (New York, 1941); and J. Paul Leonard and Alvin C. Eurich: An Evaluation of Modern Education (New York, 1942).

[8] National Survey of the Education of Teachers (6 vols., United States Office of Education, Bulletin, 1933, No. 10, Washington, 1935). See especially Vol. III, Part VII, in which R. Bruce Raup deals with the educational philosophies of faculty members in schools for the professional education of teachers.

10. Finally, administrative relationships changed, if somewhat paradoxically. As schools and school systems became larger, bureaucracy increased; school administration became a separate professional function rather than a supplementary responsibility of the senior teachers. At the same time teachers were allowed a somewhat greater role in the determination of curriculum, while parents exercised a measure of influence through parent and parent-teacher associations. At few points did school boards or administrators relinquish important powers; nonetheless, there was a perceptible growth of parent and teacher participation in policymaking.

I V

As in the period before World War I, progressivism also influenced the colleges, though neither as radically nor as extensively as the lower schools. There was a good deal of experiment during the twenties and thirties, as well as much soul-searching about the aims of liberal education, about who should go to college and why, about what studies are of most worth, and about how best to humanize and integrate knowledge for purposes of instruction.[9] By 1932 the National Society for the Study of Education could report some 128 different attempts to reform the college curriculum, and the list was admittedly far from inclusive.[1]

It was in this context of widespread protest and reform that a number of institutions—notably Sarah Lawrence, Bennington, Black Mountain, Bard, and Rollins—set out to incarnate progressive education at the undergraduate level. Each institution proceeded in its own way amidst quite different circumstances; yet all were characteristically similar at a number of points. All reorganized their curricula to take account of changing student

[9] See the special supplements to *The New Republic:* "The American College and Its Curriculum," October 25, 1922, Part II, and "Remaking the American College," XLVI (1926), 233–58; James Harvey Robinson: *The Humanizing of Knowledge* (New York, 1923); R. L. Duffus: *Democracy Enters the College* (New York, 1936); and R. Freeman Butts: *The College Charts Its Course* (New York, 1939), Part IV.

[1] National Society for the Study of Education: *Thirty-First Yearbook* (Bloomington, 1932), Part II, ch. iii.

needs; all sought to individualize instruction; and all attempted in one way or another to involve students in the making of educational policy. Equally important, perhaps, all viewed themselves, and were generally viewed by others, as consciously progressive in aims and orientation.[2]

Consider Bennington as the leading example. The initial impetus for the college came in 1923 when Dr. Vincent Ravi-Booth, Minister of the First Congregational Church in Old Bennington, Vermont, called together a group of local citizens to consider the shortage of facilities for the higher education of women and "the opportunity it presented for a departure in undergraduate education in line with best modern standards and insight." The meeting apparently generated enough interest to warrant the formation of a permanent Committee of Twenty-One to carry the idea further. Conferences were held in New York City during the winter of 1923–4; and on April 28, 1924, 500 educators and interested laymen gathered at the Colony Club to hear addresses by President Ada Comstock of Radcliffe, President William Neilson of Smith, Professor Kilpatrick of Teachers College, and Dr. Booth. A second summer conference at Bennington resulted in the securing of a charter, the creation of a board of trustees, and pledges of $646,000, including a campus site and president's house, from the residents of Bennington.[3]

In January, 1928, the trustees elected as president Dr. Robert D. Leigh, a political scientist who had assisted in a number of educational experiments while on the faculties of Reed, Columbia, Barnard, and Williams. As a first order of business, Leigh drafted *The Educational Plan for Bennington College* (1929), a document which, while admittedly tentative, decisively shaped Bennington's future.[4] The need for the new col-

[2] Ernest H. Wilkins: "What Constitutes a Progressive College?" *Bulletin of the Association of American Colleges*, XIX (1933), 108–9; and Louis T. Benezet: *General Education in the Progressive College* (New York, 1943), pp. 14–15.

[3] *The Educational Plan for Bennington College*, rev. ed. (New York, 1929).

[4] That Leigh's plan was essentially different from earlier proposals is apparent from comparing it with Vincent Ravi-Booth: "A New College

lege, Leigh contended, stemmed from the plight of the progressive schools. They had successfully discarded "the medieval intellectualist tradition" only to find themselves hamstrung by college entrance requirements imposed from above and having little relevance to their own work. There was clearly place for at least one institution "which by the nature of its entrance requirements will leave the schools free to teach what they think best; which will in its own program emphasize individuality, direct experience, serious interest, initiative, creative and independent work, and self-dependence as educational aims."

The new college would abandon the usual point-course standards for admission in favor of individual judgments based on school records, test scores, personal histories, recommendations, interviews, and the like. Tuition would be high, since students would carry their full share of instructional costs; but scholarships would be liberal. The curriculum would take cognizance of "real differences between individual students in previous work, in maturity, and in essential purposes." The work of the first two years would assist each student "to discover for herself the field of human achievement in which she possesses a marked interest combined with distinct experience." The latter two years would be devoted to intensive study in this chosen field, broadly conceived.

The college schedule would make ample allowance for nonresident activities such as field trips, laboratory research at leading centers, work, or study and travel abroad. Students would also be encouraged to participate in the community life of Bennington. The ancient separation between curricular and extracurricular activities would disappear in favor of a four-year integrated experience. And finally, the faculty would be chosen primarily on the basis of teaching ability; hence the Ph.D. would figure in neither appointment nor promotion, having proved itself "an irrelevant standard for determining teaching effectiveness."

for Women," *Progressive Education*, II (1925), 138–45. See also Robert Devore Leigh: "The Newest Experiment in American Higher Education," in Paul Arthur Schilpp, ed.: *Higher Education Faces the Future* (New York, 1930), ch. xviii.

The active life of Bennington began in the autumn of 1932 when 87 freshmen met with 19 teachers for the first classes. The story of the venture from that time until the resignation of President Leigh in 1941 has been told by Barbara Jones in her book *Bennington College* (1946). Apparently Leigh managed to recruit an extraordinarily youthful and able faculty that maintained a consistently spirited interest in the experiment. Despite the liberal scholarship policy, the students were drawn mostly from well-to-do families that could afford to pay an annual tuition of $1,000 in addition to room and board in the midst of a depression. Competition for admission was keen, however, and the average intelligence of entering freshmen as measured by the American Council on Education Psychological Test was exceedingly high. By 1935 the student body had grown to 250 and the faculty to 50, forming a closely knit and highly self-conscious community of 300 that remained fairly constant in size and character during the remainder of Leigh's administration.

From the beginning Leigh sought to avoid the parochialism of the usual departmental organization by grouping studies into four broad divisions: the arts, the social studies, the sciences, and literature. Based on the assumption that education is more likely to continue when a few things have been learned well rather than many superficially, each student was enrolled as either a trial major or a major in one of these divisions, and her counselor was a member of that divisional faculty. And based on the assumption that student interest attaches most readily to current problems, introductory work generally concerned itself with modern civilization, "the culture resulting, especially in America, from scientific discovery and the industrial revolution." [5] Classes were small, friendly, and informal, emphasizing discussion, studio, or laboratory techniques; and most students undertook a good deal of their work in conference with individual instructors. In addition, a number of the young women—78 in all between 1933 and 1941—left the college for periods of nonresident work at institutions ranging

[5] *Bennington College: Announcement for the First Year, 1932–33*, pp. 4, 8.

from Martha Graham's dance studio to the Sorbonne. Finally, students participated in the multifarious affairs of the college community through house organization committees, the Student Educational Policies Committee, ad hoc faculty-student committees, and the like.

How well did the college fulfill its aims? In 1939 Dr. Alvin C. Eurich of Stanford University was invited to lead the faculty in an appraisal of the program to date. His results, reported in 1942, indicate that in comparison with other college students Bennington women ranked quite high in general cultural knowledge and in knowledge of contemporary affairs, foreign literature, and the fine arts; average in knowledge of science and mathematics; and disappointingly low in knowledge of American history and economics. In general, students did tend to do well in their fields of specialization. "Although Bennington has not particularly stressed subject matter in its objectives," Eurich concluded, "the College is clearly making as significant a contribution, if not more so, to this aspect of the development of students as most of the better colleges of the country." [6] Granted this, the Eurich study did indicate a measure of overspecialization in Bennington's program that led the faculty to introduce a number of reforms during the 1942–43 academic year.

What of other outcomes? Here Eurich ran into the age-old difficulty of measuring more elusive changes in attitude and character. A study published in 1943 by Theodore M. Newcomb, however, threw a good deal of light on this question. [7] In researches carried on between 1935 and 1939 Newcomb found a pronounced shift in political attitudes from conservatism to progressivism as between freshmen and seniors at Bennington, a shift that was far greater than comparable shifts at similar institutions and that tended to persist well after stu-

[6] Alvin C. Eurich and Catherine Evans: "Bennington College: An Evaluation" (Unpublished manuscript in Dr. Eurich's possession), p. 164. A less systematic but quite favorable appraisal was ventured by Hubert Herring in "Education at Bennington," *Harper's Magazine*, CLXXXI (1940), 408–17.

[7] Theodore M. Newcomb: *Personality and Social Change* (New York, 1943).

dents left the college. Newcomb ascribed the particular potency of Bennington in this respect to the unique effectiveness of the college community in acculturating students to its own liberal values—testimony indeed to the validity of Leigh's *Educational Plan*.[8] Yet he also found, not surprisingly, that many of those whose attitudes had shifted most radically encountered subsequent difficulty in their home communities. Thus, one sophomore in the "throes of emancipation" wrote with particular poignancy:

> We come from fine old Tory families who believe firmly in Higher Education—God knows why. So they sent us to a well-spoken-of college with an interesting-sounding scheme of education. Mary Jane could pursue her interests at Bennington and not get a nervous breakdown over Math the way Mummie did at Wellesley. So we went to Bennington, and our friends went to Vassar, Yale, Sarah Lawrence, Harvard, finishing school, St. Paul's-to-broker's-office. They came home, changed, a little. A slightly smarter jargon, unerring taste in clothes and Things To Do, and one and all, victrola records of the conventional ideas. We came home, some of us, talking a new language, some cobwebs swept out, a new direction opening up ahead we were dying to travel. Liberal, we thought we were. "What the hell's happened to you? Become a Parlor Pink?" "Well, hardly, Ha ha." It was a little bewildering.[9]

The problem was one that too many progressives never really contended with in their efforts to refashion education as an instrument of social reform.

Less than a month after Bennington opened in the autumn of 1932, a vastly different experiment was begun a thousand

[8] Newcomb's findings concerning the role of the "college culture" in shaping attitudes are generally confirmed by Philip E. Jacob's widely quoted study: *Changing Values in College* (New York, 1957), though Jacob contends that only in rare instances is the faculty as central in the process as at Bennington.

[9] Newcomb: op. cit., p. 11. The Eurich study found that 11 per cent of the alumnae "had some difficulty in adjusting to their associates, family, or community" after leaving college.

miles to the west as 400 students registered for their first courses at the University of Minnesota's new General College. Conceived by President Lotus D. Coffman as "an adventure in the field of higher education," the new institution was specifically charged with providing "a superior intellectual opportunity for a body of university students whose needs cannot now be adequately met by the existing organization of the university." [1] Few people then or since have referred to the General College as progressive education, for the phrase by 1932 already conjured the image of a private school for the well-to-do. Yet there is no denying that Minnesota's celebrated experiment embodied as effectively as any some of the most authentic ideas and traditions of the progressive education movement.

Lotus D. Coffman was undoubtedly one of the great university presidents of the interbellum era. A rural schoolmaster who had financed his own way to a Columbia doctorate—he wrote a dissertation on *The Social Composition of the Teaching Population* (1911)—he gave continuing voice to the ideals of educational equalitarianism in an age when equalitarianism of any sort seemed strangely out of fashion. "The state universities and the public schools from the beginning have been maintained to provide freedom of opportunity . . . ," he told an NEA audience in 1928. "Long ago they learned that genius and talent do not belong to any class because of wealth or social position. The only differences they recognize are differences due to ability and to a desire to achieve. They recognize that all cannot achieve alike nor move forward at equal rates of speed. They know that some must fall by the way and that some attempt work which they are not qualified to pursue. But they are not willing to condemn those of less talent merely because they have less talent. They propose for them just what they propose for the more talented—that each shall be permitted to progress as rapidly as his abilities will permit to the approximate limits of his attainment. The student of few tal-

[1] L. D. Coffman: "Open Letter on the Junior College," *The Biennial Report of the President of the University of Minnesota to the Board of Regents, 1930–32,* p. 29.

ents will not be denied his opportunity while the student of many talents is given his." [2]

Coffman's equalitarianism was never of the Jacobin variety that absolutely denies the existence of unusual or gifted individuals. In 1930 he and his deans asked and obtained the regents' approval for a new University College at Minnesota to care for the special needs of the superior student. But the point is they did not stop there. They were equally concerned with the large number of young men and women who came to the university and floundered through a year or two of work for which they were grievously ill-prepared, only to leave in disgust —and sometimes in disgrace—with little to show for their effort. It was for this group in particular that the regents in 1932 created a new two-year undergraduate unit charged with developing challenging and imaginative forms of general education. Originally called the Junior College, it was subsequently renamed the General College because its enterprise differed so markedly from many junior colleges already in existence.

To head the new General College, Coffman brought a zealous young educator who had been a graduate student at Minnesota some years before and had since taken part in the University of Wisconsin's experiment on its Milwaukee campus: Malcolm S. MacLean. Sharing unreservedly Coffman's vision of what the university might do for its less gifted students— both Coffman and MacLean steadfastly resisted the appellation "dumbbell college," insisting that general education would be equally appropriate to superior undergraduates— MacLean moved boldly to design a curriculum that would make young people at home in the modern world. "Our objective," he wrote in his first biennial report, "is to give these students a chance to make themselves supple and adaptable to change rather than rigidly prepared for a single occupation; to enlarge their vision to see the wholeness of human life; and to foster them in acquiring a sense of values in many phases of

[2] From Lotus D. Coffman: *The State University: Its Work and Problems,* pp. 40–1. Copyright 1934 by the University of Minnesota. Reprinted by permission of the University of Minnesota Press.

adult living outside the strictly vocational. We hope that the great majority of these students may come to comprehend the problems that face them." [3]

To this end MacLean and his associates worked out a series of "overview courses" focused on "the needs, interests, desires, and capacities" of students rather than any hard and fast notion of what might be good for them. The assortment and description of the offering had a breeziness unfamiliar in the usual college catalogue. Psychology was represented under four headings: "Practical Applications of Psychology," "How to Study," "Straight and Crooked Thinking," and "Biography." Likewise, the following appeared under History and Government: "Background of the Modern World," "American Citizen and His Government," "Functions of Government," "World Politics," and "History of Minnesota." So it was also with the other eight basic areas: Euthenics (essentially family life), Current Affairs, Economics, English, Physical Sciences, Biological Sciences, Mathematics, and the Arts. To qualify for the Associate in Arts degree, students were asked to pass two comprehensive examinations in General and Contemporary Affairs and comprehensive examinations in four of the other basic areas. [4]

For the first three years MacLean had no faculty of his own but drew instead on gifted instructors from other parts of the university. His initial staff included a brilliant assortment of professors, deans, and deans-to-be who not only dreamed up experimental courses but actually taught them. MacLean also had the assistance of Alvin Eurich—the same Eurich who later appraised the Bennington effort—in designing a new sort of examination to measure effectively the outcomes of the new

[3] *The Biennial Report of the President* . . . , 1932–34, p. 275. MacLean also stated the philosophy of the General College in "A College of 1934," *The Journal of Higher Education*, V (1934), 240–6, 314–22, and "The General College: The University of Minnesota," in William S. Gray: *General Education: Its Nature, Scope, and Essential Elements* (Chicago, 1934), pp. 119–27.

[4] In addition to the annual *Bulletins* of the General College, see Malcolm S. MacLean *et al.*: *Curriculum Making in the General College* (Minneapolis, 1940); and Ivol Spafford: *Building a Curriculum for General Education* (Minneapolis, 1943).

general program.[5] Finally, there was from the beginning an unusual counseling service that made every effort to assist students in spending their time as profitably as possible and to assist the faculty in a continuing appraisal of its enterprise.[6]

The centennial historian of the University of Minnesota, James Gray, has contended that if there be any identifying characteristic of the university, it is a continuing preoccupation with self-study.[7] Certainly few pedagogical ventures had been studied and assessed as relentlessly as the General College. Under grants from the General Education Board and the Rockefeller Foundation, a succession of detailed investigations began in 1935 on who actually came to the college, what happened to them there, and what seemed to be the outcomes. By 1943 a fairly clear and detailed picture had emerged.[8] Almost three-fourths of the students between 1932 and 1940 came from the Twin City area; fewer than 10 per cent came from out-of-state high schools. The overwhelming majority were from middle-class homes; most had placed in the lower third of their high school graduating classes. Fewer than one student in five remained to complete the requirements for the Associate in Arts degree.

When queried about the strengths and weaknesses of the program, these students replied about as any group of college students, ranging from keen enthusiasm to outright antagonism. Most viewed the greatest asset of the college as its thoroughgoing concern for its students; the most common criticisms centered in the vagueness and oversimplification of subject matter and the lack of specific preparation for future jobs or advanced college work. In general, though, the college seemed to retain a slight edge over other undergraduate insti-

[5] Committee on Educational Research of the University of Minnesota: *The Effective General College as Revealed by Examinations* (Minneapolis, 1937).

[6] Staff of the General College: *Report on Problems and Progress of the General College, University of Minnesota* (Minneapolis, 1939).

[7] James Gray: *The University of Minnesota, 1851–1951* (Minneapolis, 1951), p. 308.

[8] Ruth E. Eckert: *Outcomes of General Education* (Minneapolis, 1943); C. Robert Pace: *They Went to College* (Minneapolis, 1941); and Cornelia T. Williams: *These We Teach* (Minneapolis, 1943).

tutions. "General College students actually appear a little more ready than other students to attribute positive strengths to their college experiences," Ruth Eckert concluded in 1943. "When it is remembered that the majority of young people come to the General College under some measure of compulsion [deriving from the inability to enter other preferred colleges in the university], the favorable appraisal given by most students indicates that this program of general education has made some notable strides in selling itself to its consumers." [9] Apparently it also sold itself to educators and the public, for many of the pioneering innovations of the Minnesota experiment became standard fare in the rash of community colleges that appeared in the years immediately following World War II.

V

In one of the innumerable addresses he delivered during the early years of the General College, Malcolm MacLean advanced the intriguing notion that the Civilian Conservation Corps camps might well be considered a form of general education addressed to the millions of young Americans who found themselves neither in school nor at work during the depth of the depression.[1] He thereby directed attention to the most dramatic of the sweeping pedagogical innovations associated with the New Deal. Few of these programs were conceived primarily in educational terms; most resulted only indirectly from the attack on unemployment. And certainly no explicit educational philosophy bound them together.[2] Yet seen in perspective, almost all in one way or another managed to advance the cause of pedagogical progressivism.

The Civilian Conservation Corps was one of the earliest outcomes of the frantic "hundred days" of legislative activity fol-

[9] Eckert: op. cit., p. 190.

[1] Malcolm S. MacLean: "The General College: The University of Minnesota," p. 119.

[2] Roosevelt's educational ideas are discussed by Thomas H. Greer in *What Roosevelt Thought* (East Lansing, 1958), pp. 143–50. The educational program of the New Deal, however, was conceived as pragmatically as its other political and social reforms.

lowing Franklin D. Roosevelt's inauguration. A bill for "the relief of unemployment through the performance of useful public work" was introduced into the Congress on March 21, 1933, approved by voice votes in both houses on March 29 and 30, and signed by the President on April 1.[3] The program itself went into effect almost immediately, and with a hearteningly salutary effect on morale. Government offices in many cities were swamped with applicants, and *The New York Times* reported as early as April 9: "A singing, cheering, wise-cracking crowd milled about the recruiting offices all day. Army cooks and the kitchen police dispensed liberal portions of army 'chow' while the young men sang 'Happy Days Are Here Again.' Shouts of 'Hooray for the New Deal' were also heard. . . . So enthusiastic were some of the youths over getting to work, a boon that had been denied them a long time, that they grabbed brooms from the army K.P.'s hands and swept vigorously in the face of the wind." [4]

The administration of the Corps, worked out by Roosevelt and Louis Howe, was remarkably complicated. The Department of Labor selected the enrollees; the War Department established, built, and managed the camps, caring for health, welfare, and discipline as well; and the Departments of Agriculture and of the Interior planned and directed the work projects. Policy was determined by a representative interdepartmental CCC Advisory Committee. And presiding over the whole enterprise was Director Robert Fechner, a long-time unionist and former official of the International Association of Machinists, who was himself responsible to the President.

Neither Roosevelt, nor Congress, nor the educational profession, for that matter, viewed the creation of the CCC as in any way an extension of federal educational prerogatives. As a matter of fact, the educational possibilities of the venture seem

[3] The most thorough analysis of the New Deal's educational programs is given in Harry Zeitlin: "Federal Relations in American Education, 1933–1943: A Study of New Deal Efforts and Innovations" (Unpublished Doctoral Thesis, Columbia University, 1958). For the Civilian Conservation Corps, see also Kenneth Holland and Frank Ernest Hill: *Youth in the CCC* (Washington, 1942).

[4] *The New York Times*, April 9, 1933, p. 28.

to have been missed completely during the early debates on the enabling legislation—probably a good thing for its political fortunes. Yet the men were not long in the camps before some sort of educational program began to suggest itself. Accordingly, the War Department on May 9, 1933, issued an order, approved by Fechner, to the effect that instruction in forestry would be offered by members of the Forestry Service and that "classes in general and vocational educational courses" would be conducted, when practicable, by the Army for all enrollees who desired them. Three weeks later another order authorized the establishment of camp libraries.[5]

During much of 1933 Fechner and the Army remained decidedly cool to any expansion beyond these modest beginnings. The demand for education mounted, however, and in the autumn of that year George F. Zook, United States Commissioner of Education, drafted an over-all plan for an extended program. Roosevelt approved it late in November, charging the Office of Education with staffing and policymaking, but vesting ultimate authority in the War Department. On December 29, 1933, Clarence S. Marsh, Dean of the Evening Session at the University of Buffalo, was appointed Educational Director of the CCC, to preside over a staff of nine deputies, one for each of the Army corps areas, and 1,087 camp advisers.

A *Handbook for the Educational Advisers in the Civilian Conservation Corps* was rushed into print as a first order of business, and quickly revealed the broad outlines of the program. Six dominant aims were defined: to develop powers of self-expression, self-attainment, and self-culture; to develop pride and satisfaction in cooperative endeavor; to develop an understanding of prevailing social and economic conditions, to the end that each man might cooperate intelligently in improving these conditions; to preserve and strengthen good habits of health and mental development; to assist each man, by vocational counseling and training, to meet his employment problems when he leaves camp; and to develop an appreciation of nature and of country life.

[5] Frank Ernest Hill: *The School in the Camps* (New York, 1935), p. 9.

The advisers were reminded that the program, being wholly voluntary, had to appeal to the men themselves. No formal classes as pursued in the schools and colleges would suffice. "The activities you carry on must grow out of the needs and wishes of the men," the pamphlet counseled. Vocation, social problems, home relationships, hobbies, and other matters of immediate interest were the topics on which to begin. Likewise, informal discussion, individual counseling, and instruction through radio and motion pictures were the methods most likely to elicit widespread participation. "Yours is a task without clear precedents," the advisers were told. "Your ingenuity in devising ways of meeting the situation as you find it at the camp is your real test." [6]

Apparently the advisers were indeed ingenious. By mid-1934 Marsh estimated that around 40 per cent of the enrollees were participating in the program. By 1935 he was describing it as a "great American folk-school movement," suggesting that it might well hold the key to "new ways of bridging the gap between school and job"; in any case, it had become "a recognized part of the American system of education." By 1938-9, attendance was officially estimated at 91.3 per cent of the average strength of the Corps. Almost two-thirds of the enrollees took part in some sort of job training, and about one-third attended formal classes on every conceivable subject. Over 8,000 illiterates were taught to read and write; over 5,000 of the men received eighth-grade certificates; over 1,000 received high school diplomas, and 96 actually received college degrees. In all, some 25,000 instructors took part in the enterprise.[7]

As might be expected, the continuing expansion of the CCC's educational program after 1934 aggravated many of the problems inherent in divided control. In a memorandum to Commissioner of Education John W. Studebaker in 1935—Studebaker had replaced Zook the preceding year—Marsh

[6] A Handbook for the Educational Advisers in the Civilian Conservation Corps Camps (Washington, 1934), p. 4. The United States Office of Education subsequently published A Manual for Instructors in Civilian Conservation Corps Camps (Washington, 1935) which was, for all intents and purposes, a brief exegesis of progressive pedagogy.

[7] Zeitlin: op. cit., ch. iii.

complained of a variety of "barriers" that made almost impossible attainment of the Office of Education's objectives. On closer examination the "barriers" seem to have been Fechner and the War Department. "The fact that every major recommendation to strengthen and enrich the Educational Program has been disapproved by the Director seems to indicate on his part, either lack of interest in or active hostility to the Educational Program," Marsh insisted. So far as he was concerned, the possibilities of the CCC as "an agency making for a more effective social order" had hardly been touched.

Roosevelt backed Fechner, however, and his support proved decisive. "We want CCC enrollees to be given every possible opportunity to improve themselves," he wrote Harold Ickes in 1937, "but there are natural barriers that make it impossible for a CCC camp to ever become a school in the usual understanding of that term." When Congress extended the life of the Corps that year, it did grant formal recognition to the educational program, specifically authorizing enrollees to devote ten hours a week to educational activities; but there was no essential change in the philosophy of the Corps, and no modification of the arrangement subordinating the Office of Education's program to War Department control.[8] Efforts to reorient the CCC to educational purposes persisted, but apparently to no avail.[9] The Corps remained "work-centered" to the very end.

The CCC may have been the most dramatic of Roosevelt's educational innovations, but it by no means exhausts the pro-

[8] Ibid., pp. 96–106.
[9] The principal thrust came from the American Youth Commission, created in 1935 by the American Council on Education, and the Educational Policies Commission, created in 1936 by joint action of the National Education Association and its affiliate, the Department of Superintendence. The policy statements and research monographs that issued from these Commissions, particularly the first, were legion. See Louise Arnold Menefee and M. M. Chambers: *American Youth: An Annotated Bibliography* (Washington, 1938); M. M. Chambers and Elaine Exton: *Youth—Key to America's Future* (Washington, 1949); American Youth Commission: *The Civilian Conservation Corps* (Washington, 1940); and Educational Policies Commission: *The Civilian Conservation Corps, the National Youth Administration, and the Public Schools* (Washington, 1941).

gressive thrust of the New Deal in education. The Works Progress Administration organized thousands of nursery schools for the children of families on home relief, taught well over a million illiterates to read and write, and ran a vast adult education enterprise with an annual enrollment of almost 1,500,000. In addition, WPA funds purchased school lunches, vocational and recreational equipment, and almost 6,000 new buildings for state public school systems—this over and above the 12,700 new schools built by the Public Works Administration.[1] Finally, as part of the WPA, the National Youth Administration was established in June, 1935 to provide for the nation's unemployed youth "their chance in school, their turn as apprentices, and their opportunity for jobs—a chance to work and earn for themselves." [2] During the eight years of its operation, the NYA not only enabled thousands to complete their education by providing them with part-time employment; it also developed an extraordinarily imaginative array of guidance and placement services, training opportunities, and recreational activities for young men and women who had already left the schools.

However ingenious these several programs might have been, they did tend to bypass state and local authorities on the one hand and the organized educational profession on the other; and by the late thirties there were widespread protests—the loudest from the NEA and its affiliates—about the continued federalization of the American school system.[3] World War II quickly put an end to both the threat and the controversy as most of the New Deal's emergency programs simply vanished

[1] Zeitlin: op. cit., chs. iv–vi.

[2] The history of the NYA is told by Betty and Ernest K. Lindley in *A New Deal for Youth* (New York, 1938). For the student movements that provided a backdrop for the NYA see George Philip Rawick: "The New Deal and Youth: The Civilian Conservation Corps, the National Youth Administration, and the American Youth Congress" (Unpublished Doctoral Thesis, University of Wisconsin, 1957). See also Palmer O. Johnson and Oswald L. Harvey: *The National Youth Administration* (Washington, 1938); and Doak S. Campbell, Frederick H. Bair, and Oswald L. Harvey: *Educational Activities of the Works Progress Administration* (Washington, 1939).

[3] Zeitlin traces the controversy in detail. Op. cit., ch. viii.

into history. What remained was a legacy of concern: teachers emerged from the depression sensitized as never before to the educational predicament of out-of-school youth and to the public's responsibility for contending with it. Here more than anywhere else, perhaps, lay the abiding impact of the New Deal on the subsequent course of American education.

V I

All things considered, the progressive education movement probably reached its high-water mark during the years immediately preceding World War II. The Progressive Education Association achieved its membership peak in the summer of 1938, and in October of that year *Time* ran a cover story on the organization, contending: "No U.S. school has completely escaped its influence." [4] Within the profession, progressive ideas enjoyed widespread support, and there are good grounds for Paul Woodring's recent observation that it was smart politics for an ambitious schoolman to embrace them. And a 1940 Gallup poll revealed that the public, too, was generally favorable to what was going on in the schools, though a substantial segment seemed "unaware of the objectives receiving major attention." [5]

Four years later, a much more elaborate survey by the National Opinion Research Center tended to confirm Gallup's results, though with some disturbing addenda. [6] When asked whether they were "satisfied with what children are getting from their education in school," 80 per cent of the respondents said yes, 15 per cent said no, and 5 per cent were undecided. But to the query, "Is there any kind of change you would like to see made in the public schools?" the results were of a somewhat different order. Fifty-seven per cent suggested no

[4] *Time*, October 31, 1938, p. 31.
[5] "What People Think about Youth and Education," *National Education Association Research Bulletin*, XVIII (1940), 187–219.
[6] National Opinion Research Center: *The Public Looks at Education* (Denver, 1944).

changes, though most of these were noncommittal. Of those who did suggest changes, however, 44 per cent advanced modifications in curriculum and method in directions decidedly *unprogressive* in character. Moreover, when these respondents were classified according to educational attainment, it was discovered that while 69 per cent of those with an elementary education had no changes in mind, 86 per cent of those with a college education advanced one or more suggestions. Now it may simply have been that those with sixteen years of schooling were more knowledgeable, more interested, and hence more vocal. Or indeed, it may rather have been that the more educated and articulate segments of the public were beginning to fall away from the progressive movement, and that as the college-educated population increased, progressives could expect growing opposition to their cause.

All the evidence points in the latter direction. For both within the movement and without, the more perceptive already realized that despite apparent successes, something of a crisis was brewing. Long-smouldering criticisms of progressive education for its optimistic humanitarianism, its essential naturalism, its overwhelming utilitarianism, and its persistent antiformalism suddenly burst into flame in the popular press.[7] Progressive schools were pilloried as "crimebreeders," "time-wasters," and "playhouses," and titles like "Lollypops vs. Learn-

[7] The fullest accounts of the criticisms are given in Malcolm Skilbeck: "Criticisms of Progressive Education, 1916–1930" (Unpublished Master's Thesis, University of Illinois, 1958); Sister Mary Ruth Sandifer: *American Lay Opinion of the Progressive School* (Washington, 1943); and Charles R. Foster, Jr.: *Editorial Treatment of Education in the American Press* (Cambridge, 1938), chs. ix–xiv. See also, *inter alia*, B. B. Bogoslovsky: *The Ideal School* (New York, 1936); Frederick S. Breed: *Education and the New Realism* (New York, 1939); Norman Foerster: *The Future of the Liberal College* (New York, 1938); Herman Harrell Horne: *This New Education* (New York, 1931); Robert Maynard Hutchins: *The Higher Learning in America* (New Haven, 1936); I. L. Kandel: *The Cult of Uncertainty* (New York, 1943); Jacques Maritain: *Education at the Crossroads* (New Haven, 1943); Albert Jay Nock: *The Theory of Education in the United States* (New York, 1932); Sister Joseph Mary Raby: *A Critical Study of the New Education* (Washington, 1932); and Paul Shorey: *The Assault on Humanism* (Boston, 1917).

ing" and "Treason in the Textbooks" became the order of the day.[8] More significantly, perhaps, progressive intellectuals who had once been enthusiastic supporters now turned their backs on the movement. Thus, to take one notable example, Walter Lippmann—a very different Lippmann from the one who had called *Democracy and Education* "the mature wisdom of the finest and most powerful intellect devoted to the future of American civilization"—lashed out against the superficiality and parochialism of "the modern school" in the columns of *Commonweal* magazine: "There is no common faith, no common body of principle, no common body of knowledge, no common moral and intellectual discipline. Yet the graduates of these modern schools are expected to form a civilized community. They are expected to govern themselves. They are expected to have a social conscience. They are expected to arrive by discussion at common purposes. When one realizes that they have no common culture, is it astounding that they have no common purpose? That they worship false gods? That only in war do they unite? That in the fierce struggle for existence they are tearing western society to pieces?" [9]

Within the profession too, those who took time out from drumbeating could perceive that the warring factions within the movement had come to something of an impasse. In 1938 Boyd Bode published *Progressive Education at the Crossroads*, a trenchant critique in which he charged that progressive education had never sufficiently emancipated itself from Rousseauan libertarianism, and that its failure was readily apparent in the "excrescences" that had grown up about the movement. "Progressive education stands at the parting of the ways," he warned his confreres. "The issue of democracy is becoming more insistent in all the relations of life. It implies a social and an educational philosophy which needs to be formulated and applied. If progressive education can succeed in translating its

[8] Ann L. Crockett: "Lollypops vs. Learning," *Saturday Evening Post*, March 16, 1940, pp. 29, 105–6; and O. K. Armstrong: "Treason in the Textbooks," *The American Legion Magazine*, September, 1940, pp. 8–9, 51, 70–2.

[9] Walter Lippmann: "Education without Culture," *Commonweal*, XXXIII (1940–1), 323.

spirit into terms of democratic philosophy and procedure, the future of education in this country will be in its hands. On the other hand, if it persists in a one-sided absorption in the individual pupil, it will be circumnavigated and left behind." [1]

Bode's words proved prophetic indeed. Progressives sensed the challenge, but they seemed powerless to respond. Within their own councils they devoted themselves increasingly to internecine warfare. And the continuing professionalization of the movement removed them ever further from the public. More and more they responded to criticism in the ringing rhetoric of self-justification, and in the pages of their own learned journals. The faithful were roused and reconverted, but meanwhile large uncommitted segments of the public listened attentively to the critics. In the end, it became the peculiar paradox of the movement that its dissolution began at the very floodtide of its fortunes. It took less than two decades for the tide to recede, and for Bode's bitter prophecy to be fulfilled.

[1] Boyd H. Bode: *Progressive Education at the Crossroads* (New York, 1938), pp. 43–4.

9

The Crisis in
Popular Education

THERE is a "conventional wisdom," to borrow from John Kenneth Galbraith, in education as well as in economics, and by the end of World War II progressivism had come to be that conventional wisdom. Discussions of educational policy were liberally spiced with phrases like "recognizing individual differences," "personality development," "the whole child," "social and emotional growth," "creative self-expression," "the needs of learners," "intrinsic motivation," "persistent life situations," "bridging the gap between home and school," "teaching children, not subjects," "adjusting the school to the child," "real life experiences," "teacher-pupil relationships," and "staff planning." Such phrases were a cant, to be sure, the peculiar jargon of the pedagogues. But they were more than that, for they signified that Dewey's forecast of a day when *progressive* education would eventually be accepted as *good* education had now finally come to pass.[1]

---

[1] Dewey advanced the forecast in *Experience and Education* and reiterated it in his introduction to Agnes de Lima's book *The Little Red School House* (New York, 1942).

The sources that document this view are legion: professional journals, education textbooks, school board reports, and the various publications of the Office of Education. Few are more significant, however, than a series of pronouncements issued during the middle forties by the Educational Policies Commission: *Education for All American Youth* (1944), *Educational Services for Young Children* (1945), and *Education for All American Children* (1948). Since its creation in 1936 the Commission had spoken boldly and authoritatively as the responsible voice of the teaching profession. Its membership in 1944 included the presidents of Harvard and Cornell, along with such leading pedagogical lights as George Stoddard, George Strayer, and Pearl Wanamaker; Commissioner John Studebaker and his predecessor, George Zook, were advisory members. Anything these people had to say would undoubtedly have been of interest, but their formulations as members of the Commission took on added weight because of the high prestige that body had come to command in the councils of American teachers.

The Commission's three volumes set forth a comprehensive blueprint of postwar education in Farmville and American City, both in the mythical state of Columbia.[2] The message of the analysis is clear. Americans must organize a comprehensive public school system concerned with all young people from the age of three through twenty, those in school as well as those outside. Public nursery schools in Columbia are followed by six-year elementary schools and then by eight-year secondary schools, organized as single units with three subdivisions: a junior high school, a senior high school, and a community institute. All these schools are unreservedly dedicated to the proposition "that every youth in these United States—regardless of sex, economic status, geographic location, or race—should experience a broad and balanced education which will (1) equip him to enter an occupation suited to his abilities

---

[2] The Commission insisted that it was not drawing any blueprint but rather sketching "samples of the many different possible solutions to the problem of meeting the educational needs of all American youth." What emerged, though, was willy-nilly a blueprint.

and offering reasonable opportunity for personal growth and social usefulness; (2) prepare him to assume the full responsibilities of American citizenship; (3) give him a fair chance to exercise his right to the pursuit of happiness; (4) stimulate intellectual curiosity, engender satisfaction in intellectual achievement, and cultivate an ability to think rationally; and (5) help him to develop an appreciation of the ethical values which should undergird all life in a democratic society." [3]

The nursery school, a unit defined as "an extension of educational services to include children too young for the customary reading program of grade one," is a regular part of the public school system, providing children with a supervised program of "work-play indoors and out." The youngsters experiment with clay, paints, and crayons, use simple tools, play and listen to the phonograph, and examine books and pictures. They dance and dramatize, explore the wonderland of nature and science, and make frequent trips to local stores and nearby farms. From the beginning they work at the business of learning how to behave as "participating members of a democratic group." The staff of the nursery school includes teachers, family life consultants, nursing and medical personnel, and mental hygiene and nutrition experts. Parents too, of course, play a central role in the program.

The elementary school strives toward "the discovery and full development of all the humane and constructive talents of each individual" at the same time as it nurtures "social responsibility and the cooperative skills necessary to the progressive improvement of social institutions." The staff works constantly at designing a curriculum to meet "the total needs of children." Not only the three R's, but physical well-being and mental health are prime educational responsibilities. Above all, both children and teachers are freed from a "narrow and unimaginative daily routine." The description of a typical day at "Oak Hill School" is revealing. During the early morning the six- and seven-year-olds "play house" in an alcove, imaginatively recreating the life of the world they know, using a collec-

[3] Educational Policies Commission: *Education for All American Youth* (Washington, 1944), p. 21.

tion of child-sized toys, dolls, and furniture. Another group of younger children are in the midst of a project on animal life in the Oak Hill neighborhood, and use the time to answer questions aided by a variety of reference books. Several ten- and eleven-year-olds duplicate programs for a Neighborhood Night scheduled for the coming Friday. After the mid-morning break most of the children work individually or in small groups on arithmetic skills. Lunch hour means not only a nutritious meal but the eager pursuit of various committee responsibilities. In the afternoon there is reading, followed by a half-hour of physical activity, and then a final period of group work and community singing.

In Farmville's secondary school, a new consolidated school created through the union of five formerly independent school districts, some 800 boys and girls participate in a "common secondary program" from grades seven through nine, and a "partially differentiated program" from grades ten through fourteen—differentiated, that is, with respect to occupation, intellectual pursuit, and recreational interest. New courses have been worked out cooperatively by the Farmville faculty. For example, the tenth-grade offering in "The World at Work" not only acquaints students with the economic system in Farmville and American City, but also helps them "to become familiar with the facts about the chief occupational fields, among which their choices are likely to be made." And cutting across the whole program is a continuing concern with guidance, "personal assistance to individual boys and girls in making their plans and decisions about careers, education, employment, and all sorts of personal problems." Four special counselors give full time to such assistance, but the entire staff participates. Finally, a community institute provides continuing education and services, full-time or part-time, for those adults who desire them. Needless to say, the schools of American City, making due allowances for cultural and environmental differences, reflect many of the same emphases.

Supporting these educational services are a variety of local citizens' groups that help in the formulation of educational policy, an interested legislature willing to contribute a larger share of state tax funds to equalize educational opportunity, and, at the same time, a Congress ready to use federal money to neutralize vast inequalities among the states. The mistakes of the thirties, in which federal educational programs circumvented the schools rather than assisting them, are now past history. Local, state, and federal authorities work hand in hand at maintaining the schools as a bulwark of American democracy.

Education in the Commission's world of the fifties is patently the logical outcome of the progressive education movement. In effect, the Commission was projecting the "schools of tomorrow" that the United States might have if it was willing to buy the progressive dream. The Commission's pronouncements were discussed and checked with the American Vocational Association, the National Association of Secondary School Principals, the American Association of Health, Physical Education, and Recreation, the NEA's National Department of Elementary School Principals, and a host of individual experts in and out of the educational world. Once they appeared, they were quickly incorporated into education syllabi across the nation. In retrospect, there is little doubt but that they summed up as well as any contemporary publications the best-laid plans of the teaching profession for American education in the postwar decades.[4]

I I

The conventional widsom, Galbraith tells us, is articulated at all levels of sophistication. At the highest level, that of scholarship, some novelty of statement or formulation is always encouraged, since the very vigor of minor debate preserves an aura of continuing criticism while effectively excluding any fundamental challenge. So it happened with progressive education after World War II. The movement had lost its intel-

---

[4] It is interesting to note in this respect the close similarity of the recommendations advanced by the celebrated Regents' inquiry into the character and cost of public education in the State of New York. See *Education for American Life: A New Program for the State of New York* (New York, 1938).

lectual vitality, but not its reformist thrust;[5] the presence of the one without the other resulted in a short-lived Alexandrian period in which refinements were elaborated one upon the other, but in which insistent realities were studiously ignored. What eventuated was a complex pedagogical mystique, mastered by the initiates but virtually incomprehensible to laymen concerned with the making of educational policy.

Of all the postwar refinements of progressive education— and they were legion, ranging from the preoccupation with group dynamics in the teachers colleges to the preoccupation with guidance in the schools[6]—none achieved the publicity, or indeed the notoriety, of the so-called life-adjustment movement. The ill-fated effort originated in the activities of the Vocational Education Division of the United States Office of Education. Early in 1944 that Division undertook a study of

[5] The clearest restatement of the progressive philosophy was John L. Childs: *Education and Morals* (New York, 1950). The principal theoretical reformulations came in the works of Theodore Brameld and Isaac B. Berkson. For Brameld's assessment of the progressive education movement, see *Philosophies of Education in Cultural Perspective* (New York 1955), chs. iv–vi; for his own "reconstructionism," see *Ends and Means in Education* (New York, 1950) and *Toward a Reconstructed Philosophy of Education* (New York, 1956). For Berkson's assessment of the progressive education movement, see *Education Faces the Future* (New York, 1943), chs. vi–xi; for his own reformulation, see *The Ideal and the Community* (New York, 1958).

[6] The literature on group dynamics in the postwar decade is enormous, as witness the bibliographies in "Research on Human Relations and Programs of Action," *Review of Educational Research*, XXIII (1953), 285–384. The work lent added vigor and prestige to the techniques of curriculum development Jesse Newlon had earlier introduced in Denver. When Earl C. Kelley incorporated many of these techniques into a series of teacher workshops at Wayne State University and reported the results in *The Workshop Way of Learning* (New York, 1951), John Dewey wrote: "After familiarizing myself with the activities initiated and conducted by the workshop as here described, I have concluded that it supplies the missing and much needed factor in development of the theory of progressive education. For it applies to the *training of teachers* the principles that have been set forth as applicable to and in the education of those under instruction." The clearest view of the guidance movement as an extension of progressivism is afforded by Robert Hendry Mathewson in *A Strategy for American Education* (New York, 1957); see also the penetrating review of Mathewson's volume by Paul Woodring in the *Harvard Educational Review*, XXVIII (1958), 278–80.

"Vocational Education in the Years Ahead"; and as part of the usual regimen of committee and consultant activities, a conference was organized for May 31 and June 1, 1945, at the Wardman Park Hotel in Washington. For two days there was much talk about the problems of high school students whose needs seemed to be served neither by vocational nor by college-preparatory programs; and toward the very end of the sessions Dr. Charles Prosser, the able lobbyist of the National Society for the Promotion of Industrial Education who had subsequently gone on to head the Dunwoody Institute in Minneapolis, introduced the following resolution: [7]

> It is the belief of this conference that, with the aid of this report in final form [the report on "Vocational Education in the Years Ahead"], the vocational school of a community will be able better to prepare 20 percent of the youth of secondary school age for entrance upon desirable skilled occupations; and that the high school will continue to prepare another 20 percent for entrance to college. We do not believe that the remaining 60 percent of our youth of secondary school age will receive the life adjustment training they need and to which they are entitled as American citizens—unless and until the administrators of public education with the assistance of the vocational education leaders formulate a similar program for this group.
>
> We therefore request the U.S. Commissioner of Education and the Assistant Commissioner for Vocational Education to call at some early date a conference or a series of regional conferences between an equal number of representatives of general and of vocational education—to consider this problem and to take such initial steps as may be found advisable for its solution.

The resolution was unanimously adopted by the conferees.

[7] United States Office of Education: *Life Adjustment Education for Every Youth* (Washington, n.d.), p. 15. For an earlier and fuller statement of Prosser's ideas on secondary education, see his Inglis lecture; *Secondary Education and Life* (Cambridge, 1939).

Commissioner Studebaker was agreeable, and the Office of Education began to lay plans for the proposed series of conferences. Five regional gatherings were held between April and November, 1946, bringing together secondary school principals, school superintendents, state directors and supervisors of vocational education, representatives of state departments of education, administrators and professors of teacher education institutions, and officers of national professional associations. (No arts and science professors from the universities were included.) In all, thirty-five states and the District of Columbia were represented. It was the consensus of these regional conferences (1) that secondary education was "failing to provide adequately and properly for the life adjustment of perhaps a major fraction of the persons of secondary school age"; (2) that "functional experiences in the areas of practical arts, home and family life, health and physical fitness, and civic competence" were fundamental to any educational program designed to meet the needs of youth; (3) that a supervised program of work experience was essential for most high school youngsters; (4) that those entrusted with the education of teachers needed "a broadened viewpoint and a genuine desire to serve all youth"; and (5) that sufficient public interest could be mobilized to support a nationwide program of life-adjustment education.[8] These propositions were brought before a national conference the following May, which recommended in turn that a Commission on Life Adjustment Education for Youth be created, and that a vigorous program be inaugurated to promote the purposes of life-adjustment education at the state and local levels. Commissioner Studebaker asked various professional associations to submit nominees for the Commission, and eventually a nine-member body was formed under the chairmanship of Superintendent Benjamin Willis of Yonkers.

From the beginning, the Commission saw its prime task as one of translating conventional progressive wisdom into contemporary educational practice. "National committees," stated

[8] *Life Adjustment Education for Every Youth*, p. 17.

an early report, "have been developing and extending basic theses for the past thirty years, and they have made progress in clarifying thought and securing consensus. It is the conviction of the Commission that there is available such a wealth of sound theory by which to achieve effective educational programs that at this time the great need is for action which translates the theory into school practice." [9] Based on its own reading of these reports, the Commission defined its goal as an education "designed to equip all American youth to live democratically with satisfaction to themselves and profit to society as home members, workers, and citizens." [1]

In spelling this out, the Commission reiterated most of the now time-honored phrases: life-adjustment education was concerned with "physical, mental, and emotional health," and with "the present problems of youth as well as their preparation for future living"; it recognized "the educational value of responsible work experience in the life of the community" as well as "the importance of personal satisfactions and achievements for each individual within the limits of his abilities." And as if in anticipation of the torrent of criticism that would later descend, the Commission noted that life-adjustment education "emphasizes active and creative achievements as well as an adjustment to existing conditions; it places a high premium upon learning to make wise choices, since the very concept of American democracy demands the appropriate revising of aims and the means of attaining them." [2] But the disclaimer was of little avail. The terribly unfortunate choice of name—"life-adjustment education"—coupled with the unmistakable emphasis on adjustment *to* existing conditions, was more than enough to damn the movement in the eyes of a generation increasingly concerned with conformity in American life and thought.

The first Commission on Life Adjustment Education for

[9] Ibid., p. 3.

[1] United States Office of Education: *Vitalizing Secondary Education: Report of the First Commission on Life Adjustment Education for Youth* (Washington, 1951), p. 1.

[2] Ibid., pp. 32–3.

Youth worked for three years, and turned in a report in 1951; a second Commission followed and issued its report in 1954. [3] A study of these two documents reveals that aided by the Office of Education, the movement made substantial headway in school systems throughout the nation, and probably represented the most forceful thrust of progressivism at the secondary level. The first Commission sponsored a number of regional and national conferences; it initiated cooperative efforts with several influential organizations like the National Association of Secondary School Principals and the National Catholic Education Association; and it sponsored publications that were widely distributed by the Government Printing Office. Most important, perhaps, the Commission eagerly encouraged state and local effort, and by 1950 it could report a plethora of workshops, conferences, surveys, and pilot programs in public and private schools. (At least five of the 122 Roman Catholic diocesan school systems, for example, were reorganizing in light of "life-adjustment principles" during the 1949–50 academic year.)

The second Commission, enlarged to include representatives of the American Association of Colleges for Teacher Education, the National Congress of Parents and Teachers, and the National School Boards Association, also pressed ahead at the state and local levels, and its 1954 report devoted most of its space to describing the more effective programs to date. The report ended with a section on "unfinished business" that pointed to the need for continuing study and experiment. "One may conclude," the Commission contended, "that an enormous and necessary task undertaken during the 20th century is but half finished. This is the task of providing universal secondary education for all youth that they may live in a society which must make full utilization of scientific discovery. The speed with which this assignment is completed depends in part on the resources which the public through public funds, individually or through foundations are willing to devote to

[3] United States Office of Education: *A Look Ahead in Secondary Education: Report of the Second Commission on Life Adjustment Education for Youth* (Washington, 1954).

the unfinished business of providing education for all American youth." [4]

No new commission was appointed in 1954, and no new funds were forthcoming, for the life-adjustment movement had come under sharp attack by the critics of progressive education. For all their fanfare, the two Commissions had come up with precious little in the way of original thinking or new programs; their self-appointed mission was propaganda and implementation. Yet at a time when the Progressive Education Association was rapidly disintegrating, the critics were undoubtedly accurate in their sense that here was the place to concentrate their fire. A fusillade of books and articles slammed into the various pronouncements of the Commissions, with devastating effect. The life-adjustment movement quickly disappeared, as much the victim of its own ill-chosen name as of the deeper attacks on its principles and practices.

I I I

The attack on the life-adjustment movement was no isolated phenomenon; it came rather as part of a much larger crisis in American education that had been brewing at least since the early 1940's. There were, to begin, the prosaic problems of buildings, budgets, and enrollments created by the war: few schools had been built since 1941; teachers had deserted the profession in droves; inflation was rampant; and the first of a flood of "war babies" began to enter the elementary grades as early as 1946. Then too, there were the multifarious difficulties associated with deepening public concern over communist expansionism at home and abroad. [5] And finally, though perhaps less visibly, there were the voracious demands of an expanding industrial economy for trained and intelligent manpower. [6]

[4] Ibid., p. 95.
[5] These difficulties are discussed in some detail in Theodore Brameld, ed.: *The Battle for Free Schools* (Boston, 1951); the pamphlet is a reprint of a series of articles that first appeared in *The Nation*.
[6] See in particular Dael Wolfle; *America's Resources of Specialized Talent* (New York, 1954); Education Policies Commission: *Manpower and Education* (Washington, 1956); and Eli Ginzberg: *Human Re-*

Any one of these in and of itself would have loosed fantastic pressures on the schools. Taken together, however, and compounded by a growing dissatisfaction among the intelligentsia, they held the makings of the deepest educational crisis in the nation's history. A spate of books, articles, pamphlets, radio programs, and television panels burst upon the pedagogical scene, airing every conceivable ailment of the schools, real and imaginary. One result was the most vigorous, searching, and fundamental attack on progressive education since the beginning of the movement.

The assault during the immediate postwar years was essentially continuous with the criticism of the early forties. Bernard Iddings Bell's book *Crisis in Education* and Mortimer Smith's polemic *And Madly Teach*—both of them published in 1949—furnish excellent examples.[7] Bell's stated intention was to disturb a "pseudopatriotic complacency" by asking to what extent American educational theory and practice were responsible for "the unsatisfactory state of our life and culture." His answer was a sweeping indictment of mass education for the perennial adolescence of the American people. The elementary schools had failed to transmit the elemental wisdom of the race; the high schools seemed far more interested in coddling young minds than in strengthening them; and the colleges, by surrendering to a vague utilitarian mediocrity, had deprived the nation of a humanely educated leadership. From kindergarten through the university, the school system suffered from misplaced emphases: it had taken over domestic functions that were properly parental, and it had excluded religion, without which education could have no ultimate purpose. To remedy these defects, Bell proposed a drastic series of reforms: teachers would have to be better trained, better paid, and better organ-

---

sources (New York, 1958). The celebrated "Rockefeller Brothers Report" on education in 1958 wisely located much of the pedagogical ferment of the era in "the continued pressure of an ever more complex society against the total creative capacity of its people." *The Pursuit of Excellence: Education and the Future of America* (New York, 1958), p. 10.

[7] Bell wrote as an experienced educator; Smith wrote as a " 'layman and amateur' whose eyes were opened when he happened to serve as a member of a board of education in Connecticut."

ized; educational opportunity would have to be extended by a vast program of scholarships; the school system would need to be thoroughly overhauled to remove wasteful overlap; parental responsibilities would have to be returned to parents; and religion would have to be given a central place in the curriculum, in publicly supported denominational schools if necessary.

At first glance, Smith's book seemed closely similar to Bell's. Carrying an introduction by Bell himself, it was a pointed attack on the principles and practices of "modern education." The writings of Dewey, the pronouncements of the Educational Policies Commission, and the Teachers College catalogue all came under Smith's pungent criticism. Not surprisingly, many of Bell's charges were reiterated: the schools had failed miserably in teaching the most elementary skills, and education itself had been systematically divested of its moral and intellectual content. But there were crucial differences as well; for whereas Bell sought to strengthen the teaching profession, Smith directed his ultimate indictment against it. He wrote: ". . . if anyone will take the trouble to investigate, it will be found that those who make up the staffs of the schools and colleges of education, and the administrators and teachers whom they train to run the system, have a truly amazing uniformity of opinion regarding the aims, the content, and the methods of education. They constitute a cohesive body of believers with a clearly formulated set of dogmas and doctrines, and they are perpetuating the faith by seeing to it, through state laws and the rules of state departments of education, that only those teachers and administrators are certified who have been trained in correct dogma." [8] While Bell contended in his introduction that "the fault lies not in our pedagogues but in ourselves," Smith's plea was that parents rise up in righteous indignation against the pedagogues and insist on "education's historic role as moral and intellectual teacher." It was a plea destined to resound through discussions of educational policy for at least a decade.

In retrospect, the Bell and Smith books represented the in-

[8] Mortimer Smith: *And Madly Teach* (Chicago, 1949), p. 7.

tellectual thrust of a polyglot political movement that managed to gain considerable headway during the later 1940's.[9] Yet citizens and educators alike remained only vaguely aware of what was going on until *This Happened in Pasadena* burst upon the educational scene early in 1951. Written by David Hulburd, a professional journalist, the book described the political demise of Willard Goslin, the progressive superintendent of Pasadena's progressive schools. President of the American Association of School Administrators, and widely respected among educators, Goslin had been forced out of one of the showcases of modern education by a vigorous coalition of citizens opposed to school taxes, radicalism, and progressive pedagogy. Hulburd's warning—and the warning of many who reviewed the book—was insistent: good education had been successfully subverted in one American community; it could happen in any American community; now was the time for all interested citizens to come to the aid of the schools.[1] "Most of the people constituting Goslin's opposition," proclaimed the book jacket, "were well-intentioned and sincere, and quite unaware of their true roles in a calculated, far-reaching plot. Fantastic? It can't happen here? Read this book . . . It has happened here."

The notion of "a calculated, far-reaching plot" was quickly taken up by progressives, and became the leitmotif of their counterattack during the next few years. A rash of pamphlets and articles appeared directing attention to a new genre of ultra-rightist, frequently rabble-rousing citizens' group that had entered the arena of educational policymaking.[2] Armed

[9] An early discussion of this movement took place at the Second Conference on the Scientific Spirit and Democratic Faith in New York City in 1944. Jerome Nathanson of the Ethical Culture Society wrote of the Conference: "It was in the belief that certain organized movements in education constituted a threat to the scientific spirit and democratic faith that its attention was concentrated on the educational issue." John Dewey *et al.*: *The Authoritarian Attempt to Capture Education* (New York, 1945), p. vii.

[1] See especially James B. Conant: "The Superintendent Was the Target," *The New York Times Book Review*, April 29, 1951, pp. 1, 27.

[2] This literature is collected and discussed in C. Winfield Scott and Clyde M. Hill: *Public Education under Criticism* (New York, 1954);

with charges of soft pedagogy, waste, and subversion, and cloaked with the mantle of superpatriotism, self-styled school improvement organizations like Allen Zoll's National Council for American Education and Milo McDonald's American Education Association were busily spreading the poison of pedagogical reaction in school districts across the nation. From Englewood, New Jersey, to Denver, Colorado, to Eugene, Oregon, the pattern seemed the same. A few citizens eager to keep taxes down would form a "school development council" and demand that "fads and frills" be eliminated from the system. Under the aegis of the council, the community would be showered with leaflets proclaiming the evils of modern education. Mass meetings would be held demanding immediate action. Teachers would be intimidated and the board coerced. In the end, the victims would be the nursery school, the guidance program, the teacher workshop—and almost inevitably, community morale.[3]

Whence the support for such efforts? Writing in the January, 1952, issue of *Progressive Education,* editor Archibald W. Anderson of the University of Illinois ventured an explanation. Local critics, he suggested, might be divided into two groups. One of these was composed of "honest and sincere critics" generally interested in public education. "Some of these critics take the trouble to keep themselves well informed about educational matters, are willing to work with the schools, *and generally favor the same lines of progress as the educators.* Such critics are not likely to join an organized attack." Others in this first group were generally well disposed toward public education but not so well informed. Their criticisms were usually "very specific in nature and based on some specific instances which they do not see in their total educational context." The second group of critics Anderson described as a motley assortment of "chronic tax conservationists," "congenital reactionaries," "witch hunters," "super-patriots," "dogma peddlers,"

---

and Ernest O. Melby and Morton Puner: *Freedom and Public Education* (New York, 1953). See also "Meeting the Attacks on Education," *Progressive Education,* XXIX (1951–2), 65–122.

[3] *Danger! They're After Our Schools!* (New York, 1951), pp. 6–7.

"race haters," and last but not least, "academic conservatives." [4]

Anderson's explanation fit many of the facts, but not all of them; for he ignored the growing number of citizens who were taking the trouble to keep themselves well informed about educational matters, but who did *not* generally favor the same lines of progress as the educators. What was already apparent in 1952, and what became ever more apparent as the decade progressed, was the presence of a large and articulate public ready for educational reform of a nonprogressive variety. Dean Hollis L. Caswell of Teachers College put his finger on this phenomenon in his Steinmetz Memorial Lecture of May, 1952, when he laid the "plot theory" aside and contended instead that what was happening was not merely a subversive attack on the schools but rather a searching reappraisal of the whole philosophy of progressive education. [5]

Events of the next few years generally bore out the Caswell thesis. The year 1953 brought Albert Lynd's *Quackery in the Public Schools*, Arthur Bestor's *Educational Wastelands*, Robert Hutchins's *The Conflict in Education*, and Paul Woodring's *Let's Talk Sense about Our Schools*. A year later Mortimer Smith published *The Diminished Mind*. The character of these volumes varied considerably, from Smith's uncompromising diatribe against life-adjustment education to Woodring's more moderate efforts at eclecticism; but all were fundamentally critical of progressive education. [6] Of the four, it was Bestor whose attacks were destined to exert the most telling impact on the progressive movement.

Bestor was an American historian who had taught for a num-

[4] Archibald W. Anderson: "The Cloak of Respectability: The Attackers and Their Methods," *Progressive Education*, XXIX (1951–2), 69–70. Italics mine.

[5] Hollis L. Caswell: "The Great Reappraisal of Public Education," *Teachers College Record*, LIV (1952–3), 12–22.

[6] Two acid satires added a good deal of spice to the criticism: Mary McCarthy: *The Groves of Academe* (New York, 1952) and Randall Jarrell: *Pictures from an Institution* (New York, 1954). In this respect, it is also interesting to compare the sardonic picture of the professors of education given in Virgil Scott's bitter postwar novel *The Hickory Stick* (New York, 1948) with the much more optimistic view in James M. Shields's depression novel *Just Plain Larnin'* (New York, 1934).

ber of years at Teachers College, Columbia, before going on to professorships first at Stanford and then at the University of Illinois. His criticisms of American education date from a 1952 article in *The American Scholar*, a piece on "Liberal Education and a Liberal Nation" that only vaguely foreshadowed the sharpness of subsequent writings. There followed a series of brilliantly polemical essays in *The New Republic*, *The Scientific Monthly*, and the *American Association of University Professors Bulletin* that ripped savagely into the theory and practice of the life-adjustment movement—and then in 1953, *Educational Wastelands*. The book was widely reviewed and commented upon, both within the profession and without, and a revised and enlarged version was published in 1955 under the title *The Restoration of Learning*.[7] Taken together, these writings constituted by far the most serious, searching, and influential criticisms of progressive education to appear during the fifties.

Bestor's general argument may be summed up under four broad headings: a theory of education, a conception of the historic role of the public school, a notion of the "great subversion" of American education, and a proposal for reform. In Bestor's view, the ultimate purpose of all education is intellectual training, "the deliberate cultivation of the ability to think." To think may not be the most important function in life, but it is the most important concern of the schools; likewise, intellectual training may not be the only function of the schools, but in the last analysis it is their *raison d'etre*. How is

[7] The leading professional critiques of *Educational Wastelands* were Harold C. Hand: "A Scholar's Documentation," *Educational Theory*, IV (1954), pp. 27–48, 53; William Clark Trow: "Academic Utopia?" *Educational Theory*, IV (1954), 16–26; R. Will Burnet: "Mr. Bestor in the Land of the Philistines," *Progressive Education*, XXXI (1953–4), 65–85; and R. Freeman Butts's review in the *Teachers College Record*, LV (1953–4), 340–4. Gordon K. Chalmers, President of Kenyon College, said of the 1953 volume that it was clearly reasoned, convincingly documented, and written with élan (*New York Times Book Review*, November 8, 1953, pp. 46–7) but subsequently criticized *The Restoration of Learning* for its narrow view of liberal education (*The New Republic*, October 10, 1955, pp. 18–19). See also my own review of *The Restoration of Learning* in *The Progressive*, December, 1955, p. 38.

intellectual training given? Through the academic disciplines. These, Bestor argued, have developed historically as systematic methods for solving problems. To conceive of problem-solving apart from the disciplines is to abandon man's best hope for using systematic intelligence in confronting the difficulties that beset him. True education, then, is the deliberate cultivation of the ability to think through training in the basic academic disciplines: history, English, science, mathematics, and foreign languages.

The function of the public school, Bestor continued, is to give such a basic education to all citizens. Democratic education differs from aristocratic education only in the number of persons with whom it deals, not in the values it seeks to impart. To convert the education of the common man into something other than systematic intellectual training is to rob him of his birthright; it is to vulgarize culture under the guise of democratizing it. By training all in the ability to think, the schools distribute intellectual power widely among the people. This and this alone is their distinctive way of contributing to social progress.

The great subversion of American education, Bestor contended, had been the divorce of the schools from scholarship and of teacher training from the arts and sciences. The subversives were a powerfully entrenched "interlocking directorate" composed of professors of education, the school administrators they trained, and the state departments of education that required their courses for teacher certification. Bestor pointedly attempted to distinguish between the progressive education Dewey espoused, and that he himself had received at the Lincoln School, and the life-adjustment program he so sharply criticized; but there is no denying that his attack was ultimately on the whole progressive movement and the profession that had come to support it.

Finally, there was Bestor's threefold program of reform: first, the organization of a coalition of parents and liberal arts professors who would remove the schools from the control of the "interlocking directorate"; second, the redrawing of certification requirements to strengthen academic learning and de-emphasize pedagogy; and, finally, the return of teacher training to the control of the larger university. Professional schools and departments of education had an important role as repositories of wisdom on the methods and techniques of pedagogy, Bestor granted; but it was the university as a whole that needed to determine and provide the proper education of a teacher.

It is interesting to note that in a little over half a century, Bestor had come full circle from the early progressives. Whereas Joseph Mayer Rice in the nineties had called upon the public to reform the schools by creating a new class of professionals who would manage education according to scientific principles, Bestor was now calling upon that same public to undo the damage of the professionals by returning the schools to the arts and science professors. And whereas Rice had railed against the narrowness and formalism of the curriculum, Bestor was now contending that the schools, in attempting to do everything, had ended up forsaking their own distinctive function: intellectual training. Thus swung the pendulum of reform.

For many reasons, Bestor's arguments found considerable support among the intelligentsia.[8] The academic community, long critical of goings-on in the department of education, was quite ready to blame the educationists for the crisis in the schools,[9] particularly as the tensions of popularization began to affect the colleges. So, too, were the editors of *Life* and *U.S. News & World Report*.[1] And so, too, was the public.

[8] A Council for Basic Education was founded in 1956 to advance the view that "schools exist to provide the essential skills of language, numbers, and orderly thought, and to transmit in a reasoned pattern the intellectual, moral, and aesthetic heritage of civilized man." *The Main Job of the Schools* (Washington, n.d.). Arthur Bestor and Mortimer Smith were among the first directors. For the Council's evolving position and program see its periodical, the *CBE Bulletin*.

[9] Eugene Auerbach discusses the continuing warfare in Academe in "The Opposition to Schools of Education by Professors of the Liberal Arts—A Historical Analysis" (Unpublished Doctoral Thesis, University of Southern California, 1957). See also James Bryant Conant's plea for "A Truce Among Educators," *Teachers College Record*, XLVI (1944–5), 157–63.

[1] See the "Crisis in Education" series in *Life* for March 24, 31, April 7, 14, and 21, 1958; the principal editorial contended that the

When the Russians launched the first space satellite in the autumn of 1957, a shocked and humbled nation embarked on a bitter orgy of pedagogical soul-searching.[2] "None of us is without guilt," wrote Admiral Hyman G. Rickover the following year. "But now that the people have awakened to the need for reform, I doubt whether reams of propaganda pamphlets, endless reiteration that all is well with our schools, or even pressure tactics will again fool the American people into believing that education can safely be left to the 'professional' educators. . . . The mood of America has changed. Our technological supremacy has been called in question and we know we have to deal with a formidable competitor. Parents are no longer satisfied with life-adjustment schools. Parental objectives no longer coincide with those professed by the progressive educationists. I doubt we can again be silenced."[3]

I V

The surprising thing about the progressive response to the assault of the fifties is not that the movement collapsed, but that it collapsed so readily. True, the Progressive Education Association had never been able to recoup its fortunes after the war, and slid steadily downhill after 1947. True, too, the phrase *progressive education* had itself fallen into disfavor among professionals, though progressive ideas continued to command wide assent. But even so, one is shocked by the rapidity of the

---

deeper problem in education was "to dig out educationists' debris and rediscover learning's true nature." *U.S. News & World Report* published lengthy interviews with Bestor on November 30, 1956, June 7, 1957, and January 24, 1958, around the themes "We Are Less Educated Than Fifty Years Ago" and "What Went Wrong with U.S. Schools?"

[2] An anthology of the soul-searching is Kermit Lansner, ed.: *Second-Rate Brains* (Garden City, 1958).

[3] H. G. Rickover: *Education and Freedom* (New York, 1959), pp. 189-90. Like Bestor, Rickover too had come full circle from the early progressives. Whereas they had argued that the national interest demanded an *extension* of the school's functions, he was contending that the national interest demanded a *contraction* of those functions. Both arguments tell us a good deal about the politics of American education and the kind of rhetoric it has traditionally stimulated. [Quotation used by permission of E. P. Dutton & Co., Inc.]

decline. Why this abrupt and rather dismal end of a movement that had for more than a half-century commanded the loyalty of influential segments of the American public? A number of reasons suggest themselves.

First, distortion. As frequently happens with social movements, success brought schism in the ranks. The pluralism of the nineties became the bitter ideological fragmentation of the thirties and forties. Factions developed, and within the factions cults, cliques, and fanatics. The movement became strife-ridden, given to bandwagon behavior, dominated by the feuding of minorities. The strife made headlines, and within these headlines lay the seeds of many a cartoon version of progressive education.

Second, there was the negativism inherent in this and all social reform movements. Like many protestors against injustice, the early progressives knew better what they were against than what they were for. And when one gets a true picture of the inequities of American schools during the half-century before World War I, he realizes they had much to be against; the physical and pedagogical conditions in many schools were indescribably bad, an effrontery to the mildest humanitarian sentiments. Yet, granted this, a protest is not a program. Shibboleths like "the whole child" or "creative self-expression" stirred the faithful to action and served as powerful battering rams against the old order, but in classroom practice they were not very good guides to positive action. At least the generation that invented them had an idea of what they meant. The generation that followed adopted them as a collection of ready-made clichés—clichés which were not very helpful when the public began to raise searching questions about the schools.

Third, what the progressives did prescribe made inordinate demands on the teacher's time and ability. "Integrated studies" required familiarity with a fantastic range of knowledge and teaching materials; while the commitment to build upon student needs and interests demanded extraordinary feats of pedagogical ingenuity. In the hands of first-rate instructors, the innovations worked wonders; in the hands of too many average teachers, however, they led to chaos. Like the proverbial little girl with the curl right in the middle of her forehead, progressive education done well was very good indeed; done badly, it was abominable—worse, perhaps, than the formalism it had sought to supplant.

Fourth, and this too is a common phenomenon of social reform, the movement became a victim of its own success. Much of what it preached was simply incorporated into the schools at large. Once the schools did change, however, progressives too often found themselves wedded to specific programs, unable to formulate next steps. Like some liberals who continued to fight for the right of labor to organize long after the Wagner Act had done its work, many progressives continued to fight against stationary desks in schools where movable desks were already in use. For some young people in the post-World War II generation the ideas of the progressives became inert— in Whitehead's sense of "right thinking" that no longer moves to action. Dewey in the very last essay he ever published on education likened these progressive ideas gone stale to mustard plasters taken out of the medicine cabinet and applied externally as the need arose.[4] Other young people of this same generation simply developed different preoccupations, different concerns, different rallying points. The old war cries, whatever their validity or lack of it, rang a bit hollow; they no longer generated enthusiasm.[5] Like any legacy from a prior generation, they were too easily and too carelessly spent; rarely perhaps were they lovingly invested in something new. In the end, the result was intellectual bankruptcy.

Fifth, there was the impact of the more general swing toward conservatism in postwar political and social thought. If progressive education arose as part of Progressivism writ large, it should not be surprising that a reaction to it came as a phase of

---

[4] John Dewey: "Introduction," in Elsie Ripley Clapp: *The Use of Resources in Education* (New York, 1952).

[5] Both Harold Rugg and Frederick L. Redefer found this the case when they revisited some of the older progressive schools during and after the war. See Rugg: *Foundations for American Education* (Yonkers, 1947), pp. 19–21; and Redefer: "The Eight-Year Study—Eight Years Later" (Unpublished Doctoral Thesis, Teachers College, Columbia University, 1951).

Conservatism writ large.[6] When the reaction did come, too many educators thought they would be progressives in education and conservatives in everything else. The combination, of course, is not entirely impossible, though it may well be intellectually untenable. John Dewey addressed himself to the point in *Characters and Events.* "Let us admit the case of the conservative," he wrote; "if we once start thinking no one can guarantee what will be the outcome, except that many objects, ends and institutions will be surely doomed. Every thinker puts some portion of an apparently stable world in peril, and no one can wholly predict what will emerge in its place." Dewey's comment, by the way, makes incomparably clear what he thought was progressive about good education, and gives the lie to a good deal of nonsense about his philosophy being anti-intellectual.

Sixth, there was the price the movement paid for its own professionalization; for given the political realities of American education, no program can survive that ceases assiduously to cultivate lay support. Progressives were undoubtedly right in contending that teachers needed to be better educated and better paid, and that professionalization would ultimately serve these ends. And they were right, too, in assuming that once teachers had been converted to their cause, half the battle would be won. But they committed a supreme political blunder during the thirties when they allowed the movement itself to become professionalized; for in the process the political coalition of businessmen, trade unionists, farmers, and intellectuals that had supported them in their early efforts was simply permitted to crumble. The resultant lack of nonprofessional support during the fifties was a crucial factor in the high vulnerability of the movement to widespread criticism of its policies and procedures.

Seventh, and most important, progressive education collapsed because it failed to keep pace with the continuing transformation of American society. The ultimate enemy of the con-

[6] The relationship is clearly exemplified in Russell Kirk, ed.: "The Restoration of Learning," *Modern Age,* II (1957–8), 1–111; and "Humane Schooling," Ibid., III (1958–9), 338–426.

ventional wisdom, Galbraith points out, is not so much ideas as the march of events. For the conventional wisdom accommodates itself not to the world that it is meant to interpret, but to the audience's view of that world. And since audiences tend to prefer the comfortable and the familiar, while the world moves on, the conventional wisdom is ever in danger of obsolescence.

The fact is that postwar America was a very different nation from the one that had given birth to progressive education. The great immigrations were over, and a flow of publications by David Riesman, William H. Whyte, Jr., Will Herberg, and others wrestled insistently with a redefinition of community.[7] The search for *Gemeinschaft* of the nineties had become the quest for pluralism of the fifties, while the rampant individualism that Dewey so earnestly feared was now widely applauded as nonconformity. The economy had entered upon an era marked by the harnessing of vast new sources of energy and the rapid extension of automatic controls in production, a prodigious advance that quickly outmoded earlier notions of vocational education. And new information was being generated at a phenomenal pace, thrusting to the fore the school's traditional responsibility for organizing and transmitting knowledge of every sort and variety.

Most fundamental of all, perhaps, the continued advance of the mass media, the proliferation of social welfare agencies under public and quasi-public sponsorship, and the rapid extension of industry-sponsored education programs—the "classrooms in the factories" that Harold Clark and Harold Sloan labelled the real pedagogical revolution of the time—had literally transformed the balance of forces in education.[8]

[7] See for example David Riesman *et al.*: *The Lonely Crowd* (New Haven, 1950); William H. Whyte, Jr.: *The Organization Man* (New York, 1956); Will Herberg: *Protestant-Catholic-Jew* (New York, 1955); and Henry Steele Commager: "Our Schools Have Kept Us Free," *Life*, October 16, 1950, pp. 46–7, and "A Historian Looks at the American High School," *School Review*, LXVI (1958), 1–18. For Riesman's "counter-cyclical" theory of education, see *Constraint and Variety in American Education* (Lincoln, Neb., 1956), ch. iii.

[8] Harold F. Clark and Harold S. Sloan: *Classrooms in the Factories* (Rutherford, N.J., 1958). Martin S. Dworkin has written perceptively

Whereas the central thrust of progressivism had been expansionist—it revolted against formalism and sought to extend the functions of the school—the central effort of the fifties was rather to define more precisely the school's responsibilities, to delineate those things that the school needed to do because if the school did not do them they would not get done. It was this problem more than any, perhaps, that stood at the heart of the argument over educational priorities that dominated the citizens' conferences of the decade.[9]

Granted this, however, and granted the collapse of progressive education as an organized movement, there remained a timelessness about many of the problems the progressives raised and the solutions they proposed. John Dewey once wrote in the Preface to *Schools of To-Morrow*: "This is not a text book of education, nor yet an exposition of a new method of school teaching, aimed to show the weary teacher or the discontented parent how education should be carried on. We have tried to show what actually happens when schools start to put into practice, each in its own way, some of the theories that have been pointed to as the soundest and best ever since Plato, to be then laid politely away as precious portions of our 'intellectual heritage.' "

However much progressive education had become the conventional wisdom of the fifties, there were still slum schools that could take profitable lessons from Jacob Riis, rural schools that had much to learn from the Country Life Commission, and colleges that had yet to discover that the natural curiosity of the young could be a magnificent propellant to learning. Glaring educational inequalities along race and class lines cried out for alleviation, and the vision of a democracy of culture retained a nobility all its own—Lyman Bryson restated it

---

about the educational impact of the modern film in a number of critical essays; see especially "The Family of Man," *Fundamental and Adult Education*, X (1958), 177–80, and a review of *Films in Psychiatry, Psychology, and Mental Health* in the *Teachers College Record*, LVI (1954–5), 50–2.

[9] See, for example, The Committee for the White House Conference on Education: *A Report to the President* (Washington, 1956), p. 5; and Fred M. Hechinger: *An Adventure in Education* (New York, 1956).

brilliantly in *The Next America* (1953), a book that never received the attention it deserved.[1] As knowledge proliferated, the need to humanize it only intensified;[2] while the awesome imminence of atomic war merely dramatized the difference between knowledge and intelligence.[3] Finally, the rapid transformation of the so-called underdeveloped nations lent new meaning and new urgency to Jane Addams's caveat that "unless all men and all classes contribute to a good, we cannot even be sure that it is worth having"—the point was compellingly made in C. P. Snow's widely read lecture, *The Two Cultures and the Scientific Revolution* (1959).

The Progressive Education Association had died, and progressive education itself needed drastic reappraisal. Yet the transformation they had wrought in the schools was in many ways as irreversible as the larger industrial transformation of which it had been part.[4] And for all the talk about pedagogical breakthroughs and crash programs, the authentic progressive vision remained strangely pertinent to the problems of mid-century America.[5] Perhaps it only awaited the reformulation and resuscitation that would ultimately derive from a larger resurgence of reform in American life and thought.

[1] See also Michael Walzer: "Education for a Democratic Culture," *Dissent*, VI (1959), 107–21; and Agnes E. Meyer: "The Quest for a New American Culture," *The Antioch Review*, XIX (1959–60), 437–54.

[2] I am using the term as James Harvey Robinson used it in *The Humanizing of Knowledge* (New York, 1923) to indicate the need to reorder, restate, and resynthesize new knowledge so that the average person can understand it.

[3] For exemplary discussions, see Brand Blanshard, ed.: *Education in the Age of Science* (New York, 1959); Margaret Mead: "Thinking Ahead: Why Is Education Obsolete?" *Harvard Business Review*, November-December, 1958, pp. 23–30; and Peter F. Drucker: *Landmarks of Tomorrow* (New York, 1959), ch. v.

[4] That this is so is indicated by the general direction of James Bryant Conant's proposals in *The American High School Today* (New York, 1959) and by the philosophical orientation—or lack of it—in most of the programs reported by Arthur D. Morse in *Schools of Tomorrow—Today* (Garden City, 1960).

[5] Despite the sharpness of the assault on progressive education, public opinion polls revealed a good deal of latent public support for the progressive program. See National Education Association: *Public Opinion Polls on American Education* (Washington, 1958); and Richard F. Carter: *Voters and Their Schools* (Stanford, 1960).

Bibliographical Note

WITH FEW exceptions, recent histories of the Progressive Movement have tended to ignore its educational aspects. Educational reform is not discussed in Daniel Aaron: *Men of Good Hope* (1951), Eric F. Goldman: *Rendezvous with Destiny* (1952), Richard Hofstadter: *The Age of Reform* (1955), or Henry F. May: *The End of American Innocence* (1959); likewise, it is omitted in May: "Shifting Perspectives on the 1920's," *Mississippi Valley Historical Review*, XLIII (1956–7), 405–27, and Arthur S. Link: "What Happened to the Progressive Movement in the 1920's?" *American Historical Review*, LXIV (1958–9), 833–51. The older but still useful "History of American Life" series—notably Arthur Meier Schlesinger: *The Rise of the City, 1878–1898* (1933), Harold Underwood Faulkner: *The Quest for Social Justice, 1898–1914* (1931), Preston William Slosson: *The Great Crusade and After, 1918–1928* (1930), and Dixon Wecter: *The Age of the Great Depression, 1929–1941* (1948)—includes a good deal of relevant educational material, as do Russel B. Nye: *Midwestern Progressive Politics* (1959), Arthur Mann: *Yankee Reformers in the Urban Age* (1954), and Ray Ginger: *Altgeld's America* (1958). Morton G. White devotes a brief section to education in *Social Thought in America* (1949), as does Henry Steele Commager in *The American Mind* (1950). David W. Noble ignores it in his otherwise excellent book, *The Paradox of Progressive Thought* (1958).

The fullest published histories of the progressive education movement tend to be written from a progressive point of view. Harold Rugg deals in detail with the progressive impact on elementary and secondary education in *Foundations for American Education* (1947), though his conception of the movement is at best limited. R. Freeman Butts discusses progressivism in higher education in *The College Charts Its Course* (1939). Merle Curti: *The Social Ideas of American Educators* (1935), while unmistakably a work of the thirties, is nonetheless a gold mine of information on post-Civil War educational reform; no other treatment so effectively locates education in its social context. Robert Holmes Beck: "American Progressive Education, 1875–1930" (Yale University, 1941) remains the best unpublished history of progressivism in education, though it tends to deal with individual schools and schoolmen rather than with the movement as a whole; the central themes of Beck's dissertation are reiterated in "Progressive Education and American Progressivism," *Teachers College Record*, LX (1958–9), 77–89, 129–37, 198–208. Paul Woodring includes illuminating discussions of the progressive education movement in *Let's Talk Sense about Our Schools* (1953) and *A Fourth of a Nation* (1957), but his view tends to be somewhat narrow. Louis Filler, on the other hand, advances so broad a conception of the movement in "Main Currents in Progressivist American Education," *History of Education Journal*, VIII (1957), 33–57, that it embraces virtually every pedagogical reform during the past two centuries. An early view of the range and diversity of the movement, as well as some of its internal contradictions, is given in Pedro T. Orata: " 'Fifty-Seven Varieties' of Progressive Education," *Educational Administration and Supervision*, XII (1936), 361–74. Likewise, an early view of the movement's relationship to Progressivism is given in Edward H. Reisner: "What Is Progressive Education?" *Teachers College Record*, XXXV (1933–4), 192–201.

There is no satisfactory study of the interrelations between European and American educational reform, though Adolph E. Meyer: *The Development of Education in the 20th Century* (1939) represents a good beginning. The *Yearbooks* of the International Institute of Teachers College, Columbia University—published under the editorship of I. L. Kandel between 1925 and 1944—are replete with information on a country-by-country basis, but they tend to avoid the problem of influence. Kandel's own volume, *The End of an Era* (1941), is the best point at which to begin any study of this notable series. The published reports of the New Education Fellowship's international conferences are also useful, particularly Wyatt Rawson, ed.: *A New World in the Making* (1933), E. G. Malherbe, ed.: *Educational Adaptations in a Changing Society* (1937), A. E. Campbell, ed.: *Modern Trends in Education* (1938), and K. S. Cunningham, ed.: *Education for Complete Living* (1938). William Boyd: "The Basic

Faith of the New Education Fellowship," in George Z. F. Bereday
and Joseph A. Lauwerys, ed.: *Education and Philosophy* (1957),
pp. 193–208, is an excellent introduction to the general outlook
of the NEF, as is the Fellowship's magazine, *The New Era*. John
Adams: *Modern Developments in Educational Practice* (1922)
and Adams *et al.: Educational Movements and Methods* (1924)
draw freely on American and European reform in their generalizations.

For any study of American education during the past seventy-
five years, the annual reports, bulletins, circulars, and other publications of the United States Office of Education are invaluable,
though it is always well to compare the Office's statistics with
those of the decennial census on the one hand and those of state
departments of education on the other. The annual *Addresses
and Proceedings* of the National Education Association reflect the
thinking of the teaching profession at any given time, though one
must bear in mind that the NEA's membership never exceeded
10,000 before World War I, and was frequently much smaller.
Equally useful as a guide to professional thinking and innovation
are the *Yearbooks* of the National Society for the Study of Education. Given the politics of American education, lay opinion is
always a crucial factor, a truism occasionally ignored by historians;
in this respect, *The Forum, The World's Work, The New Republic, School and Society, The New Era, The Social Frontier,
Frontiers of Democracy,* and *Progressive Education* during its
early years remain the most fruitful periodical sources for the
progressive education movement.

There is no adequate history of American education in the
twentieth century, though Edgar W. Knight: *Fifty Years of American Education* (1952) and I. L. Kandel: *American Education in
the Twentieth Century* (1957) are useful compendiums. The
series of monographs prepared for the United States exhibit at
the Paris Exposition of 1900 and published under the editorship
of Nicholas Murray Butler as *Education in the United States*
(1900) and the collection of essays edited by I. L. Kandel under
the title *Twenty-five Years of American Education* (1924) are
excellent bench-mark studies, as is Charles H. Judd's chapter on
education in Volume I of *Recent Social Trends in the United
States* (1933). The five-volume *Cyclopedia of Education* (1911–
13) edited by Paul Monroe is comprehensive and penetrating in
its coverage but is now much out of date.

As always, valuable insights may be gleaned from the accounts
of foreign visitors, though they vary tremendously in breadth,
depth, and accuracy. William W. Brickman discusses the nineteenth-century literature in "A Historical Introduction to Comparative Education," *Comparative Education Review*, III (1959–

60), 6–13. W. J. Osburn discusses the critiques prior to World War I in *Foreign Criticisms of American Education* (1922) and includes a good bibliography. Delaye Gager discusses the French commentaries between 1889 and 1914 in *French Comment on American Education* (1925). Of the English accounts, the sections on education in James Bryce: *The American Commonwealth* (1888) and the *Reports of the Mosely Education Commission to the United States of America* (1904) are probably the most widely known. William Boyd: *America in School and College* (1933), Erich Hylla: *Die Schule der Demokratie* (1928), and Harold Laski's chapter on education in *The American Democracy* (1948) are also particularly useful because of the authors' long interest in reform.

Finally, William W. Brickman: *Guide to Research in Educational History* (1949) remains the best general treatise on textbooks, encyclopedias, bibliographies, and other reference works in the history of education; while the *Harvard Guide to American History* (1954) and *A Guide to the Study of the United States of America* (1960) are standard treatises on sources in general American history.

Traditions of Popular Education

The problem of determining when the progressive education movement actually began was one of the intriguing aspects of this study. John Dewey contended in *The New Republic*, LXIII (1930), 204, that Francis W. Parker was "more nearly than any other one person" the father of the progressive education movement; and Robert Holmes Beck supports this thesis in "American Progressive Education, 1875–1930." The earliest use of the term *progressive education* in the United States probably dates from the translation of Mme. Necker de Saussure's work *L'Éducation Progressive, ou Etude du Cours de la Vie* (Paris, 1836), which appeared as *Progressive Education; or, Considerations on the Course of Life* (London, 1839). At least two doctoral theses— Leonita Mulhall: "The Genesis and Growth of the Progressive Movement in Education" (University of Cincinnati, 1931) and Ira Byrd Mosley: "The 'New Education'—A Study of Origins and Development" (Stanford University, 1939)—carry the movement back to the Renaissance and earlier, but this view cannot be taken seriously. In the end, the choice was between 1892, the date of Joseph Mayer Rice's series in *The Forum*, and 1899, the date of John Dewey's lectures on *The School and Society* (1899). I chose the earlier because Rice freely used the term *progressive* with respect to teachers, schools, and educational programs, because he clearly sensed that an educational *movement* was in the

making, and because he shared many of the political and social
ideas of the broader Progressive Movement. There is a short biography of Rice in *The National Cyclopaedia of American Biography*, XII, 203–4; otherwise, little has been written concerning his
life and work. Some of his unpublished papers are in the library
at Teachers College, Columbia University; the rest remain in the
possession of his son, Lawrence J. M. Rice, of Washington, D.C.

The American tradition of popular schooling is discussed in
R. Freeman Butts and Lawrence A. Cremin: *A History of Educa-
tion in the United States* (1953), H. G. Good: *A History of
American Education* (1956), Adolphe E. Meyer: *An Educational
History of the American People* (1957), and Paul Monroe:
Founding of the American Public School System (1940). Sidney
Jackson: *America's Struggle for Free Schools* (1942) and Law-
rence A. Cremin: *The American Common School* (1951) deal in
detail with the quarter-century preceding the Civil War. Ell-
wood P. Cubberley: *Changing Conceptions of Education* (1909),
Charles Franklin Thwing: *A History of Education in the United
States since the Civil War* (1910), and Ernest Carroll Moore:
Fifty Years of American Education (1917) deal sketchily with
the era between the Civil War and World War I but advance
some intriguing contemporary appraisals.

The standard biographical works on Horace Mann include
Mary Tyler Peabody Mann: *Life and Works of Horace Mann*
(1865–8), B. A. Hinsdale: *Horace Mann and the Common
School Revival in the United States* (1898), and E. I. F. Williams: *Horace Mann* (1937). Raymond B. Culver: *Horace Mann
and Religion in the Massachusetts Public Schools* (1929),
Robert L. Straker: *The Unseen Harvest: Horace Mann and
Antioch College* (1955), and Frank C. Foster: "Horace Mann as
Philosopher," *Educational Theory*, X (1960), 9–25, are excellent
specialized studies. Useful chapters also appear in Curti: *The
Social Ideas of American Educators*, Daniel Aaron, ed.: *America
in Crisis* (1952), and Neil Gerard McCluskey: *Public Schools
and Moral Education* (1958). Mann's twelve annual reports to
the Massachusetts Board of Education have been reprinted in a
facsimile edition by the National Education Association; selections
from the reports are presented in Lawrence A. Cremin, ed.: *The
Republic and the School: Horace Mann on the Education of
Free Men* (1957). The two principal collections of Mann's
papers are in the Massachusetts Historical Society and the Antioch
College library; the *Selective and Critical Bibliography of Horace
Mann* (1937) compiled by the Federal Writers' Project of the
WPA is standard. It is scandalous but true that there are no
satisfactory biographies of Henry Barnard, Samuel Lewis, or
John D. Pierce. Bernard C. Steiner: *Life of Henry Barnard*

(1919), Anna Lou Blair: *Henry Barnard: School Administrator* (1938), Arthur Taylor Carr: "Samuel Lewis: Educational and Social Reformer" (Western Reserve University, 1938), Charles O. Hoyt and R. Clyde Ford: *John D. Pierce: Founder of the Michigan School System* (1905), and Leroy G. Lugas: "John D. Pierce" (Temple University, 1933) represent useful beginning studies.

The career of William T. Harris is discussed in the context of late nineteenth-century American education by Brian Holmes in "Some Writings of William Torrey Harris," *British Journal of Educational Studies*, V (1956–7), 47–66, and by Curti in *The Social Ideas of American Educators*. Kurt Leidecker's *Yankee Teacher* (1946) remains the only full-length biography. Specialized aspects of Harris's career are dealt with in J. S. Roberts: *William T. Harris: A Critical Study of His Educational and Related Philosophical Views* (1924), Thomas H. Clare: "The Sociological Theories of William Torrey Harris" (Washington University, 1934), Bernard J. Kohlbrenner: "William T. Harris, Superintendent of Schools, St. Louis, Missouri, 1868–80" (Harvard University, 1942), Carl Lester Byerly: *Contributions of William T. Harris to Public School Administration* (1946), Edward L. Schaub, ed.: *William Torrey Harris, 1835–1935* (1936), Alfred Baeumler and Paul Monroe, ed.: *Studies in Honor of William Torrey Harris* (1935), and McCluskey: *Public Schools and Moral Education*. Harris wrote voluminously on every conceivable pedagogical topic; one can find the best brief statement of his educational philosophy in Ossian H. Lang, ed.: *Educational Creeds of the Nineteenth Century* (1898), and the fullest in *Psychologic Foundations of Education* (1898). Frances B. Harmon: *The Social Philosophy of the St. Louis Hegelians* (1943), Henry A. Pochmann: *New England Transcendentalism and St. Louis Hegelianism* (1948), and Charles M. Perry, ed.: *The St. Louis Movement in Philosophy: Some Source Material* (1930) are useful for the philosophic backgrounds of his pedagogy. A standard—though incomplete—bibliography is Henry Ridgley Evans: *A List of the Writings of William Torrey Harris* (1908); the principal collection of Harris's letters and unpublished papers reposes in the Library of Congress.

Education and Industry

There are a number of general histories of the industrial education movement; the best is Charles Alpheus Bennett's two-volume work *History of Manual and Industrial Education up to 1870* (1926) and *History of Manual and Industrial Education, 1870 to 1917* (1937), which deals with European as well as American developments. Paul H. Douglas: *American Apprentice-*

ship and Industrial Education (1921), Lewis F. Anderson: *History of Manual and Industrial School Education* (1926), F. Theodore Struck: *Foundations of Industrial Education* (1930), Ray Stombaugh: *A Survey of the Movements Culminating in Industrial Arts Education in Secondary Schools* (1936), and Layton S. Hawkins, Charles A. Prosser, and John C. Wright: *Development of Vocational Education* (1951) are also useful. William T. Bawden: *Leaders in Industrial Education* (1950) is a series of biographical sketches by a man who was personally acquainted with most of the central figures in the movement. The massive four-volume compilation of documents and commentary brought together by Isaac Edwards Clarke under the general title *Art and Industry: Education in the Industrial and Fine Arts in the United States* (1892–3) is a gold mine of information, as are the many government documents on industrial, trade, and vocational education; among the latter are the special reports of the United States Commissioner of Education on *Technical Education* (1870) and *Industrial Education in the United States* (1883), the *Report of the Commission on Industrial Education, Made to the Legislature of Pennsylvania* (1891), the *Report of the [Massachusetts] Commission Appointed to Investigate the Existing Systems of Manual Training and Industrial Education* (1893), and the Seventeenth and Twenty-Fifth Annual Reports of the United States Commissioner of Labor entitled respectively *Trade and Technical Education* (1902) and *Industrial Education* (1910). The *Bibliography of Industrial, Vocational, and Trade Education* published in 1913 by the United States Bureau of Education is the fullest guide to source material published before World War I.

Merle Curti: "America at the World Fairs, 1851–1893," *American Historical Review*, LV (1949–50), 833–56, documents the spirited competition for economic prestige manifested at the nineteenth-century international fairs. The details of the Philadelphia Centennial Exposition of 1876 are given in the multivolume *Report of the Director-General* (1880) of the United States Centennial Commission. Calvin M. Woodward's views on manual training are presented in two volumes: *The Manual Training School* (1887) and *Manual Training in Education* (1890). Woodward's essay on "Manual, Industrial, and Technical Education in the United States" in the 1903 report of the United States Commissioner of Education is the best guide to his later opinions. John D. Runkle's views are set forth in "The Manual Element in Education," an essay incorporated into the *Forty-First Annual Report of the Massachusetts Board of Education* (1878). There are good biographical sketches of Woodward and Runkle in the *Dictionary of American Biography*. Charles Penney Coates: *History of the Manual Training School of Washington University*

(1923) is a detailed account of the origins, founding, and early work of the first major manual-training high school in the United States. Arthur Beverly Mays: *The Concept of Vocational Education in the Thinking of the General Educator, 1845 to 1945* (1946) traces a century of controversy over the place of vocational education in the American school; the annual reports of the National Educational Association and its Department of Superintendence during the 1880's afford the best year-by-year view of the decisive decade in the controversy.

The fullest and most detailed accounts of the vocational education movement in agriculture are Alfred Charles True: *A History of Agricultural Extension Work in the United States, 1785–1923* (1928) and *A History of Agricultural Education in the United States, 1785–1925* (1929). Ann M. Keppel: "Country Schools for Country Children: Backgrounds of the Reform Movement in Rural Elementary Education, 1890–1914" (University of Wisconsin, 1960) presents a wealth of information on agrarianism in education. Useful chapters or sections are also included in James Ralph Jewell: *Agricultural Education, Including Nature Study and School Gardens* (1907), Solon Justus Buck: *The Granger Movement: 1870–1880* (1913), Theodore Saloutos and John D. Hicks: *Agricultural Discontent in the Middle West 1900–1939* (1951), and Grant McConnell: *The Decline of Agrarian Democracy* (1953). For the Morrill Act and the subsequent history of the agricultural colleges, see Earle D. Ross: *Democracy's College* (1942) and Edward Danforth Eddy, Jr.: *Colleges for Our Land and Time* (1957). The reports, bulletins, and circulars of the United States Department of Agriculture and its Office of Experiment Stations are replete with relevant material, as are the annual proceedings of the Association of American Agricultural Colleges and Experiment Stations and the National Grange and its state affiliates.

Considerable work is needed on the politics of vocational education during the period from 1890 to 1917. Philip R. V. Curoe: *Educational Attitudes and Policies of Organized Labor in the United States* (1926) covers the era but sketchily at best. Edward W. Bemis: "Relation of Labor Organizations to the American Boy and to Trade Instruction," *Annals of the American Academy of Political and Social Science*, V (1894–5), 209–41, presents the views of labor leaders toward vocational education, as do the *Fourth Annual Report of the Bureau of Statistics of Labor of the State of New York* (1886) and the *Twenty-Sixth Annual Report of the Bureau of Labor Statistics of New York State* (1908). The 1902 report of the United States Commissioner of Labor includes lengthy sections on the attitudes of employers, graduates of trade and technical schools, and labor unions toward trade and technical education in Austria, Belgium, France, Great Britain, Switzerland, and the United States. The annual proceedings of the American Federation of Labor as well as the reports of its Committee on Industrial Education between 1909 and 1912 are crucial, of course. Irvin G. Wyllie deals with the general attitudes of the business community toward education in *The Self-Made Man in America* (1954). More detailed material may be gleaned from the annual proceedings of organizations like the National Association of Manufacturers, probably the most vociferous American proponent of vocational education before the organization of the National Society for the Promotion of Industrial Education in 1906, the National Metal Trades Association, the National Association of Corporation Schools, and the Chicago Commercial Club. Needless to say, the bulletins of the National Society for the Promotion of Industrial Education are filled with relevant information of every sort and variety. Robert Ripley Clough: "The National Society for the Promotion of Industrial Education: Case Study of a Reform Organization, 1906–1917" (University of Wisconsin, 1957) reports the political efforts of the NSPIE; Lloyd E. Blauch: *Federal Cooperation in Agricultural Extension Work, Vocational Education, and Vocational Rehabilitation* (1935) is the best general account of the movement that culminated in the passing of the Smith-Hughes Act.

The earliest references to vocational education as progressive education appear in the *Fourth Annual Report of the Bureau of Statistics of Labor of the State of New York* (1886); for other views of vocational education as the core of pedagogical progressivism, see Jane Addams: *Democracy and Social Ethics* (1902), Frank Tracy Carlton: *Education and Industrial Evolution* (1908), James Phinney Monroe: *New Demands in Education* (1912), and Arthur D. Dean: *The Progressive Element in Education* (1913).

Culture and Community

Robert H. Bremner: *From the Depths* (1956) provides an excellent introduction to the problem of poverty in the United States and to the humanitarian response in the decades after the Civil War. Jacob A. Riis: *The Battle with the Slum* (1902), Joseph Lee: *Constructive and Preventive Philanthropy* (1902), Robert Hunter: *Poverty* (1905), John Spargo: *The Bitter Cry of the Children* (1908), and Charles Zueblin: *A Decade of Civic Improvement* (1905) are typical contemporary sources. Raymond Williams: *Culture and Society: 1780–1950* (1958) is illuminating on the effort of English intellectuals to redefine culture in the context of industrialism. Gertrude Almy Slichter: "European Backgrounds of American Reform: 1880–1950" (University of

Illinois, 1960) and Arthur Mann: "British Social Thought and American Reformers of the Progressive Era," *Mississippi Valley Historical Review*, XLII (1956), 672–92, deal with the crucial influence of European ideas on American reformers; neither author, however, gives more than passing mention to education. Robert A. Woods and Albert J. Kennedy: *Handbook of Settlements* (1911) and *The Settlement Horizon* (1922) remain the standard sources on the settlement movement; Arthur C. Holden: *The Settlement Idea* (1922) is also revealing. The relation of the movement to American Progressivism is treated in Allen Freeman Davis: "Spearheads for Reform—The Social Settlements and the Progressive Movement, 1890–1914" (University of Wisconsin, 1959). The educational work of the movement is discussed in detail in Morris Isaiah Berger: "The Settlement, the Immigrant and the Public School" (Columbia University, 1956). The many volumes by individual settlement leaders are indispensable for an understanding of the settlement idea; Canon and Mrs. S. A. Barnett: *Towards Social Reform* (1909), Stanton Coit: *Neighbourhood Guilds* (1891), Mary Kingsbury Simkhovitch: *Neighborhood* (1938), Lillian Wald: *The House on Henry Street* (1915), and Robert A. Woods: *The Neighborhood in Nation-Building* (1923) are excellent examples. The best biography of Jane Addams is James Weber Linn: *Jane Addams* (1935); her two autobiographical works, *Twenty Years at Hull-House* (1910) and *The Second Twenty Years at Hull-House* (1930), remain invaluable. Miss Addam's educational views are most fully stated in *Democracy and Social Ethics* (1902) and *The Spirit of Youth and the City Streets* (1909), though all of her writings bear in one way or another on the educational enterprise. For a general treatment of her educational work, see Nancy Pottishman: "Jane Addams and Education" (Columbia, 1961). There is a voluminous primary literature on the relation of child labor and educational reform but no satisfactory history. Grace Abbott's two-volume collection of documents, *The Child and the State* (1938), is an excellent introduction to the general problem; H. N. B. Meyer and Laura A. Thompson: *List of References on Child Labor* (1916) is a fairly comprehensive bibliography of the more significant pre-World War I source material. Forest Chester Ensign: *Compulsory School Attendance and Child Labor* (1921) is an introductory, but not a definitive, study. For the founding of the Children's Bureau, see Alice Elizabeth Padgett: "The History of the Establishment of the United States Children's Bureau" (University of Chicago, 1936), Josephine Goldmark: *Impatient Crusader: Florence Kelley's Life Story* (1953), and Jane Addams: *My Friend, Julia Lathrop* (1935). The annual proceedings of the National Conference of Charities and Corrections and The Na tional Child Labor Committee, as well as *The Commons, Charities, The Survey,* and *The Child Labor Bulletin* are filled with representative addresses and essays on educational reform.

Much more work is needed on the impact of immigration on the American school, especially by historians sophisticated in the relevant concepts of social psychology; W. D. Borrie *et al.*: *The Cultural Integration of Immigrants* (1959) is an excellent guide to some of these concepts. Marcus Lee Hansen: *The Immigrant in American History* (1940), Merle Curti: *The Roots of American Loyalty* (1946), Oscar Handlin: *The Uprooted* (1951), and John Higham: *Strangers in the Land* (1955) are standard works on the related problems of immigration and nationalism. Berger: "The Settlement, the Immigrant and the Public School" and Alan M. Thomas, Jr.: "American Education and the Immigrant," *Teachers College Record,* LV (1953–4), 253–67 deal in particular with the immigrant impact on the schools. Isaac B. Berkson: *Theories of Americanization* (1920) raises a crucial educational problem but limits its discussion to the first two decades of the twentieth century; a more general work dealing with a longer time span would be extraordinarily useful. The 1911 survey of the United States Immigration Commission includes invaluable information, though historians of education would do well to consider the criticisms in Maldwyn Allen Jones: *American Immigration* (1960). Edward Hale Bierstadt: *Aspects of Americanization* (1922), Edward George Hartmann: *The Movement to Americanize the Immigrant* (1948), Herbert A. Miller: *The School and the Immigrant* (1920), and Frank V. Thompson: *Schooling of the Immigrant* (1920), are useful sociological treatises. The several bulletins of the United States Bureau of Education on Americanization and related problems, especially John J. Mahoney: *Training Teachers for Americanization* (1920), are excellent guides to professional opinion.

The rural educational thought of the era must be viewed against a background of traditional agrarian ideals, for which Ann M. Keppel: "Country Schools for Country Children," A. Whitney Griswold: *Farming and Democracy* (1948), and Paul H. Johnstone: "Old Ideals Versus New Ideas in Farm Life," in United States Department of Agriculture: *An Historical Survey of American Agriculture* (1941) are illuminating sources. Liberty Hyde Bailey has never received from historians of education the attention he patently merits. The standard biography is Andrew Denny Rodgers III: *Liberty Hyde Bailey* (1949); Philip Dorf's *Liberty Hyde Bailey* (1956) is briefer, but more readable. Bailey was a prolific author whose works circulated widely in city and country alike; *The Nature-Study Idea* (1903), *The Outlook to Nature* (1905), *The State and the Farmer* (1908), *The Training of*

Farmers (1909), and *The Country-Life Movement in the United States* (1911) all have substantial sections on education. The various surveys by A. C. True and Dick J. Crosby for the Office of Experiment Stations of the United States Department of Agriculture are the best year-by-year guides to actual innovations in rural elementary and secondary education. A. C. True: *A History of Agricultural Extension Work in the United States, 1785–1923* and *A History of Agricultural Education in the United States 1785–1925*, James Ralph Jewell: *Agricultural Education, Including Nature Study and School Gardens*, and Franklin M. Reck: *The 4-H Story* (1951) are the best detailed histories. Joseph Cannon Bailey: *Seaman A. Knapp: Schoolmaster of American Agriculture* (1945) is the definitive biography of Knapp. O. B. Martin: *The Demonstration Work: Dr. Seaman A. Knapp's Contribution to Civilization* (1921) tells enthusiastically the story of Knapp's demonstration techniques. The sponsorship of these techniques in the South is recounted in *The General Education Board: An Account of Its Activities, 1902–1914* (1915), Charles William Dabney: *Universal Education in the South* (1936), and Louis R. Harlan: *Separate and Unequal* (1958). Much more work is needed on the educational aspects of Southern Progressivism. C. Vann Woodward includes a splendid chapter in *Origins of the New South, 1877–1913* (1951); Arthur S. Link ignores education in his otherwise excellent essay, "The Progressive Movement in the South, 1870–1914," *North Carolina Journal of History*, XXXIII (1946), 172–95. There is no satisfactory study of the Country Life Commission, though Grant McConnell includes a useful chapter in *The Decline of Agrarian Democracy* and Ann M. Keppel in "Country Schools for Country Children." Dewey W. Grantham, Jr.'s definitive *Hoke Smith and the Politics of the New South* (1958)deals in some detail with the history of Smith-Lever and Smith-Hughes Acts, as do Bailey in *Seaman A. Knapp* and Blauch in *Federal Cooperation in Agricultural Extension Work, Vocational Education, and Vocational Rehabilitation.*

Science, Darwinism, and Education

A general work on American educational thought is badly needed, not only for the Progressive era but for the whole span of American history. Charles Francis Donovan's "Education in American Social Thought, 1865–1900" (Yale University, 1948) is the most useful single volume for the post-Civil War decades, though his contention that religious reformers were generally uninterested in educational reform is seriously challenged by the efforts of men like Felix Adler and the Reverend William S. Rainsford of New

York. Merle Curti's *The Social Ideas of American Educators* is
replete with original information and insights on Hall, James,
Thorndike, and Dewey and is immensely valuable, along with *The
Growth of American Thought* (1951). Herbert W. Schneider:
A History of American Philosophy (1946), Richard Hofstadter:
Social Darwinism in American Thought, 1860–1915 (1945),
Ralph Henry Gabriel: *The Course of American Democratic
Thought* (1940), Harvey Wish: *Society and Thought in Modern
America* (1952), Henry Steele Commager: *The American Mind*
(1950), Morris R. Cohen: *American Thought* (1954), and Stow
Persons: *American Minds* (1958) have become standard
sources for the intellectual history of the era, as has the splendid
collection of essays edited by Persons under the title *Evolutionary
Thought in America* (1950), a collection which would have
profited immeasurably from an article on pedagogy.

Elsa Peverly Kimball: *Sociology and Education* (1932) deals in
detail with the writings of Herbert Spencer and Lester Frank
Ward as they bear on education. The standard work on Spencer's
educational views remains Gabriel Compayré: *Herbert Spencer
and Scientific Education* (1907); a review that takes account of
recent writings on social Darwinism is much needed. Spencer's
educational views are stated most fully in *Education: Intellectual,
Moral, and Physical* (1860), but many of his other volumes bear
more or less directly on the subject. It is interesting to peruse the
introductions to the many different editions of Spencer's *Education*, notably Charles W. Eliot's in the Everyman's edition of
1910. The reception to Spencer's educational ideas in the United
States could be the subject of a fascinating monograph; their
influence is patent in the reports of a number of NEA committees
between 1893 and 1918. For Charles W. Eliot's key role, see his
collected addresses and essays published under the title *Educational Reform* (1898) and Henry James's two-volume biography,
Charles W. Eliot (1930); for a commentary on the work of the
NEA's Committee of Ten, see Bernard Mehl: "The High School
at the Turn of the Century" (University of Illinois, 1954). The
standard secondary work on Lester Frank Ward is Samuel Chugerman: *Lester F. Ward: The American Aristotle* (1939). The theme
of education as an instrument of social progress runs through all
of Ward's works, from *Dynamic Sociology* (1883) to the collected
essays in *Glimpses of the Cosmos* (1913–18); there is an unpublished manuscript on education in the Brown University Library
Edward Everett Walker: "The Educational Theories of Lester
Frank Ward" (Stanford University, 1932) is a somewhat uncritical review. The pedagogical theories of Ward, William
Graham Sumner, and Albion Small are dealt with insightfully
in Donovan: "Education in American Social Thought, 1865–

1900." There are competent biographical sketches of all three men in the *Dictionary of American Biography*.

Edwin G. Boring contributes a penetrating essay on "The Influence of Evolutionary Theory upon American Psychological Thought" to Persons: *Evolutionary Thought in America*. Boring: *History of Experimental Psychology* (1950) and Edna Heidbreder: *Seven Psychologies* (1933) are useful general sources. A history of the relation of educational and psychological thought in the United States is much needed. There is no satisfactory biography of G. Stanley Hall; Lorine Pruette: *G. Stanley Hall: A Biography of a Mind* (1926) is overly psychological and at points superficial. Curti's chapter on Hall in *The Social Ideas of American Educators* is excellent, while Hall's *Life and Confessions of a Psychologist* (1923) has pungent reflections on many of the most important personalities and events of the era, as does his *Founders of Modern Psychology* (1912). G. E. Partridge: *Genetic Philosophy of Education* (1912) is a compilation of Hall's most significant pedagogical writings, while Sara Carolyn Fisher: "The Psychological and Educational Work of Granville Stanley Hall," *American Journal of Psychology*, XXXVI (1925), 1–52, is a competent but unimaginative exegesis. Hall's main works are collections of essays rather than systematic treatises. He received his first national attention for an article called "The Contents of Children's Minds," *The Princeton Review*, XI (1883), 249–72, and secured his reputation with two two-volume studies: *Adolescence* (1904) and *Educational Problems* (1911). There is a "Bibliography of the Published Writings of G. Stanley Hall" in Edward L. Thorndike: *Biographical Memoir of Granville Stanley Hall, 1846–1924* (1928). The principal collection of Hall's unpublished papers bearing on education is at Clark University. The only historical monograph on the child-study movement is Wilbur Harvey Dutton: "The Child-Study Movement in America from Its Origin (1880) to the Organization of the Progressive Education Association (1920)" (Stanford University, 1945), a compilation most valuable, perhaps, for the correspondence it includes between the author and some of the major figures of the movement. *Pedagogical Seminary* is replete with articles, notes, bibliographies, research reports, and news of the movement in all parts of the world. For the influential ideas of the Swedish feminist Ellen Key, see her own work, *The Century of the Child* (1909) and Oscar A. Winfield: "The Educational Ideals of Ellen Key" (Yale University, 1928); Oscar Cargill's comments in *Intellectual America* (1941) are pungent and highly illuminating.

Philip P. Wiener: *Evolution and the Founders of Pragmatism* (1949) provides excellent background material on the origins of James's philosophy; George Herbert Mead: "The Philosophies of

Royce, James, and Dewey in Their American Setting," *The International Journal of Ethics*, XL (1929–30), 211–31, and John Dewey: *The Influence of Darwin on Philosophy* (1910) and "The Development of American Pragmatism," in *Philosophy and Civilization* (1931) are also illuminating. Ralph Barton Perry's two-volume classic *The Thought and Character of William James* (1935) is a model of scholarship, and is nicely complemented by Henry James: *The Letters of William James* (1920). James: *Principles of Psychology* (1890) and *Talks to Teachers on Psychology: and to Students on Some of Life's Ideals* (1899) had the greatest direct impact on pedagogy, but the equally pervasive influence of the later philosophical works should not be ignored, especially *Pragmatism* (1907) and *The Meaning of Truth* (1909). Bird T. Baldwin: "William James' Contributions to Education," *Journal of Educational Psychology*, II (1911), 369–82, is a useful contemporary appraisal; later assessments include John Wesley Humphreys: "The Educational Philosophy of William James" (University of Cincinnati, 1928) and Harold Hughes Wood: "William James and Modern Public Education" (Cornell University, 1950), of which the former is by far superior. John L. Childs: *American Pragmatism and Education* (1956) deals with the larger pragmatic movement in education.

Whether or not to include Edward L. Thorndike and the scientific movement as an aspect of Progressivism in American education was an initial problem in the definition of the study, a problem resolved on three grounds: *first*, examination of *Animal Learning* (1898) and other early writings reveals them to be clearly Progressive in orientation, picturing education as an instrument of social improvement; *second*, scientism was patently a central ingredient of Progressivism in general, as, for example, in the municipal reform movement with its belief in a science of civic administration; and *third*, Thorndike and the other early pedagogical scientists thought of themselves, and were thought of by others, as Progressives. That Thorndike was essentially conservative in his social philosophy—see Curti's essay in *The Social Ideas of American Educators*—and that many of the proponents of scientism, notably Franklin Bobbitt and W. W. Charters, ended as conservatives after World War I merely indicates one of the intriguing internal contradictions of the progressive education movement. A major biography of Thorndike is needed and would constitute a fascinating research enterprise; meanwhile, the *Biographical Memoir of Edward Lee Thorndike, 1874–1949* (1952) by Robert S. Woodworth and the autobiographical sketch in *Selected Writings from a Connectionist's Psychology* (1949) must suffice. There are excellent bibliographies and commentaries on the fantastic range of Thorndike's work in the *Teachers Col-*

lege Record for February, 1926 and May, 1940. Thorndike's classic is the three-volume *Educational Psychology* (1913–14). Pedro Tamesis Orata: *The Theory of Identical Elements* (1928), H. Gordon Hullfish: *Aspects of Thorndike's Psychology in Their Relation to Educational Theory and Practice* (1926), Walter B. Kolesnik: *Mental Discipline in Modern Education* (1958), and Geraldine Joncich: "Science, Psychology, and Education: An Interpretive Study of Edward L. Thorndike's Place in the Scientific Movement in American Education" (Teachers College, Columbia University, 1961) are illuminating guides to the philosophical and psychological controversies surrounding Thorndike's contribution. James Earl Russell: *The Scientific Movement in Education* (1926), Daniel B. Leary's essay on "Development of Educational Psychology" in I. L. Kandel, ed.: *Twenty-Five Years of American Education,* and Part II of the *Thirty-Seventh Yearbook* (1938) of the National Society for the Study of Education are useful sources on the scientific movement. So far as can be determined, there is no extensive collection of unpublished Thorndike papers.

The literature on John Dewey and his relationship to American education is voluminous, but most of it is of such a character as to be of little value to the historian except as primary source material on Deweyism and anti-Deweyism. A biography of Dewey is sorely needed, and could be a landmark in American historiography. An autobiographical sketch, written in collaboration with Jane Dewey, appears in Paul Arthur Schilpp, ed.: *The Philosophy of John Dewey* (1939); another, describing his intellectual development, is included in George P. Adams and W. Pepperel Montague, eds.: *Contemporary American Philosophy* (1930). Dewey's Vermont years (1859–1882) are dealt with in Frances Littlefield Davenport: "The Education of John Dewey" (University of California at Los Angeles, 1946), George Dykhuizen: "John Dewey: The Vermont Years," *Journal of the History of Ideas,* XX (1959), 515–44, Lewis S. Feuer: "John Dewey's Reading at College," Ibid., XIX (1958), 415–21, and Feuer: "H. A. P. Torrey and John Dewey: Teacher and Pupil," *American Quarterly,* X (1958), 34–54. Morton G. White: *The Origin of Dewey's Instrumentalism* (1943) and Willinda Savage: "The Evolution of John Dewey's Philosophy of Experimentalism as Developed at the University of Michigan" (University of Michigan, 1950) deal insightfully with Dewey's early philosophical development. Feuer: "John Dewey and the Back to the People Movement in American Thought," *Journal of the History of Ideas,* XX (1959), 545–568, carries the story into the Chicago period (1894–1904). Ray Ginger: *Altgeld's America* (1958) and Robert L. McCaul: "Dewey's Chicago," *The School Review,* LXVII (1959), 258–80, provide the context in

which Dewey's pedagogical ideas developed at the University of
Chicago; Melvin C. Baker: *Foundations of John Dewey's Educa-
tional Theory* (1955) is a systematic discussion of these ideas.
Max Eastman includes a revealing portrait in *Great Companions*
(1959), as do Irwin Edman in *Philosopher's Holiday* (1938) and
Harold A. Larrabee in William W. Brickman and Stanley Lehrer,
eds.: *John Dewey: Master Educator* (1959). The literature on
Dewey must have doubled during the centennial year: Martin S.
Dworkin, ed.: *Dewey on Education* (1959) reprints a number of
Dewey's essays from "My Pedagogic Creed" to the introduction he
wrote for Elsie Ripley Clapp's *The Use of Resources in Education*
(1952), along with a thoughtful critical essay. George R. Geiger:
John Dewey in Perspective (1958) is a useful exegesis, John
Blewett, ed.: *John Dewey: His Thought and Influence* (1960)
includes a number of scholarly essays by leading Roman Catholic
authors. The standard bibliography of Dewey's works is by M.
Halsey Thomas and Herbert W. Schneider; the most recent
version of that bibliography is reprinted, along with additions by
Muriel Murray, in Schilpp, ed.: *The Philosophy of John Dewey*;
a new edition is being prepared in connection with the centennial.
There are collections of Dewey papers at the University of Michigan, the University of Chicago, and Columbia University, as well
as in the possession of Mrs. John Dewey and the many friends
and acquaintances with whom Dewey corresponded over the years.

Pedagogical Pioneers

A general picture of institutional developments in American education between 1865 and 1918 is given in Butts and Cremin: *A
History of Education in American Culture*. I. L. Kandel, ed.:
Twenty-Five Years of American Education deals in particular with
the decades following the nineties. John Elbert Stout's study of
*The Development of High-School Curricula in the North Central
States from 1860 to 1918* (1921) is illuminating, but its usefulness is limited by the author's assumption that subjects listed in
school catalogues and state syllabi are always taught; in any case,
its data should not be generalized to the nation as a whole. Forest
Chester Ensign: *Compulsory School Attendance and Child Labor*
is an introductory study in an area that needs a good deal more
work, as is W. Randolph Burgess's carefully done *Trends of School
Costs* (1920). W. H. Page *et al.*: *The School of Tomorrow* (1911)
and John Dewey and Evelyn Dewey: *Schools of To-Morrow*
(1915) are useful journalistic surveys of educational reform and
innovation. Ned Harlan Dearborn: *The Oswego Movement in
American Education* (1925) treats the influence of one significant
institution. R. Freeman Butts: *The College Charts Its Course*

deals comprehensively with progressivism in higher education. C. Hartley Grattan: *In Quest of Knowledge* (1955) advances some intriguing hypotheses about adult education as an instrument of social reform.

There is no satisfactory biography of Francis W. Parker. Charles H. Judd's sketch in the *Dictionary of American Biography* is useful, as is Parker's autobiographical commentary in William M. Giffin: *School Days in the Fifties* (1906). Ida Cassa Heffron: *Francis Wayland Parker* (1934) is an appreciation. Edward Dangler deals in detail with Parker's ideas in "The Educational Philosophy of Francis W. Parker" (New York University, 1939), as does Beck in "American Progressive Education, 1875–1930." Parker's work at Quincy is discussed in Charles F. Adams, Jr.: *The New Departure in the Common Schools of Quincy* (1879) and in Lelia E. Partridge: *The "Quincy Methods" Illustrated* (1889). His work in Chicago is reported in "An Account of the Cook County and Chicago Normal School from 1883 to 1899," *The Elementary School Teacher and the Course of Study*, II (1901–2), 752–80, and in Heffron: *Francis Wayland Parker*; Robert Eugene Tostberg: "Educational Ferment in Chicago, 1883–1904" (University of Wisconsin, 1960) includes a thoughtful appraisal. Parker published two major works on education: *Talks on Teaching* (1883) and *Talks on Pedagogics* (1894); of the two, the latter is the fuller statement of his pedagogy. His annual reports to the Quincy board of education are also edifying. There are Parker papers at the University of Chicago and in the McCormick collection at the Wisconsin State Historical Society.

Katherine Camp Mayhew and Anna Camp Edwards have published an engrossing account of the work at Dewey's Laboratory School in *The Dewey School* (1936); much of their volume is based on primary material from the *University Record*, *The Elementary School Record* for 1900, *The Elementary School Teacher and the Course of Study* for 1901 and 1902, and the June, 1903, issue of *The Elementary School Teacher*. There are unpublished papers relating to the school between 1896 and 1904 at the University of Chicago Library, the Wisconsin State Historical Society, and the Teachers College, Columbia University, Library. Dewey discusses the school in the autobiographical sketch included in Schilpp, ed.: *The Philosophy of John Dewey*, as does Max Eastman in *Great Companions*. Ella Flagg Young's association with Dewey is dealt with, though all too briefly, in John T. McManis: *Ella Flagg Young* (1916); her own views are stated most fully in *Isolation in the School* (1900).

The work at Menomonie is discussed in Ann M. Keppel and James I. Clark: "James H. Stout and the Menomonie Schools,"

Wisconsin Magazine of History, XLII (1959), 200–10, and William T. Bawden: *Leaders in Industrial Education* (1950). The best contemporary source is Adele Marie Shaw: "The Ideal Schools of Menomonie," *The World's Work*, VII (1903–4), 4540–53. For the context of the Menomonie reforms, see Ann M. Keppel: "Country Schools for Country Children."

The theory and practice of the Organic School in Fairhope, Alabama, may be gleaned from Marietta Johnson: *Youth in a World of Men* (1929), "The Educational Principles of the School of Organic Education, Fairhope, Alabama" in National Society for the Study of Education: *Twenty-Sixth Yearbook* (1926), Part I, and "Thirty Years with an Idea" (Teachers College, Columbia University, 1939). For the background of Mrs. Johnson's ideas, see Nathan Oppenheim: *The Development of the Child* (1898) and C. Hanford Henderson: *Education and the Larger Life* (1902) and *What Is It to Be Educated?* (1914). A. Gordon Melvin portrays the Parker-Henderson-Johnson stream as the authentic stream of progressive education in *Education: A History* (1946). The Deweys also include an account of Mrs. Johnson's work in *Schools of To-Morrow*, portraying it as Rousseauism incarnate.

William Paxton Burris: *The Public School System of Gary, Ind.* (1914) is an uncritical report of the early stages of the Gary development by the Dean of the University of Cincinnati's College for Teachers. Randolph S. Bourne's widely read account, *The Gary Schools* (1916), is rhapsodic in its praise, relating the innovations to Dewey's educational ideas wherever possible. The eight-volume survey carried out by the General Education Board under the supervision of Abraham Flexner and Frank P. Bachman is the most detailed study of the plan (it ends up sharply critical at a number of points); see in particular the summary volume by Flexner and Bachman entitled *The Gary Schools* (1918). The spread of the Gary Plan is documented in Charles L. Spain: *The Platoon School* (1925) and Roscoe David Case: *The Platoon School in America* (1931), but with no sense of the pitched political battles the Plan engendered; a more critical view of the Plan as the quintessence of "Taylorism" in the schools is presented by Raymond Callahan of Washington University in an unpublished manuscript entitled "The American Tragedy in Education." The biographical sketch of William Wirt by Carter V. Good in the *Dictionary of American Biography* is illuminating.

The definitive history of the University of Wisconsin is Merle Curti and Vernon Carstensen: *The University of Wisconsin: A History 1848–1925* (1949). W. H. Glover: *Farm and College* (1952), a history of the School of Agriculture, and Frederick M. Rossentretter: *The Boundaries of the Campus: A History of the*

University of Wisconsin Extension Division, 1885–1945 (1957) are also valuable. The central role of the University in the Wisconsin Progressive Movement is treated in Charles McCarthy: *The Wisconsin Idea* (1912), Frederic C. Howe: *Wisconsin: An Experiment in Democracy* (1912), and Edward N. Doan: *The La Follettes and the Wisconsin Idea* (1947). Russel B. Nye: *Midwestern Progressive Politics* (1959) includes a penetrating discussion on the relation between Progressivism and the new social sciences. For the English origins of the university extension movement, see Albert Mansbridge: *University Tutorial Classes* (1913) and William H. Draper: *University Extension: A Survey of Fifty Years, 1873–1923* (1923); for the American phase, see Grattan: *In Quest of Knowledge*.

Walter S. Monroe: *Teaching-Learning Theory and Teacher Education, 1890–1952* (1952) and Merle L. Borrowman: *The Liberal and Technical in Teacher Education* (1956) provide excellent background material on the rise of professional education for teachers. The standard history of Teachers College is Lawrence A. Cremin, David A. Shannon, and Mary Evelyn Townsend: *A History of Teachers College, Columbia University* (1954), but it tends to concentrate on internal development. Nicholas Murray Butler's two-volume autobiography, *Across the Busy Years* (1939–40), and James Earl Russell: *Founding Teachers College* (1937) afford penetrating insight into the conditions surrounding the establishment and early years of the College. Abbie Graham: *Grace H. Dodge: Merchant of Dreams* (1926) is appreciative but hardly definitive. For the widening gulf between professional teacher educators and arts and science faculties, see Howard M. Jones, Francis Keppel, and Robert Ulich: "On the Conflict Between the 'Liberal Arts' and the 'Schools of Education,'" *The ACLS Newsletter*, V (1954), 17–38, and Eugene Charles Auerbach: "The Opposition to Schools of Education by Professors of the Liberal Arts—A Historical Analysis" (University of Southern California, 1957).

Scientists, Sentimentalists, and Radicals

A number of excellent social and intellectual histories of the interbellum era complement the general works already cited. Lloyd Morris: *Postscript to Yesterday* (1947) and *Not So Long Ago* (1949) deal informally with the half-century following 1896, and are especially illuminating on the period after World War I. Frederick Lewis Allen: *Only Yesterday* (1931), Arthur M. Schlesinger, Jr.: *The Crisis of the Old Order* (1957), and William E. Leuchtenburg: *The Perils of Prosperity* (1958) are penetrating and thoroughly readable accounts of the twenties; Allen: *Since Yes-*

terday (1940) deals similarly with the thirties. Alfred Kazin: *On Native Grounds* (1942) and Oscar Cargill: *Intellectual America* are purportedly literary histories, but they range far and wide in the best tradition of Parrington. Malcolm Cowley reminisces about the literary life of the twenties in *Exile's Return* (1934); Frederick J. Hoffman deals more systematically with the same period in *The Twenties* (1955). Henry F. May disputes the common periodizing of twentieth-century intellectual history that emphasizes sharp breaks at 1919 and 1929 in *The End of American Innocence* (1959) and "Shifting Perspectives on the 1920's," *Mississippi Valley Historical Review*, XLIII (1956), 405–27. There is no satisfactory work on the educational history of the interbellum era. Norman Woelfel deals somewhat prosaically with the leading educational spokesmen of the period in *Molders of the American Mind* (1933), and Harold Rugg offers a highly personal interpretation in a number of his volumes, especially *Foundations for American Education* and *The Teacher of Teachers* (1952). Students of the period will find the serial *Review of Educational Research* an invaluable guide to sources, especially those numbers dealing with the social, historical, philosophical, and psychological foundations of education.

Harold Rugg writes of himself in the context of the intellectual life of the interbellum era in *That Men May Understand* (1941); his magnum opus on the progressive education movement—and the fullest interpretation of that movement to date—is his *Foundations for American Education*. Rugg was a prolific author, but readers will find a good deal of overlap and repetition from one work to the next. Mark Phillips deals critically with Rugg's educational position during the twenties in "*The Seven Arts* and Harold Rugg: A Study in Intellectual History" (Columbia University, 1961); otherwise, little if any work has been done on him. Rugg died in 1960, leaving a substantial collection of documents and unpublished papers relating to the progressive education movement. There is no published bibliography of Rugg's writings; aside from those already alluded to, the most significant are *Statistical Methods Applied to Education* (1917), *The Child-Centered School* (1928), *Culture and Education in America* (1931), *The Great Technology* (1933), *American Life and the School Curriculum* (1936), and the so-called Rugg social studies texts for the schools published under the general title *Man and His Changing Society*.

There is no general historical work on the scientific movement in education. Joseph Peterson: *Early Conceptions and Tests of Intelligence* (1925), Frank N. Freeman: *Mental Tests: Their History, Principles, and Applications* (1939), and Walter W. Cook's article and bibliography on achievement tests in Walter S. Monroe, ed.: *Encyclopedia of Educational Research* (1941) are useful sources on the development of mental tests. Clarence S. Yoakum and Robert M. Yerkes: *Army Mental Tests* (1920) deals in detail with the Army program during World War I. Edward L. Thorndike's publications during the 1920's and 1930's are highly significant; much of his later work is brought together in *Human Nature and the Social Order* (1940). The most eloquent statements of the progressive position on the meaning and uses of intelligence tests may be found in Walter Lippmann's series for *The New Republic*, XXXII (1922), 213–15, 246–8, 275–7, 297–8, 328–30, XXXIII (1922–3), 9–11, XXXIV (1923), 263–4, 322–3; in John Dewey's essays in the same journal, XXXIII (1922–23), 35–7, 61–3; and in William C. Bagley: *Determinism in Education* (1925). Bagley's position is notable, since throughout the interbellum period, particularly in the 1930's, he chose to identify himself with those who opposed progressive education.

The details of the early impact of scientism on educational theory may be gleaned from the *Yearbooks* of the National Society for the Study of Education beginning around 1914. The *Twenty-Sixth Yearbook* (1927) is especially useful, notably Harold Rugg's sections reviewing "A Century of Curriculum-Construction in American Schools," Part I, pp. 3–116. Much more work is needed on the Committee on Economy of Time and the curriculum movement it set in motion; the literature to date has tended to overstress the Committee on the Reorganization of Secondary Education, whose influence was more limited. Alice V. Keliher treats the controversy over grouping in *A Critical Study of Homogeneous Grouping* (1931); the NSSE's *Twenty-Fourth Yearbook* (1925), Part II and *Thirty-Fifth Yearbook* (1936), Part I are also useful on this problem. Franklin Bobbitt: *The Curriculum* (1918) and *How to Make a Curriculum* (1924) and W. W. Charters: *Curriculum Construction* (1923) are representative of the effort to develop a science of curriculum-making for the public schools. Charters's papers are at Ohio State University; I have been unable to locate any major collection of Bobbitt papers. Eugene Randolph Smith's *Education Moves Ahead* (1924) is more characteristic of private-school thinking. For a view of scientism as progressivism in education, see Charles Hubbard Judd: *Introduction to the Scientific Study of Education* (1918) and *Education and Social Progress* (1934).

Robert Holmes Beck: "American Progressive Education, 1875–1930" is exceptionally strong on the child-centered strand of the progressive education movement, and I have tended to follow his interpretations of Caroline Pratt and Margaret Naumburg. It may be unfair to label this strand *sentimentalist*, but as I read the con-

temporary literature I cannot but call to mind G. K. Chesterton's
remark that the sentimentalist, roughly speaking, "is the man who
wants to eat his cake and have it. He has no sense of honour about
ideas; he will not see that one must pay for an idea as for anything
else. . . . He will have them all at once in one wild intellectual
harem, no matter how much they quarrel and contradict each
other." The standard source on this strand is Harold Rugg and
Ann Shumaker: *The Child-Centered School*; Rugg: "The Artist
and the Great Transition," in Waldo Frank *et al.: America & Alfred Stieglitz* (1934) and Gertrude Hartman and Ann Shumaker:
Creative Expression (1932) are also useful. Caroline Pratt's autobiography, *I Learn From Children* (1948), is revealing, as are
Caroline Pratt, ed.: *Experimental Practice in the City and Country School* (1924) and Caroline Pratt and Jessie Stanton: *Before
Books* (1926). Lucy Sprague Mitchell: *Two Lives* (1953) tells
of the founding and work of the Bureau of Educational Experiments, which subsequently became the Bank Street College of Education; the *Bulletins* of the Bureau are also informative. Caroline
Ware: *Greenwich Village, 1920–30* (1935) is extraordinarily illuminating as background material. Albert Parry's breezy history
of Bohemianism, *Garrets and Pretenders* (1933), and Allen
Churchill: *The Improper Bohemians* (1959) are relevant, although they do not deal specifically with education.

There is no satisfactory discussion of Freudianism in American
pedagogical thought; the model for such a discussion would be
Frederick J. Hoffman: *Freudianism and the Literary Mind*
(1957), a scholarly work that properly emphasizes the continuing
transformation of Freudian ideas as they were taken over by
American writers. Ernest Jones's three-volume study, *The Life and
Work of Sigmund Freud* (1953–7), is the standard biography;
the standard edition of Freud's writings is edited by James Strachy
and published by the Hogarth Press in London. C. P. Oberndorf:
A History of Psychoanalysis in America (1953) tells of the dissemination of Freudian ideas in the United States; Philip Rieff:
Freud: The Mind of the Moralist (1959) is an excellent critical
appraisal, highly relevant to education. For the early effort to
apply Freudian principles to education, see William A. White:
The Mental Hygiene of Childhood (1919), A. A. Brill: *Fundamental Conceptions of Psychoanalysis* (1921), and Oskar Pfister:
Psycho-Analysis in the Service of Education (1922). For the
Bohemian popularization of Freudianism during the twenties,
see Caroline Ware: *Greenwich Village, 1920–1930* and the fourth
volume of Mark Sullivan: *Our Times: the United States, 1900–
1925* (1926–35). Margaret Naumburg's principal work on education is *The Child and the World* (1928); biographical infor-

mation on Miss Naumburg is included in Robert H. Beck: "Progressive Education and American Progressivism: Margaret Naumburg," *Teachers College Record*, LX (1958–9), 198–208.

John L. Childs: *American Pragmatism and Education* is a sympathetic commentary on the reformist stream of progressive education, including extended discussions of the life and work of William H. Kilpatrick, Boyd H. Bode, and George S. Counts. Joseph McGlade discusses the reformist stream from a particular viewpoint in *Progressive Educators and the Catholic Church* (1953). Kilpatrick's most important early publications are "The Project Method," *Teachers College Record*, XIX (1918), 319–35, *Foundations of Method* (1925), and *Education for a Changing Civilization* (1926). His writings of the thirties, notably *Education and the Social Crisis* (1932) and his contributions to *The Educational Frontier* (1933), which he edited, reflect a perceptible shift toward a stronger social orientation. He published his *Philosophy of Education* in 1951. The standard biography, Samuel Tenenbaum: *William Heard Kilpatrick: Trail Blazer in Education* (1951), is relatively uncritical. Professor Kilpatrick was generous enough to grant me access to his diary, a monumental handwritten work running over two-score volumes, his scrapbooks, his unpublished papers, and a two-volume typescript prepared from a tape he dictated for Tenenbaum in connection with the biography; the diary is invaluable for the student of the period. Childs deals with Bode's philosophic contribution in "Boyd H. Bode and the Experimentalists," *Teachers College Record*, LV (1953–4), 1–9, as well as in *American Pragmatism and Education*; Joseph James Chambliss: "The Development of Bode's Pragmatism and Its Influence on His Philosophy of Education" (University of Illinois, 1959) is also illuminating. Bode's chief works are *Fundamentals of Education* (1921), *Modern Educational Theories* (1927), *Conflicting Psychologies of Learning* (1929), and *Democracy as a Way of Life* (1948); his *Progressive Education at the Crossroads* (1938) is a brilliant critique of the progressive education movement. A number of informative essays on Bode appear in the January, 1948, issue of the *Teachers College Record*. There is no major collection of Bode papers.

Joseph Dorfman: *Thorstein Veblen and His America* (1934) includes penetrating commentaries on Veblen's critique of American education, as does David Riesman: *Thorstein Veblen: A Critical Interpretation* (1953). An autobiographical sketch of George S. Counts appears in Stanley J. Kunitz: *Twentieth Century Authors: First Supplement* (1955), along with a bibliography of major writings. Counts's most important works dealing with American education are *The Selective Character of American Secondary Education* (1922), *The Social Composition of Boards of Education*

(1927), *School and Society in Chicago* (1928), *The American Road to Culture* (1930), *The Prospects of American Democracy* (1938), and *Education and American Civilization* (1952). He is best known in many quarters for *Dare the School Build a New Social Order?* (1932), and readers will also find *The Challenge of Soviet Education* (1957) relevant to his view of American education. The story of the "Kilpatrick group" and *The Social Frontier* is recounted by Rugg in *Foundations for American Education* and *The Teacher of Teachers*; Kilpatrick's diary is obviously illuminating. I have contended that William H. Kilpatrick, ed.: *The Educational Frontier* is the characteristic progressivist work of the thirties; it should be read along with the publications of the NEA's Educational Policies Commission, the AHA's Commission on the Social Studies, the ACE's American Youth Commission, and the John Dewey Society. Dewey's critique of the progressive education movement may be found in *Experience and Education* (1938) and his Introduction to Elsie Ripley Clapp's *The Use of Resources in Education* (1952); a collection of his writings published under the title *Education Today* (1940) includes many of his essays from *The Social Frontier*. Finally, Robert W. Iversen deals intelligently with the communist educational theories of the thirties in *The Communists and the Schools* (1959).

The Organization of Dissent

There is no satisfactory history of the Progressive Education Association. Berdine Jackman Bovard tells the story to 1939 in "A History of the Progressive Education Association, 1919–1939" (University of California at Berkeley, 1941), and Beck includes a useful chapter in "American Progressive Education, 1875–1930." Apart from those, the student of the movement is thrown largely back to primary material. The story of the founding is told in Stanwood Cobb: "The Romance of Beginnings," *Progressive Education*, VI (1929), 66–73, and Ernest Cobb: *One Foot on the Ground* (1934). Stanwood Cobb: *The New Leaven* (1928) is as good a source as any on the early philosophy of the Association. The seventeen PEA *Bulletins* which appeared between 1920 and 1923 report the proceedings of the first conventions and other matters of interest to the membership. *Progressive Education*, launched in 1924 as a quarterly and subsequently converted into a monthly, carries news of policies, plans, and programs right through to the Association's demise in 1955. *The New Era* is useful for the PEA's part in the international movement for educational reform. Finally, the numerous widely circulated pamphlets published under PEA auspices during the late thirties and early forties are an excellent guide to the Association's influence on teachers at large.

The minutes of the Executive Committee from 1924 through 1946 are in the Teachers College, Columbia University, Library through the courtesy of Frederick L. Redefer, Executive Secretary and then Director between 1932 and 1943, along with a substantial unpublished history of the movement he wrote shortly after World War II entitled "Between Two Wars: An Interpretation of Progressive Education in the United States of America." The Teachers College Library also possesses files of unpublished manuscripts, autobiographical accounts, newspaper clippings, and miscellaneous printed and mimeographed documents contributed by Stanwood Cobb and Eugene Randolph Smith.

A good deal of the Association's impact during the 1930's and 1940's was made through its various Committees and Commissions. The Committee on Social and Economic Problems stirred considerable controversy with *A Call to the Teachers of the Nation* in 1933. The Commission on Secondary School Curriculum sponsored V. T. Thayer, Caroline B. Zachry, and Ruth Kotinsky: *Reorganizing Secondary Education* (1939), Caroline B. Zachry and Margaret Lighty: *Emotion and Conduct in Adolescence* (1940), and Peter Blos: *The Adolescent Personality* (1941). Similarly, the Commission on Human Relations sponsored Alice V. Keliher: *Life and Growth* (1941), Katherine Whiteside Taylor: *Do Adolescents Need Parents?* (1938), and a series of films described in *The Human Relations Series of Films* (1939). The work of the Commission on the Relation of School and College is reported in the five-volume series, *Adventure in American Education* (1942), of which Wilford M. Aikin: *The Story of the Eight-Year Study* is the summary volume. In addition, there are the printed reports of the Commission's annual conferences issued as supplements to *The Educational Record*, an occasional publication called the *Thirty Schools Bulletin*, and a large body of teacher reports, student publications (*Were We Guinea Pigs?* (1938), prepared by fifty-five students of the University High School at Ohio State University, is exemplary), and mimeographed materials issued by the schools themselves. The Commission's findings and the results as of 1950 are reviewed in Frederick L. Redefer: "The Eight-Year Study—Eight Years Later" (Teachers College, Columbia University, 1952).

Edgar B. Wesley discusses the role of the National Education Association in the progressive education movement in *NEA: The First Hundred Years* (1957); doubtless this role would expand given the larger definition of the movement I have advanced. A history of the American Federation of Teachers is much needed, as is a history of teacher unionism in general. Jack Cohn's "Attitudes and Policies of Organized Labor Toward Public Education in New York State (to 1935)" (Teachers College, Columbia University, 1952) devotes a substantial section to the AF of T. Needless to say, *The American Teacher* and the annual proceedings of AF of T conventions are rich in relevant material.

The Changing Pedagogical Mainstream

There is no comprehensive analysis of educational reform during the interbellum era, though Harold Rugg: *Foundations for American Education* and I. L. Kandel: *American Education in the Twentieth Century* present a good deal of useful information. The *Yearbooks* of the National Society for the Study of Education, the *Bulletins* of the United States Office of Education, the *Research Bulletins* of the National Education Association, the *Bulletins* of the Bureau of Educational Experiments, and *Progressive Education* are the most fertile sources of data. Partial views of the reform movement may be gleaned from Agnes de Lima: *Our Enemy the Child* (1926), which incidentally includes a list of "experimental and progressive schools" supplied by the Bureau of Educational Experiments, Harold Rugg and Ann Shumaker: *The Child-Centered School*, Henry Harap *et al.*: *The Changing Curriculum* (1937), and R. Freeman Butts: *The College Charts Its Course*. Lloyd Marcus traces the origins of a number of private progressive schools in "The Founding of American Private Progressive Schools, 1912–1921" (Harvard University, 1948). John F. Latimer describes the changes in secondary-school offerings, though without sufficient attempt at explanation, in *What's Happened to Our High Schools?* (1958). R. L. Duffus deals with innovation at the college level in *Democracy Enters the College* (1936), as do Louis T. Benezet in *General Education in the Progressive College* (1943), George P Schmidt in the latter chapters of *The Liberal Arts College* (1957), and John S. Brubacher and Willis Rudy in Part IV of *Higher Education in Transition* (1958). As might be expected, the studies of individual ventures vary considerably in character and quality; among the better are Junius L. Meriam: *Child Life and the Curriculum* (1920), Elisabeth Irwin and Louis A. Marks: *Fitting the School to the Child* (1924), Mary H. Lewis: *An Adventure with Children* (1928), Alexander Meiklejohn: *The Experimental College* (1932), Constance Warren: *A New Design for Women's Education* (1940), Agnes de Lima: *The Little Red School House* (1942), and Algo Henderson and Dorothy Hall: *Antioch College: Its Design for Liberal Education* (1946).

Agnes de Lima: *A School for the World of Tomorrow* (1939) and *Democracy's High School* (1941) are brief but illuminating introductions to the work of the Lincoln School. Flexner tells of the genesis of the experiment in *I Remember* (1940); his essay sketching a rationale for the school is reprinted in *A Modern College and a Modern School* (1923). The best single volume on what actually went on in Lincoln's classrooms and the theory behind it is afforded by James S. Tippett *et al.: Curriculum Making in an Elementary School* (1927). The most comprehensive appraisal of student achievement is reported in L. Thomas Hopkins and James E. Mendenhall: *Achievement at Lincoln School* (1934). The February, 1936, issue of the *Teachers College Record* is devoted to a survey of the school's activities. A number of individual accounts shed a good deal of light on the program as a whole, among them Hughes Mearns: *Creative Youth* (1925), Satis N. Coleman: *A Children's Symphony* (1931), Henry Emmett Brown: "The Development of a Course in the Physical Sciences for the Senior High School of the Lincoln School of Teachers College" (Teachers College, Columbia University, 1938), and Harold Rugg: *That Men May Understand.* There is an excellent collection of primary source material at Teachers College, including student poems, stories, dramas, yearbooks, newspapers, and occasional publications, faculty reports, course syllabi, administrative records, and documents relating to the controversy over the school's closing.

The extension of the country-life movement into the 1920's is a subject that needs further research. Its effects on rural education are legion, and obviously Marie Turner Harvey's work at the Porter School is merely one of many possible examples. Lucy Simmons: *History of Northeast Missouri State Teachers College* (1927) and Ferdinand Del Pizzo's "The Contributions of John R. Kirk to Teacher Education" (Washington University, 1955) provide excellent background material on the Porter experiment; the fullest account is Evelyn Dewey's enthusiastic *New Schools for Old* (1919). Mrs. Harvey's addresses in the NEA *Addresses and Proceedings* for 1918 and 1930 present her own view of her work. Ellsworth Collings: *An Experiment with a Project Curriculum* (1923) is a frequently cited appraisal of a highly similar experiment in the rural schools of McDonald County, Missouri.

The description of Frederic Burk's work at the San Francisco Normal School, reported in the NSSE's *Twenty-Fourth Yearbook* (1925), Part II, is excellent background material for the Winnetka reform of the 1920's. The genesis of the reform is discussed by Carleton Washburne and Edward Yeomans in "The Inception of the Winnetka Technique," *Journal of the American Association of University Women*, XXIII (1930), 129–36; Yeomans: *Shackled Youth* (1921) is also revealing. The fullest accounts of the Winnetka Plan are by Washburne in "Winnetka," *School and Society*, XXIX (1929), 37–50, and a subsequent volume entitled *Adjusting the School to the Child* (1932). An early comprehensive survey of results is Carleton Washburne, Mabel Vogel, and William S. Gray: *A Survey of the Winnetka Public Schools* (1926). For the spread of the Winnetka Plan on a modified basis, see City School Leaflet No. 22 of the United States Bureau of Education, *Cities Reporting the Use of Homogeneous Grouping and of the Winnetka Technique and the Dalton Plan* (1926). For a view of progressive education that casts Winnetka as the quintessential example, see Washburne: *What Is Progressive Education?* (1952).

The best descriptions of the Denver reform are given in *The Denver Program of Curriculum Revision* (1927) and *Review of Four-Year Period, August, 1923 to July, 1927: A Part of the Forthcoming Twenty-Fourth Annual Report of the Denver Board of Education* (1927). Newlon states the theory behind the reform in "Practical Curriculum Revision in the High Schools," *The North Central Association Quarterly*, I (1926), 254–63, and in Newlon and A. L. Threlkeld: "The Denver Curriculum-Revision Program," National Society for the Study of Education: *Twenty-Sixth Yearbook* (1926), Part I. For the spread of the Denver technique as well as its continuation in later years, see Hollis L. Caswell *et al.*: *Curriculum Improvement in Public School Systems* (1950).

In view of the localism of American education, the problem of assessing the influence of progressivism on the schools at large becomes extraordinarily complex. My use of *Middletown* (1929) and *Middletown in Transition* (1937) by Robert S. and Helen Merrell Lynd is in many respects a literary device at best, since there is no such thing as a typical public-school system. *Education in the United States of America* (1939), a bulletin of the United States Office of Education, is illuminating, as is the Office's *Offerings and Registrations in High-School Subjects, 1933–34* (1938). The nineteen volumes published by the President's Advisory Committee on Education in 1939 and the six-volume *National Survey of the Education of Teachers* (1932–5) are also filled with relevant data.

Part II of the *Thirty-First Yearbook* (1932) of the NSSE is probably the fullest compendium of data on college reform during the decade following World War I. Part II of the *Thirty-Eighth Yearbook* (1939) is useful on the problem of general education. *The Educational Plan for Bennington College* (1929) is the best source on the origins of Bennington. Barbara Jones: *Bennington College* (1946) recounts the history to 1941, while Alvin C. Eurich and Catherine Evans: "Bennington College: An Evaluation" (1942) is a careful survey of outcomes and achievements.

Theodore M. Newcomb's *Personality and Social Change* (1943) is a classic study on the very difficult social-psychological problem of the effects of college life on values and attitudes. It is interesting to compare Hubert Herring's picture in "Education at Bennington," *Harper's Magazine*, CLXXXI (1940), 408–17, with Charlotte Devree's in "College Girl (Progressive Education Type)," *The New York Times Magazine*, December 2, 1956, pp. 16–17, 142–4.

James Gray discusses the founding of the University of Minnesota's General College in his highly readable history, *The University of Minnesota, 1851–1951* (1951). The best source for President Lotus D. Coffman's educational philosophy is the collection of his essays and addresses published under the title *The State University: Its Work and Problems* (1934); Victor Fred Dawald: "The Social Philosophy of Lotus Delta Coffman" (University of Wisconsin, 1951) is also illuminating. For the ideas behind the General College, see Malcolm S. MacLean: "A College of 1934," *The Journal of Higher Education*, V (1934), 240–6, 314–22, and "The General College: The University of Minnesota," in William S. Gray: *General Education: Its Nature, Scope, and Essential Elements* (1934). For detailed accounts and appraisals of the actual program and its outcomes, see Committee on Educational Research of the University of Minnesota: *The Effective General College as Revealed by Examinations* (1937), Staff of the General College: *Report on Problems and Progress of the General College, University of Minnesota* (1939), Malcolm S. MacLean *et al.*: *Curriculum Making in the General College* (1940), Ruth E. Eckert: *Outcomes of General Education* (1943), C. Robert Pace: *They Went to College* (1943), Ivol Spafford: *Building a Curriculum for General Education* (1943), and Cornelia T. Williams: *These We Teach* (1943).

The educational programs of the New Deal are discussed in detail in Harry Zeitlin: "Federal Relations in American Education, 1933–1943: A Study of New Deal Efforts and Innovations" (Columbia University, 1958) and George Philip Rawick: "The New Deal and Youth: The Civilian Conservation Corps, the National Youth Administration, and the American Youth Congress" (University of Wisconsin, 1957). Kenneth Holland and Frank Ernest Hill include a thoughtful appraisal of the CCC's educational efforts in *Youth in the CCC* (1942). Betty and Ernest K. Lindley enthusiastically report the NYA's early activities in *A New Deal for Youth* (1938). Palmer O. Johnson and Oswald L. Harvey: *The National Youth Administration* (1938) and Doak S. Campbell, Frederick H. Bair, and Oswald L. Harvey:

Educational Activities of the Works Progress Administration
(1939) are useful compilations.

Of the several surveys of public attitudes toward educational
reform in general and progressive education in particular, Sister
Mary Ruth Sandifer: *American Lay Opinion of the Progressive
School* (1943) is the most directly relevant. Claude E. Arnett:
Social Beliefs and Attitudes of American School Board Members
(1932), Charles R. Foster, Jr.: *Editorial Treatment of Education
in the American Press* (1938), Doyle McClean Bortner: "A Study
of Published Lay Opinion on Educational Programs and Problems" (Temple University, 1950), and John Walton: "Major
Emphases in Education in a Selected List of General Periodicals,
1928–1947" (Johns Hopkins University, 1950) are also useful.
"What People Think about Youth and Education," *National
Education Association Research Bulletin*, XVIII (1940), 187–
219, and National Opinion Research Center: *The Public Looks
at Education* (1944) report the results of public opinion polls.

As might be expected, there is a vast literature, written from a
variety of viewpoints and on a variety of levels, critical of the
progressive education movement. Malcolm Skilbeck classifies and
summarizes part of this literature in "Criticisms of Progressive
Education, 1916–1930" (University of Illinois, 1958). Among
the more thoughtful critiques published between 1930 and 1944
are Abraham Flexner: *Universities: American, English, German*
(1930), Herman Harrell Horne: *This New Education* (1931),
Albert Jay Nock: *The Theory of Education in the United States*
(1932), Sister Joseph Mary Raby: *A Critical Study of the New
Education* (1932), B. B. Bogoslovsky: *The Ideal School* (1936),
Robert Maynard Hutchins: *The Higher Learning in America*
(1936), Howard David Langford: *Education and the Social Conflict* (1936), Frederick S. Breed: *Education and the New Realism*
(1939), I. L. Kandel: *The Cult of Uncertainty* (1943), and
Jacques Maritain: *Education at the Crossroads* (1943).

The Crisis in Popular Education

A number of anthologies document the postwar crisis in popular
education, among them Theodore Brameld, ed.: *The Battle for
Free Schools* (1951), Ernest O. Melby and Morton Puner, eds.:
Freedom and Public Education (1953), C. Winfield Scott and
Clyde M. Hill, eds.: *Public Education under Criticism* (1954),
Mortimer Smith, ed.: *The Public Schools in Crisis* (1956), Ker-
mit Lansner, ed.: *Second-Rate Brains* (1958), Henry Ehlers and
Gordon C. Lee, eds.: *Crucial Issues in Education* (1959), and
C. Winfield Scott, Clyde M. Hill, and Hobert W. Burns, eds.:

The Great Debate: Our Schools in Crisis (1959). The most important progressivist statements of the era are Sidney Hook: *Education for Modern Man* (1946), R. Bruce Raup *et al.*: *The Improvement of Practical Intelligence* (1950), John L. Childs: *Education and Morals* (1950), Theodore Brameld: *Ends and Means in Education* (1950) and *Toward a Reconstructed Philosophy of Education* (1956), and I. B. Berkson: *The Ideal and the Community* (1958). Three publications of the United States Office of Education tell the story of the ill-fated life-adjustment movement: *Life Adjustment Education for Every Youth* (n.d.), *Vitalizing Secondary Education: Report of the First Commission on Life Adjustment Education for Youth* (1951), and *A Look Ahead in Secondary Education: Report of the Second Commission on Life Adjustment Education for Youth* (1954). The most significant postwar criticisms of progressive education include Bernard Iddings Bell: *Crisis in Education* (1949), Mortimer Smith: *And Madly Teach* (1949), Albert Lynd: *Quackery in the Public Schools* (1953), Arthur E. Bestor: *Educational Wastelands* (1953), Robert Hutchins: *The Conflict in Education* (1953), Paul Woodring: *Let's Talk Sense about Our Schools* (1953), Mortimer Smith: *The Diminished Mind* (1954), Arthur Bestor: *The Restoration of Learning* (1955), Mary L. Allen: *Education or Indoctrination* (1955), Augustin G. Rudd: *Bending the Twig* (1957), and H. G. Rickover: *Education and Freedom* (1959). Mary McCarthy: *The Groves of Academe* (1952) and Randall Jarrell: *Pictures from an Institution* (1954) are eminently readable satires.

The January, 1952, issue of *Progressive Education*, published under the general title "Meeting the Attacks on Education," brings together a vast amount of information and advances the characteristic "conspiracy" explanation of the early 1950's; Archibald W. Anderson's lead essay: "The Cloak of Respectability: The Attackers and Their Methods," is especially useful. Hollis L. Caswell advances a broader and more accurate explanation of the "attacks" in "The Great Reappraisal of Public Education," *Teachers College Record*, LIV (1952–3), 12–22. *Public Opinion Polls on American Education* (1958), issued by the NEA's Research Division, summarizes the major opinion polls between 1950 and 1958; Richard F. Carter: *Voters and Their Schools* (1960) is a detailed study of attitudes in a number of California cities. Willis Haskell Umberger, Sr.: "What the Public Is Told about Schools in the Lay Magazines" (Yale University, 1951), John E. Ingalls: "A Decade of Curricular Criticism of Public School Education in the United States, 1948–57" (Bradley University, 1959), and David Ward Martin: "American Education as Seen in the Periodical Literature, 1956–1958" (Ohio State University, 1959) are useful guides to the voluminous periodical literature. *Progressive Education*, the National Education Association *Journal*, and the publications of the Association for Supervision and Curriculum Development are the best sources for proprogressive opinion; *Modern Age*, the *National Review*, *U.S. News & World Report*, and the Council for Basic Education *Bulletin* are the best sources for antiprogressive opinion.

Index

A. & M. Colleges, 43, 48n
Aaron, Daniel, 12n, 355, 359
Abbott, Grace, 71n, 364
achievement tests: see mental tests
Adams, Charles Francis, Jr., 130n, 131n, 372
Adams, Charles Kendall, 162
Adams, George P., 116n, 370
Adams, Herbert Baxter, 163
Adams, John, 357
Addams, Jane: as author in *The Forum*, 3; establishes Hull House, 60; idea of "socialized education," 61–2; on industrial education, 62–3; as member of Chicago Board of Education, 64; as member of National Child Labor Committee, 65; association with NSPIE, 88; listed in *The Red Network*, 264; writings, 363, 364
Adler, Felix, 33n, 86n, 366
adult education, 61, 64, 69–71; 145, 165–7, 230, 318–24, 331
Agard, Walter, 252
agrarianism and education, 41–50, 75–85, 143–7, 292–4, 382
agricultural education: early examples, 41–3; urged by Henry Wallace, 43–4; urged by William Dempster Hoard, 44–5; urged by farmers' organizations, 46–50; urged by Liberty Hyde Bailey, 75–8; advances to 1900, 87–9; clubs, 79–80; work of Seaman Knapp, 80–2; urged by Commission on Country Life, 82–4; at Menomonie (Wis.), 143–7; at Porter School, 293–4; at University of Wisconsin, 162–3
Aikin, Wilford M., 252–6, 380
Alberty, Harold B., 229n, 266
Allen, Frederick Lewis, 374–5
Allen, Mary L., 386

Allen, William F., 163
American Association of Colleges for Teacher Education, 337
American Association of Farmers' Institute Workers, 47n
American Association of Health, Physical Education, and Recreation, 332
American Civic Association, 78
American Education Association, 342
American Education Fellowship: see Progressive Education Association
American Farm Bureau Federation, 85n
American Federation of Teachers, 272–3
American Federation of Labor, 39, 40–1, 50, 51–4
American Society of Equity, 46
American Vocational Association, 332
American Youth Commission, 228, 322n
Americanization, 66–75
Amid, John, 291n
Anderson, Archibald W., 268n, 342–3, 386
Anderson, Lewis F., 361
Andover House (Boston), 60
Angell, James R., 141n, 287n
Antin, Mary, 69, 72n
apprenticeship, 26, 34–6, 56–7
arithmetic: see mathematics
Armory Show (1913), 179–80
Armstrong, O. K., 267n, 326n
army scale alpha, 187–8
army scale beta, 187–8
Arnett, Claude E., 201n, 385
art: see fine arts, manual training
Association for the Improvement of the Condition of the Poor, 86n

Association of American Agricultural Colleges and Experiment Stations, 42, 48–9, 50, 56
Atwood, Wallace, 141n
Auchmuty, Richard T., 34–6
Auerbach, Charles, 176n, 346n, 374
Axtelle, George E., 229n
Ayers, Mrs. Milan V., 242, 248
Ayres, Leonard P., 186n

Babcock, Stephen M., 163
Bachman, Frank P., 158–9, 373
Bacon, Francis, 93
Baeumler, Alfred, 360
Bagley, William Chandler, 191, 376
Bailey, Joseph Cannon, 80n, 81n, 366
Bailey, Liberty Hyde: education and early career, 75–6; as champion of country life, 76–7; on school reform, 78; experiments at Cornell, 78; as chairman of the Commission on Country Life, 82–5; enthuses over Menomonie (Wis.) schools, 146; writings, 365–6
Bailyn, Bernard, 176n
Bair, Frederick H., 323n, 384
Baker, G. Derwood, 287n, 307n
Baker, Melvin C., 121n, 371
Baldwin, Bird T., 109n, 369
Ball, Lester R., 270n
Bank Street College of Education, 204n
Bard College, 308
Barnard, Henry, 8, 169, 359–60
Barnett, Samuel A., 59, 364
Baron de Hirsch School, 37
Barrett, Charles Simon, 46n, 82
Bascom, John, 162
Bawden, William T., 54, 143n, 361, 373
Beard, Charles, 232
Beard, William A., 82
Beatty, Willard W., 250, 261, 262, 264, 277, 296
Beaver Country Day School (Boston), 278
Beck, Robert H., 33n, 205n, 211n, 240n, 258, 356, 358, 376, 379
Belfield, Henry, 146

Bell, Bernard Iddings, 339–40, 386
Bemis, Edward W., 35n, 37n, 362
Benezet, Louis T., 309n, 381
Benne, Kenneth D., 270n
Bennett, Charles Alpheus, 24n, 27n, 41n, 360
Bennington College: origins and founding, 309; Robert D. Leigh elected President, 309; *Educational Plan*, 309–10; early program, 311; appraised, 312–13; impact on student attitudes, 313; literature on, 383–4
Bereday, George Z. F., 357
Berger, Morris Isaiah, 64n, 70n, 364, 365
Berkson, Isaac B., 69, 270n, 333n, 365, 386
Bestor, Arthur: early criticisms of American education, 343–4; theory of education, 344–5; on the function of the public school, 345; criticisms of progressive education, 345; proposals for reform, 345–6; influence, 346–7; as director of the Council for Basic Education, 346n
Bethlehem Institute (Los Angeles), 70
Beyer, Thomas Percival, 120
Bierstadt, Edward Hale, 68n, 365
Binet, Alfred, 186
Birge, E. A., 165
Birnbaum, Lucille, 199n
Bishop, E. C., 79
Black Mountain College, 308
Blaine, Mrs. Emmons, 135n
Blair, Anna Lou, 360
Blanshard, Brand, 353n
Blauch, Lloyd E., 52n, 366
Blewett, John, 371
Bliven, Bruce, 232, 252
Bloch, Ernest, 213
Blos, Peter, 257n, 380
Bobbitt, Franklin: *How to Make a Curriculum*, 199–200; likens curriculum-maker to "great engineer," 199; as exponent of scientism, 200; conception of "educational generalist," 300n; as social conservative, 369, 376

Bode, Boyd Henry: relationship to
John Dewey, 221; comparison
with William H. Kilpatrick,
221, 223–4; early education,
221; *Fundamentals of Education*, 221–2; *Modern Educational Theories*, 222–3; criticizes scientific curriculum-making, 222; criticizes the project
method, 222; theory of education, 223; *Conflicting Psychologies of Learning*, 223–4; part
in *The Educational Frontier*,
229; *Progressive Education at
the Crossroads*, 326–7; writings on, 378
Bogoslovsky, Boris B., 325n, 385
Bok, Edward, 72n
Boring, Edwin G., 100, 104n, 368
Borrie, W. D., 365
Borrowman, Merle L., 170n, 374
Bortner, Doyle M., 385
Boston (Mass.) schools, 72
Bourne, Randolph, 120, 155,
157–9, 180, 373
Bovard, Berdine Jackman, 240n,
379
Boyd, William, 356–7
Bradbury, Dorothy E., 65n
Brameld, Theodore, 269n, 333n,
338n, 385, 386
Breadwinners' College, 70
Breed, Frederick S., 325n, 385
Bremner, Robert H., 59n, 65n,
363
Brickman, William, 357, 358, 371
Brigham, Carl C., 191n
Brill, Abraham A., 208, 211
Brim, Orville, 266
Bronxville (N.Y.) schools, 277,
295
Brookwood Workers' College (Ka-
tonah, N.Y.), 278
Brooks, Van Wyck, 180, 182, 205
Browder, Earl, 232
Brown, Elmer Ellsworth, 169
Brown, Henry Emmett, 382
Brubacher, John S., 381
Bruere, Henry, 88
Brunner, Edmund, 228
Bryan, William Jennings, 43
Bryce, James, 357
Bryson, Lyman, 352–3

Buck, Solon Justus, 42n, 362
Buffalo (N.Y.) schools, 5
Bureau of Educational Experi-
ments, 204n
Burgess, John W., 163
Burgess, W. Randolph, 175n, 371
Burk, Frederic, 295–6, 382
Burnett, R. Will, 344n
Burns, Hobert W., 385–6
Burris, William Paxton, 154n
businessmen's associations and ed-
ucation, 21, 32, 37–8, 50–3
Butler, Fred Clayton, 74n
Butler, Nicholas Murray, 86n,
171–2, 357, 374
Butterfield, Kenyon L., 48n, 82
Buttrick, Wallace, 81
Butts, R. Freeman, 161n, 189n,
308n, 344n, 356, 359, 381
Byerly, Carl Lester, 18n, 360

Caldwell, Otis, 159n
Callahan, Raymond, 158n
Cambridge (Mass.) schools, 32
Campbell, A. E., 356
Campbell, Doak S., 323n, 384
Cane, Florence, 207, 213, 214n
Cargill, Oscar, 228n, 368, 375
Carlton, Frank Tracy, 86, 363
Carnegie Foundation, 257
Carney, Mabel, 84, 176
Carr, Arthur T., 360
Carstensen, Vernon, 47n, 87n,
163, 165n, 168n, 373
Carter, Richard F., 353n, 386
Cary, Charles P., 165
Cary, Harold, 291n
Case, Roscoe David, 156n, 373
Caswell, Hollis L., 302n, 343,
383, 386
Cattell, James McKeen, 113, 186
centralization of educational con-
trol, 274–6
Chamberlain, Thomas C., 141n
Chamberlin, Dean, 253
Chamberlin, Thomas, 162, 166
Chambers, Frank, 175
Chambers, M. M., 322n
Chambliss, Joseph James, 378
Charters, Werrett Wallace, 199,
369, 376
Chautauqua movement, 166n
Cheney, Sheldon, 206n

Chesterton, G. K., 377
Chevy Chase School (Md.), 278
Chicago Commercial Club, 32,
    53n
Chicago Commons, 64
Chicago (Ill.) schools, 5, 32, 72
child labor, 65, 364–5
Child Study Association, 273
child-study movement, 102, 104–
    5, 214–5
Children's Bureau: see United
    States Children's Bureau
Children's School: see Walden
    School
Childs, John L., 215n, 221n, 228,
    229, 232, 333n, 369, 378, 386
Chugerman, Samuel, 96n, 367
Churchill, Allen, 377
Cincinnati (Ohio) schools, 32
Citizens' Union (New York City),
    88
City and Country School (New
    York City): establishment
    (1914), 204–5; clientele, 204;
    early program, 205; as charac-
    teristic progressive school of the
    1920's, 277–8
Civilian Conservation Corps:
    founding (1933), 318–19; ad-
    ministration, 319; Robert Fech-
    ner appointed Director, 319; in-
    auguration of educational pro-
    gram, 319–20; Clarence S.
    Marsh as Educational Director,
    320; educational program,
    320–2
Clapp, Elsie Ripley, 237n, 371
Clare, Thomas H., 360
Clark, Harold F., 57n, 228, 351
Clark, James I., 143n, 373
Clark, John R., 282
Clark, Jonas, 101
Clark University, 102, 104
Clark County (Ohio) schools, 79
Clarke, Isaac Edwards, 31n, 37n,
    361
Claxton, Philander P., 74
Cleveland (Ohio) schools, 32
Clough, Robert R., 363
clubs, 61, 79–80
Coates, Charles Penney, 27n,
    361–2

Cobb, Ernest, 241, 379
Cobb, Stanwood: as founder of
    Progressive Education Associa-
    tion, 240–1; invites Charles W.
    Eliot to PEA presidency, 241;
    education and early career, 241;
    early interest in educational re-
    form, 241–2; part in founding
    of the PEA, 248; as President
    of the PEA, 250; comments on
    change in PEA after 1930, 250;
    writings on PEA, 379
Coe, George, 232
Coffman, Lotus D.: conceives
    Minnesota General College,
    314; theory of education, 314–
    15, 384; view of state university,
    314–15; view of General Col-
    lege, 315
Cohen, Morris R., 367
Cohen, Sol, 158n
Cohn, Jack, 380–1
Coit, Stanton, 59, 61n, 364
Coleman, Satis, 206, 282, 286,
    382
College Settlement (New York
    City), 59, 64
Collings, Ellsworth, 294n, 382
Comings, Mr. and Mrs. H. S., 148
Commager, Henry Steele, 90,
    351n, 355, 367
Commission on Country Life,
    82–5, 145–6
Commission on Educational Free-
    dom (PEA), 251
Commission on Educational Re-
    sources (PEA), 251
Commission on Life Adjustment
    Education for Youth: origins
    and establishment, 333–5; goal,
    335–6; activities of First Com-
    mission, 336–7; activities of Sec-
    ond Commission, 337–8; criti-
    cism of Commission, 338, 345,
    347
Commission on National Aid to
    Vocational Education (1914),
    54–6
Commission on Secondary School
    Curriculum (PEA), 251, 256–7
Commission on Human Relations
    (PEA), 251, 256–7

Commission on the Relation of School and College (PEA): origins and establishment, 251–2; membership, 252; indictment of secondary education, 252; proposals, 252–3; Eight-Year Study, 253–6; foundation assistance, 257

Commission on the Reorganization of Secondary Education (NEA), 93

Committee of Fifteen (NEA), 103n

Committee of Ten (NEA), 92–3, 367

Committee on Economy of Time in Education (NEA): appointment in 1911, 193; definition of economy of time, 193; view of purpose of education, 193–4; survey of existing educational conditions, 194; view of "minimum essentials," 195–6; pedagogical recommendations, 196–7; influence on Denver curriculum revision, 300

Committee on Experimental Schools (PEA), 276

Committee on Social and Economic Problems (PEA), 251, 261–4

Commons, John R., 164, 165

Communism and education, 234n

community college, 315–18

Compayré, Gabriel, 367

compulsory attendance laws, 127–8

Comstock, Ada, 309

Comte, August, 97

Conant, James Bryant, 226n, 341n, 346n, 353n

Conference of Eastern Public Education Associations, 87n

Cook County (Ill.) Normal School, 131–3; *see also* Parker, Francis W.

Cook, Walter W., 375–6

Cooke, Flora J., 135

Cooley, Edwin G., 53n

Coonley, Mrs. Avery, 247

core program, 282–6

Coriat, Isador H., 210

Coulter, John M., 141n

Council for Basic Education, 346n

Country Life Commission, *see* Commission on Country Life

Counts, George S.: education and early career, 225; criticizes inequalities in American secondary education, 225–6; criticizes class bias in school board membership, 226; analyzes controversy concerning William McAndrew, 226; urges schools more responsive to politics, 226; urges schools to take realistic account of industrialism, 227; as editor of *The Social Frontier*, 231; criticized by Dewey, 236; "Dare Progressive Education be Progressive?" 259–60; writings, 378–9

Courtis, Stuart, 159n, 197

Covello, Leonard, 72n

Cowles, Henry C., 141n

Cowley, Malcolm, 201, 228n, 375

Cremin, Lawrence A., 8n, 66n, 73n, 93n, 169n, 170n, 227n, 282n, 289n, 344n, 359, 374

Crichton-Miller, Hugh, 209

Crockett, Ann L., 267n, 326n

Croly, Herbert, 157

Croly, Jennie Cunningham, 86n

Cromer, Marie S., 81

Crosby, Dick J., 79n, 80n, 366

Crothers, Rachel, 207n

Cubberley, Ellwood P., 41n, 67–8, 359

Culver, Raymond, 359

Cunningham, K. S., 356

Curoe, Philip R. V., 362

Curry, J. L. M., 14

Curti, Merle E., 15n, 47n, 66n, 87n, 163, 165n, 168n, 232, 261, 356, 360, 361, 365, 367, 368, 369, 373

Curtis, Nell, 282, 283–5

Cutten, George B., 188, 190

Dabney, Charles William, 81n, 366

Dalton Plan, 248, 296

Dangler, Edward, 371

Daniels, John, 70n, 73

Darwin, Charles, 93, 100

Daughters of the American Revolution, 68

Davenport, Frances L., 370

Davidson, Thomas, 70

Davies, John D., 12n

Davis, Allen F., 364

Davis Bill (1907), 51

Davis, Jerome, 270n

Dawald, Victor Fred, 384

Dean, Arthur, 180–1, 363

Dearborn, Ned, 371

DeBoer, John J., 269n

Debs, Eugene Victor, 89

Decroly Plan, 248

De Garmo, Charles, 134n, 170

De Gurowski, Adam G., 13–14

De Kruif, Paul, 163

De Leon, Daniel, 89

De Lima, Agnes, 202, 211n, 213, 279, 282n, 283n, 328n, 381

Dell, Floyd, 206n, 208, 246

Della Vos, Victor, 24–5, 27

Del Pizzo, Ferdinand, 292n, 382

Demerath, Nicholas J., III, 192n

Demolins, Edmond, 248

demonstration farms, 80–2

Dennis, Lawrence, 232

Denver (Colo.) schools, 299–303, 383

Department of Elementary School Principals (NEA), 332

Devree, Charlotte, 384

Dewey, Alice Chipman (Mrs. John), 135–6

Dewey, Evelyn, 119, 128n, 153–4, 292–3, 382

Dewey, Jane M., 116n, 135n

Dewey, John: opposes separate trade-school system, 53n; intellectual association with Jane Addams, 63n; intellectual association with Albion Small, 99; *My Pedagogic Creed*, 100; reputation compared with Edward L. Thorndike's, 115; early life and career, 115–16; influenced by William James, 115–16; role in early progressive education movement, 116–17; *The School and Society*, 117–19; views the school as *legatee* institution, 117; views the school as an embryonic community, 117–18; criticizes the methods and curriculum of "the old school," 118–19; educational writings from 1899 to 1916, 119–20; discipleship of Randolph Bourne, 119–20; *Democracy and Education*, 120ff; definition of democracy, 121–2; definition of education, 122–3; definition of growth, 122–3; relation of education and progressivism, 123; attacks historic dualisms, 123; criticizes divorce of culture and vocation, 124; urges a transformation of culture, 124–5; definition of culture, 125; discusses priorities in education, 125–6; criticized as opposed to individualism, 126; relationship to Horace Mann in history of American education, 126; *Schools of To-Morrow*, 128n, 153–4; calls Francis W. Parker "father of progressive education," 129, 358; establishes Laboratory School with Alice Chipman Dewey, 135; influenced by Ella Flagg Young, 135n; states purpose of Laboratory School, 136; theory of the curriculum, 138, 140–1; conception of the professional teacher, 138; ideas on discipline, 142; discusses Organic School at Fairhope. (Ala.), 151–2; praises Gary (Ind.) schools, 157; interest in affairs of Teachers College, Columbia University, 172–3, 176; comments on war and education, 180; views compared with Harold Rugg's, 183; attacks educational restrictionism based on tests, 190–1; appraises William H. Kilpatrick as student, 216; comments on project method, 219n; differences with William H. Kilpatrick, 219–20; agreements with William H. Kilpatrick and Boyd Bode, 224; joins Kilpatrick discussion group, 228; part in *The Educational Frontier*, 229, 230; criticizes

Dewey (*continued*)
progressive education in the 1920's, 234–5; urges systematic organization of subject matter, 235; *The Sources of a Science of Education*, 235; consistency of position during the 1930's, 235–6; criticizes George Counts, 236; *Experience and Education*, 236–7; criticizes ideological fragmentation of progressive education, 237; estimate and appraisal, 237–9; style and language, 237–8; problem of discipleship, 238; problem of influence, 238; view of philosophy as social criticism, 238–9; contemporary criticism, 239; refuses to join Progressive Education Association, 246; succeeds Charles W. Eliot as PEA Honorary President, 249; listed in *The Red Network*, 264; influence on Abraham Flexner, 280n; on laboratory schools, 290n; forecasts general acceptance of progressive education, 328; comments on teacher workshops as progressive education, 333n; last essay on progressive education, 349; writings on Pragmatism, 369; literature on, 370–1

Dewey School: *see* Laboratory School (University of Chicago)
Diederich, Paul E., 256n
Dilling, Elizabeth, 264
Dillingham Commission, *see* United States Immigration Commission
Doan, Edward N., 374
Dodge, Grace Hoadley, 170–1
Dodge, Mabel, 208
Dodge, William E., 170
Dolliver Bill (1910), 51–2
domestic science, *see* home economics
Donovan, Charles Francis, 366
Dorey, J. Milnor, 249, 251n
Dorf, Philip, 76n, 365
Dorfman, Joseph, 378
Douglas Commission (Mass.), 54
Douglas, Paul H., 57, 175n, 360

Douglas, William L., 54n
Dow, Arthur Wesley, 173
dramatics: *see* English language and literature
Draper, William H., 166n, 374
Drucker, Peter F., 353n
Duffus, R. L., 308n, 381
Dugmore, A. R., 72n
Duncan, Isadora, 206
Duluth (Minn.) schools, 72
Dunn County (Wis.): *see* Menomonie (Wis.)
Dutton, Wilbur Harvey, 104n, 368
Dworkin, Martin S., 351n, 371
Dykhuizen, George, 370

East Side House (New York City), 60
Eastman, Max, 136n, 179, 208, 371
Easton, Charles L. S., 262
Eaton, John, 14
Eckert, Ruth E., 317n, 318, 384
Eddy, Edward Danforth, Jr., 48n, 362
Edman, Irwin, 237, 371
Educational Alliance (New York City), 64, 70
Educational Policies Commission (NEA): criticism of Civilian Conservation Corps, 322n; blueprints ideal postwar education, 329–32; advances progressive education as "conventional wisdom," 332
Edwards, Anna Camp, 136n, 141n, 372
Ehlers, Henry, 385
Eight-Year Study: *see* Commission on The Relation of School and College (PEA)
elementary education: William T. Harris on, 19; Francis W. Parker on, 129–35; in the Laboratory School (University of Chicago), 137–40; at Organic School (Fairhope, Ala.), 149–50; at Gary (Ind.), 156; at Lincoln School, 283–6; at Porter School, 293–4; extension of opportunity, 306
Elementary School Record, 133n

Elementary School Teacher and the Course of Study, 139n

Eliot, Charles W.: campaigns for a "new education," 92; influenced by Herbert Spencer, 92n; chairman of Committee of Ten (NEA), 93n; comments on University of Wisconsin, 167; urges shortening and enrichment of school programs, 192; introduces *Education Moves Ahead* by E. R. Smith, 198n; Honorary President of Progressive Education Association, 241; role in founding the Lincoln School, 280; influence on Abraham Flexner, 280n; disseminates Spencer's ideas, 367

elitism in education, 188–92

Ely, Richard T., 87, 163–4

Emerson, Ralph Waldo, 12, 15

English language and literature, 129–30, 132, 138, 139, 150, 156, 196, 213, 283–6, 293–4, 296, 298, 301, 311, 316

enrollments, school, 274

Ensign, Forest Chester, 127n, 364

Ethical Culture Society, 33n, 86n

Eurich, Alvin C., 307n, 312–13, 316, 383

Evans, Catherine, 312n, 383

Evans, Henry Ridgley, 360

expressionism in education, 204–7

Exton, Elaine, 322n

Fairchild, Henry P., 232

Fairhope (Ala.), 147–53

Fairhope League, 152n

Farm Boys' and Girls' Progressive League, 79

Farmers' Cooperative Demonstration Work, 80–2

farmers' institutes, 42, 47–8

Farmers' Union, 46

Farrell, Elizabeth, 64

Faulkner, Harold U., 355

Fechner, Gustav, 100

Fechner, Robert, 319–22

Fels, Joseph, 151n

Ferenczi, Sandor, 209

Feuer, Lewis S., 116n, 370

Filler, Louis, 120n, 356

Fine, Jean, 59

fine arts, 5, 130, 133, 150, 203–5, 206–7, 213–14, 286, 311, 316

Fisher, Sara Carolyn, 102n, 368

Fiske, John, 91n

Fleming, Martha, 132n

Flexner, Abraham: undertakes survey of Gary (Ind.) schools, 158–60; criticizes the genus "educator," 160; role in founding Lincoln School, 280; "A Modern School," 280–1, 282; criticizes reorganization of Lincoln School, 290–1; *The Gary Schools*, 373

Foerster, Norman, 325n

Ford, R. Clyde, 360

foreign languages, 139, 281, 286

Foster, Charles R., Jr., 325n, 385

Foster, Frank C., 359

Fowler, Burton P., 250, 251n, 258

Francis W. Parker School (Chicago) 135, 153

Frank, Waldo, 182n, 205, 213n

Freeman, C. M., 80n

Freeman, Frank N., 375

Freud, Sigmund: lectures at Clark University in 1909, 179, 208; spread of ideas in United States, 208–9; influence on American pedagogy, 209–15; writings on, 377

Friedlaender, Israel, 69

Froebel, Friedrich, 134, 277

Froelicher, Hans, 242, 277

Frontiers of Democracy: see The Social Frontier

Gabriel, Ralph H., 367

Gager, Delaye, 358

Galbraith, John Kenneth, 328, 332

Galton, Francis, 100, 186

Gambs, John S., 261

Gans, Roma, 270n

Gary (Ind.) schools: early growth and development, 154; coming of William Wirt as school superintendent, 154; inauguration of "Gary Plan," 154–5; description of "Gary Plan," 155–7; publicizing of "Gary Plan" by Randolph Bourne, 157–8; controversy over "Gary Plan," 158;

Gary (*continued*)
    survey of Gary schools by Abraham Flexner and Frank P. Bachman, 158–60; literature on, 373
Gates, Frederick T., 82*n*
Gauss, Christian, 189
Geiger, George R., 371
"Gemeinschaft grouse," 60
General College (University of Minnesota): conceived by Lotus D. Coffman, 314; Malcolm S. MacLean as Dean, 315; curriculum, 316; faculty, 316–17; outcomes, 317–18; appraisal, 317–18; literature on, 384
General Education Board, 81–2, 257, 280–2, 290, 317
General Federation of Women's Clubs, 86*n*
geography, 133, 138, 150, 156, 196, 283–6, 296
George, Andrew, 241
George, Anne E., 242
George, Henry, 148
Gesell, Arnold, 104
Gideonse, Harry, 232
Giffin, William M., 129*n*, 372
Giles, H. H., 253*n*
Gilmore, Eugene A., 87
Ginger, Ray, 121*n*, 355, 370
Ginzberg, Eli, 338*n*
Glover, W. H., 163*n*
Goddard, H. H., 186
Goff, Emmett S., 162
Golden, John, 87
Goldenweiser, Alexander, 213
Goldman, Eric, 99, 180*n*, 355
Goldmark, Josephine, 65*n*, 364
Goldsmith, C. Elizabeth, 214
Gompers, Samuel, 37, 40, 41
Good, Carter V., 373
Good, Harry G., 359
Gordon, Milton M., 305*n*
Goslin, Willard, 341
Graham, Abbie, 374
Graham, Albert B., 79
Graham, Martha, 206
Graham, Patricia A., 240*n*
grammar: *see* English language and literature
Grange: *see* National Grange of the Patrons of Husbandry

Grantham, Dewey, W., Jr., 85*n*, 366
Grattan, C. Hartley, 166*n*, 372, 374
Gray, James, 317, 384
Gray, William S., 298, 316*n*, 383, 384
Green, George H., 209
Greenwich House (New York City), 70
Greer, Thomas H., 318*n*
Griswold, A. Whitney, 365
Grodzins, Morton, 60
Groggel, Martha, 282
Grossman, Mordecai, 231
Gruenberg, Benjamin, 109*n*
guidance services, 286, 305, 306–7, 317, 323
Gurko, Leo, 228*n*

Haeckel, Ernst, 101
Hale, G. E., 141*n*
Hall, Dorothy, 381
Hall, Granville Stanley: education and early career, 101; effort to apply Darwinism to psychology, 101; "General Psychonomic Law," 101–2; "The Contents of Children's Minds," 102; *Adolescence* and *Educational Problems*, 103; idea of the *pedocentric* school, 103–4; place in the child-study movement, 104–5; *Life and Confessions of a Psychologist*, 104; pioneer in educational psychology, 170; writings, 368
Ham, Charles H., 25*n*, 29*n*, 32
Hamilton, John, 47*n*
Hand, Harold C., 344*n*
Handlin, Oscar, 67*n*, 365
Haney, James P., 39
Hansen, Marcus Lee, 365
Harap, Henry, 291*n*, 381
Hard, William, 167*n*
Harlan, Louis R., 81*n*, 366
Harper, William Rainey, 116, 119
Harris, William Torrey: early career, 14; founds *Journal of Speculative Philosophy*, 14–15; as transitional figure in American educational thought, 15–16; influenced by Hegel, 15–16;

Harris (*continued*)
  confirms and transforms Horace
  Mann's ideas, 16–18; on moral
  education, 18; on curriculum,
  18–19; as administrator, 19; as
  apologist for urbanism and industrialism, 19–20; attacks manual training, 30–1; criticizes
  Francis W. Parker's work, 134*n*;
  pioneer in educational psychology, 170; writings on, 360
Hart, Edwin B., 163
Hartman, Gertrude, 207*n*, 247,
  248, 286
Hartmann, Edward G., 365
Hartmann, George, 232
Harvey, Marie Turner: as critic-
  teacher at State Normal School,
  Kirksville, Mo., 292; innova-
  tions at Porter School, 292–4;
  returns to Northeast Missouri
  State Teachers College, 294;
  view of progressive education,
  294–5; addresses, 382
Harvey, Oswald L., 323*n*, 384–5
Hatch Act (1887), 42
Hawkes, Herbert E., 256
Hawkins, Layton S., 361
health and physical education, 64,
  133, 144, 150, 196, 197, 286
Heberle, Rudolf, 271*n*
Hechinger, Fred M., 192*n*, 352*n*
Heffron, Ida Casa, 131*n*, 135*n*
Hegel, Georg W. F., 15–18
Heidbreder, Edna, 106*n*, 368
Helmholtz, Hermann von, 100,
  101
Helvetius, Claude-Adrien, 97
Henderson, Algo, 381
Henderson, C. Hanford, 148,
  152, 373
Hendrick, Burton J., 86*n*
Henry, William A., 162
Henry Street Settlement (New
  York), 64
Herbart, Johann Friedrich, 102*n*,
  103*n*, 134, 172, 173
Herberg, Will, 351
Herring, Hubert, 312*n*, 384
Hersey, John, 192*n*
Hervey, Walter, 171–2
Hewitt, Edwin C., 130*n*
Hicks, John D., 43*n*, 46*n*, 362

Higham, John, 67*n*
higher education: at University of
  Wisconsin, 161–8; at Benning-
  ton College, 309–13; at Gen-
  eral College, University of Min-
  nesota, 313–18
Hildreth, Gertrude, 288
Hill, Clyde M., 341*n*, 385
Hill, Frank Ernest, 319*n*, 320*n*,
  384
Hill, Marion, 72*n*
Hill, Patty Smith, 173, 176
Hinkle, Beatrice, 211
Hinsdale, B. A., 170, 359
Hirschfeld, Charles, 32*n*
history, 133, 139, 150, 163, 196,
  213, 283–6, 296, 316
Hoard, William Dempster, 44–5,
  47
Hoard's Dairyman, 44–6
Hocking, Professor and Mrs. Wil-
  liam Ernest, 278
Hoffman, Frederick J., 208*n*, 375,
  377
Hofstadter, Richard, 88*n*, 89, 90*n*,
  95, 355, 367
Hoggson, W. J., 151*n*
Holden, Arthur C., 364
Holland, Kenneth, 319*n*, 384
Holmes, Brian, 15*n*, 360
Holmes, Oliver Wendell, 237*n*
Holt, Edwin, 208
Holt, Henry, 106
Home Demonstration Work, 81
home economics, 33, 56, 64, 79,
  81, 84, 144, 286, 301
Hook, Sidney, 261, 386
Hopkins, L. Thomas, 287, 382
Horace Mann–Lincoln Institute of
  School Experimentation, 289–
  90
Horace Mann Schools (New York
  City), 287–8
Horn, Ernest, 196–7
Horne, Herman H., 325*n*, 385
Houston, David F., 81
Howe, Frederic C., 374
Howe, Louis, 319
Howe, Mark DeWolfe, 237*n*
Hoyt, Charles O., 360
Hulburd, David, 341
Hull House (Chicago): estab-
  lished, 60; educational program,

Hull House (*continued*)
61; interest of residents in child labor, 65; Labor Museum, 70; Immigrants' Protective League, 71

Hullfish, H. Gordon, 114n, 229, 270, 370

Humphrey, George C., 163

Humphreys, John Wesley, 109n, 369

Hunter, Robert, 85n, 363

Hutchins, Robert M., 232, 325n, 343, 385, 386

Hylan, John F., 158n

Ilylla, Erich, 304n, 358

Hymes, James L., Jr., 233

immigration and education, 66

Indianapolis (Ind.) schools, 5

industrial education: *see* agricultural education, manual training, vocational education

Industrial Education Association, 170

Ingalls, John E., 386

Inland Printer Technical School, 40

Intelligence Quotient: popularized by Lewis Terman, 186; as issue in social policy, 188–92

intelligence tests: *see* mental tests

International Bureau of New Schools, 248

Irwin, Elisabeth, 64

Ittner, Anthony, 52n

Iversen, Robert W., 234n, 379

Ives, Charles, 206

Jackman, Wilbur S., 131n

Jackson, Margaret W., 267n

Jackson, Sidney, 359

Jacob, Philip E., 313n

Jacobson, Augustus, 32

James, Henry (author of *Charles W. Eliot*), 92n, 368

James, Henry (editor of *The Letters of William James*), 369

James, William: as author in *The Forum*, 3; disagreement with G. Stanley Hall, 105; early career, 105–6; *Principles of Psychology*, 106ff; opposes Spen-

James (*continued*)
cer's determinism, 106; on habit, 106–7; on consciousness, 107; *Talks to Teachers on Psychology*, 107–8; philosophical ideas, 108–9; viewed by George Santayana, 109; impact on American education, 109; influences John Dewey, 115–16; discusses John Dewey's style, 237; writings, 369

Jarrell, Randall, 343n, 386

Jessup, Walter A., 287

Jewell, James Ralph, 79n, 362, 366

Jewish Theological Seminary (New York City), 69

John Dewey Society, 229, 251

Johnson, F. Ernest, 228

Johnson, Helmar G., 256

Johnson, Henry, 173

Johnson, Marietta Pierce: education and early career, 147; influenced by Nathan Oppenheim and C. Hanford Henderson, 147–8; establishes Organic School at Fairhope (Ala.), 148–9; theory of the Organic School, 149–50; program of the Organic School, 150–1; financial difficulties, 151n; praised by John Dewey, 151–2; teacher of Margaret Naumburg, 211; part in founding of Progressive Education Association 242–3; attends New Education Fellowship Conference (1925), 248; writings, 373

Johnson, Palmer O., 323n, 384

Johnstone, Paul, 365

Joncich, Geraldine, 370

Jones, Barbara, 311, 383

Jones, Edward David, 164

Jones, Ernest, 208n, 377

Jones, Howard Mumford, 12, 176n, 374

Jones, Maldwyn Allen, 67n, 365

Judd, Charles H., 182, 187, 201n, 225, 357, 372, 376

Jung, Carl, 208

junior college, 315–18

junior high school: as child of progressive movement, 306

Kahl, Joseph A., 305n
Kallen, Horace 69n
Kandel, Isaac L., 325n, 356, 357, 385
Kazin, Alfred, 375
Keliher, Alice V., 257n, 299n, 38c
Kelley, Earl C., 333n
Kelley, Florence, 65
Kelley, Oliver H., 42
Kennedy, Albert J., 60n, 64n, 70n, 364
Keppel, Ann M., 43n, 143n, 362, 366, 372-3
Keppel, Francis, 176n, 374
Kern, O. J., 79
Kerschensteiner, Georg, 52-3
Kettering, Charles, 247
Key, Ellen, 105, 368
Kilpatrick, William Heard: as faculty member at Teachers College, Columbia University, 173; education and early career, 215-16; first encounter with John Dewey, 215; studies with Dewey at Columbia University, 215-16; "The Project Method," 216-17; *Foundations of Method*, 217-19; idea of "wholehearted purposeful activity," 218; opposition to extrinsic subject matter, 218-19; *Education for a Changing Civilization*, 219n; differences with John Dewey, 219-20; influences as teacher and lecturer, 220; comparison with Boyd Bode, 221, 223-4; leads discussion group at Teachers College, Columbia University, 228-9; as editor of *The Educational Frontier*, 229; associated with *The Social Frontier*, 231; as editor of *Frontiers of Democracy*, 233; role in founding of Bennington College, 309; writings on, 378-9
Kimball, Elsa Peverly, 93n, 367
kindergarten, 19, 61, 64, 134n, 150
Kingsley, Charles, 59
Kirby, John, 52
Kirk, John R., 292n
Kirk, Russell, 350n
Kirkpatrick, John, 225

Kitchen Garden Association, 170
Klineberg, Otto, 192n
Knapp, Seaman A., 80-2
Knight, Edgar W., 357
Kohlbrenner, Bernard J., 360
Kolesnik, Walter B., 114n, 370
Kotinsky, Ruth, 257n, 380
Krug, Edward A., 93n
Kunitz, Stanley J., 378

Labaree, Benjamin, 66
labor unions and education, 32, 36-41, 50-3
Laboratory School (University of Chicago): founded by John Dewey and Alice Chipman Dewey, 135, 136n; purpose, 136; work of the youngest children, 137; connection of school, home and community, 138; work of children six through thirteen, 139-40; relation to Dewey's pedagogical theory, 140-1; consultants from the University of Chicago, 141n; estimate of the school, 141-2; literature on, 372
La Follette, Robert, 87, 89, 162
Lang, Ossian H., 17n, 360
Langford, Howard D., 385
Lansner, Kermit, 347n
LaPorte (Ind.) schools, 5
Larrabee, Harold A., 237n, 371
Laski, Harold, 358
Lathrop, Julia, 65
Latimer, John F., 306n, 381
Lauwerys, Joseph A., 357
Lay, Wilfrid, 209
League for Political Education, 86n
Learned, William S., 252
Leary, Daniel B., 370
Lee, Joseph, 85n, 363
Lehrer, Stanley, 371
Leidecker, Kurt F., 15n, 360
Leigh, Robert D.: as member of the Commission on the Relation of School and College (PEA), 252; elected President of Bennington College, 309; drafts *Educational Plan*, 309; administration at Bennington, 311-13

Leonard, J. Paul, 307n
Lerner, Max, 120n
Leuchtenburg, William E., 374–5
Levin, Willy, 206
Lewinson, Edwin, 158n
Lewis, Mary H., 381
Lewis, Samuel, 8, 359–60
Libbey, May, 243
Lieberman, Myron, 226n
Lietz, Hermann, 248
Life (magazine), 346
life-adjustment education: *see*
    Commission on Life Adjustment Education for Youth
Lighty, Margaret, 257n, 380
Lincoln School (New York City):
    conceived by Abraham Flexner,
    280–1; founding (1917), 281–
    2; faculty, 282; "units of work,"
    283; curriculum, 283–6; appraisal, 286–8; survey of 1930,
    287–8; closing, 289–91; literature on, 381–2
Lindley, Ernest K. and Betty,
    323n, 384
Link, Arthur S., 355, 366
Linn, James W., 364
Lippmann, Walter: praises *Democracy and Education*, 120n,
    publishes *A Preface to Politics*
    and *Drift and Mastery*, 180; attacks educational restrictionism
    based on tests, 190, 376; disseminates Freudian ideas, 208;
    criticizes progressive education,
    326
Locke, John, 93
Locust Point Settlement (Baltimore), 64
Lodge, Gonzalez, 173
Lodge, Henry Cabot, 3
Loeb, Jacques, 141n
Loewenberg, Bert J., 90n
Logan, S. R., 306n
Loomis, Arthur K., 277, 302n
Lovett, Robert Morss, 189–90
Low, Barbara, 210n
Ludwig, Karl, 101
Lugas, Leroy G., 360
Lynd, Albert, 343, 386
Lynd, Robert S. and Helen Merrell, 303–5, 383

MacClintock, Mr. and Mrs. William D., 141n
MacLean, Malcolm S., 315–16,
    318, 384
MacVannel, John A., 216
Mahoney, John J., 74n, 365
Malherbe, E. G., 356
Mann, Arthur, 355, 364
Mann, Horace: theory of the common school, 8–10; on curriculum, 10–11; on school discipline, 11; on moral instruction,
    11–12; influenced by phrenology, 12; as politician, 12–13; on
    "self-help," 292; writings on,
    359–60
Mann, Mary Peabody, 359
Mansbridge, Albert, 166n, 374
manual training: at Moscow Imperial Technical School, 24–5;
    as educational issue of the
    1880's, 28–32; spread in schools,
    32–4; at Cook County Normal
    School, 133; at Laboratory
    School (University of Chicago),
    140; at Menomonie (Wis.),
    143–4; at the Organic School,
    152; at Gary (Ind.), 155–6; as
    taught by Caroline Pratt, 202
Manual Training School (Washington University), 27–9, 33n
Manumit School (Pawling, N.Y.),
    278
Marble, Albert, P., 29–30
Marcus, Lloyd, 277, 381
Marin, John, 206
Maritain, Jacques, 325n, 385
Marks, Louis A., 381
Marot, Helen, 203
Marsh, Clarence S., 320–2
Martin, David Ward, 386
Martin, O. B., 80n, 366
Massachusetts Institute of Technology, 25–6
Massachusetts State Agricultural
    Board, 42
Masses (magazine), 179
mathematics, 130, 133, 138, 150,
    195–6, 281, 283–5, 286, 294,
    296, 297, 298, 301, 316
Mathewsen, Robert Hendry, 333n
Maurice, Frederick Denison, 59

Maxwell, William H., 72n
May, Henry F., 179, 355, 375
Mayhew, Katherine Camp, 136n, 139n, 141n, 372
Mayo, A. D., 130n
Mays, Arthur B., 362
McAndrew, William, 226, 246, 272n
McCall, William A., 114n
McCarthy, Charles, 164, 165, 374
McCarthy, Mary, 343n, 386
McCaul, Robert L., 121, 370
McCluskey, Neil G., 18n, 359
McConn, Max, 189
McConnell, Grant, 43n, 85n, 362, 366
McCord, William M., 192n
McDonald, Milo, 342
McDougall, William, 209
McGlade, Joseph, 377
McGuffey, William Holmes, 20
McGurk, Frank, 192n
McLaughlin Bill (1909), 51
McLellan, James Alexander, 115
McManis, John T., 372
McMurry, Charles A., 103n
McMurry, Frank, 173
Mead, George H., 141n, 368–9
Mead, Margaret, 353n
Mearns, Hughes, 206, 282, 286, 382
Mehl, Bernard, 367
Meiklejohn, Alexander, 189n
Melby, Ernest O., 342n, 385
Melvin, A. Gordon, 135n, 373
Mendenhall, James E., 287, 382
Menefee, Louise Arnold, 322n
Menomonie (Wis.) schools: innovations of James Huff Stout, 143–4; industrial education, 144; physical education, 144; normal schools and agricultural schools, 145; schools as social centers, 145–6; visited by influential observers, 146–7; literature on, 372–3
mental tests: early development in Europe and the United States, 186–7; use during World War I, 187–8; issue in debate over educational restrictionism, 188–91
Meriam, Junius, 153, 381

methods of teaching: in 1890's, 5, 20–1; with immigrants, 72–5; under Francis W. Parker, 129–35; at Laboratory School (University of Chicago), 137–41; at Organic School (Fairhope, Ala.), 149–51; at Gary (Ind.), 155–8; report of Committee on Economy of Time, 196–7; at City and Country School, 204–5; at Walden School, 213–15; William Heard Kilpatrick on, 217–19; Boyd H. Bode on, 222–4; at Lincoln School, 283–6; at Porter School, 293–4; at San Francisco State Normal School, 295–6; at Winnetka (Ill.), 296–8; in public schools generally, 307; at Bennington College, 311–12; at General College, University of Minnesota, 315–17; in the Civilian Conservation Corps, 320–1
Meyer, Adolf, 247
Meyer, Adolphe, 356, 359
Meyer, Agnes E., 353n
Meyer, H. N. B., 364
Michelson, Albert, 141n
Michigan Agricultural College, 35n
Middletown: see Muncie (Ind.) schools
Miller, Herbert A., 73n, 365
Milwaukee School of Trades, 40
Minnesota, University of, 314–18
Mitchel, John Purroy, 158n
Mitchell, H. Edwin, 195–6
Mitchell, John, 40, 52
Mitchell, Lucy Sprague, 204n, 206, 377
Monroe, Harriet, 179
Monroe, James Phinney, 87, 363
Monroe, Paul, 124n, 172, 357, 359, 360
Monroe, Walter S., 170n, 186n, 187, 195, 374
Monroe, Will S., 134n
Montague, William Pepperel, 116n, 370
Montessori, Maria, 211, 216
Moore, Ernest Carroll, 359
Moraine Park School (Dayton, Ohio), 278

Morgan, Arthur E., 249, 278
Morgan, J. P., 36
Morrill Act (1862), 35n, 42
Morris, Lloyd, 180, 374
Morse, Arthur D., 353n
Moscow Imperial Technical School, 24–5
Mosely Education Commission, 358
Mosley, Ira Byrd, 358
Mulhall, Leonita, 358
Mumford, Lewis, 213, 232
Muncie (Ind.) schools, 303–5
municipal reform and education, 86–7
Murray, Muriel, 371
music, 133, 150, 206, 207, 213, 286
Muste, A. J., 278

Nathanson, Jerome, 341n
National Association of Manufacturers, 37–8, 50, 52–3
National Association of Secondary School Principals, 332, 337
National Catholic Education Association, 337
National Child Labor Committee, 65, 86n
National Committee for Mental Hygiene, 273
National Conference on Immigration and Americanization (1916), 74
National Congress of Parents and Teachers, 273, 337
National Council for American Education, 342
National Education Association: debates industrial education, 29–34; endorses vocational education, 50; advances progressive education, 272, 275–6; rise in membership (1918–41), 275; criticizes New Deal educational programs, 323–4; as reflective of professional thought, 357
National Farm School (Doylestown, Penna.), 79
National Grange of the Patrons of Husbandry, 21–2, 42, 46, 50, 51, 80n
National Herbart Society, 141

National Municipal League, 86n
National School Boards Association, 337
National Society for the Promotion of Industrial Education, 39, 50–4, 87–8, 273
National Society for the Study of Education, 273, 291
National Youth Administration, 323
nationalism: *see* Americanization
natural sciences, 133, 138, 150, 156, 162–3, 213, 283–5, 286, 311, 316
nature-study: *see* natural sciences
Naumburg, Margaret: education and early career, 211; founds the Children's School, 211; theory of education, 212; on school program, 213; on art education, 213–14; on sex education, 214; comments on Progressive Education Association conference (1928), 249; seeks clientele for school, 277–8; writings, 377
Necker de Saussure, Mme., 358
Neighborhood House (Fort Worth), 64
Neilson, William, 309
New Deal and education, 318–24, 384–5
New Education Fellowship, 248, 356–7
New Republic, 119, 157, 225
New York (N.Y.) schools, 5, 32, 72
New York Society for Ethical Culture, 33n
New York State Normal College (Albany), 169
New York Trades Schools, 34–6
Newcomb, Theodore M., 312–13, 384
Newlon, Jesse H.: as member of Kilpatrick discussion group, 228; as contributor to *The Social Frontier*, 232; as member of the Committee on Social and Economic Problems (PEA), 261; as superintendent of schools in Denver, 299; theory of curricular reform, 299–300, 383; confidence in classroom teachers,

Newlon (*continued*)
299*n*; curricular reform in Denver, 300–2; leaves Denver for Teachers College, Columbia University, 301
Noble, David W., 88*n*, 355
Nock, Albert J., 191*n*, 325*n*, 385
North American Civic League for Immigrants, 74
Northwestern University Settlement (Chicago), 60
Nutting, Mary Adelaide, 173
Nye, Russel B., 87*n*, 164, 355, 374

Oak Lane Country Day School (Philadelphia), 278
Oberndorf, C. P., 208*n*, 377
O'Fallon Polytechnic Institute (St. Louis), 26
Ogburn, William F., 232
Ogden, Robert, 175
Ojai Valley School (Calif.), 295*n*
Oppenheim, James, 205
Oppenheim, Nathan, 147, 152, 373
Orata, Pedro Tamesis, 114*n*, 370
Organic School: *see* School of Organic Education
Osburn, W. J., 358

Pace, C. Robert, 317*n*, 384
Padgett, Alice Elizabeth, 65, 364
Page, Walter Hines: as editor of *The Forum*, 3; as editor of *The World's Work*, 21*n*; as member of the Commission on Country Life, 82; on Southern educational reconstruction, 86; *The School of Tomorrow*, 128*n*; commissions series of articles on the schools (1903), 142
Park, Robert E., 71*n*
Park School (Baltimore), 277
Parker, Francis W.: called by Dewey the father of progressive education, 21, 129; education and early career, 129; elected superintendent of the Quincy (Mass.) schools, 129; innovations at Quincy, 129–30; denies there is a "Quincy System," 131; work at Quincy criticized,

Parker (*continued*)
130–1; school supervisor in Boston, 131; principal of Cook County (Ill.) Normal School, 131ff; innovations at Cook County Normal School, 132–3; *Talks on Teaching* and *Talks on Pedagogics*, 134–5; influenced by Pestalozzi, Froebel, and Herbart, 134; failure to take account of Darwinism, 134; influenced by Rousseau, 134–5; praised by G. Stanley Hall, 135; receives gift from Mrs. Emmons Blaine to endow Chicago Institute, 135*n*; addresses students at Menomonie (Wis.), 146; writings on, 372
Parkhurst, Helen, 296
Parry, Albert, 377
Parsons, Mrs. A. J., 243
Partridge, G. E., 368
Pasadena (Calif.) schools, 295, 341
Patri, Angelo, 72*n*, 246, 247
Patridge, Lelia E., 130*n*, 372
Paulding, James K., 64
Payne, William H., 169
Pedagogical Seminary, 102, 104
Peirce, Charles, 106*n*
Perry, Charles M., 360
Perry, Ralph Barton, 105*n*, 108*n*, 369
Persons, Stow, 90*n*, 100*n*, 367
Pestalozzi, Johann Heinrich, 11, 93, 134, 277, 278
Peterson, Joseph, 186*n*, 375
Pfister, Oskar, 209, 377
Philadelphia Centennial Exposition (1876), 23
Philadelphia (Penna.) schools, 5, 32
Phillips, Mark, 206*n*, 375
Phrenology, 12
physical education: *see* health and physical education
Picht, Werner, 59*n*
Pierce, John, 8, 359–60
Pinchot, Gifford, 82
Play School: *see* City and Country School
Pochmann, Henry H., 360
Poetry (magazine), 179

Pope, Arthur Upham, 182

Populism, 43–4

Porter School (Kirksville, Mo.):
reported in *New Schools for
Old*, 292; transformed by Marie
Turner Harvey, 293; relationship with community, 293; curriculum, 293–4; literature on,
382

Portwell, B. G., 268*n*

Pottishman, Nancy, 364

Pratt, Caroline: education and
early career, 202; friendship
with Helen Marot, 203; exponent of social reform, 203; develops idea for a Play School,
203–4; establishes Play School,
204; relationship with Greenwich Village intelligentsia, 204–
6; conception of the child as
artist, 206–7; seeks clientele for
school, 277–8, 279; writings,
377

Pratt Institute, 37

Preyer, Wilhelm, 102*n*

Pritchett, Henry S., 188, 190

professional education, 168–76,
200, 307, 345

professionalization, 168–76

progressive education: initial definition, viii–ix; beginning of
movement, 21–2, 358–9; early
pluralism, 22; as manual training, 30–1; as vocational education, 36*n*, 50–1, 363; as "socialized education," 61–4, 74–5; as
aspect of Progressivism, 85–9,
179–85; influence of Herbert
Spencer, 91–4; view of Lester F.
Ward, 96–100; view of G. Stanley Hall, 100–5; view of William James, 105–9; view of Edward L. Thorndike, 110–15,
369; view of John Dewey, 115–
26, 135–42; at Quincy (Mass.),
129–31; at Cook County (Ill.)
Normal School, 131–5; view of
Francis W. Parker, 134–5; at
Laboratory School (University
of Chicago), 135–42; at Menomonie (Wis.), 142–7; view of
Marietta Johnson, 147–53, 373;
at Organic School (Fairhope,

progressive education (*continued*)
Ala.), 149–51; at Gary (Ind.),
153–60; at University of Wisconsin, 161–8; and "Wisconsin
Idea," 164–5, 167–8; at Teachers College, Columbia University, 168–76; joined to professionalism, 175–6; view of Harold Rugg, 181–4; as scientism
in education, 185–200; view of
Walter Lippmann, 190; view of
William C. Bagley, 191; view of
Committee on Economy of
Time, 193–6; view of Eugene
Randolph Smith, 197–8; view
of Franklin Bobbitt, 199–200;
as artistic expressionism in education, 201–7, 376–7; view of
Caroline Pratt, 202–6; as
Freudianism in education, 207–
15, 376–7; view of Margaret
Naumburg, 211–14; as reformism in education, 215–24; view
of William Heard Kilpatrick,
215–21; view of Boyd H. Bode,
221–4; as radicalism in education, 224–34; view of George
S. Counts, 225–7, 259–64; view
of *The Social Frontier*, 231–3;
John Dewey as critic, 234–7;
caricatures, 207, 214, 233–4,
343*n*, 348; advanced by Progressive Education Association,
240–73; early formulation by
PEA, 243–5; later formulations
by PEA, 258–67; advanced by
National Education Association,
272; advanced by American
Federation of Teachers, 272–3;
advanced by National Society
for the Study of Education,
273; in private schools after
1912, 276–91; at Lincoln
School, 280–91; in public
schools after 1912, 291–308; as
rural reformism at Porter
School, 292–5; as "individualized instruction" at Winnetka
(Ill.), 295–9; view of Frederic
Burk, 295–6; view of Carleton
Washburne, 296–8; as curriculum revision at Denver (Col.),
299–303; view of Jesse H. New-

progressive education (*continued*)
Ion, 299–302; image in *Middle-town* studies, 303–5; in colleges and universities, 308–18; as individualized education at Bennington College, 309–13; as general education at the University of Minnesota, 313–18; as advanced by the New Deal, 318–24; beginning of decline, 324–7; criticized by Walter Lippmann, 326; criticized by Boyd H. Bode, 326–7; as "conventional wisdom," 328–38; as advanced by Educational Policies Commission, 329–32; reformulations after 1945, 343*n*; as conceived by Commission on Life Adjustment Education for Youth, 333–8; criticisms after 1945, 338–47; criticisms of Bernard Iddings Bell, 338–9; criticisms of Mortimer Smith, 340, 343; criticisms of Arthur Bestor, 343–6; criticisms of Hyman G. Rickover, 347; collapse as a movement, 347–53

Progressive Education (magazine), 247–8

Progressive Education Association: founding (1918–19), 240–3; first platform, 243–5; early activities, 245–50; international concerns, 248; transformation after 1930, 250–1; commissions and committees 251, 256–7; Commission on the Relation of School and College, 251–6; foundation support, 257; search for a philosophy, 258ff; Committee on Social and Economic Problems, 261–5; Committee on Educational Philosophy, 265; Committee on Philosophy of Education, 266–7; conversion into American Education Fellowship, 268–9; final years, 269–70; reconversion to Progressive Education Association, 270; appraisal, 270–3; literature on, 379–80

Prosser, Charles A.: as secretary of NSPIE, 54; as member of Com-

Prosser (*continued*)
mission on National Aid to Vocational Education, 54–5; proposes resolution on life-adjustment education, 334; writings, 360

Pruette, Lorine, 368

psychoanalysis and education, 207–15

Public Education Association (New York City), 64, 86–7

Public Works Administration, 323

Puner, Morton, 342*n*, 385

Quick, Herbert, 245–6

Quincy (Mass.) schools, 128–31; *see also* Parker, Francis W.

Raby, Sister Joseph Mary, 325*n*, 385

Rainsford, William S., 85, 86*n*, 366

Rankine, Mrs. A. K., 206

Raup, R. Bruce, 228, 229, 235–6, 307*n*, 386

Ravage, Marcus, 67*n*

Ravi-Booth, Vincent, 309

Rawick, George Philip, 323*n*, 384

Rawson, Wyatt, 356

Raymond, Jerome, 164

reading: *see* English language and literature

Reber, Louis E., 166–7

Reck, Franklin M., 80*n*, 366

Reddie, Cecil, 248

Redefer, Frederick L.: reviews Eight-Year Study, 256*n*; comments on response to 1932 address by George Counts, 260–1; as member of the Committee on Social and Economic Problems (PEA), 262; comments on "respectability" of progressive education, 276; revisits older progressive schools after World War II, 349*n*; writings on PEA, 380

Regents' Inquiry (New York State), 332*n*

Rein, Wilhelm, 172

Reinsch, Paul Samuel, 87, 164, 165

Reisner, Edward H., 356

released-time religious instruction, 158

Rensselaer Polytechnic Institute, 35n

retardation, 186n

Reynolds, James B., 64

Rice, Joseph Mayer: education and early career, 3–4; writes series of articles on the schools (1892), 4–6; criticism of series, 6–7; subsequent career, 7–8; as pedagogical progressive, 21–2; comments on demand for Quincy (Mass.) teachers, 131; comments enthusiastically on Cook County (Ill.) Normal School, 133n; comments on teacher incompetence, 169; acquaintance with James Earl Russell, 172; marks beginning of progressive education movement, 358–9

Richards, Charles R., 39, 52n, 88, 159n, 176

Richman, Julia, 64

Rickover, Hyman G., 347, 386

Rieff, Philip, 377

Riesman, David, 351, 378

Riis, Jacob, 3, 58, 72n, 85, 86n, 169n, 184, 363

Roadside Settlement (Des Moines), 64

Robbins, Jane, 59, 64

Roberts, J. S., 360

Robertson, James, 146

Robinson, James Harvey, 308n, 353n

Rockefeller, John D., 81

"Rockefeller Brothers Report," 339n

Rockefeller Foundation, 317

Rodgers, Andrew Denny, III, 76n, 365

Rollins College, 308

Roosevelt, Eleanor, 264

Roosevelt, Franklin, 318–24

Roosevelt, Theodore, 58, 82, 168, 180, 184

Rosenfeld, Paul, 205

Ross, Earle D., 48n, 362

Rossentreter, Frederick M., 166n, 373–4

Rosten, Leo, 73n

Rousseau, Jean Jacques, 11, 93, 103, 120, 152, 277

Rudd, Augustin G., 268n, 386

Rudy, Willis, 381

Rugg, Harold: education and early career, 181; *Statistical Methods Applied to Education*, 182; joins Committee on the Classification of Personnel, 182; friendship with Arthur Upham Pope, 182; career at Teachers College, Columbia University, 182ff; social science texts, 182; *The Child-Centered School*, 183, 279; influenced by the Depression, 183; *Foundations for American Education*, 183–4; describes Kilpatrick discussion group, 228–9; as editor of *Frontiers of Democracy*, 233; as member of Commission on the Relation of School and College (PEA), 252; frames policy statement for American Education Fellowship, 270n; comments on leading progressive schools (1870–1930), 276–7; on faculty of Lincoln School, 282; revisits older progressive schools in 1940's, 349n; writings, 355–6, 375, 376, 377

Runkle, John D., 25–6, 27, 29, 33, 361

Rusk, Ralph L., 12n

Ruskin, John, 59, 63

Russell, James Earl: brings Edward L. Thorndike to Teachers College, Columbia University, 113; education and early career, 172; as Dean of Teachers College, Columbia University, 172ff; conception of professional education, 173–4; ideas on democracy and education, 174; interest in southern reconstruction, 174; interest in social service, 175; synthesis of professionalism and progressivism, 175; *The Scientific Movement in Education*, 370; *Founding Teachers College*, 374

Ryan, W. Carson, Jr., 265

Sachs, Julius, 173
Sage, Russell, 175
St. Louis (Mo.) schools, 19
St. Paul (Minn.) schools, 32
Salisbury, Rollin D., 141n
Salutos, Theodore, 43n, 46n, 362
Sandifer, Sister Mary Ruth, 325n, 385
Sanford, Charles W., 344n
San Francisco State Normal School, 295–6
Santayana, George, 109n
Sarah Lawrence College, 308
Sarton, Mrs. George, 278
Savage, Willinda, 116n, 370
Sayers, E. V., 270n
Schaub, Edward L., 360
Schiff, Jacob, 3
Schilpp, Paul Arthur, 116n, 310n, 370
Schlesinger, Arthur M., 355
Schlesinger, Arthur M. Jr., 374–5
Schmidt, George P., 381
Schneider, Herbert W., 367, 371
School of Organic Education (Fairhope, Ala.), 149–52
school-lunch program, 64, 323
sciences: see natural sciences
scientific movement in education, 114–15, 185–200
Scott, C. Winfield, 341n, 385
Scott, Virgil, 343n
Scott, William A., 164
Scott, Mrs. William C. D., 87n
Search, Preston W., 296n
Search, Theodore C., 37–8
Sears, Barnas, 14
"Second Morrill Act" (1890), 43
secondary education: William T. Harris on, 19; John Dewey on, 140; at Fairhope (Ala.), 150–1; at Gary (Ind.), 156; at Lincoln School, 283–6; reorganization, 306; extension of program, 306
Seeds, Nellie, 261
Seven Arts, 205–6
Shady Hill School (Cambridge, Mass.), 278
Shaker Heights (Ohio) schools, 277, 295
Shane, Harold G., 270n
Shannon, David A., 170n, 282n, 289n, 374

Shaw, Adele Marie, 21n, 71n, 142ff, 373
Sheed, F. J., 232
Sheldon, Edward A., 14, 134n
Shields, James M., 343n
Shorey, Paul, 280n, 325n
Shumaker, Ann, 207, 279, 286
Simkhovitch, Mary Kingsbury, 61n, 64n
Simmons, Lucy, 292n, 382
Simon, Théodore, 186
Simpson, James, 12n
Sinclair, Upton, 225, 272
Skilbeck, Malcolm, 325n, 385
Slichter, Gertrude A., 363
Sloan, Harold S., 57n, 351
slöjd (handwork usually in wood), 33
Slosson, Preston W., 355
Small, Albion, 98–100, 225, 367
Smiles, Samuel, 29n
Smith, Alexander, 141n
Smith, David Eugene, 173
Smith, Eugene Randolph: education and early career, 197; work in arithmetic in Montclair (N.J.), 197; *Education Moves Ahead*, 197–8; part in founding of Progressive Education Association, 242; as PEA President, 250; role in Eight-Year Study, 253n; as first headmaster of Park School, 277; as characteristic private-school educator, 376
Smith, Hoke, 85
Smith, Mortimer, 339–40, 343, 346, 386
Smith, Ruby Green, 77n
Smith, W. H., 81
Smith-Hughes Act (1917), 56–7
Smith-Lever Act (1914), 56, 82n, 84, 85n
Snow, C. P., 353
Snyder, Morton, 248–9
social Darwinism, 93–6, 99–100, 367
Social Frontier: established in 1934, 231; editorial board, 231; editorial policy, 231–2; leading contributors, 232; later history, 232–3; name changed to *Fron-*

Social Frontier (*continued*)
   tiers of Democracy, 232–3; appraisal, 233
Social Gospel, 67
social settlements and education, 58–65, 69–70
social studies, 182, 286, 311
social work, 59–65
Society for Curriculum Study, 291
Soltes, Mordecai, 71n
Spafford, Ivol, 316n, 384
Spain, Charles L., 156n, 373
Spalding, Willard B., 270n
Spargo, John, 85n, 363
Sparling, Samuel, 164
Spaulding, Edward G., 237n
Spencer, Herbert: influence in the United States, 91; *Education, Intellectual, Moral, and Physical*, 91–2; influence on Charles W. Eliot, 92; influence on Committee of Ten (1893) and Commission on the Reorganization of Secondary Education (1918), 92–3; on scientific pedagogy, 93–4; on the futility of social reformism, 94; discipleship of William Graham Sumner, 94–6; influence on Lester Frank Ward, 96–100; influence on American psychology, 100; influence on G. Stanley Hall, 101; writings on, 367
Stanford-Binet test, 186–7
Stanton, Jessie, 204n, 205n, 377
Starr, Ellen Gates, 60
Starr, Frederick, 141n
"steamer classes," 71
Stearns, Harold E., 190n, 225
Steenbock, Harry, 163
Steffens, Lincoln, 167
Stein, Maurice R., 305n
Steiner, Bernard C., 359
Stern, Bernhard J., 98n
Stieglitz, Alfred, 182, 206
Stoddard, George, 192, 329
Stoddard, Lothrop, 188n
Stombaugh, Ray, 361
Stout, James Huff, 143–6
Stout, John Elbert, 371
Stover, Charles B., 64
Strachey, James, 208n
Straker, Robert L., 359

Strayer, George, 159n, 329
Struble, George G., 201n
Struck, F. Theodore, 361
Studebaker, John W., 321–2, 329, 335
Sullivan, Mark, 72n, 377
Sumner, William Graham: as professor at Yale, 94; as disciple of Herbert Spencer, 95; bias against educational reform, 95–6; writings on, 367–8

Taft, William Howard, 65
Talbot, Winthrop, 72n, 74n
Taylor, Carl C., 46n
Taylor, Katherine Whiteside, 257n, 380
"Taylorism," 158n
teacher education, 168–76, 200, 307, 345
Teachers College, Columbia University: origins and founding, 170–1; alliance with Columbia University, 171; administration of James Earl Russell, 172–6; early faculty, 172–3, 175–6; marriage of professionalism and progressivism, 175; advantages and disadvantages of autonomy, 176; literature on, 374
teaching methods: *see* methods of teaching
technical education: *see* agricultural education, vocational education
Tenenbaum, Samuel, 215n, 378
Terman, Lewis M., 104, 186, 192
tests: *see* mental tests
Thayer, V. T., 224, 229, 256n, 257n, 380
Thomas, Alan M., Jr., 73n, 365
Thomas, M. Halsey, 371
Thomas, W. I., 141n
Thompson, Frank V., 72n, 365
Thompson, Laura A., 364
Thorndike, Edward L.: education and early career, 110; *Animal Intelligence*, 110ff; problem-box experiments, 111; theory of learning, 111–12; critique of G. Stanley Hall, 112–13; career at Teachers College, Columbia University, 113ff, 172, 176; on

Thorndike (*continued*)
transfer of training, 113; on individual differences, 114; *Principles of Teaching*, 114; idea of a science of education, 114–15; reputation compared with John Dewey's, 115; states *credo* of educational measurement movement, 185; develops achievement scales, 186; place in progressive education movement, 369; writings on, 369–70

Thornton, Charles S., 133n

Threlkeld, Archie L., 299n, 301–2, 383

Thwing, Charles, 359

Tibbetts, Vinal H., 268n

Tippett, James S., 283n, 382

Toepfer, Kenneth H., 172n

Toledo (Ohio) schools, 32

Tostberg, Robert Eugene, 372

Townsend, Mary Evelyn, 170n, 282n, 289n, 374

Toynbee Hall, 59

trade education: *see* vocational education

Trow, William Clark, 344n

True, Alfred Charles, 42n, 48n, 79n, 80n, 362, 366

Tucker, William J., 60

Tufts, James H., 119, 141n

Turner, Frederick Jackson, 161n, 163

Tyler, Ralph W., 255

Ulich, Robert, 176n, 374

Umberger, Willis H., 386

unions: *see* labor unions

United States Children's Bureau, 65

United States Department of Agriculture, 80–2

United States Immigration Commission (1907–11), 72

United States Office of Education: Americanization effort, 74–5; disseminates progressive education, 275; sponsors Commission on Life Adjustment Education for Youth, 333–7

university extension, 165–7

University Settlement (New York City), 64

Upton, Albert, 192n

U.S. News & World Report (magazine), 346

Vanderbilt, George W., 170–1

Vandewalker, Nina C., 134n

Van Hise, Charles: inaugural address of 1904, 161; idea of the state university, 161–2; idea of "service to the state," 162; promotes union of academic and practical studies, 163; supports university extension, 165–6; praised in popular press, 167–8

Van Loon, Hendrik, 213

Van Rensselaer, Mrs. Schuyler, 86n

Veblen, Thorstein, 124, 224–5

Vincent, George E., 99, 141n

vocational education: early examples, 34–6; as issue dividing business and labor, 36–41; rural phase, 41–50; as movement culminating in Smith-Hughes Act (1917), 50–7; at Gary (Ind.), 156–7; affected by World War I, 180–1; in the Civilian Conservation Corps, 321

Vogel, Mabel, 298, 383

Wald, Lillian, 61n, 64, 65, 364

Walden School (New York City): establishment (1915), 211; early program, 212–14; as characteristic progressive school of the 1920's, 277–8

Walker, Edward Everett, 367

Wallace, Henry, 43–4, 45, 82

Wallace's Farmer (magazine), 43–4, 45, 79

Walters, Raymond, 252

Walton, John, 385

Walzer, Michael, 353n

Wanamaker, Pearl, 329

Ward, Lester Frank: education and early career, 96; view of mind as "telic," 96–7; view of education as the "great panacea," 97; influenced by August Comte and Claude-Adrien Helvetius, 97; supports public education, 97–8; discipleship of Albion Small, 98–9; influences

Ward (*continued*)
  Charles Van Hise, 166; writings, 367
Warde, William F., 89n
Ware, Caroline, 205n, 208n, 377
Warren, Constance, 381
Washburne, Carleton: comments on report of Committee on Social and Economic Problems (PEA), 262; comments on conversion of PEA into AEF, 270n; invited to school superintendency at Winnetka (Ill.), 295; as disciple of Frederic Burk, 295–6; ideas on curriculum, 296–7; view of progressive education, 297n; writings, 382–3
Washington University (St. Louis), 27–9
Watson, Goodwin, 228, 252, 262
Wattenberg, William, 229n
Weber, Max, 206
Wecter, Dixon, 355
Weisz, Howard Ralph, 181n
Wells, H. G., 245
Wesley, Edgar B., 272n, 275n, 380
Wheaton, H. H., 71n
Wheeler, Benjamin Ide, 172
Wheeler, Everett, 60
White, Emerson, 29
White, Morton G., 116n, 355, 370
White, William A., 209, 377
Whitman, Charles O., 141n
Whittemore, Richard, 171n
Whittier House (Jersey City), 64
Whyte, William H., Jr., 351
Wiener, Philip P., 109n, 368
Wilkins, Ernest H., 287, 309n
Williams, Cornilia T., 317n, 384
Williams, E.I.F., 8n, 359
Williams, Laura C., 242, 246
Williams, Raymond, 63n, 124n, 363
Willis, Benjamin, 335
Wilson, Woodrow, 56
Winfield, Oscar A., 368
Winnebago County (Ill.) schools, 79
Winnetka Plan, 296–9
Winnetka (Ill.) schools, 295, 296–9, 382–3

Winsor, Charlotte, 289
Wirt, William: education and early career, 154; appointed superintendent of schools for Gary (Ind.), 154; develops "Gary Plan," 155–7; consultant to New York City Board of Education, 158; writings on, 373
Wisconsin, University of: relation to "Wisconsin Idea," 87; under presidency of Charles Van Hise, 161ff; agricultural program, 162–3; School of Economics, Political Science and History, 163–4; relationship to state government, 164–5; extension program, 165–7; praised in popular press, 167–8; literature on, 373–4
Wish, Harvey, 367
Woelfel, Norman, 201n, 231, 232n, 375
Wolfle, Dael, 338n
Women's Municipal League, 86n
Wood, Harold Hughes, 369
Woodring, Paul, 324, 333n, 343, 356, 386
Woods, Robert A., 60, 64n, 70n, 88, 364
Woodward, C. Vann, 366
Woodward, Calvin M.: education and early career, 26; criticizes public schools, 26–7; founds Manual Training School at Washington University, 27; ideas on manual training, 28–9; challenged in National Educational Association, 29–32; espouses vocational education, 34; influences James Huff Stout, 143; writings, 361
Woodworth, Robert S., 110n, 113, 369
Works Progress Administration, 323
World's Work, 82
Wright, Chauncey, 106n
Wright, John C., 361
Wright, Lula, 282
Wrightstone, J. Wayne, 287n
writing: *see* English language and literature

Wundt, Wilhelm, 100, 101, 172
Wyllie, Irvin G., 363

Yeomans, Edward, 295n, 382
Yerkes, Robert, 187–8, 376
Yoakum, Clarence S., 187n, 376
York County (Neb.) schools, 78
Youmans, Edward L., 91
Young, Ella Flagg, 135–6, 372

Zachry, Caroline B., 256n, 257n, 380
Zangwill, Israel, 68
Zeitlin, Harry, 233n, 319n, 321n, 323n, 384
Zoll, Allen, 342
Zook, George F., 320–1, 329
Zorach, William, 206
Zueblin, Charles, 60, 363

VINTAGE WORKS OF SCIENCE AND PSYCHOLOGY

V-286   **ARIES, PHILIPPE** / Centuries of Childhood

V-292   **BATES, MARSTON** / The Forest and The Sea

V-267   **BATES, MARSTON** / Gluttons and Libertines

V-994   **BERGER, PETER & BRIGITTE AND HANSFRIED KELLNER** / The Homeless Mind: Modernization & Consciousness

V-129   **BEVERIDGE, W. I. B.** / The Art of Scientific Investigation

V-837   **BIELER, HENRY G., M. D.** / Food Is Your Best Medicine

V-414   **BOTTOMORE, T. B.** / Classes in Modern Society

V-742   **BOTTOMORE, T. B.** / Sociology: A Guide to Problems & Literature

V-168   **BRONOWSKI, J.** / The Common Sense of Science

V-419   **BROWN, NORMAN O.** / Love's Body

V-877   **COHEN, DOROTHY** / The Learning Child: Guideline for Parents and Teachers

V-972   **COHEN, STANLEY AND LAURIE TAYLOR** / Psychological Survival: The Experience of Long-Term Imprisonment

V-233   **COOPER, DAVID** / The Death of the Family

V-43   **COOPER, D. G. AND R. D. LAING** / Reason and Violence

V-918   **DAUM, SUSAN M. AND JEANNE M. STELLMAN** / Work is Dangerous to Your Health: A Handbook of Health Hazards in the Workplace & What You Can Do About Them

V-638   **DENNISON, GEORGE** / The Lives of Children

V-671   **DOMHOFF, G. WILLIAM** / The Higher Circles

V-942   **DOUGLAS, MARY** / Natural Symbols

V-157   **EISELEY, LOREN** / The Immense Journey

V-874   **ELLUL, JACQUES** / Propaganda: The Formation of Men's Attitudes

V-390   **ELLUL, JACQUES** / The Technological Society

V-802   **FALK, RICHARD A.** / This Endangered Planet: Prospects & Proposals for Human Survival

V-906   **FARAGO, PETER AND JOHN LAGNADO** / Life in Action: Biochemistry Explained

V-97   **FOUCAULT, MICHEL** / Birth of the Clinic: An Archaeology of Medical Perception

V-914   **FOUCAULT, MICHEL** / Madness & Civilization: A History of Insanity in the Age of Reason

V-935   **FOUCAULT, MICHEL** / The Order of Things: An Archaeology of the Human Sciences

V-821   **FRANK, ARTHUR, & STUART** / The People's Handbook of Medical Care

V-866   **FRANKL, VIKTOR D.** / The Doctor & The Soul: From Psychotherapy to Logotherapy

V-132   **FREUD, SIGMUND** / Leonardo da Vinci: A Study in Psychosexuality

V-14   **FREUD, SIGMUND** / Moses and Monotheism

V-124   **FREUD, SIGMUND** / Totem and Taboo

V-491   **GANS, HERBERT J.** / The Levittowners

V-938   **GARDNER, HOWARD** / The Quest for Mind: Piaget, Levi-Strauss, & The Structuralist Movement

V-152   **GRAHAM, LOREN R.** / Science & Philosophy in the Soviet Union

V-221   **GRIBBIN, JOHN AND STEPHEN PLAGEMANN** / The Jupiter Effect: The Planets as Triggers of Devastating Earthquakes (Revised)

V-602   **HARKINS, ARTHUR AND MAGORAH MARUYAMA (eds.)** / Cultures Beyond The Earth

V-372   **HARRIS, MARVIN** / Cows, Pigs, Wars, and Witches: The Riddles of Culture

V-453   **HEALTH POLICY ADVISORY COMMITTEE** / The American Health Empire

V-283   **HENRY, JULES** / Culture Against Man

V-73   **HENRY, JULES & ZUNIA** / Doll Play of the Pilaga Indian Children

V-970   **HENRY, JULES** / On Sham, Vulnerability & Other Forms of Self-Destruction

V-882   **HENRY, JULES** / Pathways to Madness

V-663   **HERRIGEL, EUGEN** / Zen in the Art of Archery

V-879   **HERSKOVITS, MELVILLE J.** / Cultural Relativism

V-566   **HURLEY, RODGER** / Poverty and Mental Retardation: A Causal Relationship

V-953   **HYMES, DELL (ed.)** / Reinventing Anthropology

V-2017   **JUDSON, HORACE FREEDLAND** / Heroin Addiction: What Americans Can Learn from the English Experience

V-268   **JUNG, C. G.** / Memories, Dreams, Reflections

V-994   **KELLNER, HANSFRIED AND PETER & BRIGITTE BERGER** / The Homeless Mind: Modernization & Consciousness

V-210   **KENYATTA, JOMO** / Facing Mount Kenya

V-823   **KOESTLER, ARTHUR** / The Case of the Midwife Toad

V-934   **KOESTLER, ARTHUR** / The Roots of Coincidence

V-361   **KOMAROVSKY, MIRRA** / Blue-Collar Marriage

V-144   **KRUEGER, STARRY** / The Whole Works: The Autobiography of a Young American Couple

V-906   **LAGNADO, JOHN AND PETER FARAGO** / Life in Action: Biochemistry Explained

V-776   **LAING, R. D.** / Knots

V-809   **LAING, R. D.** / The Politics of the Family & Other Essays

V-43   **LAING, R. D. AND D. G. COOPER** / Reason and Violence

V-280   **LEWIS, OSCAR** / The Children of Sánchez

V-634   **LEWIS, OSCAR** / A Death in the Sánchez Family

V-421   **LEWIS, OSCAR** / La Vida: A Puerto Rican Family in the Culture of Poverty —San Juan and New York

V-370   **LEWIS, OSCAR** / Pedro Martinez

V-727   **MANN, FELIX, M. D.** / Acupuncture (rev.)

V-602   **MARUYAMA, MAGORAH AND ARTHUR HARKINS (eds.)** / Cultures Beyond the Earth

V-816   **MEDVEDEV, ZHORES & ROY** / A Question of Madness

V-427   **MENDELSON, MARY ADELAIDE** / Tender Loving Greed

V-442   **MITCHELL, JULIET** / Psychoanalysis and Feminism

V-672   **OUSPENSKY, P. D.** / The Fourth Way

V-524   **OUSPENSKY, P. D.** / A New Model of The Universe

V-943   **OUSPENSKY, P. D.** / The Psychology of Man's Possible Evolution

V-639   **OUSPENSKY, P. D.** / Tertium Organum

V-558   **PERLS, F. S.** / Ego, Hunger and Aggression: Beginning of Gestalt Therapy

V-462   **PIAGET, JEAN** / Six Psychological Studies

V-221   **PLAGEMANN, STEPHEN AND JOHN GRIBBIN** / The Jupiter Effect (Revised)

V-6   **POLSTER, ERVING & MIRIAM** / Gestalt Therapy Integrated: Contours of Theory & Practice

V-70   **RANK, OTTO** / The Myth of the Birth of the Hero and Other Essays

V-214   **ROSENFELD, ALBERT** / The Second Genesis: The Coming Control of Life

V-301   **ROSS, NANCY WILSON (ed.)** / The World of Zen

V-441   **RUDHYAR, DANE** / The Astrology of America's Destiny

V-464   **SARTRE, JEAN-PAUL** / Search for a Method

V-806   **SHERFEY, MARY JANE, M. D.** / The Nature & Evolution of Female Sexuality

V-918   **STELLMAN, JEANNE M. AND SUSAN M. DAUM** / Work is Dangerous to Your Health

V-440   **STONER, CAROL HUPPING** / Producing Your Own Power: How to Make Nature's Energy Sources Work for You

V-972   **TAYLOR, LAURIE AND STANLEY COHEN** / Psychological Survival

V-289   **THOMAS, ELIZABETH MARSHALL** / The Harmless People

V-800   **THOMAS, ELIZABETH MARSHALL** / Warrior Herdsmen

V-310   **THORP, EDWARD O.** / Beat the Dealer

V-588   **TIGER, LIONEL** / Men in Groups

V-810   **TITMUSS, RICHARD M.** / The Gift Relationship From Human Blood to Social Policy

V-761   **WATTS, ALAN** / Behold the Spirit

V-923   **WATTS, ALAN** / Beyond Theology: The Art of Godsmanship

V-853	**WATTS, ALAN** /	The Book: On the Taboo Against Knowing Who You Are
V-999	**WATTS, ALAN** /	Cloud-Hidden, Whereabouts Unknown
V-665	**WATTS, ALAN** /	Does It Matter?
V-299	**WATTS, ALAN** /	The Joyous Cosmology
V-592	**WATTS, ALAN** /	Nature, Man, and Woman
V-609	**WATTS, ALAN** /	Psychotherapy East and West
V-835	**WATTS, ALAN** /	The Supreme Identity
V-904	**WATTS, ALAN** /	This Is It
V-298	**WATTS, ALAN** /	The Way of Zen
V-468	**WATTS, ALAN** /	The Wisdom of Insecurity
V-813	**WILSON, COLIN** /	The Occult
V-313	**WILSON, EDMUND** /	Apologies to the Iroquois
V-197	**WILSON, PETER J.** /	Oscar: An Inquiry into the Nature of Sanity
V-893	**ZAEHNER, R. C.** /	Zen, Drugs & Mysticism

VINTAGE CRITICISM: LITERATURE, MUSIC, AND ART

V-570 ANDREWS, WAYNE / American Gothic
V-418 AUDEN, W. H. / The Dyer's Hand
V-887 AUDEN, W. H. / Forewords and Afterwords
V-161 BROWN, NORMAN O. / Closing Time
V-75   CAMUS, ALBERT / The Myth of Sisyphus and Other Essays
V-626 CAMUS, ALBERT / Lyrical and Critical Essays
V-535 EISEN, JONATHAN / The Age of Rock: Sounds of the American Cultural Revolution
V-4   EINSTEIN, ALFRED / A Short History of Music
V-13   GILBERT, STUART / James Joyce's Ulysses
V-407 HARDWICK, ELIZABETH / Seduction and Betrayal: Women and Literature
V-114 HAUSER, ARNOLD / Social History of Art, Vol. I
V-115 HAUSER, ARNOLD / Social History of Art, Vol. II
V-116 HAUSER, ARNOLD / Social History of Art, Vol. III
V-117 HAUSER, ARNOLD / Social History of Art, Vol. IV
V-610 HSU, KAI-YU / The Chinese Literary Scene
V-201 HUGHES, H. STUART / Consciousness and Society
V-88   KERMAN, JOSEPH / Opera as Drama
V-995 KOTT, JAN / The Eating of the Gods: An Interpretation of Greek Tragedy
V-685 LESSING, DORIS / A Small Personal Voice: Essays, Reviews, Interviews
V-677 LESTER, JULIUS / The Seventh Son, Vol. I
V-678 LESTER, JULIUS / The Seventh Son, Vol. II
V-720 MIRSKY, D. S. / A History of Russian Literature
V-118 NEWMAN, ERNEST / Great Operas, Vol. I
V-119 NEWMAN, ERNEST / Great Operas, Vol. II
V-976 QUASHA, GEORGE AND JEROME ROTHENBERG (eds.) / America A Prophecy: A New Reading of American Poetry from Pre-Columbian Times to the Present
V-976 ROTHENBERG, JEROME AND GEORGE QUASHA (eds.) / America A Prophecy: A New Reading of American Poetry from Pre-Columbian Times to the Present
V-415 SHATTUCK, ROGER / The Banquet Years, Revised
V-435 SPENDER, STEPHEN / Love-Hate Relations: English and American Sensibilities
V-278 STEVENS, WALLACE / The Necessary Angel
V-100 SULLIVAN, J. W. N. / Beethoven: His Spiritual Development
V-166 SZE, MAI-MAI / The Way of Chinese Painting
V 162 TILLYARD, E. M. W. / The Elizabethan World Picture

VINTAGE POLITICAL SCIENCE AND SOCIAL CRITICISM

V-568   **ALINSKY, SAUL D.** / Reveille for Radicals

V-736   **ALINSKY, SAUL D.** / Rules for Radicals

V-726   **ALLENDE, PRESIDENT SALVADOR AND REGIS DEBRAY** / The Chilean Revolution

V-286   **ARIES, PHILIPPE** / Centuries of Childhood

V-604   **BAILYN, BERNARD** / Origins of American Politics

V-334   **BALTZELL, E. DIGBY** / The Protestant Establishment

V-571   **BARTH, ALAN** / Prophets With Honor: Great Dissents & Great Dissenters in the Supreme Court

V-791   **BAXANDALL, LEE (ed.) AND WILHELM REICH** / Sex-Pol.: Essays 1929-1934

V-60   **BECKER, CARL L.** / The Declaration of Independence

V-563   **BEER, SAMUEL H.** / British Politics in the Collectivist Age

V-994   **BERGER, PETER & BRIGITTE AND HANSFRIED KELLNER** / The Homeless Mind: Modernization and Consciousness

V-77   **BINZEN, PETER** / Whitetown, USA

V-513   **BOORSTIN, DANIEL J.** / The Americans: The Colonial Experience

V-11   **BOORSTIN, DANIEL J.** / The Americans: The Democratic Experience

V-358   **BOORSTIN, DANIEL J.** / The Americans: The National Experience

V-501   **BOORSTIN, DANIEL J.** / Democracy and Its Discontents: Reflections on Everyday America

V-414   **BOTTOMORE, T. B.** / Classes in Modern Society

V-742   **BOTTOMORE, T. B.** / Sociology: A Guide to Problems & Literature

V-305   **BREINES, SIMON AND WILLIAM J. DEAN** / The Pedestrian Revolution: Streets Without Cars

V-44   **BRINTON, CRANE** / The Anatomy of Revolution

V-30   **CAMUS, ALBERT** / The Rebel

V-966   **CAMUS, ALBERT** / Resistance, Rebellion & Death

V-33   **CARMICHAEL, STOKELY AND CHARLES HAMILTON** / Black Power

V-2024   **CARO, ROBERT A.** / The Power Broker: Robert Moses and The Fall of New York

V-862   **CASE, JOHN AND GERRY HUNNIUS AND DAVID G. CARSON** / Workers Control: A Reader on Labor and Social Change

V-98   **CASH, W. J.** / The Mind of the South

V-555   **CHOMSKY, NOAM** / American Power and the New Mandarins

V-248   **CHOMSKY, NOAM** / Peace in the Middle East? Reflections on Justice and Nationhood

V-815   **CHOMSKY, NOAM** / Problems of Knowledge and Freedom

V-788   **CIRINO, ROBERT** / Don't Blame the People

V-17   **CLARKE, TED AND DENNIS JAFFE (eds.)** / Worlds Apart: Young People and The Drug Problems

V-383   **CLOWARD, RICHARD AND FRANCES FOX PIVEN** / The Politics of Turmoil: Essays on Poverty, Race and The Urban Crisis

V-743   **CLOWARD, RICHARD AND FRANCES FOX PIVEN** / Regulating the Poor: The Functions of Public Welfare

V-940   **COBB, JONATHAN AND RICHARD SENNETT** / Hidden Injuries of Class

V-311   **CREMIN, LAWRENCE A.** / The Genius of American Education

V-519   **CREMIN, LAWRENCE A.** / The Transformation of the School

V-808   **CUMMING, ROBERT D. (ed.)** / The Philosophy of Jean-Paul Sartre

V-2019   **CUOMO, MARIO** / Forest Hills Diary: The Crisis of Low-Income Housing

V-305   **DEAN, WILLIAM J. AND SIMON BREINES** / The Pedestrian Revolution: Streets Without Cars

V-726   **DEBRAY, REGIS AND PRESIDENT SALVADOR ALLENDE** / The Chilean Revolution

V-638   **DENNISON, GEORGE** / The Lives of Children

V-746   **DEUTSCHER, ISAAC** / The Prophet Armed

V-748   **DEUTSCHER, ISAAC** / The Prophet Outcast

V-617   **DEVLIN, BERNADETTE** / The Price of My Soul

V-671   **DOMHOFF, G. WILLIAM** / The Higher Circles
V-812   **ELLUL, JACQUES** / The Political Illusion
V-874   **ELLUL, JACQUES** / Propaganda: The Formation of Men's Attitudes
V-390   **ELLUL, JACQUES** / The Technological Society
V-143   **EMERSON, THOMAS I.** / The System of Freedom of Expression
V-396   **EPSTEIN, EDWARD JAY** / Between Fact and Fiction: The Problem of Journalism
V-998   **EPSTEIN, EDWARD JAY** / News from Nowhere: Television and The News
V-405   **ESHERICK, JOSEPH W. (ed.) AND JOHN S. SERVICE** / Lost Chance in China: The World War II Despatches of John S. Service
V-803   **EVANS, ROWLAND JR. AND ROBERT D. NOVAK** / Nixon in the White House: The Frustration of Power
V-802   **FALK, RICHARD A.** / This Endangered Planet: Prospects and Proposals for Human Survival
V-2002   **FERNBACH, DAVID AND KARL MARX** / Political Writings Vol. I: The Revolutions of 1848
V-2003   **FERNBACH, DAVID AND KARL MARX** / Political Writings Vol. II: Surveys from Exile
V-2004   **FERNBACH, DAVID AND KARL MARX** / Political Writings Vol. III: The First International and After
V-225   **FISCHER, LOUIS (ed.)** / The Essential Gandhi
V-927   **FITZGERALD, FRANCES** / Fire in the Lake: The Vietnamese and the Americans in Vietnam
V-316   **FREEMAN, S. DAVID** / Energy: The New Era
V-368   **FRIEDENBERG, EDGAR Z.** / Coming of Age in America
V-409   **FRIENDLY, FRED W.** / Due to Circumstances Beyond Our Control
V-378   **FULBRIGHT, J. WILLIAM** / The Arrogance of Power
V-846   **FULBRIGHT, J. WILLIAM** / The Crippled Giant
V-491   **GANS, HERBERT J.** / The Levittowners
V-167   **GANS, HERBERT J.** / More Equality
V-862   **GARSON, DAVID G. AND GERRY HUNNIUS AND JOHN CASE** / Workers Control: A Reader in Labor and Social Change
V-2018   **GAYLIN, WILLARD** / Partial Justice: A Study of Bias in Sentencing
V-183   **GOLDMAN, ERIC F.** / The Crucial Decade—and After: America 1945-1960
V-31   **GOLDMAN, ERIC F.** / Rendezvous With Destiny
V-174   **GOODMAN, PAUL AND PERCIVAL** / Communitas
V-325   **GOODMAN, PAUL** / Compulsory Mis-education and The Community of Scholars
V-32   **GOODMAN, PAUL** / Growing Up Absurd
V-932   **GRAUBARD, ALLEN** / Free the Children: Radical Reform and The Free School Movement
V-457   **GREENE, FELIX** / The Enemy: Some Notes on the Nature of Contemporary Imperialism
V-430   **GUEVERA, CHE** / Guerilla Warfare
V-33   **HAMILTON, CHARLES AND STOKELY CARMICHAEL** / Black Power
V-453   **HEALTH/PAC** / The American Health Empire
V-635   **HEILBRONER, ROBERT L.** / Between Capitalism and Socialism
V-283   **HENRY, JULES** / Culture Against Man
V-482   **HETTER, PATRICIA AND LOUIS O. KELSO** / Two-Factor Theory: The Economics of Reality
V-465   **HINTON, WILLIAM** / Fanshen: A Documentary of Revolution in a Chinese Village
V-328   **HINTON, WILLIAM** / Iron Oxen
V-2005   **HOARE, QUINTIN (ed.) AND KARL MARX** / Early Writings
V-95   **HOFSTADTER, RICHARD** / The Age of Reform: From Bryan to FDR
V-795   **HOFSTADTER, RICHARD** / America at 1750: A Social Portrait
V-9   **HOFSTADTER, RICHARD** / The American Political Tradition
V-686   **HOFSTADTER, RICHARD AND MICHAEL WALLACE (eds.)** / American Violence: A Documentary History
V-317   **HOFSTADTER, RICHARD** / Anti-Intellectualism in American Life

V-540   **HOFSTADTER, RICHARD AND CLARENCE L. VER STEEG (eds.)** / Great Issues in American History: From Settlement to Revolution, 1584-1776

V-541   **HOFSTADTER, RICHARD (ed.)** / Great Issues in American History: From the Revolution to the Civil War, 1765-1865

V-542   **HOFSTADTER, RICHARD (ed.)** / Great Issues in American History: From Reconstruction to the Present Day, 1864-1969

V-385   **HOFSTADTER, RICHARD (ed.)** / The Paranoid Style in American Politics and Other Essays

V-591   **HOFSTADTER, RICHARD (ed.)** / The Progressive Historians

V-201   **HUGHES, H. STUART** / Consciousness and Society

V-862   **HUNNIUS, GERRY, DAVID G. GARSON AND JOHN CASE** / Workers Control: A Reader on Labor and Social Change

V-514   **HUNTINGTON, SAMUEL F.** / The Soldier and the State

V-566   **HURLEY, ROGER** / Poverty & Mental Retardation: A Causal Relationship

V-17   **JAFFE, DENNIS AND TED CLARKE (eds.)** / Worlds Apart: Young People and The Drug Programs

V-241   **JACOBS, JANE** / Death and Life of Great American Cities

V-584   **JACOBS, JANE** / The Economy of Cities

V-433   **JACOBS, PAUL** / Prelude to Riot

V-459   **JACOBS, PAUL AND SAUL LANDAU WITH EVE PELL** / To Serve the Devil: Natives and Slaves Vol. I

V-460   **JACOBS, PAUL AND SAUL LANDAU WITH EVE PELL** / To Serve the Devil: Colonials and Sojourners Vol. II

V-2017   **JUDSON, HORACE FREELAND** / Heroin Addiction: What Americans Can Learn from the English Experience

V-790   **KAPLAN, CAROL AND LAWRENCE (eds.)** / Revolutions, A Comparative Study

V-337   **KAUFMANN, WALTER (trans.) AND FRIEDRICH NIETZSCHE** / Beyond Good and Evil

V-369   **KAUFMANN, WALTER (trans.) AND FRIEDRICH NIETZSCHE** / The Birth of Tragedy and The Case of Wagner

V-985   **KAUFMANN, WALTER (trans.) AND FRIEDRICH NIETZSCHE** / The Gay Science

V-401   **KAUFMANN, WALTER (trans.) AND FRIEDRICH NIETZSCHE** / On the Genealogy of Morals and Ecce Homo

V-437   **KAUFMANN, WALTER (trans.) AND FRIEDRICH NIETZSCHE** / The Will to Power

V-994   **KELLNER, HANSFRIED AND PETER AND BRIGITTE BERGER** / The Homeless Mind: Modernization and Consciousness

V-482   **KELSO, LOUIS O. AND PATRICIA HETTER** / Two-Factor Theory: The Economics of Reality

V-708   **KESSLE, GUN AND JAN MYRDAL** / China: The Revolution Continued

V-510   **KEY, V. O.** / Southern Politics

V-764   **KLARE, MICHAEL T.** / War Without End: American Planning for the Next Vietnams

V-981   **KLINE, MORRIS** / Why Johnny Can't Add: The Failure of the New Math

V-361   **KOMAROVSKY, MIRRA** / Blue Collar Marriage

V-675   **KOVEL, JOEL** / White Racism

V-459   **LANDAU, SAUL, PAUL JACOBS WITH EVE PELL** / To Serve the Devil: Natives and Slaves Vol. I

V-460   **LANDAU, SAUL, PAUL JACOBS WITH EVE PELL** / To Serve the Devil: Colonials and Sojourners Vol. II

V-560   **LASCH, CHRISTOPHER** / The Agony of the American Left

V-367   **LASCH, CHRISTOPHER** / The New Radicalism in America

V-46   **LASCH, CHRISTOPHER** / The World of Nations

V-987   **LEKACHMANN, ROBERT** / Inflation: The Permanent Problem of Boom and Bust

V-880   **LERNER, GERDA (ed.)** / Black Women in White America: A Documentary History

V-280   **LEWIS, OSCAR** / The Children of Sanchez

V-634   **LEWIS, OSCAR** / A Death in the Sanchez Family
V-421   **LEWIS, OSCAR** / La Vida
V-370   **LEWIS, OSCAR** / Pedro Martinez
V-533   **LOCKWOOD, LEE** / Castro's Cuba, Cuba's Fidel
V-787   **MALDONADO-DENIS, DR. MANUEL** / Puerto-Rico: A Socio-Historic Interpretation
V-406   **MARCUS, STEVEN** / Engels, Manchester and The Working Class
V-480   **MARCUSE, HERBERT** / Soviet Marxism
V-2002 **MARX, KARL AND DAVID FERNBACH (ed.)** / Political Writings, Vol. I: The Revolutions of 1848
V-2003 **MARX, KARL AND DAVID FERNBACH (ed.)** / Political Writings, Vol. II: Surveys from Exile
V-2004 **MARX, KARL AND DAVID FERNBACH (ed.)** / Political Writings, Vol. III: The First International and After
V-2005 **MARX, KARL AND QUINTIN HOARE (trans.)** / Early Writings
V-2001 **MARX, KARL AND MARTIN NICOLOUS (trans.)** / The Grundrisse: Foundations of the Critique of Political Economy
V-619   **McCONNELL, GRANT** / Private Power and American Democracy
V-386   **McPHERSON, JAMES** / The Negro's Civil War
V-928   **MEDVEDEV, ROY A.** / Let History Judge: The Origins & Consequences of Stalinism
V-112   **MEDVEDEV, ZHORES A.** / Ten Years After Ivan Denisovitch
V-427   **MENDELSON, MARY ADELAIDE** / Tender Loving Greed
V-614   **MERMELSTEIN, DAVID (ed.)** / The Economic Crisis Reader
V-307   **MIDDLETON, NEIL (ed.) AND I. F. STONE** / The I. F. Stone's Weekly Reader
V-971   **MILTON, DAVID & NANCY AND FRANZ SCHURMANN (eds.)** / The China Reader IV: People's China
V-905   **MITCHELL, JULIET** / Woman's Estate
V-93   **MITFORD, JESSICA** / Kind and Usual Punishment
V-539   **MORGAN, ROBIN (ed.)** / Sisterhood is Powerful
V-389   **MOYNIHAN, DANIEL P.** / Coping: On the Practice of Government
V-107   **MYRDAL, GUNNAR** / Against the Stream: Critical Essays on Economics
V-730   **MYRDAL, GUNNAR** / Asian Drama: An Inquiry into the Poverty of Nations
V-170   **MYRDAL, GUNNAR** / The Challenge of World Poverty
V-793   **MYRDAL, JAN** / Report from a Chinese Village
V-708   **MYRDAL, JAN AND GUN KESSLE** / China: The Revolution Continued
V-834   **NEWTON, HUEY P.** / To Die for the People
V-2001 **NICOLOUS, MARTIN (trans.) AND KARL MARX** / The Grundrisse: Foundations of the Critique of Political Economy
V-377   **NIETZSCHE, FRIEDRICH AND WALTER KAUFMANN (trans.)** / Beyond Good and Evil
V-369   **NIETZSCHE, FRIEDRICH AND WALTER KAUFMANN (trans.)** / The Birth of Tragedy and The Case of Wagner
V-985   **NIETZSCHE, FRIEDRICH AND WALTER KAUFMANN (trans.)** / The Gay Science
V-401   **NIETZSCHE, FRIEDRICH AND WALTER KAUFMANN (trans.)** / On the Genealogy of Morals and Ecce Homo
V-437   **NIETZSCHE, FRIEDRICH AND WALTER KAUFMANN (trans.)** / The Will to Power
V-803   **NOVAK, ROBERT D. AND ROWLAND EVANS, JR.** / Nixon in the White House: The Frustration of Power
V-689   **AN OBSERVER** / Message from Moscow
V-383   **PIVEN, FRANCES FOX AND RICHARD CLOWARD** / The Politics of Turmoil: Essays on Poverty, Race & The Urban Crisis
V-743   **PIVEN, FRANCES FOX AND RICHARD CLOWARD** / Regulating the Poor: The Functions of Public Welfare
V-128   **PLATO** / The Republic
V-719   **REED, JOHN** / Ten Days That Shook the World

V-791	**REICH, WILHELM AND LEE BAXANDALL (ed.)** / Sex-Pol.: Essays 1929-1934
V-159	**REISCHAUER, EDWIN O.** / Toward the 21st Century: Education for a Changing World
V-622	**ROAZEN, PAUL** / Freud: Political and Social Thought
V-204	**ROTHSCHILD, EMMA** / Paradise Lost: The Decline of the Auto-Industrial Age
V-954	**ROWBOTHAM, SHEILA** / Women, Resistance and Revolution
V-288	**RUDOLPH, FREDERICK** / The American College and University
V-226	**RYAN, WILLIAM** / Blaming the Victim, (Revised edition)
V-130	**SALE, KIRKPATRICK** / Power Shift
V-965	**SALE, KIRKPATRICK** / SDS
V-902	**SALOMA, JOHN S. III AND FREDERICK H. SONTAG** / Parties: The Real Opportunity for Effective Citizen Politics
V-375	**SCHELL, ORVILLE AND FRANZ SCHURMANN (eds.)** / The China Reader, Vol. I: Imperial China
V-376	**SCHELL, ORVILLE AND FRANZ SCHURMANN (eds.)** / The China Reader, Vol. II: Republican China
V-377	**SCHELL, ORVILLE AND FRANZ SCHURMANN (eds.)** / The China Reader, Vol. III: Communist China
V-738	**SCHNEIR, MIRIAM (ed.)** / Feminism
V-375	**SCHURMANN, FRANZ AND ORVILLE SCHELL (eds.)** / The China Reader, Vol. I: Imperial China
V-376	**SCHURMANN, FRANZ AND ORVILLE SCHELL (eds.)** / The China Reader, Vol. II: Republican China
V-377	**SCHURMANN, FRANZ AND ORVILLE SCHELL (eds.)** / The China Reader, Vol. III: Communist China
V-971	**SCHURMANN, FRANZ AND NANCY AND DAVID MILTON (eds.)** / The China Reader, Vol. IV: People's China
V-89	**SENNETT, RICHARD** / Families Against the City: Middle Class Homes of Industrial Chicago 1872-1890
V-940	**SENNETT, RICHARD AND JONATHAN COBB** / The Hidden Injuries of Class
V-308	**SENNETT, RICHARD** / The Uses of Disorder
V-974	**SERRIN, WILLIAM** / The Company and the Union
V-405	**SERVICE, JOHN S. AND JOSEPH W. ESHERICK (ed.)** / Lost Chance in China: The World War II Despatches of John S. Service
V-798	**SEXTON, BRENDAN AND PATRICIA** / Blue Collars and Hard Hats
V-279	**SILBERMAN, CHARLES E.** / Crisis in Black and White
V-353	**SILBERMAN, CHARLES E.** / Crisis in the Classroom
V-850	**SILBERMAN, CHARLES E.** / The Open Classroom Reader
V-681	**SNOW, EDGAR** / Red China Today: The Other Side of the River
V-930	**SNOW, EDGAR** / The Long Revolution
V-902	**SONTAG, FREDERICK H. AND JOHN S. SALOMA III** / Parties: The Real Opportunity for Effective Citizen Politics
V-388	**STAMPP, KENNETH** / The Era of Reconstruction 1865-1877
V-253	**STAMPP, KENNETH** / The Peculiar Institution
V-959	**STERN, PHILIP M.** / The Rape of the Taxpayer
V-547	**STONE, I. F.** / The Haunted Fifties
V-307	**STONE, I. F. AND NEIL MIDDLETON (ed.)** / The I. F. Stone's Weekly Reader
V-231	**TANNENBAUM, FRANK** / Slave and Citizen: The Negro in the Americas
V-312	**TANNENBAUM, FRANK** / Ten Keys to Latin America
V-984	**THOMAS, PIRI** / Down These Mean Streets
V-322	**THOMPSON, E. P.** / The Making of the English Working Class
V-810	**TITMUSS, RICHARD** / The Gift Relationship: From Human Blood to Social Policy
V-848	**TOFFLER, ALVIN** / The Culture Consumers
V-980	**TOFFLER, ALVIN (ed.)** / Learning for Tomorrow: The Role of the Future in Education

V-686   **WALLACE, MICHAEL AND RICHARD HOFSTADTER (eds.)** / American Violence: A Documentary History
V-957   **WHALEN, CHARLES** / Your Right to Know
V-313   **WILSON, EDMUND** / Apologies to the Iroquois
V-483   **ZINN, HOWARD** / Disobedience and Democracy

V-286   **ARIES, PHILIPPE** / Centuries of Childhood

V-563   **BEER, SAMUEL H.** / British Politics in the Collectivist Age

V-620   **BILLINGTON, JAMES H.** / Icon and Axe: An Interpretive History of Russian Culture

V-44   **BRINTON, CRANE** / The Anatomy of Revolution

V-391   **CARR, E. H.** / What Is History?

V-628   **CARTEY, WILFRED AND MARTIN KILSON (eds.)** / Africa Reader: Colonial Africa, Vol. 1

V-629   **CARTEY, WILFRED AND MARTIN KILSON (eds.)** / Africa Reader: Independent Africa, Vol. 1

V-522   **CHINWEIZU** / The West and the Rest of Us: White Predators, Black Slavers and the African Elite

V-888   **CLARK, JOHN HENRIK (ed.)** / Marcus Garvey and the Vision of Africa

V-507   **CLIVE, JOHN** / Macauley

V-261   **COHEN, STEPHEN F.** / Bukharin and the Bolshevik Revolution: A Political Biography

V-843   **DAUBIER, JEAN** / A History of the Chinese Cultural Revolution

V-227   **DE BEAUVOIR, SIMONE** / The Second Sex

V-726   **DEBRAY, REGIS AND SALVADOR ALLENDE** / The Chilean Revolution

V-746   **DEUTSCHER, ISAAC** / The Prophet Armed

V-748   **DEUTSCHER, ISAAC** / The Prophet Outcast

V-617   **DEVLIN, BERNADETTE** / The Price of My Soul

V-471   **DUVEAU, GEORGES** / 1848: The Making of A Revolution

V-702   **EMBREE, AINSLIE (ed.)** / The Hindu Tradition

V-2023   **FEST, JOACHIM C.** / Hitler

V-225   **FISCHER, LOUIS** / The Essential Gandhi

V-927   **FITZGERALD, FRANCES** / Fire in the Lake: The Vietnamese & The Americans in Vietnam

V-914   **FOUCAULT, MICHEL** / Madness & Civilization: A History of Insanity in the Age of Reason

V-935   **FOUCAULT, MICHEL** / The Order of Things: An Archaeology of the Human Sciences

V-97   **FOUCAULT, MICHEL** / The Birth of the Clinic: An Archaeology of Medical Perception

V-152   **GRAHAM, LOREN R.** / Science & Philosophy in the Soviet Union

V-529   **HALLIDAY, FRED** / Arabia Without Sultans

V-114   **HAUSER, ARNOLD** / The Social History of Art (four volumes—through 117)

V-979   **HERZEN, ALEXANDER** / My Past and Thoughts (Abridged by Dwight Macdonald)

V-465   **HINTON, WILLIAM** / Fanshen

V-328   **HINTON, WILLIAM** / Iron Oxen

V-2005   **HOARE, QUINTIN (ed.) AND KARL MARX** / Early Writings

V-878   **HOLBORN, HAJO (ed.)** / Republic to Reich: The Making of the Nazi Revolution

V-201   **HUGHES, H. STUART** / Consciousness and Society

V-514   **HUNTINGTON, SAMUEL P.** / The Soldier and the State

V-790   **KAPLAN, CAROL AND LAWRENCE** / Revolutions: A Comparative Study

V-708   **KESSLE, GUN AND JAN MYRDAL** / China: The Revolution Continued

V-628   **KILSON, MARTIN AND WILFRED CARTEY (eds.)** / Africa Reader: Colonial Africa, Vol. I

V-629   **KILSON, MARTIN AND WILFRED CARTEY (eds.)** / Africa Reader: Independent Africa, Vol. II

V-728   **KLYUCHEVSKY, V.** / Peter the Great

V-246   **KNOWLES, DAVID** / Evolution of Medieval Thought

V-939   **LEFEBVRE, GEORGES AND JOAN WHITE (trans.)** / The Great Fear of 1789: Rural Panic in Revolutionary France

V-533   **LOCKWOOD, LEE** / Castro's Cuba, Cuba's Fidel

V-787   **MALDONADO-DENIS, MANUEL** / Puerto Rico: A Socio-Historic Interpretation

V-406   **MARCUS, STEVEN** / Engels, Manchester & The Working Class
V-480   **MARCUSE, HERBERT** / Soviet Marxism
V-2002 **MARX, KARL AND DAVID FERNBACH (ed.)** / Political Writings, Vol. I: The Revolutions of 1848
V-2003 **MARX, KARL AND DAVID FERNBACH (ed.)** / Political Writings, Vol. II: Surveys from Exile
V-2004 **MARX, KARL AND DAVID FERNBACH (ed.)** / Political Writings, Vol. III: The First International and After
V-2005 **MARX, KARL AND QUINTIN HOARE (ed.)** / Early Writings
V-2001 **MARX, KARL AND MARTIN NICOLOUS (trans.)** / Grundrisse: Foundations of the Critique of Political Economy
V-92   **MATTINGLY, GARRETT** / Catherine of Aragon
V-928   **MEDVEDEV, ROY A.** / Let History Judge: The Origins & Consequences of Stalinism
V-816   **MEDVEDEV, ROY & ZHORES** / A Question of Madness
V-112   **MEDVEDEV, ZHORES** / Ten Years After Ivan Denisovich
V-971   **MILTON, DAVID & NANCY AND FRANZ SCHURMANN** / The China Reader IV: People's China:
V-905   **MITCHELL, JULIET** / Woman's Estate
V-730   **MYRDAL, GUNNAR** / Asian Drama: An Inquiry into the Poverty of Nations
V-793   **MYRDAL, JAN** / Report from a Chinese Village
V-708   **MYRDAL, JAN AND GUN KESSLE** / China: The Revolution Continued
V-2001 **NICOLOUS, MARTIN (trans.) AND KARL MARX** / The Grundrisse: Foundations of the Critique of Political Economy
V-955   **O'BRIEN, CONOR CRUISE** / States of Ireland
V-689   **OBSERVER, AN** / Message From Moscow
V-525   **PARES, SIR BERNARD** / A History of Russia
V-719   **REED, JOHN** / Ten Days That Shook the World
V-677   **RODINSON, MAXIME** / Mohammed
V-954   **ROWBOTHAM, SHEILA** / Women, Resistance & Revolution: A History of Women & Revolution in the Modern World
V-2067 **SAKHAROV, ANDREI** / My Country and The World
V-303   **SANSOM, GEORGE B.** / The Western World & Japan
V-745   **SCHAPIRO, LEONARD** / The Communist Party of the Soviet Union
V-738   **SCHNEIR, MIRIAM (ed.)** / Feminism
V-375   **SCHURMANN, F. AND O. SCHELL (eds.)** / The China Reader, Vol. Imperial China
V-376   **SCHURMANN, F. AND O. SCHELL (eds.)** / The China Reader, Vol. II: Republican China
V-377   **SCHURMANN, F. AND O. SCHELL (eds.)** / The China Reader, Vol. III: Communist China
V-971   **SCHURMANN, F. AND DAVID & NANCY MILTON** / The China Reader, Vol. IV: People's China
V-405   **SERVICE, JOHN S. AND JOSEPH H. ESHERICK (ed.)** / Lost Chance in China: The World War II Despatches of John S. Service
V-847   **SNOW, EDGAR** / Journey to the Beginning
V-930   **SNOW, EDGAR** / The Long Revolution
V-681   **SNOW, EDGAR** / Red China Today: The Other Side of the River
V-220   **SOBOUL, ALBERT** / The French Revolution, 1787-1799: From the Storming of the Bastille to Napoleon
V-411   **SPENCE, JONATHAN** / Emperor of China: Self-Portrait of K'ang-hsi
V-962   **STERN, FRITZ** / The Varieties of History: From Voltaire to the Present
V-312   **TANNENBAUM, FRANK** / Ten Keys to Latin America
V-387   **TAYLOR, A. J. P.** / Bismarck: The Man and the Statesman
V-322   **THOMPSON, E. P.** / The Making of the English Working Class
V-298   **WATTS, ALAN** / The Way of Zen
V-939   **WHITE, JOAN (trans.) AND GEORGES LEFEBVRE** / The Great Fear of 1789: Rural Panic in Revolutionary France
V-627   **WOMACK, JOHN JR.** / Zapata and the Mexican Revolution

VINTAGE HISTORY—AMERICAN

V-570   **ANDREWS, WAYNE** / American Gothic
V-604   **BAILYN, BERNARD** / The Origins of American Politics
V-334   **BALTZELL, E. DIGBY** / The Protestant Establishment
V-832   **BARNET, MIGUEL (ed.) AND ESTEBAN MONTEJO** / The Autobiography of a Runaway Slave
V-571   **BARTH, ALLEN** / Prophets With Honor: Great Dissents and Great Dissenters in the Supreme Court
V-60   **BECKER, CARL L.** / The Declaration of Independence
V-494   **BERNSTEIN, BARTON J. (ed.)** / Towards a New Past: Dissenting Essays in American History
V-512   **BLOCH, MARC** / The Historian's Craft
V-513   **BOORSTIN, DANIEL J.** / The Americans: The Colonial Experience
V-11   **BOORSTIN, DANIEL J.** / The Americans: The Democratic Experience
V-358   **BOORSTIN, DANIEL J.** / The Americans: The National Experience
V-501   **BOORSTIN, DANIEL J.** / Democracy and Its Discontents: Reflections on Everyday America
V-44   **BRINTON, CRANE** / The Anatomy of Revolution
V-33   **CARMICHAEL, STOKELY AND CHARLES HAMILTON** / Black Power
V-2024   **CARO, ROBERT A.** / The Power Broker: Robert Moses and The Fall of New York
V-98   **CASH, W. J.** / The Mind of the South
V-888   **CLARKE, JOHN HENRIK (ed.)** / Marcus Garvey and the Vision of Africa
V-311   **CREMIN, LAWRENCE A.** / The Genius of American Education
V-872   **DILLARD, J. L.** / Black English: Its History and Usage in the United States
V-190   **DONALD, DAVID** / Lincoln Reconsidered
V-707   **DORSEN, NORMAN (ed.)** / The Rights of Americans
V-143   **EMERSON, THOMAS I.** / The System of Freedom of Expression
V-803   **EVANS, ROWLAND, JR. AND ROBERT D. NOVAK** / Nixon in the White House: The Frustration of Power
V-368   **FRIEDENBERG, EDGAR Z.** / Coming of Age in America
V-400   **GENOVESE, EUGENE D.** / The Political Economy of Slavery
V-676   **GENOVESE, EUGENE D.** / The World the Slaveholders Made
V-31   **GOLDMAN, ERIC F.** / Rendezvous with Destiny
V-183   **GOLDMAN, ERIC F.** / The Crucial Decade—and After: America 1945-1960
V-33   **HAMILTON, CHARLES AND STOKELY CARMICHAEL** / Black Power
V-95   **HOFSTADTER, RICHARD** / The Age of Reform: From Bryan to F. D. R.
V-795   **HOFSTADTER, RICHARD** / America at 1750: A Social Portrait
V-9   **HOFSTADTER, RICHARD** / The American Political Tradition
V-317   **HOFSTADTER, RICHARD** / Anti-Intellectualism in American Life
V-385   **HOFSTADTER, RICHARD** / The Paranoid Style in American Politics and Other Essays
V-540   **HOFSTADTER, RICHARD AND CLARENCE L. VER STEEG (eds.)** / Great Issues in American History, From Settlement to Revolution 1584-1776
V-541   **HOFSTADTER, RICHARD (ed.)** / Great Issues in American History, From the Revolution to the Civil War, 1765-1865
V-542   **HOFSTADTER, RICHARD (ed.)** / Great Issues in American History, From Reconstruction to the Present Day, 1864-1969
V-591   **HOFSTADTER, RICHARD** / Progressive Historians
V-514   **HUNTINGTON, SAMUEL P.** / The Soldier and the State
V-459   **JACOBS, PAUL AND SAUL LANDAU WITH EVE PELL** / To Serve the Devil: Natives and Slaves, Vol. I
V-460   **JACOBS, PAUL AND SAUL LANDAU WITH EVE PELL** / To Serve the Devil: Colonials and Sojourners, Vol. II
V-242   **JAMES, C. L. R.** / The Black Jacobins
V-527   **JENSEN, MERRILL** / The New Nation
V-933   **KAMMEN, MICHAEL** / People of Paradox: An Inquiry Concerning the Origins of American Civilization

V-996   KAMMEN, MICHAEL / A Rope of Sand: The Colonial Agents, British Politics, and the American Revolution
V-510   KEY, V. O. / Southern Politics
V-560   LASCH, CHRISTOPHER / The Agony of the American Left
V-367   LASCH, CHRISTOPHER / The New Radicalism in America
V-46   LASCH, CHRISTOPHER / The World of Nations
V-459   LANDAU, SAUL AND PAUL JACOBS WITH EVE PELL / To Serve the Devil: Natives and Slaves, Vol. I
V-460   LANDAU, SAUL AND PAUL JACOBS WITH EVE PELL / To Serve the Devil: Colonials and Sojourners, Vol. II
V-38   LEFCOURT, ROBERT (ed.) / Law Against the People: Essays to Demystify Law, Order and The Courts
V-880   LERNER, GERDA (ed.) / Black Women in White America: A Documentary History
V-315   LEWIS, ANTHONY / Gideon's Trumpet
V-937   MAIER, PAULINE / From Resistance to Revolution: Colonial Radicals and the Development of American Opposition to Britain, 1765-1776
V-386   McPHERSON, JAMES / The Negro's Civil War
V-832   MONTEJO, ESTEBAN & MIGUEL BARNET (ed.) / The Autobiography of a Runaway Slave
V-803   NOVAK, ROBERT D. AND ROWLAND EVANS, JR. / Nixon in the White House: The Frustration of Power
V-285   RUDOLPH, FREDERICK / The American College and University: A History
V-965   SALE, KIRKPATRICK / SDS
V-89   SENNETT, RICHARD / Families Against the City: Middle Class Homes of Industrial Chicago, 1872-1890
V-279   SILBERMAN, CHARLES E. / Crisis in Black and White
V-353   SILBERMAN, CHARLES E. / Crisis in the Classroom
V-388   STAMPP, KENNETH M. / The Era of Reconstruction, 1865-1877
V-253   STAMPP, KENNETH M. / The Peculiar Institution
V-547   STONE, I. F. / The Haunted Fifties
V-908   STONE, I. F. / The Truman Era
V-231   TANNENBAUM, FRANK / Slave and Citizen: The Negro in the Americas
V-110   TOCQUEVILLE, ALEXIS DE / Democracy in America, Vol. I
V-111   TOCQUEVILLE, ALEXIS DE / Democracy in America, Vol. II
V-540   VER STEEG, CLARENCE L. AND RICHARD HOFSTADTER (eds.) / Great Issues in American History 1584-1776
V-699   WALLACE, ANTHONY F. C. / The Death and Rebirth of the Seneca
V-362   WILLIAMS, T. HARRY / Lincoln and His Generals
V-313   WILSON, EDMUND / Apologies to the Iroquois

VINTAGE FICTION, POETRY, AND PLAYS

V-814   **ABE, KOBO** / The Woman in the Dunes
V-2014 **AUDEN, W. H.** / Collected Longer Poems
V-2015 **AUDEN, W. H.** / Collected Shorter Poems 1927-1957
V-102   **AUDEN, W. H.** / Selected Poetry of W. H. Auden
V-601   **AUDEN, W. H. AND PAUL B. TAYLOR (trans.)** / The Elder Edda
V-20   **BABIN, MARIA-THERESA AND STAN STEINER (eds.)** / Borinquen: An Anthology of Puerto-Rican Literature
V-271   **BEDIER, JOSEPH** / Tristan and Iseult
V-523   **BELLAMY, JOE DAVID (ed.)** / Superfiction or The American Story Transformed: An Anthology
V-72   **BERNIKOW, LOUISE (ed.)** / The World Split Open: Four Centuries of Women Poets in England and America 1552-1950
V-321   **BOLT, ROBERT** / A Man for All Seasons
V-21   **BOWEN, ELIZABETH** / The Death of the Heart
V-294   **BRADBURY, RAY** / The Vintage Bradbury
V-670   **BRECHT, BERTOLT (ed. by Ralph Manheim and John Willett)** / Collected Plays, Vol. 1
V-759   **BRECHT, BERTOLT (ed. by Ralph Manheim and John Willett)** / Collected Plays, Vol. 5
V-216   **BRECHT, BERTOLT (ed. by Ralph Manheim and John Willett)** / Collected Plays, Vol. 7
V-819   **BRECHT, BERTOLT (ed. by Ralph Manheim and John Willett)** / Collected Plays, Vol. 9
V-841   **BYNNER, WITTER AND KIANG KANG-HU (eds.)** / The Jade Mountain: A Chinese Anthology
V-207   **CAMUS, ALBERT** / Caligula & Three Other Plays
V-281   **CAMUS, ALBERT** / Exile and the Kingdom
V-223   **CAMUS, ALBERT** / The Fall
V-865   **CAMUS, ALBERT** / A Happy Death: A Novel
V-626   **CAMUS, ALBERT** / Lyrical and Critical Essays
V-75   **CAMUS, ALBERT** / The Myth of Sisyphus and Other Essays
V-258   **CAMUS, ALBERT** / The Plague
V-245   **CAMUS, ALBERT** / The Possessed
V-30   **CAMUS, ALBERT** / The Rebel
V-2   **CAMUS, ALBERT** / The Stranger
V-28   **CATHER, WILLA** / Five Stories
V-705   **CATHER, WILLA** / A Lost Lady
V-200   **CATHER, WILLA** / My Mortal Enemy
V-179   **CATHER, WILLA** / Obscure Destinies
V-252   **CATHER, WILLA** / One of Ours
V-913   **CATHER, WILLA** / The Professor's House
V-434   **CATHER, WILLA** / Sapphira and the Slave Girl
V-680   **CATHER, WILLA** / Shadows on the Rock
V-684   **CATHER, WILLA** / Youth and the Bright Medusa
V-140   **CERF, BENNETT (ed.)** / Famous Ghost Stories
V-203   **CERF, BENNETT (ed.)** / Four Contemporary American Plays
V-127   **CERF, BENNETT (ed.)** / Great Modern Short Stories
V-326   **CERF, CHRISTOPHER (ed.)** / The Vintage Anthology of Science Fantasy
V-293   **CHAUCER, GEOFFREY** / The Canterbury Tales (a prose version in Modern English)
V-142   **CHAUCER, GEOFFREY** / Troilus and Cressida
V-723   **CHERNYSHEVSKY, N. G.** / What Is to Be Done?
V-173   **CONFUCIUS (trans. by Arthur Waley)** / Analects
V-155   **CONRAD, JOSEPH** / Three Great Tales: The Nigger of the Narcissus, Heart of Darkness, Youth
V-10   **CRANE, STEPHEN** / Stories and Tales
V-126   **DANTE, ALIGHIERI** / The Divine Comedy
V-177   **DINESEN, ISAK** / Anecdotes of Destiny

V-431 **DINESEN, ISAK** / Ehrengard
V-752 **DINESEN, ISAK** / Last Tales
V-740 **DINESEN, ISAK** / Out of Africa
V-807 **DINESEN, ISAK** / Seven Gothic Tales
V-62   **DINESEN, ISAK** / Shadows on the Grass
V-205 **DINESEN, ISAK** / Winter's Tales
V-721 **DOSTOYEVSKY, FYODOR** / Crime and Punishment
V-722 **DOSTOYEVSKY, FYODOR** / The Brothers Karamazov
V-780 **FAULKNER, WILLIAM** / Absalom, Absalom!
V-254 **FAULKNER, WILLIAM** / As I Lay Dying
V-884 **FAULKNER, WILLIAM** / Go Down, Moses
V-139 **FAULKNER, WILLIAM** / The Hamlet
V-792 **FAULKNER, WILLIAM** / Intruder in the Dust
V-189 **FAULKNER, WILLIAM** / Light in August
V-282 **FAULKNER, WILLIAM** / The Mansion
V-339 **FAULKNER, WILLIAM** / The Reivers
V-412 **FAULKNER, WILLIAM** / Requiem For A Nun
V-381 **FAULKNER, WILLIAM** / Sanctuary
V-5   **FAULKNER, WILLIAM** / The Sound and the Fury
V-184 **FAULKNER, WILLIAM** / The Town
V-351 **FAULKNER, WILLIAM** / The Unvanquished
V-262 **FAULKNER, WILLIAM** / The Wild Palms
V-149 **FAULKNER, WILLIAM** / Three Famous Short Novels: Spotted Horses, Old
       Man, The Bear
V-45   **FORD, FORD MADOX** / The Good Soldier
V-7   **FORSTER, E. M.** / Howards End
V-40   **FORSTER, E. M.** / The Longest Journey
V-187 **FORSTER, E. M.** / A Room With a View
V-61   **FORSTER, E. M.** Where Angels Fear to Tread
V-219 **FRISCH, MAX** / I'm Not Stiller
V-842 **GIDE, ANDRE** / The Counterfeiters
V-8   **GIDE, ANDRE** / The Immoralist
V-96   **GIDE, ANDRE** / Lafcadio's Adventures
V-27   **GIDE, ANDRE** / Strait Is the Gate
V-66   **GIDE, ANDRE** / Two Legends: Oedipus and Theseus
V-958 **von GOETHE, JOHANN WOLFGANG (ELIZABETH MAYER, LOUISE BOGAN
       & W. H. AUDEN, trans.)** / The Sorrows of Young Werther and Novella
V-300 **GRASS, GUNTER** / The Tin Drum
V-425 **GRAVES, ROBERT** / Claudius the God
V-182 **GRAVES, ROBERT** / I, Claudius
V-717 **GUERNEY, B. G. (ed.)** / An Anthology of Russian Literature in the Soviet
       Period: From Gorki to Pasternak
V-829 **HAMMETT, DASHIELL** / The Big Knockover
V-2013 **HAMMETT, DASHIELL** / The Continental Op
V-827 **HAMMETT, DASHIELL** / The Dain Curse
V-773 **HAMMETT, DASHIELL** / The Glass Key
V-772 **HAMMETT, DASHIELL** / The Maltese Falcon
V-828 **HAMMETT, DASHIELL** / The Red Harvest
V-774 **HAMMETT, DASHIELL** / The Thin Man
V-781 **HAMSUN, KNUT** / Growth of the Soil
V-896 **HATCH, JAMES AND VICTORIA SULLIVAN (eds.)** / Plays by and About
       Women
V-15   **HAWTHORNE, NATHANIEL** / Short Stories
V-610 **HSU, KAI-YU** / The Chinese Literary Scene: A Writer's Visit to the People's
       Republic
V-910 **HUGHES, LANGSTON** / Selected Poems of Langston Hughes
V-304 **HUGHES, LANGSTON** / The Ways of White Folks
V-158 **ISHERWOOD, CHRISTOPHER AND W. H. AUDEN** / Two Plays: The Dog
       Beneath the Skin and The Ascent of F6
V-295 **JEFFERS, ROBINSON** / Selected Poems

V-380 **JOYCE, JAMES** / Ulysses
V-991 **KAFKA, FRANZ** / The Castle
V-484 **KAFKA, FRANZ** / The Trial
V-841 **KANG-HU, KIANG AND WITTER BYNNER** / The Jade Mountain: A Chinese Anthology
V-508 **KOCH, KENNETH** / The Art of Love
V-915 **KOCH, KENNETH** / A Change of Hearts
V-467 **KOCH, KENNETH** / The Red Robbins
V-82 **KOCH, KENNETH** / Wishes, Lies and Dreams
V-134 **LAGERKVIST, PAR** / Barabbas
V-240 **LAGERKVIST, PAR** / The Sibyl
V-776 **LAING, R. D.** / Knots
V-23 **LAWRENCE, D. H.** / The Plumed Serpent
V-71 **LAWRENCE, D. H.** / St. Mawr & The Man Who Died
V-329 **LINDBERGH, ANNE MORROW** / Gift from the Sea
V-822 **LINDBERGH, ANNE MORROW** / The Unicorn and Other Poems
V-479 **MALRAUX, ANDRE** / Man's Fate
V-180 **MANN, THOMAS** / Buddenbrooks
V-3 **MANN, THOMAS** / Death in Venice and Seven Other Stories
V-297 **MANN, THOMAS** / Doctor Faustus
V-497 **MANN, THOMAS** / The Magic Mountain
V-86 **MANN, THOMAS** / The Transposed Heads
V-36 **MANSFIELD, KATHERINE** / Stories
V-137 **MAUGHAM, W. SOMERSET** / Of Human Bondage
V-720 **MIRSKY, D. S.** / A History of Russian Literature: From Its Beginnings to 1900
V-883 **MISHIMA, YUKIO** / Five Modern Nō Plays
V-151 **MOFFAT, MARY JANE AND CHARLOTTE PAINTER** / Revelations: Diaries of Women
V-851 **MORGAN, ROBIN** / Monster
V-926 **MUSTARD, HELEN (trans.)** / Heinrich Heine: Selected Works
V-925 **NGUYEN, DU** / The Tale of Kieu
V-125 **OATES, WHITNEY J. AND EUGENE O'NEILL, Jr. (eds.)** / Seven Famous Greek Plays
V-973 **O'HARA, FRANK** / Selected Poems of Frank O'Hara
V-855 **O'NEILL, EUGENE** / Anna Christie, The Emperor Jones, The Hairy Ape
V-18 **O'NEILL, EUGENE** / The Iceman Cometh
V-236 **O'NEILL, EUGENE** / A Moon For the Misbegotten
V-856 **O'NEILL, EUGENE** / Seven Plays of the Sea
V-276 **O'NEILL, EUGENE** / Six Short Plays
V-165 **O'NEILL, EUGENE** / Three Plays: Desire Under the Elms, Strange Interlude, Mourning Becomes Electra
V-125 **O'NEILL, EUGENE, JR. AND WHITNEY J. OATES (eds.)** / Seven Famous Greek Plays
V-151 **PAINTER, CHARLOTTE AND MARY JANE MOFFAT** / Revelations: Diaries of Women
V-907 **PERELMAN, S. J.** / Crazy Like a Fox
V-466 **PLATH, SYLVIA** / The Colossus and Other Poems
V-232 **PRITCHETT, V. S.** / Midnight Oil
V-598 **PROUST, MARCEL** / The Captive
V-597 **PROUST, MARCEL** / Cities of the Plain
V-596 **PROUST, MARCEL** / The Guermantes Way
V-600 **PROUST, MARCEL** / The Past Recaptured
V-594 **PROUST, MARCEL** / Swann's Way
V-599 **PROUST, MARCEL** / The Sweet Cheat Gone
V-595 **PROUST, MARCEL** / Within A Budding Grove
V-714 **PUSHKIN, ALEXANDER** / The Captain's Daughter and Other Stories
V-976 **QUASHA, GEORGE AND JEROME ROTHENBERG (eds.)** / America a Prophecy: A New Reading of American Poetry from Pre-Columbian Times to the Present

V-80   **REDDY, T. J.** / Less Than a Score, But A Point: Poems by T. J. Reddy
V-504   **RENAULT, MARY** / The Bull From the Sea
V-653   **RENAULT, MARY** / The Last of the Wine
V-24   **RHYS, JEAN** / After Leaving Mr. Mackenzie
V-42   **RHYS, JEAN** / Good Morning Midnight
V-319   **RHYS, JEAN** / Quartet
V-2016   **ROSEN, KENNETH (ed.)** / The Man to Send Rain Clouds: Contemporary Stories by American Indians
V-976   **ROTHENBERG, JEROME AND GEORGE QUASHA (eds.)** / America a Prophecy: A New Reading of American Poetry from Pre-Columbian Times to the Present
V-366   **SARGENT, PAMELA (ed.)** / Bio-Futures: Science Fiction Stories about Biological Metamorphosis
V-876   **SARGENT, PAMELA (ed.)** / More Women of Wonder: Science Fiction Novelettes by Women about Women
V-41   **SARGENT, PAMELA (ed.)** / Women of Wonder: Science Fiction Stories by Women About Women
V-838   **SARTRE, JEAN-PAUL** / The Age of Reason
V-238   **SARTRE, JEAN-PAUL** / The Condemned of Altona
V-65   **SARTRE, JEAN-PAUL** / The Devil & The Good Lord & Two Other Plays
V-16   **SARTRE, JEAN-PAUL** / No Exit and Three Other Plays
V-839   **SARTRE, JEAN-PAUL** / The Reprieve
V-74   **SARTRE, JEAN-PAUL** / The Trojan Women: Euripides
V-840   **SARTRE, JEAN-PAUL** / Troubled Sleep
V-443   **SCHULTE, RAINER AND QUINCY TROUPE (eds.)** / Giant Talk: An Anthology of Third World Writings
V-607   **SCORTIA, THOMAS N. AND GEORGE ZEBROWSKI (eds.)** / Human-Machines: An Anthology of Stories About Cyborgs
V-330   **SHOLOKHOV, MIKHAIL** / And Quiet Flows the Don
V-331   **SHOLOKHOV, MIKHAIL** / The Don Flows Home to the Sea
V-447   **SILVERBERG, ROBERT** / Born With the Dead: Three Novellas About the Spirit of Man
V-945   **SNOW, LOIS WHEELER** / China On Stage
V-133   **STEIN, GERTRUDE** / Autobiography of Alice B. Toklas
V-826   **STEIN, GERTRUDE** / Everybody's Autobiography
V-941   **STEIN, GERTRUDE** / The Geographical History of America
V-797   **STEIN, GERTRUDE** / Ida
V-695   **STEIN, GERTRUDE** / Last Operas and Plays
V-477   **STEIN, GERTRUDE** / Lectures in America
V-153   **STEIN, GERTRUDE** / Three Lives
V-710   **STEIN, GERTRUDE & CARL VAN VECHTEN (ed.)** / Selected Writings of Gertrude Stein
V-20   **STEINER, STAN AND MARIA-THERESA BABIN (eds.)** / Borinquen: An Anthology of Puerto-Rican Literature
V-770   **STEINER, STAN AND LUIS VALDEZ (eds.)** / Aztlan: An Anthology of Mexican-American Literature
V-769   **STEINER, STAN AND SHIRLEY HILL WITT (eds.)** / The Way: An Anthology of American Indian Literature
V-768   **STEVENS, HOLLY (ed.)** / The Palm at the End of the Mind: Selected Poems & A Play by Wallace Stevens
V-278   **STEVENS, WALLACE** / The Necessary Angel
V-896   **SULLIVAN, VICTORIA AND JAMES HATCH (eds.)** / Plays By and About Women
V-63   **SVEVO, ITALO** / Confessions of Zeno
V-178   **SYNGE, J. M.** / Complete Plays
V-601   **TAYLOR, PAUL B. AND W. H. AUDEN (trans.)** / The Elder Edda
V-443   **TROUPE, QUINCY AND RAINER SCHULTE (eds.)** / Giant Talk: An Anthology of Third World Writings
V-770   **VALDEZ, LUIS AND STAN STEINER (eds.)** / Aztlan: An Anthology of Mexican-American Literature

V-710   **VAN VECHTEN, CARL (ed.) AND GERTRUDE STEIN** / Selected Writings of Gertrude Stein
V-870   **WIESEL, ELIE** / Souls on Fire
V-769   **WITT, SHIRLEY HILL AND STAN STEINER (eds.**) / The Way: An Anthology of American Indian Literature
V-2028 **WODEHOUSE, P. G.** / The Code of the Woosters
V-2026 **WODEHOUSE, P. G.** / Leave It to Psmith
V-2027 **WODEHOUSE, P. G.** / Mulliner Nights
V-607   **ZEBROWSKI, GEORGE AND THOMAS N. SCORTIA (eds.)** / Human-Machines: An Anthology of Stories About Cyborgs

VINTAGE BELLES—LETTRES

V-418	**AUDEN, W. H.** / The Dyer's Hand
V-887	**AUDEN, W. H.** / Forewords and Afterwords
V-271	**BEDIER, JOSEPH** / Tristan and Iseult
V-512	**BLOCH, MARC** / The Historian's Craft
V-572	**BRIDGE HAMPTON** / Bridge Hampton Works & Days
V-161	**BROWN, NORMAN O.** / Closing Time
V-544	**BROWN, NORMAN O.** / Hermes the Thief
V-419	**BROWN, NORMAN O.** / Love's Body
V-75	**CAMUS, ALBERT** / The Myth of Sisyphus and Other Essays
V-30	**CAMUS, ALBERT** / The Rebel
V-608	**CARR, JOHN DICKSON** / The Life of Sir Arthur Conan Doyle: The Man Who Was Sherlock Holmes
V-407	**HARDWICK, ELIZABETH** / Seduction and Betrayal: Women and Literature
V-244	**HERRIGEL, EUGEN** / The Method of Zen
V-663	**HERRIGEL, EUGEN** / Zen in the Art of Archery
V-201	**HUGHES, H. STUART** / Consciousness & Society
V-235	**KAPLAN, ABRAHAM** / New World of Philosophy
V-337	**KAUFMANN, WALTER (trans.) AND FRIEDRICH NIETZSCHE** / Beyond Good and Evil
V-369	**KAUFMANN, WALTER (trans.) AND FRIEDRICH NIETZSCHE** / The Birth of Tragedy and the Case of Wagner
V-985	**KAUFMANN, WALTER (trans.) AND FRIEDRICH NIETZSCHE** / The Gay Science
V-401	**KAUFMANN, WALTER (trans.) AND FRIEDRICH NIETZSCHE** / On the Genealogy of Morals and Ecce Homo
V-437	**KAUFMANN, WALTER (trans.) AND FRIEDRICH NIETZSCHE** / The Will to Power
V-995	**KOTT, JAN** / The Eating of the Gods: An Interpretation of Greek Tragedy
V-685	**LESSING, DORIS** / A Small Personal Voice: Essays, Reviews, Interviews
V-329	**LINDBERGH, ANNE MORROW** / Gift from the Sea
V-479	**MALRAUX, ANDRE** / Man's Fate
V-406	**MARCUS, STEVEN** / Engels, Manchester and the Working Class
V-58	**MENCKEN, H. L.** / Prejudices (Selected by James T. Farrell)
V-25	**MENCKEN, H. L.** / The Vintage Mencken (Gathered by Alistair Cooke)
V-151	**MOFFAT, MARY JANE AND CHARLOTTE PAINTER (eds.)** / Revelations: Diaries of Women
V-926	**MUSTARD, HELEN (trans.)** / Heinrich Heine: Selected Works
V-337	**NIETZSCHE, FRIEDRICH AND WALTER KAUFMANN (trans.)** / Beyond Good and Evil
V-369	**NIETZSCHE, FRIEDRICH AND WALTER KAUFMANN (trans.)** / The Birth of Tragedy and the Case of Wagner
V-985	**NIETZSCHE, FRIEDRICH AND WALTER KAUFMANN (trans.)** / The Gay Science
V-401	**NIETZSCHE, FRIEDRICH AND WALTER KAUFMANN (trans.)** / On the Genealogy of Morals and Ecce Homo
V-437	**NIETZSCHE, FRIEDRICH AND WALTER KAUFMANN (trans.)** / The Will to Power
V-672	**OUSPENSKY, P. D.** / The Fourth Way
V-524	**OUSPENSKY, P. D.** / A New Model of the Universe
V-943	**OUSPENSKY, P. D.** / The Psychology of Man's Possible Evolution
V-639	**OUSPENSKY, P. D.** / Tertium Organum
V-151	**PAINTER, CHARLOTTE AND MARY JANE MOFFAT (eds.)** / Revelations: Diaries of Women
V-986	**PAUL, DAVID (trans.)** / Poison & Vision: Poems & Prose of Baudelaire, Mallarme and Rimbaud
V-598	**PROUST, MARCEL** / The Captive
V-597	**PROUST, MARCEL** / Cities of the Plain
V-596	**PROUST, MARCEL** / The Guermantes Way

V-594   **PROUST, MARCEL** / Swann's Way
V-599   **PROUST, MARCEL** / The Sweet Cheat Gone
V-595   **PROUST, MARCEL** / Within a Budding Grove
V-899   **SAMUEL, MAURICE** / The World of Sholom Aleichem
V-415   **SHATTUCK, ROGER** / The Banquet Years (revised)
V-278   **STEVENS, WALLACE** / The Necessary Angel
V-761   **WATTS, ALAN** / Behold the Spirit
V-923   **WATTS, ALAN** / Beyond Theology: The Art of Godmanship
V-853   **WATTS, ALAN** / The Book: On the Taboo Against Knowing Who You Are
V-999   **WATTS, ALAN** / Cloud-Hidden, Whereabouts Unknown: A Mountain Journal
V-665   **WATTS, ALAN** / Does it Matter?
V-951   **WATTS, ALAN** / In My Own Way
V-299   **WATTS, ALAN** / The Joyous Cosmology
V-592   **WATTS, ALAN** / Nature, Man and Woman
V-609   **WATTS, ALAN** / Psychotherapy East & West
V-835   **WATTS, ALAN** / The Supreme Identity
V-298   **WATTS, ALAN** / The Way of Zen
V-870   **WIESEL, ELIE** / Souls on Fire